Viva Nuestro Caucus

WORKING AND WRITING FOR CHANGE
Series Editors: Steve Parks and Jessica Pauszek

The Writing and Working for Change series began during the 100th anniversary celebrations of NCTE. It was designed to recognize the collective work of teachers of English, Writing, Composition, and Rhetoric to work within and across diverse identities to ensure the field recognize and respect language, educational, political, and social rights of all students, teachers, and community members. While initially solely focused on the work of NCTE/CCCC Special Interest Groups and Caucuses, the series now includes texts written by individuals in partnership with other communities struggling for social recognition and justice.

Books in the Series

CCCC/NCTE Caucuses
History of the Black Caucus National Council Teachers of English by Marianna White Davis
Listening to Our Elders: Working and Writing for Social Change by Samantha Blackmon, Cristina Kirklighter, and Steve Parks
Building a Community, Having a Home: A History of the Conference on College Composition and Communication edited by Jennifer Sano-Franchini, Terese Guinsatao Monberg, K. Hyoejin Yoon
Viva Nuestro Caucus: Rewriting the Forgotten Pages of Our Caucus, edited by Romeo García, Iris D. Ruiz, Anita Hernández and María Paz Carvajal Regidor

Community Publications

Other People's English: Code-Meshing, Code-Switching, and African American Literacy by Vershawn Ashanti Young, Rusty Barrett, Y'Shanda Young-Rivera, and Kim Brian Lovejoy
Becoming International: Musings on Studying Abroad in America, edited by Sadie Shorr-Parks
Dreams and Nightmares: I Fled Alone to the United States When I Was Fourteen by Liliana Velásquez. Edited and translated by Mark Lyon
The Weight of My Armor: Creative Nonfiction and Poetry by the Syracuse Veterans' Writing Group, edited by Ivy Kleinbart, Peter McShane, and Eileen Schell
PHD to PhD: How Education Saved My Life by Elaine Richardson

Viva Nuestro Caucus

REWRITING THE FORGOTTEN PAGES
OF OUR CAUCUS

Edited by:
Romeo García
Iris D. Ruiz
Anita Hernández
María Paz Carvajal Regidor

PARLOR PRESS
Anderson, South Carolina
www.parlorpress.com

Parlor Press LLC, Anderson, South Carolina, USA
Copyright © 2019 New City Community Press
Printed on acid-free paper
Manufactured in the United States of America

No part of this book may be reproduced or transmitted in any form, by any means electronic or mechanical, including photocopying and recording, or by any information storage or retrieval system, without written permission from the publisher.

Library of Congress Cataloging-in-Publication Data on File

1 2 3 4 5

978-1-64317-118-0 (paperback)
978-1-64317-119-7 (PDF)
978-1-64317-120-3 (ePub)

WORKING AND WRITING FOR CHANGE
An Imprint Series of Parlor Press
Series Editors: Steve Parks and Jessica Pauszek

Cover photograph by Mónica Carvajal Regidor
Interior design by Elizabeth Parks, elizabethannparks@gmail.com

Parlor Press, LLC is an independent publisher of scholarly and trade titles in print and multimedia formats. This book is available in paper and eBook formats from Parlor Press on the World Wide Web at http://www.parlorpress.com or through online and brick-and-mortar bookstores. For submission information or to find out about Parlor Press publications, write to Parlor Press, 3015 Brackenberry Drive, Anderson, South Carolina, 29621, or email editor@parlorpress.com.

A Note on Terminology

In *Viva Nuestro Caucus*, we use CTE to refer to the Chicano Teachers of English. We also use Caucus (capitalized) to encompass the CTE, Hispanic Caucus, Latino Caucus, Latin@ Caucus, and Latinx Caucus of the National Council of Teachers of English and of the College Composition and Communication Conference. When referring to the Chicano and Chicana Movement as well as the Chicanos and Chicanas who were instrumental in this movement, we use both identity markers, "Chicano and Chicana." Similarly, when referring to the broader population of Latinos and Latinas, we also offer both the masculine and feminine "o" and "a." We don't negate the importance of the neutral purpose of the "x" in the identity marker, "Chicanx" and "Latinx," as is more common among the millennial Chicanx/Latinx populations, but we do recognize the debate is permanently changing Chicano/Chicano, Latino/Latina to Chicanx/Latinx. As such, we don't use "Chicanx" and "Latinx" until we begin talking about our Latinx Caucus at the present moment.

CONTENTS

1   INTRODUCTION: AN IMPETUS FOR VIVA NUESTRO CAUCUS
Romeo García

PART I
HISTORIES: THE STORY OF THE CAUCUS

9   CHAPTER ONE: SIDESTEPPING RADICAL CHANGE: A SHORT HISTORY OF NCTE
Romeo García

25   CHAPTER TWO: CREATING A "NEW HISTORY" WITHIN NCTE/CCCC: CIVIL RIGHTS, THE CHICANO MOVEMENT, AND HONORING FELIPE DE ORTEGO Y GASCA
Iris D. Ruiz

46   CHAPTER THREE: FOUNDING FIGURE FORGING A PATH: FELIPE DE ORTEGO Y GASCA
María Paz Carvajal Regidor

62   CHAPTER FOUR: FOUNDING FIGURE DESPITE SETBACKS: CARLOTA CÁRDENAS DE DWYER
Romeo García

68   CHAPTER FIVE: FOUNDING FIGURE
     INSURING INCLUSION OF LATINO AND LATINA LITERATURE:
     ROSEANN DUEÑAS GONZÁLEZ
     Anita Hernández

80   CHAPTER SIX: GENERATIONS OF LEADERSHIP
     Anita Hernández and Iris D. Ruiz

92   CHAPTER SEVEN: THE EVOLUTION OF THE LATINX CAUCUS
     IN THE NCTE AND CCCC
     Anita Hernández and Romeo García

116 CHAPTER EIGHT: WE'RE HERE TO STAY: THE CURRENT
     STATE OF THE CAUCUS AND FUTURE DIRECTIONS
     *Romeo García, Iris D. Ruiz, Anita Hernández,
     and María Paz Carvajal Regidor*

PART II
EXPERIENCES: IN THEIR OWN WORDS

127   FELIPE DE ORTEGO Y GASCA

131   CARLOTA CÁRDENAS DE DWYER

139   ROSEANN DUEÑAS GONZÁLEZ

146   VICTOR VILLANUEVA

153   CECILIA RODRÍGUEZ MILANÉS

163   BOBBIE HOUTCHENS AND MARY CARMEN CRUZ

173   CRISTINA KIRKLIGHTER

180   DAMIAN BACA

192   STEVEN ALVAREZ

199   CRISTINA RAMÍREZ

202   AJA MARTINEZ

209   TRACEY FLORES

PART III
RESULTS: WORK AND WORKS ACHIEVED

215   ANNOTATED CAUCUS ARCHIVE
          Maria Paz Carvajal Regidor, Romeo García, and Anita Hernández

256   SELECTED LIST OF CAUCUS MEMBERS' PUBLICATIONS

276   APPENDIX: FULL INTERVIEW TRANSCRIPTS

INTRODUCTION
An Impetus for Viva Nuestro Caucus

Romeo García

NONETHELESS WE PERSEVERED

Almost fifty years have passed since the Chicano Teachers of English (CTE) formed out of dissatisfaction with their lack of representation within the National Council of Teachers of English (NCTE). Before this formation, conversations had already been taking place between CTE founders Carlota Cárdenas de Dwyer, Felipe de Ortego y Gasca, and Roseann Dueñas González since they had first "spotted each other a mile away" (See Dwyer, 2011) as fellow Chicanos. During this time, the social dynamics of the 1960s had sounded a call in and across the U.S. for equity and inclusion. For educators such as Cárdenas de Dwyer, Ortego y Gasca, and González, they recognized Chicano students were never represented in assigned textbooks and that there was little-to-no curricular or pedagogical support provided to enable their success. As Cárdenas de Dwyer recalls, for them, the challenges of meeting the call for action in the 1960's included finding, establishing, and/or creating literature, criticism, and textbooks to meet this need. Speaking of Ortega y Gasca and Dueñas González, Cárdenas de Dwyer recognized "We would be the ones to write the criticism and pedagogy." They would have to be the ones to create CTE.

Yet, they often faced resistance. Members of CTE had to reach out to textbook publishers who were not very interested in publishing Chicano or Mexican American literature. They were questioned by educators about the need to include Chicanos and Mexican Americans into the national curriculum. And scholarly venues, such as *College English*, were also resistant. Indeed,

Ortego y Gasca's 1970 "Huevos con Chorizo: A Letter to Richard Ohmann," is a reminder how difficult it can be to publish within an academic outlet whose editor and audience were predominately white. And though NCTE and CCCC accommodated CTE during annual conventions, neither organization provided strong support. "Nonetheless we persevered," stated Cárdenas de Dwyer. Working together, despite being geographically separated, Cárdenas de Dwyer, Ortego y Gasca, and Dueñas González would meet in hotel lobbies and hotel rooms at NCTE conventions, plotting and strategizing their next "guerrilla actions," intentionally, "rejecting the tactic of subtle sotto voce" ("Working for Change Founders Panel Part 1: 1960s-1970s").

As a result, the founders of CTE created literature, criticism, and textbooks, such as *Chicano Voices* and *Chicano Literature* (Cárdenas de Dwyer), *Backgrounds of Mexican American Literature*, "Chicano Renaissance," *Selective Mexican American Biography* (Ortego y Gasca), and "Chicanos and American Literature" (Carrasco and Ortego y Gasca). They participated on the *NCTE Task Force on Racism and Bias in the Teaching of English*, the *Textbook Review Committee*, and *"Students' Rights to Their Own Language"* (SRTOL). They presented at NCTE conferences, speaking on the conditions and needs of Latino students during pre-convention workshops and individual presentations. Moreover, CTE would continually call attention to Latinx issues, advocate for curricular and pedagogical support for Chicanx and all Latinx students, and create an agenda with which Latinx educators could engage in social activism and advocacy within the spheres of classrooms as well as in organizations such as NCTE/CCCC. Such an agenda put students of color, and not NCTE or CCCC, first. A vision for social justice and social change, thus, did not simply emerge from NCTE and CCCC, but rather from minority caucuses such as CTE. Despite obstacles and many setbacks, CTE persevered.

"Nonetheless we persevered," is a fitting way to pay homage to the early founders of the Latinx Caucus, the latest incarnation of CTE. It also resonates with Cárdenas de Dwyer's statement, "I do not feel alone on this stage. I stand with Roseann Dueñas González, Felipe Ortego, Kris Gutiérrez, and numerous others from the past" ("Working for Change Founders Panel Part 1: 1960s-1970s"). The impetus for *Viva Nuestra Caucus* echoes that sentiment of perseverance and historical acknowledgement of collective labor. For as we write this partial history, we do not feel alone. We stand with past and current members of both the NCTE and CCCC (now titled) Latinx Caucus to tell a story to future caucus members and general members of NCTE and CCCC about how "we persevered." And we stand with those who recognize that there remains an imperative to call attention to Latinx issues, advocate for curricular and pedagogical support for Latinx students, and advance an agenda by which to engage in social activism and advocacy within the spheres of the classroom and organizations such as NCTE and CCCC. *Viva Nuestra Caucus* thus gives the NCTE and CCCC readership a partial history of the agendas and activities of the Caucus from its formation to the present as well as a renewed call to action.

AN IMPETUS FOR VIVA NUESTRO CAUCUS

Over the past 50 years, much has changed. The CTE is now known as the Latinx Caucus. Its membership has grown. The collective voice of the Caucus has become more significant within NCTE and CCCC where its members now undertake prominent roles. Two visions remain central to the Caucus, however. First, the Caucus is committed to Latinx issues writ-large; the changes in identity terms reflect this important mission towards coalitional building. Second, the Caucus keeps at the forefront the voices of our elders because without their words, advocacy, or commitment to better the educations and lives of Latinx people, there would be no platform for the Caucus to exist. As noted, these visions have led to the Latinx Caucus playing a pivotal role within both NCTE and CCCC.

But in 2011, when NCTE celebrated its 100th year as an organization, the identity-based caucuses did not have a prominent role in in this celebratory narrative. NCTE had established the *Task Force on Council History* for its 100th year celebration and the committee recommended a centennial volume documenting the history of the NCTE—their role in literacy education and their advocacy efforts in providing support for teachers of English. *Reading the Past, Writing the Future*, as it would be titled, focused on this celebratory narrative of progress. Yet, it failed to account for identity-based caucuses, such as the Latinx Caucus, and how catalytic such caucuses have been in fighting for social change and political justice alongside and within NCTE. Thus, *Reading the Past, Writing the Future* became a reminder of the work NCTE still had before it. The publication also demonstrated the need for caucuses, such as the Latinx Caucus, to remind NCTE of their central role within the national organization. Finally, it reminded many of how seductive and misleading a narrative of progress can be.

In response to *Reading the Past, Writing the Future* failing to account for the importance of caucuses and special interest groups, NCTE supplied initial funding for the *Working and Writing for Change* series, initially edited by

Samantha Blackmon, Cristina Kirklighter, and Steve Parks. The first publication in this series was *Listening to Our Elders: Working and Writing for Change*. *Listening to Our Elders* attempted to provide a platform for those NCTE and CCCC members who were pivotal in creating the caucuses and special interest groups, highlighting the need to preserve and expand the collective work of teachers working for equity and inclusion within and across diverse identities and languages. It was always understood by Blackmon, Kirklighter, and Parks that there needed to be additional volumes focusing on the history of each caucus and special interest groups and that there was still work left to be done to ensure that these histories were not forgotten. *Viva Nuestro Caucus* emerges from that effort.

Viva Nuestro Caucus is a historical account of the emergence of CTE as well as a celebration of the achievements of the caucus and its members. Echoing *Working and Writing for Change,* this volume includes interviews with founding and current caucus members who discuss the importance of the caucus to their professional growth as well as to the work of NCTE and CCCC. Here, we recognize the need to preserve and make visible a history, which until now has remained on the margins of invisibility. Indeed, if a history of the Latinx Caucus was not undertaken that history would be lost. The voices of founding members of CTE such as Cárdenas de Dwyer, Ortego y Gasca, and Dueñas González would not be recorded. Another impetus for publishing *Viva Nuestro Caucus* is our mindfulness of future members and leadership. However partial, preserving these voices and articulating our history, gives future members of the caucus a foundation on which to continue to build, whether that means new caucus initiatives or new roles within NCTE/CCCC. Finally, we continue to be mindful of the ramifications and implications the NCTE centennial volume had on the Latinx Caucus. The NCTE history relegated identity-based caucuses to the margins, as an afterthought. *Viva Nuestro Caucus* thus became a collective effort to recover and re-center our history, our accomplishments, and our vital presence in NCTE and CCCC.

Viva Nuestro Caucus was not completed without challenges, however. To move the Latinx Caucus to the central place which visibility affords would take time, patience, collaboration, and passion: We had to persevere. We began, then, so as not to allow invisibility to be the default. We began in the name of our past members, current members, and future members. One question we constantly contemplated throughout the development of the project was how to begin. The oral histories of the founders as well as long-time members are slowly vanishing. With no official archive, a history recorded on notebook paper, conference booklets, and letters would deteriorate in individuals' houses. Indeed, we did not get a chance to interview or explore the personal archives of all whom should be represented here. Thus, we realize our reconstructed history could in no way be complete. *Viva Nuestro Caucus*, fundamentally, is a practice of listening—listening to our elders and continuing to breathe life into the history and future of the Caucus. And we hope this volume creates a call to continue to listen to the history of our caucus, continue to attempt to fully articulate its importance. For as stated above, we see this volume as just a beginning.

We intend that *Viva Nuestro Caucus* stands as a reminder of how collective voices engage in knowledge-making and meaning-making practices. We have tried to enact this collectively throughout this volume. The cover image for *Viva Nuestro Caucus* comes from Ortego y Gasca's bibliography of Mexican American scholarship. This bibliography reflected what was available at the time, which was not much. We conclude *Viva Nuestro Caucus* in a similar fashion by including a working bibliography that actualizes a vision Ortego y Gasca had of having more scholarship by Mexican Americans. This volume's title also pays homage to Cárdenas de Dwyer, who concluded a letter back in the 1970s with this phrase, "Viva Nuestro Caucus," which translates into "Our Caucus lives and may it continue to live vibrantly!" Indeed, this title reflects our own disposition, *Viva Nuestro Caucus*.

Finally, we understand there is a need to continue this historical work. Throughout *Viva Nuestro Caucus*, our work has been to consider what historical exigencies led to the formation of CTE, how initiatives undertaken by past and present Caucus members reflect the presence of discriminatory and sometimes racist practices within NCTE/CCCC, as well as how critical the Latinx Caucus has been and continues to be within both these organizations. We asked readers to consider the implications for *Viva Nuestro Caucus* as a working document that speaks back to a national education organization. We realize, however, that different emphases and frameworks will need to be articulated by other scholars and volumes to fully articulate our collective history. Our hope is that *Viva Nuestro Caucus* is a beginning to efforts to bring more visibility to the Latinx Caucus. We are more than just a brief mention in the history of NCTE and CCCC. This volume is a testament that the Caucus has indeed "been here before" and that nonetheless "we persevere."

WORKS CITED

Blackmon, Samantha, Kirklighter, Cristina, and Steve Parks, editors. *Listening to Our Elders: Working and Writing for Change*. Utah State University Press, 2010.

de Dwyer, Carlota Cárdenas. *Chicano Voices*. Houghton Mifflin, 1975.

---. *Chicano Literature: An Introduction and An Annotated Bibliography*. U of Texas Press, 1973.

Ortego y Gasca, Philip. "Huevos con Chorizo: A Letter to Richard Ohmann." *Nosotros: Newsletter of the Chicano Caucus of NCTE*, 1970.

---. "The Chicano Renaissance." *Social Casework*, 1971, pp. 294-307.

---. *Selective Mexican American Bibliography*. Border Regional Library Association, 1972.

---. *Backgrounds of Mexican American Literature*. Caravel Press, 1981.

Ortego y Gasca, Philip, and José Carrasco. "Chicanos and American Literature." *Searching for America*, edited by Ernece Kelly, CCCC and NCTE, 1972.

PART I
Histories: The Story of the Caucus

CHAPTER ONE

Sidestepping Radical Change: A Short History of NCTE

Romeo García

This chapter is dedicated to contextualizing the history of NCTE from the early 1900s to late 1970s. This contextualization of mission statements and goals by NCTE, as well as a discussion of social and political transformations both within society and NCTE, helps provide insight into the formation of Chicano Teachers of English (CTE) in NCTE. What will be argued is that when NCTE celebrated its 100th year anniversary with the publication of its centennial volume—*Reading the Past, Writing the Future*—it would not be the first time it had denied the significance of activist groups such as the Latinx Caucus. It reflects the ability of an organization, such as NCTE, to graft itself upon the politics of the CTE by adopting but never fully committing to the caucus goals. Therefore, while the Task Force on Council History sought out to accomplish three goals—(1) document the history of NCTE, (2) document NCTE's role in literacy and English education, and (3) document its role in advocacy—what becomes evident through the work of this chapter is NCTE's inability to initiate and sustain actual radical change or become a leader for social change.

NCTE: A READING OF ITS RISE IN A TIME OF CHANGE

The idea of a national society of teachers of English percolated for some time. A growing concern about the differences between K-12 and college/university education,[1] coupled with the concern that there was not a true platform for K-12 educators, led to the NCTE being formed in 1911. In *A Long Way*

---

1   The history of Harvard and its grip upon education is well documented (see Pollock; Stewart; Brereton).

Together: A Personal View of NCTE's First Sixty-Seven Years J.N. Hook notes that in December of 1911, NCTE passed a resolution for there to be a "national society of teachers of English," a representative body "which could reflect and render effective the will of the various local associations and of individual teachers, and, by securing concern of action, greatly improve the condition surrounding English work."

NCTE would initially work to establish itself as a legitimate professional organization. One of NCTE's strategies was to speak on behalf of English teacher's conditions, presenting concerns regarding English education as a representative organization. NCTE would also demonstrate its abilities both by connecting English teachers within their particular states and across the country as well as by representatively vocalizing concerns of colleges and universities hands-on approaches of managing and controlling secondary curricula.

NCTE also legitimized itself through publications focused on student's backgrounds and interests. It also argued for the necessity to separate secondary schooling and higher education influences. This can be observed in publications such as *The Reorganization of English in Secondary Schools* (1917), *Experience Curriculum in English* (1935), "Basic Aims for English Instruction in American Schools" (1942), and *The National Interest and the Teaching of English* (1961). These publications would become significant for the teachers of English and the profession of English as it would not only justify curricula and pedagogical choices of teachers of English, but these publications would also offer support for teachers of English.

NCTE would acknowledge and respect the need for experiential learning and student-centered curricula. *The Reorganization of English in Secondary Schools* (1917) and *Experience Curriculum in English* (1935) are two primary examples of this. In *The Reorganization of English in Secondary Schools* (1917), a collaboration between NCTE and the National Education Association (NEA), it is noted that the creation of the committee is to bring about reform around such beliefs as:

- The college-preparatory function of the high school is a minor one.

- English is not a merely formal subject.

- Language is social in nature.

- The need for properly trained teachers (26-29).

What the report simultaneously does, though, is call out higher education's management and control of secondary schooling. For instance, the committee states, "The entire doctrine of 'preparation' for higher institutions is fallacious. The best preparation for anything is real effort and experience in the present (5). This is further discussed the section entitled, "The History of the Study of English in American Secondary Schools" (12). Under the heading, "The Aims of High-School English," the committee calls attention to the need for development of effective communication, the need to connect teachings and praxis to aspects of life, and the need for teachings and praxis to be conducive to "knowledge born of experience and reflection" (4).

The importance of *The Reorganization of English in Secondary Schools* (1917) is its care with considering the state of English education for elementary and high school and its provisions to making suggestions on topics anywhere from the aims of English education to grading. This is evidenced in the section, "The Aims of the English Course":

> Stated broadly, it should be the purpose of Every English teacher, first, to quicken the spirit and kindle the imagination of his pupils, open up to the potential significance and beauty of life, and develop habits of weighing and judging human conduct and of turning to books for entertainment, instruction, and inspiration as the hours of leisure may permit; second to supply the pupils with an effective tool of thought and of expression for use in their public and private life, i.e., the best command of language which, under the circumstances, can be given to them (30).

The report reflects much of what is now accepted as best practice within composition courses: combining lower and higher order concerns, relating education to student's knowledges and experiences, and demonstrating the centrality of reading, writing, and speaking to student's future endeavors. This is evidenced furthermore in the section, "The Organization of the English Course," in which the committee argues that the "subject matter of English consists primarily of activities, not of information" (33). The committee asserts that English studies is an "art, not as a science" that is meant to "be learned by practice rather than by generalization" (33). The rest of the report moves forward by discussing the role of English education within grade levels, weaving in their point of views on topics such as literature and grammar and including their suggestions for educators and administrators.

The concern for primary and secondary school students continues with a commissioned report by NCTE President Ruth Mary Weeks, entitled *An Experience Curriculum in English* (1935), which would build on *The Reorganization of English in Secondary Schools*. Reminiscent of John Dewey, report author W. Wilbur Hatfield reflects the sentiment of experiential learning:

> The place of English in this program is obvious; to provide the communication (speaking, writing, listening, reading) necessary to the conduct of social activities, and to provide indirect experiences where direct experiences are impossible or undesirable. An effective program in English must make provision for carrying the literary and linguistic activities beyond the confines of the English classroom (4).

Hatfield illuminates the role of English within the everyday in his publication and argues that English is essential to a student's education:

> Experience is the best of all schools. And experience need not be a dear school, if it is competently organized and conducted by a capable teacher who illuminates each situation in prospect and retrospect. The school of experience is the only one which will develop the flexibility and power of self-direction requisite for successful living in our age of swift industrial, social, and economic change (3).

For Hatfield, English need not be used for the sole preparation of students for entrance to college, but rather, should be "adapted" for the study and practice of everyday life. At the heart of any good education, as Hatfield discusses above, is experience. Hatfield asserts that in regard to experience and English studies, students "should be given experiences that have intrinsic worth" (18). Not everyone agreed, though, with the idea of experience. NCTE found itself in a predicament, that of supporting student-centered approaches and confronting criticism regarding skill-based practices.

In a 1937 publication entitled "An Experience Curriculum in English," Preston Farrar disagrees with Hatfield. Farrar agrees that experience is central and significant, but argues, "In many cases the preparation most needed is not an ordinary experience at all but a technical exercise devised by educators" (136). Farrar continues by taking issue with Hatfield's conversation of grammar, logic, and argumentation, and asserts that "if there is one thing that every experienced and observant teacher does know it is that average high school pupils do not read literature of ordinary difficulty with intelligence" (138). The whole argument presented by Farrar is that Hatfield's report lacks guidance and that it is unreasonable in approach. Farrar concludes, "I have said enough to show the dangers of accepting a theory without sufficient thought and then riding it to death no matter how hard the going" (139). NCTE would foreshadow the resistance NCTE would face to its core values and missions as social, political, and economic shifts remade the United States landscape.

The effects of WWII and the affective culture it created within education is undeniable. The study and teaching of English was greatly changed during this period. Rhetoricians such as Kenneth Burke, Richard Weaver, and I.A. Richards all demonstrate in their works the influence of WWII and post-WWII America. But, it was changes within the educational pipeline that had the greatest effects on the study and teaching of English. For example, when the Victory Corps was established on September 25, 1942 by Commissioner of Education John Studebaker, its emphasis was on science, mathematics, and physical education, as well as the preparation of Americans for military service. In this context, English was deemed as not necessary and its future was threatened.

David England's "With Grammar on My Left" provides insight of this looming threat and how it led to English leaders gathering for an emergency conference in Washington. The result of this meeting would be a letter that would explain how English teaching could become an "effective instrument in the successful prosecution of the war, in winning the peace, and furthering the activities of the Victory Corps" (67). Amending "The Communication Arts and the High School Victory Corps," Commissioner Studebaker would recognize English as "an important contributor to the war effort" (68). England's conversation on one of NCTE's pamphlets entitled "Teaching English in Wartime" (and journals such as *The English Journal*) demonstrate the extent to which war dominated English instruction. NCTE would also step up efforts to demonstrate the need for English studies, the need for research regarding English, and English' role in society, by lobbying and advocating for the public and federal government to recognize and acknowledge its merits. However, this would come at a heavy price.

In the late 1940s and early 1950s, English would be caught up in what was then known as the life adjustment movement, which started in the wake of WWII. Between the 1950's and 1960's, NCTE would align itself with the life adjustment movement and would publish works such as *The English Language Arts* (1952), *Language Arts for Today's Children* (1954), and *English Language Arts in the Secondary School* (1956), which reflected conversations stemming from this movement. *The English Language Arts* (1952), though controversial, would place emphasis on growth, social identity, citizenry, and on "language arts." *English Language Arts in the Secondary School* (1956) provided a framework for language arts, grounded within the ideas of effective communication (in writing, speaking, and listening) and the world (the everyday) of 1956. However, as criticism continued to be carried out against NCTE for prescribing to life adjustment principles, NCTE began changing its focus. This became evident in a 1959 presidential address.

In 1959, NCTE president Brice Harris in "Act Well Your Part" argues that it is important to convince the public that English studies is vital as well as to consider the future of the discipline. Harris states, "The truth of the matter is that the public's idea of our function as English teachers if confused, hazy, uninformed, and oftentimes medieval and maudlin" (118). Harris makes two arguments thus: (1) "English teachers and the public are going to have to understand each other a great deal better in the years ahead" and (2) English teachers are going to have to work together more harmoniously" (119). What Harris' address does is call for a professionalization of the English profession. But amidst social, political, and economic changes in society, this professionalization of the English profession would graph and map itself upon education reform of the 1950s and early 1960s.

The 1950s and 1960s is of particular importance because social, political, and economic issues would impact NCTE which would translate into changes within its mission and role as spokes-organization for the study and teaching of English. Criticism on education, particularly the role and value of English education as compared to science by U.S. leadership (Dwight D. Eisenhower), political conditions (the Cold War, Sputnik), and the establishment of the National Science Foundation and National Defense Education Act, would lead to education reform. An emphasis on science education and science-based educators would result in a particular approach that focused on science, foreign language, and mathematics. J.J. McPherson in, "Let's Look at the Systems Concept of Educational Planning," refers to this approach as a systems approach, which McPherson described as: (1) the relationality of subjects in student's educational experience, (2) the establishment of student learning objectives and outcomes, and (3) the establishment of assessment and evaluation that would ensure curricula effectiveness (66-68; also see Lilienfield). Such a systems approach would reform curricula with science being the focal point and be justified and rationalized with the rhetoric of nationalism as well as national security (also see Rudolph). Cold War democracy would have implications for NCTE, especially in regard to how they would garner the attention of the government to support the study and teaching of English.

The National Defense Education Act (NDEA), according to NCTE president Albert Kitzhaber in "Reform in English," subjugated English to a status of unimportance. Kitzhaber recalls in his presidential address, "We in English protested vigorously when English was excluded from the National Defense Education Act of 1958" (338). In his presidential speech, Kitzhaber talks about the legitimization of the English (and rhetoric) profession, the possibilities of the discrediting of the English profession, and the need for a moral wakening and collaborative undertaking between secondary and college English teachers. NCTE would begin to legitimize itself by re-articulating a definition of English as that concerned with content, skills, and college preparation. This is in contrast to its commitments in previous years. Again, NCTE would do so through congressional lobbying efforts and publications on the state of English teachers and English studies.

In 1958, NCTE, MLA, College English Association (CEA), and American Studies Association (ASA) collaborated together at the Basic Issues Conference which resulted in the 1958 publication, *The Basic Issue in the Teaching of English*. In the publication, the impetus for the study and teaching of English is provided in the preface:

- English has a practical value.

- English is more than a group of skills and has its own subject matter.

- English has a civilizing value.

- English can provide the opportunity for self-education and development (4-5).

Moreover, the publication highlighted the perceived state of the reading and writing skills of students, the pursuit of solving the literacy problem, and the problematics of the teaching of English (5-6). Indeed, this is undergirded in some of their concluding statements, "English teaching is a part of the educational system of this country, undramatized to date by the scientific and political crises which have aroused the interest and concern of the public" (15).

Beyond the preface, the committee engaged in a conversation of the goals, content, and teaching problems of English education. The committee poses the question, "Has the fundamental liberal discipline of English been replaced, at some levels of schooling, by ad hoc training in how to write a letter, how to give a radio speech, manners…" (7). As the committee continues to pose various questions, thirty-five to be exact, the committee concludes with conversations on what the individual teacher can do, what English departments can do, and what the professional organization can do. Undergirding the posed questions and concluding statements by the committee is the idea that "There is as much reason to believe that English teaching can be radically improved, given the right approaches to the problems…as there is to suppose that we can strengthen education in mathematics, science, and foreign languages" (5). *The Basic Issue in the Teaching of English* would foreshadow NCTE's role in trying to garner the attention of the federal government to reconsider English as a necessary study of all students.

Cold War democracy would continue into the 1960s. The 1961 report, *The National Interest and the Teaching of English: A Report on the Status of the Profession,* is one such example, which echoed the 1958 report on *The Basic Issue in the Teaching of English,* which called for the need to increase the "extension of democratic rights and responsibilities to most of our citizens" (23). This is to say, as organizations such as NCTE attempted to establish a civic relationship between the instruction of students in English and national democracy, it also sought out to create an image of an English student as one who could, as a civic participant in democracy, carry on the struggle over democracy. Three points are made in *The National Interest and the Teaching of English*:

- Support all national efforts to obtain support for the teaching of English and the other humanities on a national scale.

- Direct its Executive Committee to inform the nation's leaders in government, business, and education of the Council's mounting concern over the neglect of English and the other humanities in current educational efforts; and furthermore.

- Direct its Executive Committee to inform the Congress of the United States and the United States Office of Education of the compelling need for an extension of the National Defense Education Act of 1958 to include English and the humanities as a vital first step toward improving instruction in English and of stimulating program development in this important area (n.p.).

The report would highlight what the NCTE referred to as the "National problem" (preserving human values, poorly prepared educators, deficiencies of English instruction, etc.) and the "status of English teaching" (better English teachers, better teaching conditions, better research in English). What NCTE effectively did was announce that English teachers, the teaching of English, and the state of English studies needed to be improved and reformed. For example, the committee writes, "Poorly prepared teachers of English have created a serious national problem" (27) and argues, "Teaching by persons who cannot meet this standard will not produce the communication skills or the sense of human values needed so urgently in our nation" (39). NCTE, though, suggests that it has solutions to these problems (e.g., standards of preparation) and argue that better research in English can help in resolving such problems as well. In 1965, NCTE would publish *The National Interest and the Continuing Education of Teachers of English*, which called attention to the education teachers received. The point is, NCTE would present itself as an organization that could usher in improvements and reforms.

NCTE would ultimately garner the attention from the Committee of the National Defense Education Act (NDEA) in 1964 as part of the NDEA reauthorization process. Acknowledgment by the NDEA would come, however, at the expense of conceding to criticism on English education. That is, NCTE would have to acknowledge there were problems with English teachers and with the teaching of English. Fighting on the front of establishing the discipline of English' vitality within this framework would have several implications. It would mean that 1) English could be taught as a set of skills, 2) English would be the keystone language to use and practice in the learning processes of students, and 3) fluency of English would determine the success of non-native English speakers (English could be taught as a foreign language). These three areas of emphasis would be proposed as an appeal for federal funding in the revised NDEA. Though NCTE's lobbying efforts at times failed, this did not halt efforts for governmental support. This becomes evident with the creation of Project English (coordinated by J.N. Hook) by the Department of Health, Education, and Welfare for example. Project English (1964) would advocate for English curriculum within the profession of English, once more attempting to establish a civic relationship between the instruction of students in English and national democracy.

NCTE historically and presently continues to play an important role in the study and teaching of English. In this 100-year history, between 1911 and 2011, NCTE advocated for English teachers and the profession of English as well as helped guide the profession throughout the eras. It truly was a leader in guiding the meaning of English during periods of social change. However, it is important to note NCTE irregularly took a stance on issues related to racism and discrimination. This is not only significant because of the rhetoric that surrounds whether or not NCTE should be involved in politics, but also because it reflects, as Deborah Brandt notes in her foreword for *Reading the Past, Writing the Future*, a legacy in which NCTE has fallen silent and thus has failed.

NCTE'S EARLY STANCE ON RACISM AND DISCRIMINATION

In a post-100th-year anniversary, it is important to reflect upon NCTE's stance on racism and discrimination. In NCTE's centennial volume, *Reading the Past, Writing the Future*, Leila Christenbury concedes to two historical issues within NCTE: (1) equal gender representation and (2) racial inequality. Lindemann writes, "Though NCTE has not always been in the forefront of social change, it has had leaders who strongly objected to racial inequality" (23). This is a bit misleading. What Lindemann needed to say was that while NCTE has indeed been at the forefront of social change, as the above history demonstrates, those intentions have often been underwritten by various postulations (e.g., Standard English, Nationalism, Capitalism). These postulations hindered NCTE's ability to fully commit to radical reform. This is not to take away from the instances when NCTE advocated for racial equity. Rather, it is to suggest, or more specifically to argue, it has inadequately maintained a commitment to radical reform.

Returning to J.N. Hook's *A Long Way Together* it is true that NCTE had no representatives of minority groups. In fact, his choice words—"pure Anglo-Saxon"—is indicative of the type of organization NCTE was when it first formed and emerged. As Hook reflects on the 1922 Chattanooga NCTE Convention, he remembers thinking, "apparently no thought at all was given to the matter of segregation" (127). Hook also recalls an interview between Robert Pooley and Alfred Grommon about the 1932 Memphis NCTE convention:

> Now we did have a problem in Memphis. We had two Council meetings. One Council meeting went on in a hotel [the Peabody] and auditorium on one side of the street, and the black members met in another

building on the other side of the street...there was really no joint meeting at that time and in that place. (qtd. in *A Long Way Together* 127)

Pooley, in 1941, as president of NCTE proposed the convention to be held in Atlanta. But, even in Atlanta, as Pooley recalls, African-Americans "could not stay as residents in the hotels" (128). There is no doubt that NCTE witnessed racial inequity at its conventions. It could have been an opportunity to be a leader in racial equity. Yet, it took nearly nine years, as Hook notes, for NCTE to take a firm stance on matters of segregation and adopt the following policy and resolution: "no council convention would thereafter be held in any place in which any Council member would be discriminated against in any way" (129).

Christenbury does mention initiatives thereafter by NCTE that attempt to combat racism and discrimination, but they are inconsistent. Perhaps, one reason for NCTE's inconsistency is its own history of complicities with discriminatory and borderline racist language. Indeed, Deborah Brandt foreshadows this in her foreword of the centennial volume by suggesting NCTE has fallen silent and has failed in some places. An example of such failure can be found within a 1917 statement produced by NCTE for National Speech Week:

I love the United States of America. I love my country's flag. I love my country's language. I promise:

- That I will not dishonor my country's speech by leaving off the last syllable of words.

- That I will say a good American "yes" and "no" in place of an Indian grunt "un-hum" or a foreign "ya" or "yeh" and "nope."

- That I will do my best to improve American speech by avoiding loud rough tones, by enunciating distinctly, and by speaking pleasantly, clearly, and sincerely.

- That I will learn to articulate correctly as many words as possible during the year.

(qtd. in *The Skin That We Speak* 33)

What is problematic is NCTE's conceit to nationalism, what it means to be a "good American," and what it means to "improve American speech." Moreover, the references to the "Indian grunt" and the "foreign" grunt is embedded with cultural logics that scream discrimination and borderline racism. Though not a stretch by any means, this type of nationalist rhetoric would be echoed in NCTE's 1961 report, *The National Interest and the Teaching of English: A Report on the Status of the Profession*, which would focus on how America is a major world power (136). The concluding statements in the report are short but important, because the idea of "national interests" is always embedded within the ideology of post-war capitalism/global power.

The social and political milieu of the 1960s and 1970s would offer new opportunities and demands for NCTE/CCCC to address racism in society. There would be the formation of the Student Nonviolent Coordinating Committee (SNCC) in 1960, The Port Huron Statement of 1962, the assassination of Malcolm X, the Watts Rebellion, the birth of open admissions at CUNY (and remedial education) in 1965, and the assassination of Martin Luther King, Jr. and the rise of the Black Panther Party in 1968.

The 1960s was a time of social change, but also a time of complicities. Indeed, in *The Black Campus Movement* Ibram Rogers' critical account of what changed in regard to the black community focuses on how black people questioned whether a "non-violent" platform was effective. What becomes evident is how student organizations on campus played a critical role in the rallying cry of Black Power. As a result, Massimo Teodori, in *The New Left*, argued, "The student, who had been raised to believe the myth of the great American democracy, found here—no less than in other aspects of their life—a contradiction between fact and principle" (21). The university, a microcosmic reproduction of society, Teodori notes, played a central role in the development of American society and power structures. What the New Left and other social movements stressed on campus was the idea of participatory democracy that could only create radical change through collaboration. This democracy focused on all elements of the university and society from economic to ideology to addressing a racist America—though alliances between white New Left organization and Black Power organizations failed to sustain themselves.

As a result of this social activism, there emerged conversations on the role of composition and rhetoric in regard to the political and social activity ongoing outside of the academy. Louis Kampf in "Must We Have a Cultural Revolution," for example, focused on the on the role freshman English courses play in stratifying students. Kampf writes, the "responsibility of the Freshmen English Teacher seems to be to protect the class system" (248). An important question Kampf asks is, "Can we change the social context within which students are taught?" (249). Ultimately, Kampf suggests that the freshmen English course be a site of resistance culture and concludes by offering some words of wisdom, "there can be no revolution in the realm of culture without a revolution in the realm of politics" (249). These words echo Donald Murray's examination of what education revolution might look for composition teachers in "Finding Your Own Voice: Teaching Composition in an Age of Dissent." In this article, Murray ultimately argues that the teacher of composition should welcome dissent and teach effective and responsible argumentation (123). Another important conversation emerges from in "The Rhetoric of the Open Hand and the Rhetoric of the Closed Fist," wherein Edward Corbett traces the differences between "traditional" rhetoric and "new" rhetoric. His critique is that the closed fist "prompts" another "closed fist to be raised" rather than "moved" to take an ethical approach (295-296). Between the 1960s and 1970s there were critical conversations being had by scholars such as Mina Shaughnessy, David Bartholomae, Ira Shor, and countless others.

NCTE/CCCC responded in a variety of fashions to this new political situation. There would be the establishment of the Task Force on Teaching English to the Disadvantaged (1964), a Special Issue of *The English Journal* focused on the underserved and underrepresented (1965), and the Task Force on Racism and Bias in the Teaching of English (1969). The 1970s brought about a wider framework for the work to be done. In Geneva Smitherman's "CCCC's Role in the Struggle for Language Rights," she argues the period brought attention to the "academic exclusion of and past injustices inflicted upon Blacks, Browns, women, and other historically marginalized groups" (354). The inception of the CCCC (then NCTE) Students Rights to their Own Language (SRTOL) Resolution, thus, was significant. The resolution had three goals: 1) heighten the consciousness of language attitudes, 2) promote the value of linguistic diversity, and 3) increase effectiveness in teaching students of diverse languages. But, the resolution did not pass without controversy and resistance. Indeed, if one traces the archival correspondences in regard to SRTOL by members of NCTE and CCCC, the tension and resistance towards this resolution becomes evident—as discussed in Smitherman's article.

It was also during this period that the Black Caucus was formed. Between the 1960s and 1970s, within education, there was an increase in minority presence on campuses, but a decrease in minority teachers/scholars presenting at NCTE/CCCC. In, *History of the Black Caucus*, Marianna Davis (1994) discusses the concerns with "instant scholars" who "grossly misrepresent the Black experience" (11). What Davis is referring to is a statement made from the Black Caucus, who in 1968 at the NCTE's Convention in Milwaukee, Wisconsin came together to discuss the absence of Blacks on the convention program and the problem with "instant scholars." The emergence of the Black Caucus in the 1970s would forever change NCTE and CCCC, as it was attentive to increases in minority presence and decrease in minority teachers, interest of Black issues without any Black representation, and lack of representation of Black literature or studies.

And it is at this point in NTCE/CCCC history that the CTE is formed in 1968. And unlike the NCTE centennial history, which erases our legacy, this volume intends to show "we" have always been here. We've been here in our struggle for securing civil rights (e.g., the Mexican American Movement of the early 1900s and the Chicano Movement of the 1960s); we've been here as organizations (e.g., The Orden Hijos de America, LULAC, American G.I. Forum); we've been here through conventions focused on issues facing the Mexican American population (e.g., El Primer Congreso Mexicanista, The Harlingen Convention, National Chicano Youth Liberation Conference); we've been here in the fight for desegregation in education (e.g., Del Rio ISD v. Salvatierra; Alvarez v. Lemon Grove School District; Mendez v. Westminster; Delgado v. Bastrop ISD); we've been here as social and political activists (e.g., Jose Thomas Canales, The Idar family, Hector P. Garcia, Reies López Tijerina, César Chávez); we've been here as academic activists (e.g., Cárdenas de Dwyer; Ortego y Gasca; Dueñas González); and, we've been here as student activists (MAYO, MASA, UMAS, MASC, MECHA). We've been here before!

And it is to redress the absence of that history and collective effort that this volume now turns to the following chapter by Iris D. Ruiz entitled, "Creating a "New History" within NCTE/CCCC: Civil Rights, The Chicano Movement, and Honoring Felipe de Ortego y Gasca." Moving initially outside of NCTE, only to return, Ruiz historicizes the Chicano Movement as well as the professionalization of Composition Studies to give further context to the emergence of the CTE within NCTE and CCCC.

WORKS CITED

Anderson, Harold A., et al. "Basic Aims for English Instruction in American Schools." *The English Journal*, vol. 31, no. 1, 1942, pp. 40-55.

Brandt, Deborah. Foreword. *Reading the Past, Writing the Future: A Century of American Literacy Education and the National Council of Teachers of English*, edited by Erika Lindemann, NCTE, 2010, pp. ix-1.

Brereton, John, editor. *The Origins of Composition Studies in the American College, 1875-1925*. U of Pittsburgh Press, 1995.

Corbett, Edward P.J. "The Rhetoric of the Open Hand and the Rhetoric of the Closed Fist." *College Composition and Communication*, vol. 20, no. 5, 1969, pp. 288-296.

Davis, Marianna W. *History of the Black Caucus*. Parlor Press, 1994.

Delpit, Lisa, and Joanne K. Dowdy, editors. *The Skin that We Speak: Thoughts on Language and Culture in the Classroom*. The New Press, 2002.

England, David A. "With Grammar on My Left: English Teaching and the Second World War." *The English Journal*, vol. 68, no. 4, 1979, pp. 67-72.

Farrar, Preston C. "An Experience Curriculum in English." *The High School Journal*, vol. 20, no. 4, 1937, pp. 133-139.

Harris, Brice. "Act Well Your Part." Presidential Address. Convention of the National Council of Teachers of English, Pittsburgh, 1958. *The English Journal*, vol. 48, no. 3, 1959, pp. 115-122.

Hatfield, Wilbur W. *An Experience Curriculum in English: A Report of the Curriculum of the National Council of Teachers of English*. The National Council of Teachers of English, 1935.

Hook, J.N. *A Long Way Together: A Personal View of NCTE's First Sixty-Seven Years*. National Council of Teachers of English, 1979.

Hosic, James F. *Reorganization of English in Secondary Schools*. Department of the Interior Bureau of Education, 1917.

Kampf, Louis. "Must We Have a Cultural Revolution." *College Composition and Communication*, vol. 21, no. 3, 1970, pp. 245-249.

Kitzhaber, Albert R. "Reform in English." Presidential Address. Convention of the National Council of Teacher of English, Cleveland, 1964. *College English*, vol. 26, no. 5, 1965, pp. 337-344.

Lilienfeld, Robert. *The Rise of Systems Theory: An Ideological Analysis: An Ideological Analysis*. John Wiley & Sons, 1978.

Lindemann, Erika. (ed.). *Reading the Past, Writing the Future: A Century of American Literacy Education and the National Council of Teachers of Eng-*

lish. National Council of Teachers of English, 2010.

McPherson, J.J. "Let's Look at the Systems Concept of Educational Planning!" *The High School Journal*, vol. 44, no. 2, 1960, pp. 66-72.

Musgrave, Marian E. "Failing Minority Students: Class, Caste, and Racial Bias in American Colleges." *College Composition and Communication*, vol. 22, no. 1, 1971, pp. 24-29.

Murray, Donald M. "Your own Voice: Teaching Composition in an Age of Dissent." *College Composition and Communication,* vol. 20, no. 2, 1969, pp. 118-123.

The National Interest and the Continuing Education of Teachers of English. The National Council of Teachers of English, 1964.

Pollock, Thomas C. "The Profession in Perspective: Two Reminiscences of the NCTE. *The English Journal*, vol. 66, no. 4, 1977, pp. 6-9.

Rogers, Ibram H. *The Black Campus Movement: Black Students and the Racial Reconstruction of Higher Education, 1965-1972*. Palgrave-MacMillan, 2012.

Rudolph, John L. *Scientists in the Classroom: The Cold War Reconstruction of American Science Education*. Palgrave, 2002.

Smitherman, Geneva. "CCCC's Role in the Struggle for Language Rights." *College Composition and Communication*, vol. 50, no. 3, 1999, pp. 349-376.

Squire, James, R., et al. *The National Interest and the Teaching of English*. The National Council of Teachers of English, 1961.

Stewart, Donald C. "Two Model Teachers and the Harvardization of English Departments." *The Rhetorical Tradition and the Teaching of Writing*, edited by James J. Murphy, MLA, 1982, pp.118-129.

Teodori, Massimo. *The New left: A Documentary History*. Bobbs Merill, 1975.

The National Interest and the Teaching of English. NCTE, 1958.

United States Department of Health, Education, and Welfare, Office of Education. "Project English." CCC, vol. 13, no. 1, 1962, pp. 39-42.

CHAPTER TWO

Creating a "New History" within NCTE/CCCC: Civil Rights, The Chicano Movement, and Honoring Felipe de Ortego y Gasca

Iris D. Ruiz

> Key to teaching minority American literatures (including Chicano literature), besides obvious preparation, is the objective to make American literature what it should be—the literature of the American people not just the literature of dominant white America. This may have the ring of stridency but inclusivity needs to be the watchword not just in the reformation and teaching of American literature but in all categories of American life.
>
> —Felipe de Ortego y Gasca

Half of a century has passed since Felipe de Ortego y Gasca, late Chicano literary icon, pioneer, and civil rights historian, began to reflect upon a need to provide more visibility for Chicano literary figures in American Literature. As a Chicano scholar-activist who committed himself to ensuring that this inclusion took place, Ortego y Gasca has gained a reputation as an activist who is no stranger to standing on the front lines of the civil rights movement, battling against the exclusion of and resistance to Chicano literary representation. There is no doubt that Ortego y Gasca's activism within NCTE is partially motivated by his experience with editorial rejections of his own scholarly work on at least three occasions by one of English Studies' flagship journals, *College English*, while he was also engaged in the struggle for equal intellectual representation for Chicano scholars in the discipline of English Studies and its representative textbooks.[1]

Analogous to the way that Ortego y Gasca's above quote alludes to needed disciplinary reformation and inclusion of Chicano literary figures in the traditional American literary canon, decolonial and disciplinary historian, Iris D. Ruiz, points to similar educational and theoretical changes that took place in the discipline of History after the second civil rights movement of the 1960's.[2] Such changes are evident with the recognition of "New Histories," (Foner) which were aimed at providing a more nuanced and accurate view of histories previously limited by Eurocentric dominated rhetorical frameworks within the United States. These "New Histories" challenged such narrow conception of historical production and highlighted the "struggle for freedom, equality of opportunity, and equal rights, in both the popular and the political arena . . . [and were] also known for the legitimation and recovery of various 'alternative' knowledges within institutions of higher education. These disciplinary changes, not quite paradigmatic as politically expedient, brought about the creation of Ethnic Studies programs and a move toward considering 'social histories,' also known as 'new histories'" (Ruiz, *Reclaiming* 16). When taken together, both Ruiz and Ortego y Gasca can be seen as "creating" alternative representations within their respective disciplines: both History and English.

This chapter seeks to carve out a space that does what both Ortego y Gasca and Ruiz have accomplished in their scholarly careers, namely, enter an otherwise invisible population in a new history of Composition Studies. While Latinos and Latinas are absent within "old" (read traditional and Eurocentric) Composition Studies disciplinary histories, this chapter seeks to enter Chicanos and Chicanas into a "new" history of the field where Chicanos and Chicanas are finally integrated into the history of Composition Studies. As the introduction notes, the Chicano Teachers of English (CTE) was formed in 1968. As also noted in introduction, it was necessary for the earliest CTE members to engage in "guerrilla actions" that pushed NCTE/CCCC to recognize literary and scholarly contributions of its Latino and Latina members and literacy practitioners, scholars, and educators. This chapter aims to give a historical context that informs the impetus for those actions, which led to the creation of CTE—a time when Chicanos and Chicanas were in the midst of forging a presence within higher education and the national consciousness at large.

CIVIL RIGHTS, COMPOSITION STUDIES, AND THE CHICANO EMERGENCE

Looking back to 1949, at the start of CCCC as a professional organization, reveals that its historical context begins within a conservative moment, and while CCCC was a major force in helping to create a nationalist consciousness firmly rooted in American identity, Chicanos were not recognized as contributing to this professional and national consciousness. During the time when the Cold War[3][4] was sparked by major political differences between two superpowers, the U.S. and Russia, Chicanos were still seen as a negligent presence even when they fought to defend the U.S. in both World Wars I and II. While the U.S was edging for prominence on the global stage of aeronautic advancement as part of the "space race," and the launch of Sputnik, on the home front, our country was not able to reconcile its own internal issues of being embedded in a long colonial history of racism against various immigrant, colonized, and minority populations, many of whom were Latino and Latina. Not long before the creation of CCCC, for example, both African Americans and Mexican Americans were victims of blatant public segregation and Jim Crow laws (1930's) that legally segregated neighborhoods and public and educational spaces such as schools, libraries, and museums. Race relations were very tense all throughout this time and seemed to heighten with the Brown v. Board of Education decision of 1954. However, with the rise of racial tensions, the resultant student and community activist movements, and the election of John F. Kennedy, racial minorities began to fight for and realize racial equality and integration into a more realistic American Dream, one that was marked by inclusion, diversity, and activism.

Solidified in the late 1960s, the fight for political and social representation by African Americans, Mexican Americans, women, the working-class poor, and scorned farm workers, just to name a few, spilled directly into Composition Studies. During this time, mass and local protests were gaining momentum through the success of civil disobedience, leftist ideologies, and activist demonstrations, many of which were sparked by racial unrest. Berkeley protests, The New Left political movement, student protests and civil leader hunger strikes, sit-ins such as the Greensboro lunch sit-in, and boycotts such as the Consumer League Boycott in New Orleans (1960) are just of few manifestations of this civil unrest; there were also four assassinations (MLK Jr., John F. Kennedy, Malcom X, and Robert F. Kennedy), and a bloody war. However, due to the extreme actions of political activists and the FBI's orders to quell civil rights leaders who were threatening to change the social order, such as Dr. Martin Luther King Jr., death was not an uncommon fate for political leaders who were known as dissidents. As a matter of fact, compositionist, Lester Faigley noted that on April 4, 1968, during the annual Conference on College Composition and Communication (CCCC) meeting in Minneapolis, Martin Luther King Jr. was assassinated in Memphis.[8] Immediately after this incident, a letter, written by Richard Braddock on behalf of the CCCC, was sent to Coretta Scott King, King's widow. In this letter, he laments that

> only recently we have realized that we have been hurting ourselves by not discovering and utilizing the rich resources of our Negro members we have not known well or of non-member Negro colleagues we have not known at all... After all these years, we are finally taking steps to identify and establish closer communication with all our colleagues and to broaden the representation on our Executive Committee and, very soon, among our officers. (Braddock quoted in Faigley 59)

One can discern in Braddock's words the language of remorse, regret, and hope for future change within a field that, from its beginning, dealt with and still deals with acculturation and accommodation to a white mainstream. However, it was not until this moment that other cultures began to be given serious consideration. Here, the importance of Ernece Kelly's speech at CCCC following King's death cannot be underestimated. The delay in reconsidering racist practices came to an end, in part, as a reaction to the complex milieu of social issues which came to the fore in the sixties and MLK's resultant death by assassination. The outrage of MLK Jr's' murder as well as the struggles within the legal sphere and educational institutions produced a space to launch an ongoing critique of racial attitudes and unfair civil rights laws that legitimized discrimination against Blacks, Latinos, and Latinas. This critique led to the passage of new educational and legal policies (e.g. Fair Housing Act of 1968 and the Higher Education Act of 1965). The rise of Civil Rights movements in the 60s, thus, made a profound impact on the field of Composition and Rhetoric, marked by intense changes that were brought upon by the availability of more equal educational opportunities such as Open Admissions, the response by CUNY,[5] and efforts by intersectional, identity-based groups such as Latinos and Latinas to create groups with unifying political issues such as the Chicano Teachers of English (CTE).[6] If it had not been for the wide-reaching Chicano Nationalist ideologies that were being nationally spread, directly coming out of the Chicano Movement, for example, such efforts would not have had the impetus to come to be. However, even with an increasingly "brown power" movement, the integration of Chicano and Chicana scholars and their unique concerns within NCTE and CCCC[7] would still be met with resistance today.

CHICANOS/AS' SEARCH FOR VISIBILITY: THE FIELDS, THE SCHOOLS, THE IVORY TOWER

One unjust phenomenon remains unchanged since the 1960's; we have noticed, with the help of our elders, that over the past 60 years there has been a lack of Latino and Latina representation in the field's most respected publications, such as *College English* and *CCC*. Further, while NCTE and CCCC have recognized the need to engage in political activism through efforts such as the creation of the Task Force on Racism and Bias and the Committee Against Racism and Bias in 1969, this has not precluded the necessity for "guerrilla" tactics, aka "going rogue." These tactics, however, have proven to be challenging due to limited numbers of Latino and Latina members. However, this lack of numbers did not fetter Chicanos and Chicanas and Latinos and Latinas in search of an intellectual and professional identity as well as scholarly representation after the Chicano Movement and the broader Civil Rights Movement. In Ortego y Gasca's essay, "Shaping the Chicano Literary Canon," he notes one such successful effort to gain professional visibility:

> One such effort at organizing a Chicano group occurred in 1968 when as a member of the National Council of Teachers of English (NCTE) I organized the Chicano Caucus of NCTE. That Caucus played a significant role as a member of the NCTE Task Force on Racism and Bias in the Teaching of English and in its contribution to the Task Force document *Searching for America*, 1973. (2)

Such successes were ignited in part by some essential victories of the Chicano and Chicana people during the Chicano Movement. These victories happened in the fields, the high schools, and in the ivory tower. The 1960s gave hope for social justice within the Chicano community, as civil rights leaders across the nation demanded change and equal opportunities for people of color. Leaders like César Chávez, Reiss López Tijerina and Rodolfo "Corky" Gonzáles were shaking up injustices in the labor system, presenting Chicano youth in Los Angeles with role models to emulate. Meanwhile, a developing "iconography of cultural pride and beauty was empowering Chicanos with art and murals throughout East Los Angeles communities" (Simpson). Below, I provide a brief synopsis of each of these moments, as I am aware that not all readers will know the history and impetus for the Chicano Movement. It is beyond the scope of this chapter's purpose to go into great depth in each of these areas, and there are countless resources available to study each one of them. The purpose here is to carve out a space in a history that, while parts are written in visible words on a page, has either unknowingly or unjustly rendered Latino and Latina experiences invisible by failing to account for them in words and failing to create a historical memory for those same people (Ruiz *Reclaiming*).

On the fields, where a large portion of southwestern Chicanos and Chicanas worked, the creation and success of the United Farm Workers was led by César Chávez and Dolores Huerta. They both engaged communities through acts of civil disobedience, boycotts, worker strikes, hunger strikes, marches, and even theatrical performances (Luis Valdez) and were the main players in the grape boycott, which led to the success of the farm workers' movement. It was through this success that many Chicano and Chicana youth could, not only hope for a better future, but could actually attain a better future through communal unity, boundless courage, and both basic and higher education (Rosales, Haney-Lopez, and Pulido).

The growth of the youth's role in the Chicano and Chicana Movement was largely facilitated by Vickie Castro, who helped to organize a group of Chicano and Chicana teenagers to form the Young Citizens for Community Action, which eventually evolved into Young Chicanos For Community Action, then later as the Brown Berets, who are still fighting for Mexican-American equality in California. Further adding to this youth-led Chicano movement, starting in 1967, Moctezuma Esparza, along with eleven friends, played a large role in starting a group called United Mexican American Students (UMAS). UMAS traveled around to universities recruiting Chicano students who wanted to help increase Chicano and Chicana enrollment in colleges. Esparza and a few other UMAS members, along with teacher Sal Castro, and Vickie Castro helped organize hundreds of students to walkout of classes in 1968 protests to highlight the economic and unequal educational conditions that they faced (Simpson). In East Los Angeles, California high schools, victory was won. The success of the "walkouts," also known as "blowouts,"[9] took place the same year that MLK Jr. was assassinated. Vicki Castro and the YCCA (Young Chicanos for Community Action) helped organize the East LA high school walkouts in which fifteen thousand Chicano students walked out of five different East L.A. high schools in order to protest unfair and unequal treatment such as: vocational tracking practices, little attention to Chicano history and literature in the school curriculum, and little efforts to hire Chicano and Chicana faculty and staff (Chavez 43). These efforts were a direct response to growing a Chicano student consciousness, which was due to preceding events leading up to the East L.A. walkouts. Chicanos and Chicanas noticed and became dissatisfied with their substandard social position. For example, they demanded accountability from public schools because close to half of Chicanos and Chicanas were dropping out of high school and ending up in the unemployment office (Simpson). It is clear that Chicanos, as well as African Americans, came to realize that they could become social justice advocates in areas that lacked attention to their civil rights through their engagement in these civil rights actions.

NCTE AND CHICANO LITERATURE: FELIPE ORTEGO Y GASCA

Along with the creation of UMAS, in March of 1969, hundreds of Chicano and Chicana student activists met on the campus of the University of California at Santa Barbara to draw up a course of action committed to Chicano and Chicana cultural nationalism, self-determination, and education of Chicano and Chicana youth. This plan came to be known as, El Plan de Santa Barbara[10] and from it MEChA—*El Movimiento Estudiantíl Chicano de Aztlán* (The Chicano Student Movement of Aztlán)—was formed. The establishment of MEChA marked a significant shift in Chicano and Chicana youth activism and the Chicano movement at large in the late 1960s. By bringing together such prominent Chicano student organizations as UMAS (United Mexican American Students), MAYO (Mexican American Youth Organization), and MASC (Mexican American Student Confederation) under one unified organizing body, soon, Chicano and Chicana youth's militancy and commitment to *el movimiento*, or the Chicano movement, would electrify the struggles taking place in Chicano and Chicana communities while simultaneously politicizing the university sphere.

However, at this time, Chicano Studies had not yet been established, and it was not until 1969, a year after the walkouts, that El Plan Espiritual de

Aztlán,[11] the Chicano manifesto for seeking and affecting change for the Chicano community and beyond, was written. However, while Chicano Studies had yet to be established, Chicano and Chicana scholars began to take note of the absence of Chicano voices in their disciplines' scholarship, which was coupled with little attention being paid to Chicano concerns and their unique identities and history. As mentioned early on in this chapter, Felipe de Ortego y Gasca was a pioneering Chicano scholar in the discipline of English Literature. As noted in chapter one, NCTE formed in the early 1900s, and also served to open possibilities for minorities to be heard, albeit to a limited degree. However, with the growth of American patriotism, the National Defense Fund, and Project English, Chicanos were beginning to take note of academia's stubbornness to include their voices especially; yet, they persevered.

Chicanos who were educated just before and during the Civil Rights era began to question the lack of Chicano authors and voices in literature survey texts and courses. Felipe de Ortego y Gasca is credited with creating the beginnings of what is now known as the Literary Chicano epistemological tradition and Chicano Studies. As an early member of NCTE, he was also involved in the scholarly and political pursuit of critical Mexican American representation in the NCTE organizational structure and became one of the early founders of the Chicano Teachers of English (CTE). He also became an important member of the Task Force on Racism and Bias in the Teaching of English (see following chapter for more information).

These successful attempts at disrupting the hegemony of English studies demonstrate that, during the time of the creation of CTE (1968), a Chicano renaissance was taking place, also known as the broader Chicano Movement. Furthermore, identity-based political movements of the 1960s and 70s were being explored in ways that called upon these groups to make a visible difference for their people in ways that would grant them equal recognition, equal economic opportunities, and equal educational opportunities. Ortego y Gasca was one such activist, and he critically engaged with minority scholars in the field who were also writing about minority issues. He critiques Walter Ong's mention of "double identities," for example, and, instead, advocates for a more holistic identity. He writes, "Growing up in the United States as the child of Mexican immigrants I never felt as if, dysphorically, I was growing up with double identities even though in Spanish I was Felipe and in English I was Philip" (para. 7). Scholars began grappling with issues of identity and ways to navigate the academy even while the academy was not so welcoming of them. Of course, efforts at inclusion were not always welcome and often felt like an uphill battle: the struggle was "real." Chicano integration into and representation in English Studies would not be easy because racial injustices ensued despite the passage of the Civil Rights Act of 1964, and de facto segregation continued in education in southern and southwestern states. Taking matters into their own hands, it was educational activists and pioneers, such as Ortego y Gasca, who struggled for representation when they realized that their demands were not going to be simply granted through legal means. For example, the 1954 Supreme Court decision was not an effective means to end segregation and unequal educational opportunities. Integration had to be, instead, forced, and activists had to be very calculating with their efforts to make their concerns heard and addressed.

CARVING OUT SPACE FOR A "NEW" HISTORY: THE LIMITS OF NEW CRITICISM:

While it should not come as a surprise, NCTE and CCCC were directly affected by this history as noted by Ortego y Gasca. He recounts the history of the need and formation of compositionists of color into necessary collectivities:

> In 1968 on the death of Martin Luther King, Jr. the National Council of Teachers of English (NCTE) at its national convention in Chicago approved a resolution by the membership to establish a Task Force on Racism and Bias in the Teaching of English as a memorial to the slain civil rights leader. [...] Our charge was to survey high school and college anthologies and readers (collections) of American literature for their content–to ascertain how inclusive they were vis-a-vis the minorities represented by the participating caucuses. Needless to say, that inclusiveness was non-existent. The scathing Report of the Task Force [on Racism and Bias] published in 1972 entitled *Searching for America* gave all the anthologies F's for inclusiveness. That was 1972. (Somos Primos)

As Ortego y Gasca notes, NCTE had its work cut out for them because there was virtually no representation of minorities in "high school and college anthologies and readers (collections) of American literature." Ortego y Gasca would help to fill in this gap by writing the report (*Searching for America*) and then beginning to create what we now know as the Chicano Literary and Theoretical tradition. In an article titled, "Searching for America: Living on the Margins of American Literature," Ortego y Gasca discusses the structure of the report of the task force. I quote him at length:

> The report *Searching for America* was structured in two parts: the first part Critical Evaluations critiqued the twelve college-level textbooks of American literature; and the second part featured Background Essays providing information about the current state then of literary progress attained by the writers of the marginalized groups. This was certainly not a bias-free exposition. Nevertheless, it was our hope that in the hands of teachers and administrators *Searching for America* would be a catalyst for change. Additionally, our hope was that the Critiques and Essays would offer the reader a rudimentary familiarity with the names of marginalized writers and some of their works. (para. 14)

However, it should be noted that, not only was Ortego y Gasca carving out a space for Chicano Literature, he also had to face entering a literary field that was dominated by New Critical approaches to texts. Susan Miller confirms this focus on New Criticism in her book *Textual Carnivals*. She states that in the beginning of the 50's "American literary curricula were almost exclusively New Critical in orientation" (Miller 21). The discipline of English Studies was a prime target for change, as its normative functions were called into question for their New Critical approaches to English Literature and its focus upon close readings of texts. Such textual approaches were basically hindrances for people of color (POC) at this time, and the likes of T.S. Eliot, I.A. Richards, and William Buckley, Cleanth Brooks dominated the ides of textual analysis for many years to come while reviving a discipline that was in decline. These reading tactics were seen as being too prescriptive for POC who were just coming into their own definitions of their own literary tradition. In a recent interview with Ortego y Gasca, I asked him how he came to be a pioneering figure in a traditional and largely white discipline. He stated:

> What I know is that growing up and my first years in academia, I just assumed that I was supposed to follow a particular path. That path, unfortunately now, on reflection, that path was an all-white path. It wasn't until 1966 that I really, thanks to Octavio Romano, who organized *El Grito* and the Quinto Sol Publications. In *El Grito* Volume 1 Number 1, the emphasis there was that we should stop as Chicanos trying to get the white publishers, white publications to give us an opportunity. We should stop . . . asking, begging for anything. We were the ones that had to determine what the parameters or the worth of the works that we wrote."

The members of the CTE, then, played a significant role in questioning these formalist approaches to texts because New Criticism was disinterested in representation and efforts to include a multiplicity of voices. The CTE criticized the educational institution as it carried on its acculturating mission through New Critical means. The rejection of ahistorical New Critical readings of texts contributed to turbulent historical realities for racial minorities and limited their scholarly contributions. As a result of these limitations, the fight for Chicano and Chicana and other minority textual visibility became much pronounced. In his interview, Ortego Y Gasca confirms that philosophies stemming out the Chicano movement aided in this battle for visibility. He said, "It's part of that philosophy and commitment that grew out of the Chicano Movement, that we began, at that time, to realize that we needed to be more assertive, aggressive, and more in your face with a lot of white people." Ortego y Gasca further noted how he navigated expectations of the academy for him to follow the "white track" with a dissertation on European literary figures that he later scrapped for one that would establish the first published scholarly study of Chicano Literature.

Another limitation exacerbating the problem of New Criticism and whiteness was institutional neglect on matters of bilingual education, an area researched by Ortego y Gasca. In his interview, he noted that that the absence of Chicano literary voices was not a result of the absence of research on how to educate Spanish-speaking children. Although his work is absent from mainstream Composition Studies journals, Ortego y Gasca published "Issues in Language and Reading Instruction of Spanish-speaking Children," "Problems and Strategies in Teaching the Language Arts to Spanish Speaking Mexican American Children," and "Language and Reading Problems of Spanish Speaking Children in the Southwest." Through this institutional neglect of Ortego y Gasca's work and other scholars of color like him, a common disciplinary vocabulary that deals specifically with the literacy needs, concerns, and attributes of Spanish speakers is lacking. This absence hindered productive progress in combating racism and bias in Composition Studies scholarship.

The aforementioned institutional and intellectual limitations made the task of Chicano educational representation one of resistance against imposed limitations and called upon a small number of Chicano scholars to combat the stubbornness of old traditions and definitions that hesitated to give way to Chicano and Chicana voices. In the time of a growing national consciousness, Chicano scholars began gaining momentum, and although it was apparent that there was no such thing as Chicano Literature because it had not been created, legitimized, or theorized yet, Chicano Literature, and later Chicano Rhetoric, was successfully created from the "bottom up" (this book contains archival documents related to the creation of a legitimate Chicano literary tradition).

Ortego y Gasca had a prominent role in the creation of Chicano Literature. However, he and others committed to legitimizing Chicano Literature, such as Octavio Romano, have had to engage in advocacy work that took them beyond the scope of their everyday faculty positions in pursuit of social justice and racial equity. Ortego Y Gasca commented on his close relationship with Romano as one that grew out of being opposites to one another:

> In 1966, Octavio Romano organized *El Grito* and *Quinto Sol*. It was then that I became a Chicano. I had a flannel suit, I was supposed to follow the white track. He and I are nemesis to each other. If it weren't for Romano, I would have been Richard Rodriguez, he and I are nemesis to each other.

Ortego y Gasca became heavily influenced by early Chicano literary figures such as Octavio Romano, who was committed to bringing the Chicano voice into literary and textual representation through newspapers such as *El Grito* and *Quinto Sol*. In an essay titled, "Chicano/Latino Literature and the American Literary Canon" Ortego y Gasca notes that such publications led to the creation of a Chicano Renaissance. He is worth quoting at length here:

> Since 1960 there has been an efflorescence of American Latino literature highlighted by the Chicano Renaissance of the 60's and 70's. Consciousness of their exclusion from the American literary mainstream produced an avalanche of American Latino publications dedicated to the diffusion of American Latino literature, spearheaded by the Chicano publishing efforts of *Quinto Sol* in Berkeley, California, and its *Journal of Mexican American Thought* which they called *El Grito*. In the mid 70's a joint publication out of Gary, Indiana, entitled *Revista Chicano/Riqueña* promoted Chicano and Puerto Rican writers, first consciousness of U.S. Latinicity.
>
> These efforts to promote American Latino literature has led to a stream of anthologies focusing on the Latino literary heritage of the United States. In 1979, Nicolas Kanellos founded *Arte Publico* Press at the Uni-

versity of Houston specifically to showcase American Latino writers. Out of these concerns emerged the University of Houston project: *Recovering the U.S. Hispanic Literary Heritage* to show how integral U.S. Hispanic writers are to American literature. (4)

Composition Studies, however, still has a long way to go before they can claim to have engaged with a critically historically informed understanding of Chicano and Chicana textual representations and literacy histories (Ruiz). An engagement with the vast collection of Ortego y Gasca archives, only lightly touched upon in this chapter is one place to begin (see below).

THE FUTURE OF CCCC AND CHICANO/CHICANA INVISIBILITY

Given such territorial claims to the field, also reminiscient of the academic culture wars of the 1950's and 1990's, it should be obvious why Latinidad needs better representation and inclusion in our field; however, this presumption of obviousness will not adequately provide a well-rounded accounts of the role of Latinos and Latinas in both the history of Composition Studies, and in the history of NCTE and CCCC. This recovery work won't happen by itself, in other words. Currently, this burden of inclusion has been placed upon mostly Latino and Latina composition scholars who have entered a quest for reclamation of "New Histories:" those that account for geographical regions and populations not recorded in traditional historical account of Composition Studies. Eric Foner's description of a "New History," mentioned early on in this chapter and supported by Ruiz is one that is still under construction in the field of Composition Studies and both NCTE and CCCC.

As Ruiz notes, in the 1870s, when Composition courses appeared at Harvard to address the flawed literacy skills of a growing white middle-class, Chicanos and Chicanas (the majority of the U.S. Latino and Latina population)[12] were heavily concentrated in the southwest[13] due to their prolonged historical presence and their internal colonization (see Irene Blea on "internal colonialism"). However, early histories of Composition Studies often refer to the first composition courses being taught at Eastern Elite universities such as Harvard, where Latinos/Latinas were virtually absent and overlooked due to their recently colonized status (with Florida being colonized in the late 1700s and the Southwest being officially colonized in 1848). Surely these populations had complex literacy histories, yet these were not the population present in official histories of Yale and Harvard. Instead, these universities were attended almost exclusively by white, middle-class men. Given this historical absence, and despite integration of the Southwest into the U.S., the absence of Chicano scholarly contributions to the field is still apparent, and this history is just the beginning of providing much needed attention to a "New History" that accounts for the role of Chicanos within the field.

Today, two 21st century digital phenomena have made the need for Composition Studies to attend to their diverse practitioners and scholars necessary, namely, the world wide web and the blatant racism that this ubiquitous digital network has allowed the world to witness, along with the stark absence of racial topics in mainstream Composition Studies journals, visible through open access, digital venues (discussed as Imperial Scholarship by Richard Delgado). As a field, we need to find new ways to achieve social justice through literacy in an era where technology enables everyone to expose the enduring Jim Crow (blatant) and New Jim Crow (latent) racism taking place all too often—visible in continued gatekeeping practices of the field's main flagship journals. Such technologies demonstrate that, as a nation that is more race conscious and constantly being fed images of racial injustice, we have yet to achieve racial equality in our field evidenced by the lack of attention to supporting scholarship focused specifically on exploring the role race plays in our subject selections, research designs, and data analysis, communication of findings, and the articulation of broader implications of such studies to publics inside and outside of the field.

In addition, as our student populations are becoming more diverse, Composition and Rhetorical Studies would benefit tremendously by paying attention to what their members of color have been working toward since their beginning engagements with NCTE and CCCC. Both organizations have a long way to go in their white, male dominated publication venues. As Ortego y Gasca notes in response to the question, "Do you see any progression in terms of publications?":

> I don't see lots of Chicanos in *College English*. The tone and attitude of [name omitted] seems like the same attitude of Richard Ohmann [sic] in 1970. I did not bother after that. I am not at all keen if I can publish in a white magazine. We have a great network, and we have several Latino outlets available to us. *Arte Publico Press*, Houston, *Hispanic Vista*. There are at least 15 outlets and these are the same as publications for us. Those essays are posted in the Latino outlets, they are the same as publications for us. (Interview)

Let's continue to work on Chicano and Chicana representation within the field. This chapter has focused upon the Chicano movement, located in the southwestern United States, which is shown to be directly tied to the creation of the Chicano Teachers of English and to the field of Composition Studies and its affiliate professional organizations: NCTE and CCCC.

SELECTED WORKS BY FELIPE DE ORTEGO Y GASCA (AND FRIENDS)

I include below what is just the tip of the iceberg of an archive of works that should have been included in mainstream Composition and Rhetoric journals. As has been mentioned in this chapter and in the next, Ortego y Gasca was denied the opportunity to legitimately contribute to the field's most well-known publishing spaces for unknown reasons, but we deduce that when the reader goes through each one of these sources, available in the e-book version of this book, they will formulate their own opinions as to why this archive is crucial to the field's historical identity. I have been fortunate to work with Ortego y Gasca for the past three years, starting with my election as the co-chair of the Latinx Caucus in 2015. This was, indeed, a great moment for me, but I want to stress how much I have learned from the work that Felipe has shared with me over the past three years. It is due to his work that I have realized the importance of the Caucus work, antiracist work, and decolonial work. I, therefore, honor his work, his life, and his labor through the inclusion of a selected publications that are my favorites.

Adios Chaucer, Adios Shakespeare
https://drive.google.com/file/d/0B5olU_f6-ZxxT0M5aUNx-TEs2XzNaek5CLTFuTHJJOGkzSnlj/view?usp=sharing

American Latinos in Contemporary American Literature
https://drive.google.com/file/d/0B5olU_f6-ZxxbUJqV1cwYllfd2Z-VNVh4X3prTm4za19DN1NN/view?usp=sharing

Arizona English Bulletin
https://drive.google.com/file/d/0B5olU_f6-ZxxdHNmc2ozcl9M-b24zN091VUJ1dTJjU1dWeFZV/view

Faculty News Ortego
https://drive.google.com/file/d/0B5olU_f6-ZxxOUc2b1JFYUhzZn-BlSXFSZnFlbU9yS2ctYVZj/view?usp=sharing

Folger Shakespeare Library
https://drive.google.com/file/d/0B5olU_f6-ZxxLU1kYjlVZVps-MnFsM3l4WUNXaUphY0tQT0dR/view?usp=sharing

Chicano Latino Literature and the American Literary Canon
https://drive.google.com/file/d/0B5olU_f6-Zxxd1dxSExsS-WFuZy1jYnVBTVRKbXY2TjlKTmJ3/view?usp=sharing

A Writer's Life: A Literary Journey
https://drive.google.com/file/d/0B5olU_f6-Zxxb3RDYkN4N2lD-c1o5Q193am5DcUhvak9BN0JR/view?usp=sharing

Bravo Road with Don Felipe
https://drive.google.com/file/d/0B5olU_f6-ZxxaGQ5YkwxVXowN-VJoV192MFZ4YU9QLXBaQXln/view?usp=sharing

Linguistic Imperative in TESOL
https://drive.google.com/file/d/0B5olU_f6-ZxxbXZ4T0c5aTR5M-WJPSUUyNmFQNVZHMDlTeE9n/view?usp=sharing

Literatura Contemporanea del otro Mexico
https://drive.google.com/file/d/0B5olU_f6-ZxxRG5Cci1JT3JlOXRn-ZmZJb1ZWaGx6UjdwaG9B/view?usp=sharing

Into the Wild Blue Yonder
https://drive.google.com/file/d/0B5olU_f6-ZxxSWg0THA-2OHN6TUdBSi1KRlpvTWNPV3hoSlRz/view?usp=sharing

On Turning 90, Life, Literacy, and Legacy
https://drive.google.com/file/d/0B5olU_f6-ZxxNGpEc1BIVjdHUn-dRVmhVX0ZZMW1yWXVqLVM0/view?usp=sharing

Profile: Chronicle of Higher Education
https://drive.google.com/file/d/0B5olU_f6-ZxxWXI3VmJKa3FBNz-E4SG1zUHI1SXQ3ZTNwd0FF/view?usp=sharing

Race on Campus and Historically White Colleges and Universities
https://drive.google.com/file/d/0B5olU_f6-ZxxWXI3VmJKa3FBNz-E4SG1zUHI1SXQ3ZTNwd0FF/view?usp=sharing

Towards a Cultural Interpretation of Literature
https://drive.google.com/file/d/0B5olU_f6-ZxxVkY3d0JvS0w1M-2phZ3ZuR0Q0TkJlSGFCUHRr/view?usp=sharing

Writing and Cultural Dissonance: Chicanos/Latinos, Freshman English, and Writing Centers
https://drive.google.com/file/d/0B5olU_f6-ZxxQXRsa2RYSjQzM-29fYWxUbmN3bTBFZndEcHNB/view?usp=sharing

Octavio Romano and the Chicano Literary Renaissance
http://plumafronteriza.blogspot.com/2006/11/octavio-romano-and-chicano-literary.html

Reflections on Chicanos and The Teaching of American Literature
http://latinostories.com/Brown_Latino_Literature_Project/Essays/Chicanos_and_the_Teaching_of_American_Literature.htm

A Chicano in Viking Land
https://drive.google.com/file/d/0B5olU_f6-ZxxeERHV1BhakswME-hBeXQzRnZGZllnc1B1Y0k4/view?usp=sharing

The Colonial Syllabus in Literature
https://www.academia.edu/37301154/The_Syllabus_a_vehicle_for_academic_colonialism_The_Colonial_Syllabus_in_Literature_and_First_Year_Composition

ENDNOTES

1. While the introduction mentions Ortego y Gasca's essay, "Huevos con Chorizo: A Letter to Richard Ohmann" where Ortego divulges his editorial rejection and resultant conversation with then, Richard Ohmann, he also discussed his reaction to these rejections in his interview, which is included in part III of this book.

2. Scholars interested in equal representation were challenging the discipline of history as well by calling out the methods in which historical texts were being written. Referring the Civil Rights era as the second reconstruction era, Reconstruction historian, Eric Foner (*"The New American"* 18).

3. See chapter 1 for a more in-depth discussion of the relationship between Project English, the National Defense Fund and NCTE Also see Mariana White Davis' *History of the Black Caucus: National Council Teachers of English* (1994) and Scott Wible's Shaping *Language Policy in the United States: The Role of Composition Studies.* James Berlin's "Rhetoric and Ideology in the Writing Classroom" the field's "radical departure" from current-traditional rhetoric and scientism's influence on its eminence.

4. Interestingly, the first Conference on College Composition and Communication was held in 1949, just eight years before the launch of Sputnik and in the thick of the Cold War. With the threat of communism, the spread of the McCarthy Era, and The Red Scare, just after WWII, the U.S. was involved in political turmoil both in the global spectrum and within its own nation.

5. New York tends to lead on policy discussions, and because NYC is so diverse and has implications for all other minority serving students it becomes a model for how we think about basic writing, ESL, Language diversity etc. See http://www.nyc.gov/html/records/rwg/cuny/pdf/history.pdf for more on the history of open admissions at CUNY.

6. In addition, the Cold War (1947) was largely responsible for the growth of communication as a disciplinary field, which inevitably allowed col-

lege composition to flourish once more, from its bounded history to "standardized" writing to something more technical and even radical.

7. In 1949, the CCCC was founded; however, Stephen North dates modern composition and its new modes of inquiry back to 1963 in response to the reform movement associated with the Cold War and the National Defense Education Act of 19585 (North 11). In Kitzhaber's 1963 CCCC address, he cited studies and conferences that had taken place during Project English, a U.S. Department of Education effort involving a number of Curriculum Study Centers at locations throughout the country (Gage xvi). As such, Composition Studies as a field with a contemporary research agenda can be traced back to the early 1960s. These National Defense influences on the field of Composition and education in general led to curricular reactions to a growing emphasis on scientism and research in Composition. James Berlin explains some pedagogical responses to the restrictions placed upon Composition scholarship and practice.

8. Donna Burns Phillips, Ruth Greenberg, and Sharon Gibson also discuss Composition as a changing field during the time period of 1965 through 1979 in response to social movements, social needs, and the assassination of MLK Jr. They explain that [n]ot surprisingly, the political and social upheaval of this era had a direct effect on the composition scene: many CCC [*College Composition and Communication*] articles focused on social and educational concerns as they related to the teaching of writing—Martin Luther King Jr's assassination, minorities and teaching correctness, remedial teaching, democratizing freshman English, students' right to their own language, ethnic literature, and sexism (Ruiz *Reclaiming* 101).

9. For more information on the "60's Blowouts" see: *LA Times* article: "'60s 'Blowouts' : Leaders of Latino School Protest See Little Change" by Elaine Woo. March 7, 1988. http://articles.latimes.com/1988-03-07/local/me-488_1_lincoln-high-school-graduate.

10. See: http://mechadeucdavis.weebly.com/uploads/9/7/0/4/9704129/el_plan_de_santa_barbara.pdf

11. El Plan Espiritual de Aztlán was written by Rodolfo Corky Gonzáles at the Denver Youth Conference in 1969.

12. https://www.census.gov/prod/cen2010/briefs/c2010br-04.pdf

13. Important to note is that there were some parts of the Southwest that did not want to cooperate in the Chicano movement. Parts of the Southwest did, and this is mainly because, as Carlos Munoz talks about, we have evolved in disparate ways. The Chicano movement of the West of the Southwest was about identity politics but not so much for other parts of the Southwest.

WORKS CITED

Acuña, Rudolfo. *Occupied America*. 8th Edition. Pearson, 2014.

Chávez, Ernesto. *Mi Raza Primero: Nationalism, Identity, and Insurgency in the Chicano Movement in Los Angeles, 1966-1978*. UC Press, 2002.

Dwyer, Carlota Cárdenas. "Working for Change Founders Panel Part 1: 1960-70s". NCTE Centennial/Early History of the Latino/Chicano Caucus.

Faigley, Lester. *Fragments of Rationality*. U Pittsburgh Press, 1992.

Foner, Eric. *The New American History*. Temple U Press, 1997.

---. *Who Owns History?: Rethinking the Past in a Changing World*. Macmillan, 2003.

Kelly, Ernece B. "Murder of the American Dream". *College Composition and Communication*. 19.2 (1968), 106-108.

Miller, Susan. *Textual Carnivals: The Politics of Composition*. Southern Illinois UP, 1991.

Ortego y Gasca, Felipe. "Chicano/Latino Literature and the American Literary Canon." Caravel Press Online Encyclopedia of Latino Issues Today. Web.

---. "La Leyenda Negra//The Black Legend: Historical Distortion, Defamation, Slander, Libel, and Stereotyping of Hispanics." *Somos Primos*. 111 issue. Part 8, 2008. Web.

---. "Reflections on Chicanos and the Teaching of American Literature." Prepared for the Conference on American Literature, Texas A&M University, October 21, 2001. Web.

---. "Searching for America: Living on the Margins of American Literature." Latinopia.com, Nov. 10, 2014. Web.

---. Interview. Full text included in chapter 8 of this book.

Kelly, Ernece B. "Murder of the American Dream". *College Composition and Communication*. 19.2 (1968), 106-108.

Pulido, Laura. *Black, Brown, Yellow, and Left: Radical Activism in Los Angeles*. UC Press, 2006.

Ruiz, Iris D. *Reclaiming Composition for Chicano/as and other Ethnic Minorities: A Critical History and Pedagogy*. Palgrave, 2016.

Rosales, Arturo. *Chicano! The History of the Mexican American Civil Rights Movement*. Houston: Arte Publico Press, 1997.

Simpson, Kelly. "East L.A. Blowouts: Walking Out for Justice in the Classrooms." *KCET*. Web. November 6, 2016. Web.

CHAPTER THREE
Forging a Path: Felipe de Ortego y Gasca

María Paz Carvajal Regidor

As Iris Ruiz states in the previous chapter, The Chicano Teachers of English (CTE) was founded in 1968 when a small group of educators within the National Council of Teachers of English (NCTE), including Carlota Cárdenas de Dwyer, José Carrasco, and Felipe de Ortego y Gasca, began working together to increase the visibility of Chicano and Mexican American scholars and literature (Meztli 122). The work of this group, which eventually led to the formation of what we know today as the Latinx Caucus, had important implications for NCTE and for the teaching of English across the nation as they set out to create change in the classroom and in the textbook industry (Dwyer 7) by advocating for the inclusion of Chicano and Chicana and Latino and Latina literature in teaching materials and ensuring that the experiences of these groups were better represented in the field. As discussed throughout *Viva Nuestro Caucus*, as we celebrate over 50 years of the CTE, it's imperative that we look back at its origins and the goals of its founders to ensure that we continue to learn from Caucus members that came before us. To do so, in this chapter I provide a case study of Felipe de Ortego y Gasca and his early work in CTE and NCTE starting in the late 1960s through the mid 1970s. While the previous chapter explores Ortego y Gasca's career and scholarship within the larger context of the Chicano movement, my chapter draws heavily from materials in the NCTE archive to better understand how this founding member helped shape the Caucus and NCTE. Recovering the earliest parts of our Caucus' history allows us to see how members of the Latinx Caucus—as exemplified by Ortego y Gasca—leverage their membership to create change beyond the group, ultimately influencing NCTE and the field.

Ortego y Gasca is central to CTE's history not only as a founding member but also because he worked on a number of fronts to ensure that NCTE and the field embraced similar goals to those of CTE. Furthermore, his work within and beyond CTE helps us recover the early history of the Caucus and contextualize the experiences of minority scholars who were involved with NCTE. Ortego y Gasca's emphasis on the need of strengthening the visibility of Chicanos and Chicanas and Mexican American scholars and literature and of fighting racism can be seen in his involvement in a number of initiatives within NCTE, including the establishment of CTE and his work on NCTE's Task Force on Racism and Bias in the Teaching of English (henceforth, TFRB). While there is relatively little that pertains directly to the early history of CTE in the NCTE archive, some of Ortego y Gasca's and other members of CTE's work is preserved in the NCTE archive[1] because of their involvement in the TFRB (see the "Annotated Caucus Archive" for examples of materials from the NCTE archive). Due to the lack of archived materials regarding CTE, this chapter mainly explores NCTE's archived materials on the TFRB, but also moves beyond the institutional archive, using interviews with Ortego y Gasca and his own scholarly work over the years to trace his work in NCTE and his accomplishments.

Ortego y Gasca's own experiences with education offer a glimpse into some of the obstacles minority students faced in attempting to gain access to and succeed in higher education. Ortego y Gasca's birth name is Felipe, but, as he recalls, "when I began to attend the segregated schools in San Antonio, Texas, my name was changed to Philip" (qtd. in Rosales 140). In 1966, Ortego y Gasca reclaimed the name Felipe, but continued to publish under Philip for some time. Recovering Ortego y Gasca's involvement in NCTE and his work beyond it during the late 1960s and early 1970s has been particularly hard for this reason. In the NCTE archives he is referred to as Philip Ortego, but in other texts and publications he appears as Felipe Ortego, or Felipe de Ortego y Gasca, or sometimes Felipe D. Ortego y Gasca.

More recently, when asked what name he would prefer when referring to him and his work, he said he prefers Felipe de Ortego y Gasca (interview, 2016).[2] Regardless of the names he has published under, Ortego y Gasca has dedicated most of his scholarly career to advancing Mexican-American and Chicano and Chicana literature and literacy. Speaking about his education, Ortego y Gasca explains that 'I never got my GED or a high school diploma, but I ended up getting a PhD in English [. . .] pretty good for a kid who never graduated high school' (qtd. in Batoon). His dissertation, *Backgrounds of Mexi-*

can American Literature, was the first study of Mexican-American literary history (Ortego y Gasca, "Reflections" 120), and he has continued to champion the work of Chicano and Chicana and Latino and Latina writers ever since. As he explains, by the time his article "The Chicano Renaissance" was published in 1971, "expanding the American literary canon to include Chicano literature" was his "life's mission" (Ortego y Gasca, "Reflections" 118). His scholarly work allowed him to discover his roots, but reaching a scholarly path was complicated for him.

Ortego y Gasca's academic achievements are inseparable from his service to the country during World War II. As a Marine in World War II, Ortego y Gasca worked on airplane engines as an Aviation Machinist Mate in the Pacific (personal communication, 2017) and also served in China after the war (Battoon). After serving, Ortego y Gasca worked in the steel mills in Pittsburgh for two years until he "decided to do something with my life" (Ortego y Gasca, qtd. in Rosales 141). Despite only having completed one year of high school, he began attending the University of Pittsburgh in 1948 because it allowed veterans to enroll regardless of previous education (Rosales 141). In 1952, he joined an Air Force reserve unit, which was mobilized in 1953. He served in Europe for four years and eventually ended his Air Force career at El Paso, Texas in 1962 after ten years of service (Battoon; Rosales 142). Two years later, Ortego y Gasca began working towards a Master's in Shakespearean literature (Battoon; Rosales 143). After earning his Master's degree, he began his PhD at the University of New Mexico with the goal of writing his dissertation on Chaucer. In 1969, having written three chapters of his dissertation, he was asked to teach a class on Mexican-American literature (Rosales 144). This turned out to be the first course in Mexican-American literature in the nation. His experience planning for and teaching this course led to his decision to change his dissertation topic to a study of Mexican-American literary history and served as a springboard for his goal of opening up the American literary canon to Chicano and Chicana literature (Rosales 144-145; Ortego y Gasca, "Reflections" 118). Although this goal is reflected across his scholarly work in literature, it also left a mark on NCTE through Ortego y Gasca's involvement in CTE, the TFRB, and NCTE conventions and meetings.

NCTE'S TASK FORCE ON RACISM AND BIAS: WORKING TOWARDS INCLUSION

Before tracing Ortego y Gasca's involvement in the TFRB, it's important to know more about the context in which it was formed and why NCTE deemed it necessary in the late 1960s. NCTE's Executive Committee passed a resolution to establish the Task Force on Racism and Bias in the Teaching of English in 1969 (NCTE Board of Directors Meeting Minutes, Nov. 26, 1969). The responsibilities outlined for the TFRB on that date included:

- "immediate preparation of a statement on the nature and frequency of racism in English Textbooks"

- "a longer range examination of the complex ramifications surrounding the general questions of bias and racism in the teaching of English"

- "a concise report on the effectiveness and the fairness or unfairness of presently used tests for evaluation, placement, and college admission pertaining to English"

- "such recommendations for specific action on matters pertinent to racism as may be desirable for the Council or for any agency or affiliate of the Council" (NCTE Board of Directors Meeting Minutes, Nov. 26, 1969).

Even though the Executive Committee believed in the importance of creating a task force and outlined clear goals for it, finding members for the TFRB was not an easy task. Robert F. Hogan, Executive Secretary of NCTE, explained that when it was time to appoint a director and members of the TFRB, "past practice did not seem right [because] the more we accepted the charge of racism, the surer we became that many of us were culpable, or ignorant, or both" (ix). It was for this reason that NCTE's identity caucuses were central to the creation of the TFRB. Ernece B. Kelly was invited to become the director of the TFRB in part because Hogan and other NCTE members felt that she was able to use "her own resources..." to recruit members for the TFRB (Hogan ix). In addition, as a member of the Executive Committee of the Conference on College Composition and Communication (CCCC) and as a member of the Black Caucus, Kelly had previously voiced many of the TFRB's concerns (Hogan ix; Kelly, "letter to Nancy"). From the early work of the TFRB, it is clear that it not only set out to serve educators, but also to widen and expand the definition of English literature to include literature by ethnic minorities. Some of the most important goals of the TFRB were clearly similar to the goals of CTE. However, the TFRB had more institutional backing and therefore the ability to attempt to reach these goals at the national level.[3]

Once Kelly found members for the TFRB, one of its first accomplishments was putting together a document titled "Criteria for Teaching Materials in Reading and Literature" (henceforth Criteria). Kelly and the other members of the TFRB hoped that the Criteria "could be a force in giving both students and teachers curriculum materials which express the truth of the social and cultural world in which we live" (NCTE Board of Directors Meeting Minutes, Nov. 25, 1970). The Criteria, officially adopted by the Board of Directors in November 1970, emphasizes that those involved in English and Language Arts Programs have a responsibility to ensure that the materials schools provide can help students develop "attitudes grounded in respect for and understanding of the diversity of American society" (NCTE Criteria). The Criteria goes on to say that "it is the obligation and responsibility of teachers, curriculum planners, textbook selection committees, local and state education authorities, designers of learning systems and publishers" to ensure that teaching materials include a variety of voices and authors and fair representation of America's minorities (NCTE Criteria). The naming of so many parties was meant to distribute responsibility among individuals and groups that could create the changes the TFRB and like-minded educators and scholars sought.

The Criteria also outlines the "crucial deficiencies" in education materials, including "the inadequate representation of literary works by members of non-white minorities in general anthologies" used in the majority of English courses across all educational levels and the "representation of minority groups which is demeaning, insensitive, or unflattering to the culture" (NCTE Criteria). In order to resolve these and other issues, the Criteria calls for the creation of anthologies which "commit themselves to fair . . . and balanced . . . inclusion of the work of non-white minority group members" and for the representation of non-white minorities that respect "their dignity as human beings and mirrors their contributions to American culture, history and letters" (NCTE Criteria). The Criteria made visible some of the most important concerns that the CTE and other identity caucuses had, providing a national platform for enacting change in the teaching of English that would make it more accurate and inclusive.

Importantly, many of the changes the Criteria called for also aligned with one of the main goals of the TFRB—to enact change in the publishing industry. As Carlota Cárdenas de Dwyer, a member of the TFRB and one of the founders of CTE, explained years later, it was up to the emerging teachers in the 1960s to "make contact and persuade textbook publishers to change *everything* they were doing" because literature "needed to be transformed into a curriculum with pedagogical support on a national level" (5). It wasn't until 1976 that an editor was interested in making changes to textbooks, but through the work of the TFRB, publishers slowly began making some changes (Dwyer 9-10). Similarly, in 1977, while still discussing potential changes to the Criteria at the NCTE Board of Directors Meeting, Vivian Davies speaking for Kelly, who was unable to attend, told board members that "progress has been made in that many publishers are attempting to include wider representation of writers in literature anthologies" (NCTE Board of Directors Meeting Minutes, Nov. 24, 1977). Davies expanded by noting that "publishers have not been hostile to the task force's ideas and occasionally have called upon the group for guidance" (NCTE Board of Directors Meeting Minutes, Nov. 24, 1977). In other words, the TFRB, led by members of CTE and other identity caucuses, instigated changes in the publishing industry, an important step toward creating change in the classroom which would, in turn, help ensure the continuation of the fight against racism and bias.

ORTEGO Y GASCA AND NCTE: WORKING ACROSS PLATFORMS TO CREATE CHANGE

Ortego y Gasca's involvement with NCTE is most visible in archived materials related to the TFRB, but the TFRB was only one of a number of platforms he used to advocate for the publication and inclusion of Latino and Latina and Chicano and Chicana literature in teaching materials. In January 1971, Kelly sent an official letter asking Ortego y Gasca to become a member of the TFRB. In this letter Kelly states that the TFRB seeks to "expand [its] membership . . . to include others who are interested in fighting against racism . . . ." and asks whether Ortego y Gasca "would be willing to work with us for a period of two years" as part of the group's "core-group, which is made up only of urban minority persons [and] is most responsible for work and decisions" (Kelly, letter to Philip). Ortego y Gasca responds to Kelly's letter on February 7, 1971 stating that:

> I accept with pleasure, for indeed the question of racism and bias in

> the teaching of English is a professional issue of great important [sic] to me and other Chicano English teachers. Sad to say that literary historians and anthologies have not yet caught up with us. (Ortego, letter to Ernece)

In 1971, Ortego y Gasca was finishing up his dissertation, which he also mentions in his acceptance letter to demonstrate his

> ... concern for the fact that Mexican American Literature is but another aspect of American literature which has been neglected. American lit textbooks, like Norton, for example, focus only on the literature of the Atlantic frontier and of Anglo American writers. This is thus one area I'd be very much interested in exploring with the Task Force. (Ortego, letter to Ernece)

Ortego y Gasca shows from the beginning of his correspondence with Kelly that he is eager to join the TFRB because he deems the work it sought to do as important for teachers like him and as necessary to ensure that literature by Chicano and Chicana and Latino and Latina is included in the canon. He even provides an explanation of where his expertise and scholarship might match the TFRB's goals, demonstrating how his own expertise and positionality might be beneficial for the overall work of the TFRB. His letter also shows his attempts at creating local change by actively engaging members of the English Department at El Paso to heed the TFRB's Criteria:

> Since receipt of your letter I've been making plans to get with the Chairman of our English department and to establish new criteria for our selection of American literature texts, one which will reflect the multiethnic composition of the United States. Perhaps if we indicate to publishers our intent to seek such texts, they'll undertake revising their present practices. A ver? (Ortego, letter to Ernece)

From the start of his involvement with the TFRB, Ortego y Gasca fully engages with its mission and is eager to make changes within the publishing industry, within the English Department in which he works, and in the field by providing avenues for the dissemination of Chicano and Chicana and Latino and Latina literature. Ortego y Gasca's correspondence with Kelly demonstrates that he had important experiences, interests, and knowledge that he sought to leverage as a member of the TFRB. While Ortego y Gasca doesn't mention his work with CTE in this particular letter, he does discuss some of his general interests, ones that overlap with his own academic trajectory and the goals of CTE. It's likely that Ortego y Gasca saw the TFRB as another way to work towards increasing minority involvement in NCTE and fighting for the inclusion of Chicano and Chicana and Latino and Latina literature in teaching materials.

Indeed, one of the ways Ortego y Gasca was most involved with the TFRB was through his work in changing attitudes and practices within the publishing industry. An important contribution Ortego y Gasca made to the TFRB was his co-authored chapter in *Searching for America*, a publication of the Textbook Review Committee part of the TFRB published in 1972. As Kelly explains in the introduction to the book, the goal of the members of this committee included two main tasks: "they wrote critical evaluations of twelve books widely used as college-level American literature texts, using as a principal touchstone the NCTE policy statement, 'Criteria for Teaching Materials in Reading and Literature'" and "they wrote essays commenting on the literature, culture, or history of those racial and ethnic groups which have been systematically excluded from American literature collections" (xii). This book, in accordance with other goals of the TFRB, was intended to act as "a catalyst for change, both in individuals and in groups, as they go about the business of selecting and criticizing literary texts" (Kelly, "Introduction" xiii).

While the emphasis is on change by instructors and publishers, Kelly reminds readers that the most fundamental concern "is with our students" because "American literature anthologies today give students only a skewed and deceptive portrait of American life and letters" (xiv). Although at times it may seem like the work of the TFRB was too broad to create real change, we see from published and archived materials the dedication members of this group had toward students and education. Ortego y Gasca also shared these concerns, which are visible in his co-authored chapter in *Searching for America*.

Ortego y Gasca's chapter, titled "Chicanos and American Literature," was co-authored with José A. Carrasco, then assistant professor at San Jose State College. In this chapter, Ortego y Gasca and Carrasco argue that the reason Mexican-American and Chicano and Chicana writers aren't included in literature anthologies is not because they don't exist, but because of ignorance about them and "of a thoroughly ethnocentric literary point of view that has placed Anglo-American literature and Anglo-American writers at the top of the literary heap in the United States" (79). In addition to criticizing the state of literary publishing and studies of the time, Ortego y Gasca and

Carrasco outline the history of Chicanos and Chicanas and make clear the importance of their ability to use Spanish and English in their writing, which they see as a means of expanding creativity (81). Ortego y Gasca and Carrasco point to the depiction of Chicanos and Chicanas and Mexican Americans in literature as a central reason for racism against them and conclude by arguing that "if we are to truly overcome the 'color' problem, editors and publishers of American literary texts *must* be forced to assume responsibility for the perpetuation of racism towards Chicanos and Chicanas in American society and to take swift and immediate corrective action" (94). With this statement, they nicely capture what was at stake and the importance of having accurate representation of Chicanos and Chicanas and Latinos and Latinas in educational materials and how this representation (or lack of) had important implications that went well beyond educational spaces.

Ortego y Gasca viewed this chapter as an important piece that explained the lack of representation and the mistreatment of Chicanos and Chicanas and Latinos and Latinas, as exemplified by the fact that he continued to share its findings many years after its publication. During a keynote presentation in 2009, he explained that members of the TFRB "did not find just token representation in the texts of American literature--we found NO representation in those texts. We were invisible" (emphasis in original; "La Tarea" 4). Although Ortego y Gasca and Carrasco don't put it in these words, in addition to arguing for change in the publishing and use of teaching materials, they are working toward breaking down stereotypes of Chicano and Chicana and Latino and Latina writers by arguing that the language they use is not only a vital component of U.S. literature, but also a part of their cultural identity and in no way deficient. Instead, they highlight the benefits to creativity derived from the ability to write in two languages. This discussion of the mixing of languages in writing demonstrates its importance to Chicano and Chicana and Latino and Latina writers and helps to put readers at ease regarding the literacy skills of the writers Ortego y Gasca and Carrasco argue should be included in teaching materials. Although combating racism and bias in teaching materials is central to this piece, Ortego y Gasca and Carrasco were also in some ways setting the stage for providing students materials that might reflect their own language use, a necessary aspect of respecting students' rights to their own language, even before the passing of the Students Right to their Own Language Resolution in 1974 (see Chapter 1 for more on this resolution). Ortego y Gasca and Carrasco use this chapter and their work as members of the TFRB to attempt to work toward equality while acknowledging the complexity of this task, especially given stereotypes and misconceptions about Chicanos and Chicanas and Latinos and Latinas at the time.

In addition to publishing important scholarship through the TFRB, Ortego y Gasca was involved in NCTE conferences. His attendance at these helped to influence NCTE in meaningful ways. Ortego y Gasca was brought on to the TFRB because of his experiences as a Chicano, but he was not content with being one of a few minorities. Instead, he used his position as member of the TFRB and as member of CTE to help diversify NCTE and its conferences and conventions. For example, Ortego y Gasca worked alongside Carlota Cárdenas de Dwyer to bring the poet Ricardo Sanchez for a presentation at the NCTE national convention in 1972 (Ortego, letter to Nancy). After the convention, he asked that NCTE use some of the money allocated for the improvement of Chicano and Chicana representation at NCTE activities to help Sanchez cover the cost of attending the convention (Ortego, letter to Nancy). Ortego y Gasca was aware of NCTE's goal of including more Chicanos and Chicanas in its activities and he and other members of CTE advocated for the inclusion of Chicanos and Chicanas and Latino and Latina artists and scholars and for reimbursement for their participation. Through actions like these, Ortego y Gasca and other members of the CTE would call attention to the lack of minority involvement in NCTE at the time and would continue to argue for greater representation.

Beyond the CTE and conferences, Ortego y Gasca also successfully used his attendance at NCTE meetings to create change in the organization. During the annual business meeting in 1971 Ortego y Gasca "spoke on the lack of visibility of Chicano members and the lack of substance in programs on topics of concern to Chicano members" and proposed a sense of the house motion (NCTE Annual). In this motion, Ortego y Gasca recommended "that presentations about Southwest literature include the whole range of Southwest literature rather than literature by only one group of the Southwest population" (NCTE Annual). He also suggested "that NCTE national conferences provide a significant forum for expression about minority affairs in the teaching of English, and that, in addition to bringing various minorities into the Executive structure of NCTE, the Executive Committee establish a Minority Affairs Advisory Committee to promote and foster greater minority participation in NCTE" (NCTE Annual). When Ortego y Gasca was asked what "a significant forum" meant, he responded by saying that it meant "'more than tokenism'" and "pointed out that blacks were better represented not only in the convention program but in the present meeting than were Chicanos and

Chicanas, Native Americans or Asian-Americans" (NCTE Annual). Ortego y Gasca was well aware of the need to diversify NCTE and assisted in accomplishing that goal at this and other events. It was in part through his participation in this meeting that a Minority Affairs Advisory Committee[4] was established. Through this committee, NCTE members would continue to work towards more diversity and inclusion.

Just as Ortego y Gasca and other members of the Latinx Caucus have done since its formation, we still continue to fight for representation. The work of increasing minority representation and of combating racism and bias isn't over, nonetheless past and present Latinx Caucus members have helped create changes that extend beyond the Caucus. These changes have positively influenced NCTE and have opened doors for Latinx scholars. For example, Ortego y Gasca's involvement with NCTE led to the publication of his anthology *We are Chicanos*. After taking part in a meeting with publishers during the 1971 national convention, Ortego y Gasca was approached by a representative of Simon & Schuster who asked if he would edit an anthology of Chicano literature (Rosales 145). Ortego y Gasca accepted and two years later *We are Chicanos*, the first anthology of Chicano and Chicana literature to "include a critical literary perspective," was published (Rosales 145). Ortego y Gasca also wrote for and edited *La Luz Magazine*, the "first national magazine serving sixteen million Hispanos" (*La Luz Magazine*, cover). Each issue of *La Luz* included featured stories, current events, and a section covering issues in education, which often included book lists and annotated bibliographies of works by Chicano and Chicana and Latino and Latina writers. Although this magazine was labeled a "general interest" publication, it is clear that one of its emphases was on education and literacy.

Ortego y Gasca acknowledges that publishing in the late 60s and 70s wasn't easy. He has been transparent throughout his career about the difficulties he has faced in publishing in mainstream publications, most notably in his letter to the editor "Huevos con Chorizos: A Letter to Richard Ohmann.[5]" Due to the difficulty in changing publishing practices, Ortego y Gasca published extensively in what he calls "the public affairs arena of Chicano issues" (Ortego y Gasca, "Reflections" 118). His work has appeared in *The Nation, Saturday Review, La Luz Magazine,* and *El Grito* (Ortego y Gasca, "Reflections"). He has written and edited a number of books, including *We are Chicanos: An Anthology of Mexican-American Literature* and *The Tejano Yearbook, 1519-1978: A Selective Chronicle of the Hispanic Presence in Texas* (see Chapter 2 for more on his publishing record). In addition, among literary circles, he is well known for coining the term "the Chicano Renaissance" and for his poetry, fiction, and literary criticism. Through academic and more mainstream avenues, Ortego y Gasca ensured that his ideas reached a variety of audiences and continued to disseminate his message of the importance of supporting Latino and Latina writers and literature.

CONCLUSION: FOLLOWING PAST LEADERS' FOOTSTEPS, FORGING AHEAD

Ortego y Gasca passed away in December 2018, but he continued to teach, publish, and be a great mentor to many until the very end. He graciously shared his knowledge to those of us who are interested in recovering the early history of the Latinx Caucus and who want to know more about Latinx scholars who have helped forge paths that we can continue to shape according to our evolving goals. Ortego y Gasca remained steadfast in achieving his goal of opening up the literary canon to marginalized voices and his work will continue to serve as an example for emerging and for future Chicano and Chicana and Latino and Latina students, writers, teachers, and scholars. Ortego y Gasca and other members of CTE were devoted to expanding representation across NCTE and worked tirelessly to bring positive change to the Council. In Ortego y Gasca's case, this meant being present and vocal not only within the CTE and the TFRB, but more broadly at NCTE meetings and conventions. In addition, even as he worked to change publishing practices, he was able to publish his own work, often in non-scholarly or lesser-known publications and still gain recognition for it within scholarly circles. Ortego y Gasca's ability to work within the constraints of a system that hasn't always valued diverse voices made it possible to begin to change this system, eventually opening up doors for the Latinx Caucus' current members and their goals.

Uncovering and recovering figures like Ortego y Gasca through archival research helps us piece together the Caucus' history and to give credit to its founding members, but even more importantly, it exposes the ways in which their work seeped into and influenced NCTE, often also positively influencing the field as a whole. As this chapter demonstrates, we often have to be creative in the ways in which we recover histories such as those of the CTE because they're not often given the recognition they deserve and their histories aren't always recorded in lasting ways. The archive provides some insight, but we often must rely on other materials, including interviews and other published work, to create a full picture. Many of the chapters in *Viva Nuestro Caucus* are made possible in large part by the generosity of CTE's founding members and other Caucus leaders, who graciously agreed to be interviewed in order to help us recover the early history of the Caucus and thanks to whom we can better understand today's Caucus. Ultimately, the work of fighting for representation and for a better understanding of ethnic minorities within NCTE and the field is not over, but knowing the history of the Latinx Caucus provides us with an opportunity to celebrate the accomplishments of members like Ortego y Gasca and the change they have facilitated and to continue working toward ensuring that voices that have historically been silenced are given the recognition they deserve.

END NOTES

1. The National Council of Teachers of English (NCTE) archive is located at the University of Illinois at Urbana Champaign.

2. I use this name except for when I'm citing work that he has published under a different version of his name. See Ortego y Gasca's "Octavio Romano and the Chicano Literary Movement" for more on his decision to begin using his birth name.

3. The TFRB was more visible to a larger number of NCTE's membership and bigger than the CTE, which likely contributed to there being much more information on the TFRB in the NCTE archive than there is on CTE.

4. At the 1972 annual business meeting, when it was resolved to appoint a Minority Affairs Advisory Committee, Ortego y Gasca asked to change the wording of the resolution so that the Committee would work "in consultation with [the] Task Force on Racism and Bias in the Teaching of English . . . " (Second Session of the Annual Business Meeting, November 25, 1972). He understood that the TFRB could help diversify NCTE and he helped ensure that the work of the TFRB was taken seriously and that its members influenced as many other NCTE initiatives as possible.

5. See Ortego y Gasca "Reflections," and Dwyer for more on the obstacles Ortego y Gasca and other minority scholars faced in publishing in mainstream journals.

WORKS CITED

Batoon, Nathan. "Felipe de Ortego y Gasca." Voices: *Oral History Project.* University of Texas at Austin, 2015, www.lib.utexas.edu/voces/template-stories-indiv.html?work_urn=urn%3Autlol%3Awwlatin.628&work_title=Ortego%2C+Felipe. Accessed 15 April 2015.

Dwyer, Carlota Cárdenas. "Working for Change Founders Panel Part 1: 1960s-1970s." *National Council of Teachers of English*, 2013, p. 1-10, www.ncte.org/library/NCTEFiles/Press/Carlota_Cárdenas_Dwyer.pdf. Accessed 1 May 2015.

Hogan, Robert F. "Foreword." *Searching for America.* Edited by Ernece B. Kelly, National Council of Teachers of English, 1972, pp. Ix-xi.

Kelly, Ernece B. "Introduction." *Searching for America*, National Council of Teachers of English, 1972, pp. Xii-xiv.

---. Letter to Nancy Prichard. March 10, 1970. Record Series 15/73/8, box 1. University of Illinois Archives, University of Illinois at Urbana-Champaign, Urbana, IL.

---. Letter to Philip Ortego. January 27, 1971. Record Series 15/73/8, box 1. University of Illinois Archives, University of Illinois at Urbana-Champaign, Urbana, IL. *La Luz Magazine.* La Luz Publications, Inc. 3.10-11 (1975). Record Series 15/73/08 Box 9. University of Illinois Archives, University of Illinois at Urbana-Champaign, Urbana, IL.

Meztli, Itzcóatl Tlaloc. "Latino/a Caucus: Chicana Trailblazer in NCTE/CCCC An Interview with Carlota Cárdenas de Dwyer." *Listening to Our Elders: Working and Writing for Change*, edited by Samantha Blackmon, Cristina Kirklighter, and Steve Parks, New City Community Press, 2011, pp 122-144.

NCTE. Annual Business Meeting Minutes November 27, 1971. Record Series 15/70/1, box 1. University of Illinois Archives, University of Illinois at Urbana-Champaign, Urbana, IL.

---. Board of Directors Meeting Minutes. Nov. 26, 1969. Record Series 15/70/1, box 1. University of Illinois Archives, University of Illinois at Urbana-Champaign, Urbana, IL.

---. Board of Directors Meeting Minutes. Nov. 25, 1970. Record Series 15/70/1, box 1. University of Illinois Archives, University of Illinois at Urbana-Champaign, Urbana, IL.

---. Board of Directors Meeting Minutes. November 27, 1971. Record Series 15/70/1, box 1. University of Illinois Archives, University of Illinois at

Urbana-Champaign, Urbana, IL.

---. Second Session of the Annual Business Meeting. November 25, 1972. 15/70/1. Box 1. University of Illinois Archives, University of Illinois at Urbana-Champaign, Urbana, IL.

---. Board of Directors Meeting Minutes, Nov. 24, 1977. Record Series 15/70/1, box 1. University of Illinois Archives, University of Illinois at Urbana-Champaign, Urbana, IL.

---. Criteria for Teaching Materials in Reading and Literature. Record Series 15/73/9, box 1.University of Illinois Archives, University of Illinois at Urbana-Champaign, Urbana, IL.

Ortego y Gasca, Felipe de. "Octavio Romano and the Chicano Literary Movement." *Pluma Fronteriza,* 6 Nov. 2006, plumafronteriza.blogspot.com/2006/11/octavio-romano-and-chicano-literary.html. Accessed 16 August 2016.

---. "La Tarea y el Trabajo: Summary and Assessment of Contemporary Latino American Literature. Keynote Presentation. *LatinoStories.com,* 2009, http://latinostories.com/Brown_Latino_Literature_Project/Essays/Keynote_Speech_by_Felipe_de_Ortego_y_Gasca.htm

---. Interview. 14 August 2016.

---. Personal communication. 6 July 2017.

Ortego y Gasca, Philip D. *We are Chicanos: An Anthology of Mexican-American Literature,* Washington Square Press, 1973.

Ortego y Gasca, Philip D., and Arnoldo De León, eds. *The Tejano Yearbook, 1519-1978: A Selective Chronicle of the Hispanic Presence in Texas,* Carvel, 1978.

---."Reflections On The 'Chicano Renaissance.'" *Camino Real: Estudios De Las Hispanidades Norteamericanas,* vol. 1, no. 1, 2009, pp. 117-133. *MLA International Bibliography.* Accessed. 20 April 2015.

Ortego, Philip. Letter to Ernece B. Kelly. February 7, 1971. Record Series 15/73/8, box 1. University of Illinois Archives, University of Illinois Archives, University of Illinois at Urbana-Champaign, Urbana, IL.

Ortego, Philip D., and Jose A. Carrasco. "Chicanos and American Literature." *Searching for America,* edited by Ernece B. Kelly, The National Council of Teachers of English, 1972, pp. 78-94.

Rosales, Jesús. "Felipe de Ortego y Gasca: The Chicano Renaissance Man." *Thinking en Español: Interviews with Critics of Chicana/o Literature,* U of Arizona Press, 2014, pp. 138-149.

CHAPTER FOUR
Despite Setbacks: Carlota Cárdenas de Dwyer

Romeo García

Carlota Cárdenas de Dwyer has had fruitful career. As she recalls at her presentation at the Working for Change Founders Panel in 2011, it was 1962 at St. Michaels High school that she realized little-to-no literature, criticism, or textbooks existed for students of color. No curricular or pedagogical support was there for such students. She notes, "students understood that they no longer recognized themselves in their teachers or in their textbooks, and they would start to ask for change." She reflects:

> At that time to step into an English class was to enter a self-perpetuating, self-referencing world--the teacher, the textbooks, the curriculum, a veritable house of wax figures, all produced annually, like prototypes of an unyielding world view, repeated but never renewed. The breadth and depth of our national literary reserves, if sketched by means of reverse engineering from this perspective, would be rather anemic. The revered canon of U.S. literature, the bedrock of eleventh-grade English classes across the entire country, managed to group without expanding its vision of the nation. By extension, one could view the NCTE as a microcosm of American culture for the first half of the twentieth century. It was a narrow path that wound its way through the materials and methods of our profession.

It was at this time, 1962, that Cárdenas de Dwyer decided to pursue an M.A. degree in English at the University of Illinois at Urbana Champaign. The impetus behind this career choice included creating and providing curriculum and pedagogical support for the students of color being taught in English classrooms. Her inspiration to do so was sustained over the years by what she observed during those years as a graduate student. On the one hand, she accounts, "From the fields of Delano to the barrio communities of Denver, Chicago, Detroit...it was a time of an outpouring of cultural and social expression." On the other, she notes, "No surprise that in those days, I did not see the Mejicano/Latino culture, history, or language of my home and family in Chicago in anything I ever read or taught in an English classroom."

Cárdenas de Dwyer became part of the "voices" that "rose into a chorus of the many" when she set out to gather and assemble Chicano resources. This would not be an easy task. But in the years to come, since entering graduate school to pursue an M.A. degree in English, she would be taken to her first NCTE conference by a mentor where she realized that the question was not only "what to teach" but also "how to teach it." Both the "what" and "how," once more, revolved around Mejicano and Latino culture. As she discussed in her presentation, to gather and assemble Chicano resources, she "embarked on an excursion" from New York to Chicago to Detroit and Denver. This was because, as she notes, "we were still technologically in BC with no pdfs, no email, not even a fax." She recalls in an interview conducted by Romeo García and Jaime Mejía how she'd pick up community newspapers, poetry, and Chicano literature to begin creating a contemporary literature that could be used in the classrooms. Cárdenas de Dwyer would become instrumental in the assembling and accumulation of Chicano literature to be used within the classrooms, eventually resulting in the publications of *Chicano Voices* and *Chicano Literature*.

After her first NCTE conference, Cárdenas de Dwyer related even more with her students in Chicago. She notes, "Just as my students in Chicago did not view themselves reflected...so I did not perceive myself or my culture represented in the first convention of the NCTE that I attended Milwaukee 1967." For this reason, Cárdenas de Dwyer decided to pursue a Ph.D. degree in English at SUNY Stony Brook. When she decided to write a dissertation on contemporary Chicano literature, "I was told that I would be accepted to the program, but that there was no SUNY faculty that could assist me with the dissertation." Still she persevered. As a result, Cárdenas de Dwyer would become fundamental in creating and anchoring a space by which to research and talk about Chicano literature and the importance of developing curricular and pedagogical support for students of color in English classrooms. She was not alone, however. It would be during these years that she'd meet Ortego y Gasca and Roseann Dueñas González, sometimes in the hotel lobbies and sometimes in hotel rooms.

The social milieu of the 1960s had sounded a call in and across the U.S. Cárdenas de Dwyer recalls the effect the assassination of MLK in 1968 had on her and others during a 4Cs meeting, "We were instantly activated, as prepared to mobilize ourselves into taking meaningful steps to impel changes we knew could be delayed no longer." NCTE became the platform by which to begin dialogue about the needs of Latino students in the English teaching profession and textbook industry. As discussed in previous chapters, Cárdenas de Dwyer, Ortego y Gasca, and González would be active on many fronts—the Task Force on Racism and Bias, *Searching for America* Report, the Students' Rights to their Own Language. Despite these efforts, as Cárdenas de Dwyer notes, "progress was not smooth or even without some rancor." This is where the dictum, "Nonetheless we persevered," enters the discourse of CTE. And they persevered by "plotting" and "strategizing," via guerilla actions—plotting and strategizing for the next convention, the next pre-convention workshop, the next presentation, and the next textbook for multi-cultured students and schools. Cárdenas de Dwyer notes, "Rejecting the tactic of subtle sotto voce, we would cause heads to turn..." In many ways, Cárdenas de Dwyer was instrumental in bucking the status quo.

Cárdenas de Dwyer was never one to remain silent or quiet, which caused heads to turn during her tenure at the University of Texas at Austin. She was recruited by Jose Limon and Américo Paredes. Cárdenas de Dwyer would enter as an ABD and eventually would be promoted to Assistant professor. She recalls when she got there, she checked into the office and she said, "My name is Carlota Cárdenas de Dwyer." She notes, "I don't know what they expected," speaking to the fact that they were all silent. Along the ways, she would bump heads with the chair James Kinneavey. This is what she was known for, as Cárdenas de Dwyer recalls being told, "Oh, you are the pushy Chicana." "At first, they had to accept me, I spoke their language," she recalled. But as Cárdenas de Dwyer protested the "Q" designation marker on her student sheet, which defined Mexican American students from the Lower Rio Grande Valley" in a Freshman English course as foreign, she found herself in a predicament. The administration kept informing her that the "Q" label would change, but never did. Finally, Cárdenas de Dwyer decided to protest further by refusing to submit grades. She recalls, "I went up and told the secretary you can tell James Kinneavey I will not be submitting grades." Cárdenas de Dwyer remembers the look on the secretary's face as she turned around and left. Later that evening she would receive a call letting her know that the designation was changed.

Years after causing heads to turn, Cárdenas de Dwyer would face her toughest setback, being denied tenure. There existed a culture at the University of Texas that was misogynistic, racist, and discriminatory. Despite her active participation on "10,000 committees," she noted, "None of it was good enough and I was denied tenure." She refused to play "their" game, because to her it was more important to serve the students and to advocate for them. For her, and her husband Walter Dwyer, it all comes back to that moment where she bumped heads with Kinneavey. She recalls Walter stating that he knew they would deny her tenure because "they found out they could not control you" (García, Mejía, Cárdenas de Dwyer). Some of this would be chalked up to the pedagogy/English literary studies divide, where because Cárdenas de Dwyer focused on curricular and pedagogical support, instead of corridos and folklore like Americo Paredes or Jose Limon, she was seen as inferior—there was MLA and there was NCTE. She was too interested in advocating for students, because it was in the classrooms where real change could occur. This did not set well with colleagues. "They told me I should do a certain type of scholarship," she recalls, and she continues, "Don't tell me what to do, you do what you do and I do what I do." "All I did was work...I was doing most of the scholarship [reference to Chicano scholarship]," Cárdenas de Dwyer recalls. This was looked down upon because it was not the literary traditions of corridos and folklore. She remembers thinking, "My whole world came down and for that I will never forgive them." Despite these setbacks, Cárdenas de Dwyer would enjoy a lustrous life as an educator in the San Antonio school district.

Cárdenas de Dwyer also would play a critical role in the emergence of CTE and helped bring awareness to issues facing Mexican American students, scholars, and educators. There are many correspondences referencing Carlota Cárdenas de Dwyer, conversations Dwyer has with other NCTE members, and recognitions of Dwyer.

- 1970: In a correspondence by Ernece Kelly with the members of the Task Force on Racism and Bias in the Teaching of English, Carlota Cárdenas de Dwyer is recognized for her hard work in compiling a bibliography of minority writers.

- 1970: In a correspondence with Nancy Prichard, Carlota Cárdenas de Dwyer discusses content with Ernece Kelly and describes to Prichard several of the things she will be working on in relation to the Task Force on Racism and Bias in the Teaching of English. One of her points is to continue working the Chicago based Mexican American Council on Education.

- 1972: In a correspondence with James Lape, Carlota Cárdenas de Dwyer discusses the "progress" made by Chicanos in NCTE (Las Vegas) and CCCC (Boston) and the references briefly the process of establishing the Chicano Teachers of English. Dwyer concludes with "Viva Nuestras Caucus."

- 1972: In a correspondence with Felipe de Ortego y Gasca about a May meeting in Chicago for the NCTE Task Force on Racism and Bias in the Teaching of English, Carlota Cárdenas de Dwyer goes over the topic of the meeting—an annotated bibliography of minority literature. Dwyer states, "A Chicano bibliography is something we all have wanted to see in NCTE for a long time and here is our opportunity--let's make the most of it, hermanos!" In concluding correspondence, Dwyer includes her suggestions of how this bibliography could look like.

- 1972: In a correspondence with William Stafford, Carlota Cárdenas de Dwyer promotes the work of a Chicano poet. She concludes the correspondence with a final statement: "Since the NCTE has pledged to promote all aspects of American literature, it seems especially important for us to insure a truly representative variety of writers in an official program, such as the Poets Festivals."

There are other correspondences regarding Carlota Cárdenas de Dwyer. The point being made is that Dwyer was instrumental and active within CTE, NCTE, and the English classroom. Cárdenas de Dwyer believed that "every generation has its own battle." Her battle was advocating for Chicano resources and creating curricular and pedagogical support. "The bottom line, we have to change the country," she notes, as she refers to the import of her contribution—the invention of Chicano curriculum—and she makes a last sounding call for the future generation—"every generation has its own battle."

Cárdenas de Dwyer left a footprint that cannot begin to be captured by this short discussion or even the materials below. As Mejia argues, "Had you gotten tenure as you should have gotten tenure you would have been such a landmark iconic figure to so many Chicano/as at UT since then, since 1982 there would have been so many people you would have influenced, you would have been, I think in my view, legendary. Because they turned you down though, they just lost an opportunity."

CHAPTER FIVE

Inclusion of Latino and Latina Literature: Roseann Dueñas González

Anita Hernández

> I realized from my own experience that unless there is a connection with school created by a teacher, a text, a theme, a set of lessons, there is no chance of academic achievement and every chance of alienation from the larger society and their own communities. The lack of a home-school connection through recognition of language, culture, and integration of familiar cultural ideas and themes fosters a passive acceptance of the school and the larger culture's conception of a student's place in the world.
>
> —Roseann Dueñas González

Just as Felipe de Ortego y Gasca and Carlota Cárdenas de Dwyer had a passion for Chicano and Mexican literary works, cultural connections, and students' bilingualism, Roseann Dueñas González, too, shared this fervor and commitment. The opening quote for this chapter, clearly illustrates her beliefs about schools recognizing students' funds of knowledge as well as their language and culture as a key factor to their academic success. This was her driving force in her presentations at the NCTE conference workshops. She, also, had a long career of scholarship, commitment to her own Latino community, and service to the Caucus and to the NCTE organization. Her motivation was not only from her experiences as a student teacher watching the unfairness students of color had to endure, but also from her experience growing up in a immigrant family in Tucson. In speaking of her students, she critically reflects on the situation high school students of color tolerated:

> When I did my student teaching at a Tucson secondary school with a Latino, African American, and Native American population . . . I experienced firsthand the second-class treatment of students of color and a curriculum that did not include their histories, literature, texts, or images of any kind. Particularly abhorrent to me was the institutional mistreatment of Mexican American students who were Spanish dominant English language learners.
>
> In fact, in 1969 and 1970, during my teaching experience as a student teacher at a local Tucson high school, I saw literally hundreds of students whose educational opportunities had been severely limited by their misclassification as special education students and their substandard pedagogical treatment in alleged ESL classrooms, where no content of any kind was presented and time was passed watching movies and doing endless crossword puzzles with limited learning value, as well as learning parts of speech and the mindless drilling of sentence patterns. (Baca & Kirklighter 15-16)

Roseann Dueñas González was the granddaughter of immigrant grandparents who settled in Ajo, Arizona from Sonora, Mexico. When her grandmother dies, her daughter Maria Luisa at age 11 takes on the duties of family caretaker and can no longer attend school. Roseann Dueñas González was the youngest daughter of Maria Luisa and Jesus González. Not having finished school, her mother, Maria Luisa, was determined to teach herself English. She grew up watching her mother learn English through reading the newspaper and looking up words using a Webster's Dictionary. While learning English herself, her mother was determined to also teach Roseann English so that she would not be punished in school for speaking Spanish. Roseann Dueñas González's love of English grew from her experiences growing up watching her mother teach herself English. Her lived experiences coupled with her student teaching experience and as a secondary English Education supervisor in Phoenix high schools were the impetus for the commitment to Latino students during her entire career as a Professor of English and Language, her service to the CTE, and the committees she served on in the NCTE.

Roseann Dueñas González first attended an NCTE conference in 1971, where she met Felipe de Ortego y Gasca, Carlota Cárdenas de Dwyer, and

José Carrasco, and instantly became a part of the founding CTE group, which had been initiated three years earlier in 1968. In her own words, her immediate commitment to CTE and NCTE had solidified. She had begun to think differently about English education:

> In 1971, I had already come to the conclusion that the only way to change the outcome for Latino students was to change the pedagogical model and recognize and respect the students' and parents' culture and language and incorporate them into the school culture. I realized that discriminatory treatment and poor expectations of students lead to academic poor self- concept, academic underachievement, separation from school, through failure or dropout, and alienation from family, ethnicity group, and mainstream society. The key was to create a multicultural, tolerant, respectful classroom environment and to introduce curriculum, materials, literature, and topics that spoke to the students' experience. (Baca & Kirklighter 17)

She went on to be a Chicana English professor, researcher, and a leader of the NCTE's Chicano Teachers of English. She reflects on her role in influencing both the NCTE and publishers to integrate Latino and Latina authored literary works in American literature anthologies—a vision that Ortego de Gasca also had. As a longtime member of NCTE, Roseann Dueñas González was central to the effort that the Chicano Teachers of English (CTE) initially put forth and throughout the Caucus history into the 2000s. Roseann Dueñas González was not just a lone scholar, she was a collaborator, working in partnership with Ortego y Gasca and Cárdenas de Dwyer. The three together did so much to push CTE forward to makes its mark on the NCTE and CCCCs organizations. Roseann Dueñas González's integration continued to solidify CTE at a critical historical moment that paralleled the Chicano Movement's trajectory. She was also an active member and officer of the NCTE for over forty years, taking up the work that made the CTE and the Caucus visible and important to the NCTE.

AS A SCHOLAR

Roseann Dueñas González was the first in her family to attend college. In 1966 she was admitted to the University of Arizona, where she was an English Education major. She graduated cum laude. She immediately entered the university's graduate school and completed her Master's degree in English as a Second Language in the English Department in 1972. With her MA degree in hand, she was appointed Lecturer at Arizona State University (ASU), where she taught composition and the practicum for student teachers in English Education and supervised student teachers in the Phoenix high schools. While at ASU, she established a writing clinic for the athletes. After a year, Roseann was recruited back to the University of Arizona in 1973 as a lecturer and in 1974 immediately began her doctoral studies in linguistics. While completing her dissertation, in 1976, she became the Assistant Director of Freshman English under the direction of Dr. Charles Davis, the Director of Freshman English at the University of Arizona. Upon completing her dissertation on court interpretation in 1977, the administrative office of the U.S. Courts used her dissertation to develop the Court Interpreters Act of 1978.

After earning her doctoral degree in 1977, Roseann Dueñas González was promoted to Assistant Professor of English. At the time she was one of the six women professors in the Department of English out of 90 faculty at the University of Arizona. In 1991, Roseann Dueñas González became the first Mexican American woman to earn full professor status at the University of Arizona. For her, the tenure and promotion process of the professorship was a relatively smooth process, unlike her Latino colleagues at other universities. Much of this was due to a combination of factors, including her talents, her longtime attendance at the University of Arizona as a student earning her BA, MA, and Ph.D. degrees, and the mentoring she received from Professor Charles Davis. In contrast, see Chapter 4 to read about the tenure and promotion process for Cárdenas de Dwyer.

In 1982, to further assist limited English-speaking individuals, Roseann Dueñas González created the Medical Interpreter Training Institute in Arizona, and, in 1983, she founded the three-week Summer Institute for Court Interpretation. In 1982, Agnese Haury became interested in the federal project that Roseann Dueñas González was leading in developing and validating a federal court interpreter certification exam. Haury herself was a researcher, historian, editor, author and philanthropist who remained connected and endowed several projects that Roseann Dueñas González led. Hence, in 1983, she named the Institute for Interpretation after Agnese Haury and National Center for Interpretation, which Roseann Dueñas González led until her retirement in 2012 (Everett-Haynes 2012). Few professors have opportunities for receiving endowments, let alone Chicano and Chicana professors. For Roseann Dueñas González this was a feather in her professional cap and an honor for her institution, the University of Arizona. For more specifics about the interpreter institute go to https://nci.arizona.edu/about-us/.

While conducting the medical interpreters institute and the summer institutes for court interpretation, Roseann Dueñas González and other colleagues developed a book that has become a seminal text in interpretation *Fundamentals of Court Interpretation: Theory, Policy and Practice* (González, Vasquez, & Mikkleson 1992). This text established the standards for the field of interpretation. Roseann Dueñas González's commitment to the development of standards, validation of the examinations, and the certification process in medical and court interpretation is a testimony to her vision of what is equitable and possible for individuals who were limited in their English-speaking abilities. Currently, every federal and state course uses this text to teach the fundamentals of court interpretation; the text is also considered the standard for informed practice in the field.

Aside from initiating the institutes and creating a national center, Roseann Dueñas González was also publishing through the NCTE. In the 1980s, she wrote two articles for the NCTE's *English Journal*: "Teaching Mexican American Students to Write: Capitalizing on the Culture" (González 1982) and "The English Language Amendment: Examining Myths" (González 1988). The topic of this latter article on the English language amendment was expanded into a two-volume edited collection, which was first accepted as a book proposal and then published through the NCTE, titled *Language Ideologies: Critical Perspectives on the Official English Movement Vol 1, Education and the Social Implications of Official Language* and *Language Ideologies: Critical Perspectives on the Official English Movement, Vol. 2: History, Theory, and Policy* (González 2001). The volumes address the complexity of the debate over the rights of language diversity and the English-only movement in the United States at the policy, pedagogy, and classroom level. Language ideology and the English language amendment was an important issue that members brought to the CCCC leadership in 1974 with the CCCC Position Statement on Students' Rights to Their Own Language and in 2001 CCCC Position Statement on Second Language Writing and Writers (NCTE, 1974; 2001). Roseann Dueñas González uniquely brought together essays written by NCTE/CCCC scholars, and well-known scholars in bilingual education, second language education, legislative, and policy. Under her editorship, the essays in the second volume critically examined the political, legislative, and social complexities and their implications of English-only and language diversity/language as a resource policies. The essays used theories of social justice and critical perspectives about language beliefs and their policy consequences. Both volumes speak about the media's influence in framing the debate on language and those moments of language panic, the legal systems bias against Spanish speakers, and problems faced by educators when educating students who are native speakers of other languages.

Roseann Dueñas González included NCTE members in both volumes. Gail Okawa, longtime Caucus and NCTE member, wrote about preservice English teachers' reflections about their own language ideologies to include their students' who are from diverse language backgrounds. In the second volume, Amanda Espinosa-Aguilar, also a longtime Caucus and NCTE member, includes a rhetorical analysis of the English-Only literature and how the language in their literature instills fear and anxiety within our society. Both volumes illustrate the care and thoughtfulness that Roseann Dueñas González put into the creation of the two volumes that were well received by the research community (Kleifgen 2002). During her forty-one years as a scholar at the University of Arizona, Roseann Dueñas González also mentored many graduate students—among them, Mary Carmen Cruz, who was then a high-school English teacher in the Tucson Unified School District and became a long-time active member of the Caucus between 1990 and 2012. Through Roseann Dueñas González's persistence, Cruz became more involved in various roles within NCTE. She was a key Caucus NCTE planning committee member. Following in the footsteps of her mentor, Cruz spent many years ensuring that proposals involving Latinos and Latinas were evaluated fairly and that those proposals that addressed Latinos and Latinas incorporated assets-based perspectives.

AS A LEADER IN THE CAUCUS AND WITH THE NCTE

Not only was Roseann Dueñas González a pioneering member during the early years of the CTE, but she was also an active NCTE member and leader. Roseann Dueñas González entered the NCTE just when Ernece Kelly was chairing the Task Force on Racism and Bias in the Teaching of English (1969 to 1972). While she was an active member with the CTE, Roseann Dueñas González served as the CTE vice-president from 1974 to 1976.

She credits her mentor at the University of Arizona for her becoming involved with the NCTE. In her own words from her 2017 interview, she states:

> The only reason that I was going to conferences, getting out there, is because I had an incredibly tremendous mentor, Charles Davis, who

was responsible for hiring me. He was my undergraduate professor, and then I went away and taught at Arizona State University, where I graduated with my master's. Then I was recruited back to U of A as a lecturer. I was recruited by him, as he was the head of the program in freshman composition.

Because of him, I began going to the Arizona English Teachers Association and becoming a really active participant in our state affiliate of NCTE, and eventually I made it to the national convention at his behest and with funding from the university for the first time. That was my beginning with the NCTE, and that's when I met Felipe and Carlota. I credit them as the ones who recruited me into Chicano Teachers of English, which later became the Caucus. (Hernández, February 7, 2017 Interview)

Her mentor was most likely a white ally who saw the talent and potential in Roseann Dueñas González, as he recruited her back to the University of Arizona and guided her to become involved in the profession's professional organizations—the state-wide Arizona NCTE and the NCTE. These experiences widened her professional stature and assisted her in the tenure and promotion process.

After meeting Ortego y Gasca and Cárdenas de Dwyer in 1971 at Las Vegas convention, Roseann Dueñas González immediately became a part of the team. The three immediately began to remedy the lack of Chicano representation within the organization, its conference program, and beyond to the profession as a whole. The following year they presented at NCTE's 1972 Minneapolis Convention, a three-hour focus group (#AB21), which was described in the convention program as follows:

- *Cochairmen*: [Carlota] Cárdenas Dwyer, State Univ. of New York, Stony Brook, Philip [Felipe] D. Ortego, University of Texas at El Paso

- *Associate Chairmen*: Donald F. Castro, University of Texas at El Paso,

- Gilbert Narro Garcia, Texas Lutheran College

- *Consultants*: Roseann Dueñas González, Arizona State University (20 minutes)

- Francisco H. Ruiz, Penn Valley Community College (20 minutes)

- Ricardo Sanchez, Mictla Publishing, "Chicano Literature: A Tertiary Perspective" (20 minutes)

- Marcello Trujillo, University of Colorado, "Approaches to Teaching Chicano Literature" (20 minutes). (NCTE 1972)

This 1972 presentation was an example of the many preconvention and postconvention workshops, seminars, and talks the three Caucus leaders gave to help English teachers across the nation be better prepared to teach Latino students. The above convention presentation was a highlight for the founding members when they first started.

> Something really exciting is that, right from the beginning the [now named] Hispanic Caucus used to have some input into the program, even before the Rainbow Sessions began, and that was one of the most inspiring and one of the most important things that we were able to do. Every year we were able to propose a program. …We felt we were really blessed because we had four hours to be able to talk to teachers about, let's say five or six important Chicano literature works and be able to get into how best to approach their teaching and what the major things of literature are in their work, something about the author and the context and the key for teachers to bring this work to their students in the most efficacious way. That was something that I remember with lot of excitement in terms of giving us the opportunity to invite major authors.... With the support of NCTE, we were able to bring major authors in Chicano literature to the attention of classroom teachers wherever NCTE might be held. (Hernández, 2017, February 7 Interview)

However, the idea of including ethnic literature within English departments was controversial. According to Roseann Dueñas González "there were battles in NCTE, within academia, in English departments" (Baca & Kirklighter 2013). During the 1970s, the Chicano literary cannon had begun to be published in larger numbers. Luis Valdez's *Actos*, Tomás Rivera's *...y no se lo tragó la tierra*, and Ernesto Galarza's *Barrio Boy* had just been published in 1971. Rodolfo Anaya's *Bless Me Ultima* was published the following year. *Macho* by Edmund Villaseñor and *We are Chicanos* by Felipe de Ortego y Gasca were published in 1973. Moreover, through the CTE, poets and novelist were invited to talk. See Chapters 2 and 3 for more information on Ortego y Gasca and his literary trajectory and Chapters 4 and 5 for more on Cárdenas de Dwyer.

During the 1978 NCTE convention in Dallas, Roseann Dueñas González was a contributing presenter for the Theory into Practice demonstrations with students in simulated classrooms for the Secondary School English Conference. She worked with scholars in the field of English Education and writing to expand the focus to include Latinos and multilingual writers:

> George Hillocks, Jr., University of Chicago, language; Robert Shafer, Arizona State University, composition; Roseann González, University of Arizona, multiethnic studies; and William Strong, Utah State University, linguistics. (NCTE 1977)

The following year, in 1979, Roseann became a member of the NCTE Executive Committee; and in 1994, she was in a pivotal position as chair of the NCTE's Committee on Resolutions. In those capacities, she encouraged many of the Caucus members to become involved within the organization by volunteering their time and expertise (González 1995). In the 1990s, Roseann Dueñas González was nominated as president of the NCTE, but was not elected. The NCTE recognized her with a Distinguished Service Award in 1999. In sum, Roseann Dueñas González used her NCTE positions to increase Latino and Latina involvement within the organization at large.

AS AN EDITOR

In the late 1970s, Roseann Dueñas González and Carlota Cárdenas de Dwyer were invited by publisher Scott Foresman to be editors of the Latino/Latina contributions to the Medallion America Reads Literature series for secondary schools, which was to include stories, poems, essays, and dramas by Latino/Latina authors (Miller, González, and Millett 1979; Miller, Cárdenas de Dwyer, Hayden, Hogan, and Wood 1982). The *Question and Form in Literature* anthology, which Roseann Dueñas González edited included, for example, a short story, "*Back to Bachimba*" by Enrique Hank López and several poems, among them, *"Eulogy for a Man from Jalostitlan"* by Rita Gutierrez-Christensen. This anthology was divided into eight units with a total of 600 pages of short stories, poetry, drama (Greek, Shakespearean, and modern), prose, and a novella. Of these units, the introduction included a poem written by Villanueva, the poetry section included three poems written by Peñaranda, Salazar and Gutiérrez-Christensen, and a story by López in the prose section. The anthology also included Native American and African American authors.

The anthology that Carlota Cárdenas de Dwyer co-edited, *United States in Literature*, was an anthology for eleventh-grade students, with also eight literary units and a total of 665 pages of stories, poetry, and essays. This anthology included, for example, a short story, *"El retrato"* ("The Portrait"), which was an excerpt from the book *"Y no se lo tragó la tierra/And the Earth Did Not Part"* by Tomás Rivera and *"El Corrido de Gregorio Cortez"* ("The Ballad of Gregorio Cortez") by Américo Paredes. By the 1979 standards, the inclusion of Latino and Latina authors, and authors of color enhanced the literature anthologies greatly, however, by today's standards' the number of included poems and short stories by Latino and Latina poets and authors would pale in comparison.

CONCLUSION

Through Roseann Dueñas González's efforts and her scholarship, English education shifted to include Chicano and Chicana literature and language ideologies. Her initial participation in the profession was due to her talent as an English Education major and the vision of her mentor, Charles Davis, the Director of Freshman Composition at the University of Arizona in the 1970s and 1980s. When she began her career, she was the lone Chicana professor and one of the few women in the English department at the University of Arizona. Her commitment to the Caucus and NCTE over forty years was noteworthy and recognized by the 1999 NCTE Service Award. She published books and articles, and established the center for interpretation while setting national standards for court interpretation. Just as Roseann Dueñas González was mentored, she mentored many students and scholars in the Caucus and at the University of Arizona. Caucus members are indebted to her for her dedication to graduate students, to the profession, and to the Caucus. Her legacy is peerless.

WORKS CITED

Anaya, Rodolfo. *Bless Me Ultima*. TQS Publishers, 1972.

Baca, Isabel, and Cristina Kirklighter. Interview with Roseann Dueñas González. *Reflections,* vol.13, no. 1, 2013, pp. 13-51.

Cárdenas de Dwyer, Carlota, and Robert Hayden. *United States in Literature: Grade Eleven*. Scott Foresman, 1979.

Everett-Haynes, La Monica. A Visionary Supporter from the Start. *UANews*, November 15, 2012. Available from https://uanews.arizona.edu/blog/visionary-supporter-start

Galarza, Ernesto. *Barrio Boy*, Ballentine, 1971.

González, Roseann Dueñas. "Teaching Mexican American Students to Write: Capitalizing on the Culture," *English Journal*, vol. 71, no. 7, 1982, pp. 20–24.

---. "The English Language Amendment: Examining Myths." *English Journal*, vol. 77, no. 3, 1988, pp. 24–30.

---, Victoria Vasquez, and Holly Mikkleson. *Fundamentals of Court Interpretation: Theory, Policy and Practice*. Urbana, IL: National Council of Teachers of English, 1992.

---, editor. *Language Ideologies: Critical Perspectives on the Official English Movement*, vol. 1: *Education and the Social Implications of Official Language*. Urbana, IL: National Council of Teachers of English, 2001.

---, editor. *Language Ideologies: Critical Perspectives on the Official English Movement*, vol. 2: *History, Theory, and Policy*. Urbana, IL: National Council of Teachers of English, 2001, 2012.

Hernández, Anita. Interview with Roseann Dueñas González. Writing and Working for Change project. February 7, 2017. *Viva Nuestro Caucus: Rewriting the Forgotten Pages of Our Caucus*.

Kleifgen, Jo Anne. Reviewed Work(s): Education and the Social Implications of Official Language. Vol. 1 of Language Ideologies: Critical Perspectives on the Official English Movement by Roseann Dueñas González and Ildikó Melis; History, Theory, and Policy. Vol. 2 of Language Ideologies: Critical Perspectives on the Official English Movement by Roseann Dueñas González and Ildikó Melis *Rhetoric Review*, vol. 21, no. 1, 2002, pp. 109-114.

National Council of Teachers of English (NCTE). CCCC Position Statement on Students' Rights to Their Own Language, *CCC* Special Issue, Fall 1974, Vol. XXV. Also available at http://www2.ncte.org/blog/2015/03/students-right-to-their-own-language/

National Council of Teachers of English (NCTE). Expanding Opportunities: Academic Success for Culturally and Linguistically Diverse Students, December 1998. Also available at http://www2.ncte.org/statement/expandingopportun/

National Council of Teachers of English (NCTE). CCCC Position Statement on Second Language Writing and Writers, 2001. Available at http://cccc.ncte.org/cccc/resources/positions/secondlangwriting

Ortego y Gasca, Felipe de. *We are Chicanos*. Pocket, 1973.

Valdez, Luis. *Actos*, Menyah Productions, 1971.

Villaseñor, Edmund. *Macho*. Jaca Books, 1973.

CHAPTER SIX
Generations of Leadership

Anita Hernández and Iris D. Ruiz

The work of founding members Ortego de Gasca, Cárdenas de Dwyer, and Dueñas González was built upon and expanded by the Caucus chairs who followed. This chapter describes the principal achievements of several of the Caucus chairs who are acknowledged for their leadership and activism.

KRIS GUTIÉRREZ'S LEADERSHIP (1977 - PRESENT)

Kris Gutiérrez grew up in Miami, Arizona, in a bilingual home where great-grandparents, grandparents, and parents spoke Spanish. Her father worked in the copper mines and "was very involved in the Veterans of Foreign Wars like many Chicanos who fought in WWII and were very patriotic" (Turner 309). At one point, when her father was a weekly contributor on Americanism for the local newspaper, Gutiérrez was asked to help compose, write, and edit his column. These lived experiences led to her interest in English, rhetoric, composition, and bilingualism. Currently, Gutiérrez is a professor of Language, Literacy, and Culture at University of California, Berkeley where she holds the Carol Liu Chair in Educational Policy. Previous to Berkeley, she was the Inaugural Provost's Chair and a professor of Learning Sciences/Literacy, University of Colorado, Boulder and a Professor of Social Research Methodology at Graduate School of Education and Information Science at UCLA. Kris Gutiérrez earned her Ph.D. in Rhetoric and Composition from the University of Colorado, Boulder in 1986 and earned her MA degree in English from Arizona State University in 1982. After earning her Master's degree, she took a position as the Director of Freshman Composition for provisionally admitted, underrepresented minority students, including children from poor white migrant workers (Turner 1996). She was greatly influenced by the gatekeeping role that writing held (Turner).

Gutiérrez became involved in CCCC in 1977, when she was the local coordinator for the 1978 conference, which was held in Denver, Colorado. By 1979, Gutiérrez had been elected to the Executive Committee and had joined the Caucus. For eleven years, from 1981 to 1992, she led the Hispanic Caucus as a co-chair and simultaneously was a member of the Task Force on Racism and Bias in the Teaching of English from 1981 to 1988. She was also a member of NCTE's Standing Committee on Testing and Evaluation (1980 and 1986) and for many years (1982 to 1996) Kris Gutiérrez was a member of NCTE's college section.

Gutiérrez contributed intellectually to the profession through her articles in *College Composition and Communications* (Coe and Gutiérrez, 1981; Gutiérrez, 1982) and in *College English* (Gutiérrez, 1987). In her early work she co-authored an article, with Coe, about helping students resolve writing problems while developing their writing abilities; the other two articles were written within the context of NCTE/CCCCs committees. The 1982 article was written with the Committee on the Teaching of English and its Evaluation, which recommended six observational instruments writing directors could use to evaluate writing instruction. The 1987 article was written with the Task Force on Racism and Bias and it focused on expanding opportunities for student academic success of culturally and linguistically diverse students. Gutiérrez went on to write a seminal article on sociocritical literacy theory and the third space (Gutiérrez, 2008). Gutiérrez is also a prolific writer and contributor of new ideas in the field of English education and to the education of bilingual Latino and Latina students in the U.S. Through her collaborations with colleagues across the disciplines she has contributed new ways of thinking and new concepts in research.

Kris Gutiérrez continued to be an active NCTE and CCCC leader by chairing the Standing Committee on Research from 2002 to 2004 and was a member of this committee until 2007. During the 2016 NCTE conference, Gutiérrez was honored for her many contributions to the NCTE by being awarded the Advancement of People of Color Leadership Award during the 2016 NCTE conference. Kris Gutiérrez was and continues to be a prolific scholar and a staunch supporter of the Caucus and NCTE and CCCCs.

VICTOR VILLANUEVA (1984–PRESENT)
Victor Villanueva is a Regents Professor in the Department of English at Washington State University. He, too, is a longtime dedicated member of the NCTE and CCCC. He began as an Assistant Professor at Northern Ari-

zona University in 1987 after completing his dissertation at the University of Washington in 1986. Both Dueñas González and Gutiérrez first recruited Victor Villanueva to the Latino Caucus in the mid-1980s. By 1986, he was a member of the NCTE Resolutions Committee and a member of the Minority Affairs Advisory Council. From 1987 to 1990, he was a member of the NCTE's Commission on Language. He became co-chair of the Caucus in 1988, and served in that capacity until 1994. He was a member of the NCTE's Task Force on Involving People of Color in the Council in 1995, Program Chair of the CCCC in 1997, and a member of the NCTE's Publications Committee of the Studies on Writing and Rhetoric Series. By 1998, Victor Villanueva was a member on the NCTE's Executive Committee. He has continued to serve both the NCTE and the CCCC on various committees. One of Villanueva's crowning achievements is his mentorship of many Latino scholars. One only has to look at the acknowledgement pages of the articles and literary works to appreciate his dedication to Caucus scholars.

Victor Villanueva is also a prolific scholar. Through his initial experiences at NCTE and CCCCs, Villanueva saw the need to write *Bootstraps: From an American Academic of Color,*

> You see, part of the reason why I ended up writing *Bootstraps* was because of these people that I met at CCCCs and NCTE, almost exclusively because of them. Because the intentions were always good, the real bigots are few and far between, but for all of the good intention there was also this phenomenal ignorance (Ruiz Interview 2016).

While the book has been popular, the book proposal at first was not. Villanueva has commented about how the proposal was accepted: "When Boots was first proposed [to NCTE], there was some resistance to it by the editorial board, but the editorial board also included Keith Gillyard and I think he had more to do with convincing the editorial board to go with *Boots* than anyone." Once published in 1993, the book became award-winning text. He has received two prestigious awards: the Conference on English Education's (CEE) Richard A. Meade Award for Distinguished Research in English Education was awarded in 1994, then two years later, the book was awarded the David H. Russell Award for Distinguished Research in the Teaching of English. It has been translated into several languages.

Twelve years later, Villanueva's book, *Bootstraps,* continued to be relevant and became a recommended text in NCTE's position statement on Supporting Linguistically and Culturally Diverse Learners in English Education

(NCTE, 2005). In the position statement, *Bootstraps* supports the Crossing Cultural Boundaries Belief in that "teachers and teacher educators must be willing to cross traditional, personal and professional boundaries in pursuit of social justice and equity" (11). Since *Bootstraps* was published, Villanueva continued to publish a myriad of articles, book chapters, and two other books: *Cross-Talk Comp Theory: A Reader* and with Geneva Smitherman *Language Diversity in the Classroom: From Intention to Practice*. Following in Cárdenas de Dwyer's and Dueñas González's footsteps, Victor Villanueva also began consulting with publishers, such as Harcourt from 1995 to 1997; Allen and Bacon, in 1996; and Longman in 1998. Like Gutiérrez, he also served on several editorial boards, including *College Composition and Communication*; *Composition Studies*; and *College English*. In 2008, Villanueva was the first Caucus member to be honored for his contributions to the NCTE and CCCC with the Advancement of People of Color Leadership Award in 2008.

CECILIA RODRÍGUEZ MILANÉS (1989-2012)

Cecilia Rodríguez Milanés has been a Professor in the Department of English at the University of Central Florida since 1999. She was promoted to the rank of professor in 2015 at the University of Central Florida. Previous to this, she was at the Indiana University of Pennsylvania, where she taught writing and multicultural literature and was later named interim director of the Women's Studies. While Rodríguez Milanés was at each of her institutions, her deans supported the Caucus Newsletter, *Capirotada,* with additional resources, such as a student assistant.

Rodríguez Milanés was a dedicated member of the Caucus, the NCTE, and CCCC. She sustained her leadership throughout her 23 years of involvement. She first attended NCTE as a graduate student in 1989, when she had earned her degree from State University of New York at Albany, where she studied writing with Toni Morrison. Rodríguez Milanés was the co-chair of the Caucus from 1995 to 2010. She first co-chaired the Caucus with Mary Carmen Cruz from 1995 to 1996 and at the end of her tenure with Cristina Kirklighter. In addition to co-chairing the Caucus, her leadership extended into heading the Caucus Newsletter, *Capirotada,* as editor and writer for a period of 14 years from 1994 to 2008. See the Annotated Archive for examples of the *Capirotada* Newsletters.

Rodríguez Milanés encouraged many Caucus members to write literary works, such as poems, book reviews, short stories, and professional news for *Capirotada*. She herself wrote a number of articles for *Capirotada*. For example, in 1996, Rodríguez Milanés shared with the Caucus her professional and personal experiences in Cuba. At one point, she was helping the University of Puerto Rico create a women's studies program, given her own experiences as interim director. Through *Capirotada* several articles were written by the members to stand up for Latino students across the nation.

When asked what issues she experienced while a member of NCTE/CCCC and the Caucus, she focused on who NCTE was publishing and not publishing.

> Well, Victor has always been a leader and it is because he's been around a long time and because he knows everybody. Victor was a shining star example for us as someone who could navigate the publishing world within NCTE, but even his book 'Bootstraps' didn't come out right away. I can't remember right now when that was published, but we were a long time waiting for that book to be published. And it was a long time that it was by itself and there were no other books by Latino colleagues published by NCTE (Hernández, 2016a Interview August 17).

In reviewing books written by Latinos and published by NCTE as Rodríguez Milanés has pointed out, Villanueva's *Bootstraps From an American Academic of Color* was published in 1993. Four years later, in 1997 NCTE published *CrossTalk Comp Theory: A Reader*, a second edition in 2003 and a third edition in 2011. In 2001, NCTE published Dueñas González's two-volume collection on *Language Ideology*. Later in 2003, NCTE/CCCC published an edited collection on language awareness by Smitherman and Villanueva titled *Language Diversity in the Classroom: From Intention to Practice*. Since this time, NCTE has published books by both Raúl Sánchez and Steven Alvarez, Caucus leaders, in 2017. Clearly, more books on Chicano and Latino literature can be and should be published by NCTE.

As an author, Rodríguez Milanés published a collection of short stories in *Marielitos, Balseros and Other Exiles* about the Cuban immigrants who traveled from Cuba's Mariel Harbor to Florida and were received by relatives living in the U.S. with the 1980 Boat Lift program (Rodríguez Milanés2009). A year later she published a book of poetry *Everyday Chica* (Rodríguez Milanés 2010) about growing up Cuban American in New Jersey and Miami, Florida to parents who could not return to Cuba. This book received the Longleaf Press Poetry Chapbook Award. Most recently she published a second collection of short stories of growing up ethnic in Miami and in New Jersey and born to Cuban exile parents in *Oye What I'm Gonna Tell You* (Rodríguez Milanés 2015). A reading of her book *Oye* is available at https://vimeo.com/20089369. While she is not presently attending the NCTE nor CCCC because of her position, her heart is with the Caucus.

BOBBI CIRIZA HOUTCHENS (1987–2015)

Bobbi Ciriza Houtchens was a high-school English teacher at Arroyo Valley High School in San Bernardino, California as well as a longtime member of the NCTE. In 1987, when she was a graduate student working on her Master's degree, her mentor, Dr. Barbara Flores, recruited her into the NCTE. For many years, Houtchens co-chaired the Latino Caucus at CCCC (2004 to 2006 with Cecilia Milanés Rodriguez; 2013 to 2015 with Cristina Kirklighter and Renee Moreno). She was also an active Caucus member from 1987 to 2015. She is currently retired from public school teaching, but she consults with various organizations including the National Academy of Science (Houtchens 2017).

In 1993, Bobbi was the first recipient of the NCTE's Teachers for the Dream Award (NCTE, 2017b). She later wrote an article in the NCTE's *English Journal* about the impact of her project award (Houtchens, 1997). In her Teachers for the Dream program, Houtchens had her high school students volunteer to tutor elementary school students, with the goal of having students of color consider teaching as a future profession. Her Teachers of the Dream program was so successful, the school district recognized her success and expanded her program to all five high schools. Houtchens first began working on the NCTE's convention planning through the Rainbow Strand. From 1998 to 2003, she was an editor of the Rainbow Teachers' column in the *English Journal*, in which she selected and published short news articles about Latino and Latina literary scholars, language, and advocacy for Latino and Latina students. From 2001 to 2004, she was the chair of the Committee Against Racism and Bias in the Teaching of English, which reviewed the NCTE's program for stereotypical views of Latino and Latina students; and from 2009 to 2014, she was a member of that committee. Houtchens was also an active member of the Secondary Steering Committee from 2003 to 2007. Furthermore, through the Co-Sponsored Speakers Program, she spoke to NCTE affiliates around the country. In 2002 and 2003, Houtchens was one of the featured English teachers in the NCTE's *Beyond the Canon: Teaching Multicultural Literature in High School*, which debuted in the 2003–2004 school year as a professional development series for English teachers, funded by the

Annenberg Foundation and the Corporation for Public Broadcasting, and produced by New York Public Television, Channel 13/WNET (Houtchens, 2002; 2003). In 2008, she was selected as a Washington Fellow at the Department of Education.

As Houtchens looks back at her involvement in the Caucus and in the NCTE, she noticed the overall lack of commitment to identity caucuses and, in particular, the Latinx Caucus. By 2011, the NCTE's centennial year, Houtchens noted that there were many resolutions to improve diversity, equity, and a recognition of Chicano and Chicana and Latino and Latina literature and issues, however, their impact within NCTE and CCCC has not been as influential as Houtchens would have liked. In a review of the resolutions, there are a total of twenty-nine statements: nineteen NCTE and CCCC resolutions, five position statements, four NCTE guidelines, and one research policy brief, all about diversity within the organization; students' language rights; teacher recruitment; and opposition to racism. Many of these statements were written by Caucus members as they tried to make significant change within the NCTE and CCCCs.

MARY CARMEN CRUZ (1986–2013)

Mary Carmen Cruz was a high-school English teacher at Cholla High Magnet School and later was a Teacher Mentor in the Tucson Unified School District in Tucson, Arizona as well as a longtime member of the NCTE and a strong advocate for all students of color and in particular Latino and Latina students. Mary Carmen Cruz credits Dueñas González, her mentor, for her joining the NCTE in 1986, when she was a graduate student at the University of Arizona, working on her Master's degree. After that, she was an active member of the NCTE for twenty-seven years. From the inception of the *Rainbow Strand* in 1987, Cruz was an active committee member, endorsing presentations that supported Latino and Latina students in schools across the nation. In the 1990s, Cruz was the editor of the *English Journal*'s *Rainbow Teacher/Rainbow Students* column. From 1994 to 1998, she was elected for and was as a member of the NCTE's secondary section steering committee. From 1999 to 2000 she was a co-chair of the Caucus alongside Cecilia Rodríguez Milanés. During that time, and as a Caucus member, from the 1990s into the 2000s she addressed four major issues that were important to the Caucus:

1. Advocating for rights of students to be bilingual.

2. Recruiting teachers of color.

3. Opposing racism and bias in the teaching of English.

4. Supporting diverse and multicultural education. (Hernández, 2016d)

In 2001, Cruz became a member of the NCTE's Committee on Racism and Bias in the Teaching of English, and chaired the committee the following year. In 2003 and 2004, she was elected as the NCTE's representative-at-large and was the secondary representative on the Executive Committee. When asked how teachers are meeting the needs of diverse literacy learners in classrooms, Cruz had this to say:

> "Ultimately, says Mary Carmen Cruz, Chair of the Adolescent and Young Adult Literacy Subcommittee of the NCTE Executive Committee, "we need to look at the prior literacy experiences of the adolescents and young adults in our classrooms, and if they're positive, we need to enrich them. If students have been limited in those or have other experiences that aren't traditional in our academic setting, then we tap that and we guide them into developing a literacy that ensures more importantly academic competencies and knowledge. (Council Chronicle, 2004)

Cruz was also one of the featured English teachers in the *Developing Writers: A Workshop for High School Teachers*, which debuted in 2004 as a professional development series for English teachers, funded by the Annenberg Foundation and produced by Maryland Public Television (Annenberg, 2004). In sum, Cruz was a strong Caucus leader and she advanced the Caucus agenda through her service on the many NCTE secondary committees and as an editor of *Rainbow Teacher/Rainbow Students* column of *English Journal*. She is emblematic of the previous Caucus Leaders who also were committed to both the Caucus and to the issues of diversity in the NCTE and CCCC committees.

CONCLUSION

Of course, there are many more luminaries who have not been featured in this chapter, such as Isabel Baca, Damián Baca, Aurelia Davila de Silva, Maria Franquiz, Alfredo Lujan, Renee Moreno, Amanda Espinoza-Aguilar, Jaime Mejía, and others. Each has made strong contributions to the Caucus. An in-depth analysis of their work would enhance the history of the Caucus and its leaders' contributions to the fields of English Education, Rhetoric and Composition, and to the education of Latino and Latina students. Still the accomplishments and activism of those featured has demonstrated how the Caucus leadership has influenced the field of English education, Composition and Rhetoric, as well as the education of Latino and Latina students in schools across the nation. Each scholar brought their own unique perspective and, through their involvement, moved the Caucus forward to advocate for improving the poor educational quality that Latino and Latina students have received over the past decades. Their articles, books, pedagogical recommendations, and projects are a testimony to the educational equity they all desired for Latino and Latina students.

WORKS CITED

Annenberg VideoSeries. (Mary Carmen Cruz, Classroom Teacher). "*Developing Writers: A Workshop for High School Teachers*: Workshop two. Annenberg - Corporation for Public Broadcasting Professional Development Video Series, 2004. Available at http://www.learner.org/workshops/hswriting/support/

Coe, Richard and Kris Gutiérrez. "Using problem-solving procedures and process analysis to help students with writing problems". *College Composition and Communications*, vol. 32, 1981, pp. 262-27.

Council Chronicle. Adolescent literacy captures the spotlight. National Council of Teachers of English (NCTE), September 2004. Available at http://www.ncte.org/library/magazines/archives/117631

Gutiérrez, Kris with CCC Committee on the Teaching of English and its Evaluation. Evaluating instruction in writing: Approaches and instruments. *College Composition and Communication*, vol. 33, 1982, pp. 213-229.

--- with Task Force on Racism and Bias. Expanding opportunities: Academic success for culturally and linguistically diverse students. *College English*, vol. 49, 1987. pp. 550-552. (principal author)

---. Developing a Sociocritical Literacy in the Third Space. *Reading Research Quarterly*, vol. 43, no. 2, 2008, pp. 148-164.

---. Remarks to the Latinx Caucus. E-mail sent to the members of the Latinx Caucus, 19 November, 2016. (Reproduced in the Appendix)

Hernández, Anita. Interview with Cecilia Rodríguez Milanés. Writing and Working for Change project. 2016a, August 17. *Viva Nuestro Caucus: Rewriting the Forgotten Pages of Our Caucus.*

---. Interview of Bobbi Houtchens and Mary Carmen Cruz for the Writing and Working for Change Project, 2016b. *Viva Nuestro Caucus: Rewriting the Forgotten Pages of Our Caucus.*

Houtchens, Bobbi Ciriza. "Teachers for the Dream." *English Journal*, vol. 86, no. 4, 1997, pp. 64–66. Available at http://www.ncte.org/library/NCTEFiles/Resources/Journals/EJ/0864-april97/EJ0864Rainbow.pdf/.

--- (consensus committee member). Promoting the Educational Success of Children and Youth Learning English: Promising Futures. National Academies of Science, Engineering, and Medicine. 2017.

---. "Case Study for Arroyo Valley High School." In "Secondary School

Courses Designed to Address the Language Needs and Academic Gaps of Long-Term English Learners". Edited by Laurie Olsen. Californians Together, 2012.

---. "Finding Ourselves in Antonio: Teaching Bless Me, Ultima," Engaging American Novels: Lessons from the Classroom. In Joseph O. Milner & C. Pope, ed. National Council of Teachers of English, 2011.

---. Research Review: New Study Addresses Impact of the English Only Movement in Boston Public Schools. *AccELLerate, National Clearinghouse for English Language Acquisition.* vol. 1, no. 3, 2009.

---, Contributing Consultant: Ballantyne, K.G., A.R. Sanderman, et al. *Dual Language Learners in the Early Years: Getting Ready to Succeed in School.* Washington, D.C.: National Clearinghouse for English Language Acquisition, 2008. Available at http://www.ncela.gwu.edu/resabout/ecell/earlyyears.pdf

---. "La Pluma es Lengua del Alma: Using Writing to Chronicle the Soul's Journey." California English, Summer, 2006. Available at http://www.nwp.org/cs/public/print/resource/2332

---. *English Learners And High School Reform: A Classroom Teacher's Perspective.* Council of Chief State School Officers, 2003.

---. (On-Camera Master Teacher). "Literacy Development of Latino Students: Using Our Present Realities to Shape The Expanding Canon Annenberg - Corporation for Public Broadcasting Professional Development Video Series, 2003. Available at http://www.learner.org/workshops/hslit/about.html.

---. "Literacy Development of Latino Students: Using Our Present Realities to Shape (On-Camera Master Teacher) Conversations in Literature. Annenberg - CPB Professional Development Video Series, 2002. Available at http://www.learner.org/workshops/conversations/

---. "Literacy Development of Latino Students: Using Our Present Realities to Shape Our Futures." In *The Best for Our Children: Critical Perspectives on Literacy for Latino Students.* Edited by María De la Luz Reyes and J. Halcón. Teachers College Press, 2000.

---, editor. "English in the News" column. *The English Journal.* National Council of 1997-2003 Teachers of English.

National Council of Teachers of English (NCTE). *CCCC Chair's Letter*, December 1998. Available at http://www.ncte.org/library/NCTEFiles/Resources/Journals/CCC/0502dec98/CO0502Chairs.PDF.

---. Supporting Linguistically and Culturally Diverse Learners in English Education, July 31, 2005. Available at http://www2.ncte.org/statement/diverselearnersinee/

Rodríguez Milanés, Cecilia. *Marielitos, Balseros, and Other Exiles.* Ig Publishers. 2009.

---. *Oye What I am gonna tell you.* Ig Publishers. 2015.

Ruiz, Iris. Interview of Victor Villanueva for the Writing and Working for Change Project, 2016. *Viva Nuestro Caucus.*

Smitherman, Geneva and Villanueva, Victor, editors. *Language Diversity in the Classroom: From Intention to Practice:* National Council Teachers of English. 2003.

Turner, Myrna Gwen. Interview with Kris Gutiérrez. *Issues in Applied Linguistics*, vol. 7, no. 2, 1996, pp. 308-314.

Villanueva, Victor. *Bootstraps: From an American Academic of Color.* National Council Teachers of English. 1993.

---. *Cross-Talk Comp Theory: A Reader.* National Council Teachers of English. 1997; 2003; 2011.

CHAPTER SEVEN

The Evolution of the Latinx Caucus in the NCTE and CCCC

Anita Hernández and Romeo García

Previous chapters of this book provide the historical context of the NCTE/CCCCs, the emergence of a Chicano political/cultural movement, and the emergence of the CTE through the work of Felipe de Ortego y Gasca, Carlota Cárdenas de Dwyer, and Roseann Dueñas González (also highlighting their scholarly work and careers). This chapter continues that discussion by tracing the trajectory of the Caucus, including how its founding leaders and those that followed perceived the Caucus, their vision for the Caucus, its successes and struggles in ensuring that the voices of the Caucus would be incorporated within the NCTE and CCCCs. In order to recover the history of the Caucus, the editorial team interviewed Caucus chairs and members about their perspective and their work in the Caucus, in NCTE, and CCCCs, as well as drew upon the previous work of the *Working and Writing for Change* project. Archival documents were also reviewed, including the Caucus newsletters and NCTE documents, such as resolutions and documents regarding the Task Force Against Racism and Bias in the Teaching of English.

In reflecting on the state of the Latinx Caucus before and after NCTE's Centennial year, it became clear the Caucus has evolved into its present form with new members and new leaders influenced by the passion and persistence of a small group of individuals who spent 25 to 40 years spearheading the rights of Chicano and Chicana and Latino and Latina students to their own language, literary heritage, and an equitable education. This small group of Caucus leaders fought not only for excellent English and Language Arts courses, but for American Literature anthologies to be inclusive of Chicanos, Puerto Ricans, Cubans, and Latinos and Latinas across the nation in higher education, high schools, junior high schools, and elementary schools.

The scholarly work produced by both the founding Caucus leaders and those leaders who came later, along with the resolutions, are a testament to this struggle for equity and diversity in schools and within the NCTE and CCCCs (Cárdenas de Dwyer, & Hayden; González, 1995; Houtchens; NCTE 1972, 1975, 1978, 1996; 2007, 2015c; Ortego y Gasca, 2001). This chapter traces the history and development of the CTE to the Latinx Caucus, highlighting the important contributions of the caucus during this period.

FROM CHICANO TO LATINX

The early chapters of this book describe the emergence of the CTE and the effort as well as projects by Ortego y Gasca, Cárdenas de Dwyer, and Dueñas González directed through the Caucus and NCTE. By the late 1970s, the CTE had become the Chicano Caucus. During this time, Kris Gutiérrez was an integral leader of the Caucus. According to Gutiérrez, the Chicano Caucus evolved to fill a void in the scholarship presented at the NCTE. In her own words:

> Roseann Dueñas González, Carlota Cárdenas de Dwyer, and I, with the help of the Black Caucus, formed what was then termed the Chicano Caucus to fill a significant void for an important constituency in NCTE. There were only three of us and we would caucus with the Black Caucus and began to contribute important and consequential practices to NCTE, including the creation of the *Rainbow Strand*. (Gutiérrez, 2016)

As more members joined who had Puerto Rican, Cuban, or Central American cultural ties, the name of the Caucus also evolved. In the early 1990s, the name was changed by its members to the Hispanic Caucus to reflect the larger group of colleagues. Longtime Caucus leader Alfredo Lujan succinctly noted the further transformation of the name to reflect the unity and respect that the members felt for each other:

> Our NCTE Caucus was once called the Chicano Caucus; then it was the Hispanic Caucus. At the Pittsburgh NCTE Convention (1993), we became the Latino Caucus; this seems more inclusive—a term [that] most of us are comfortable [with]. It has become clear that we are diverse, and we need to embrace and respect each Latino other, brother and sister. Somos quien somos..., juntos. (Lujan 2)

The Caucus name continued to evolve. From Latino Caucus to Latino/Latina Caucus, then to Latin@ Caucus, and, as of 2016, it is known as the Latinx

Caucus—a gender-neutral alternative. Latinx also represents a critique of nationalism, cultural imperialism, structural racism/sexism, Eurocentrism, and heteronormativity. Over time, as Caucus members' conceptions of who we are and who we were were discussed and critiqued, the Caucus name changed to encompass members' critical consciousness or *conscientization*. This larger historical context, in regard to the filtering of identity terms, can be seen as a strategic articulation of representation. This becomes evident in the larger scope of Mexican American and Chicano and Chicana civil rights.

Despite the identity transformations, the Caucus has remained true to its original purpose. The following is its published mission:

> The Latinx Caucus of NCTE/CCCC is a network of Latinx educators in English studies, literacy, and language arts. Our purpose is to:
>
> - exchange ideas
>
> - serve as a resource for members, the educational community, and the general public,
>
> - and support activities that promote the learning and advancement of students and teachers of color.
>
> Any Latinx educator, or like-minded educator, or preservice educator who is a member of NCTE is invited to join us. (NCTE, 2017a)

The Caucus today, continues to attract Latinx scholars in K-12 English education (NCTE) and those interested in composition and rhetoric at the college level (CCCCs). The Caucus continues to elect co-chairs that represent those who attend the NCTE and those who attend CCCCs, ensuring that the Caucus represents the collective and that colleagues in both groups have their voices heard, a similar practice to the functioning of the Black Caucus. If the co-chairs can only attend one conference and not the other, there is a channel of communication amongst each other.

In the next sections of this chapter, the leaders that followed Ortego y Gasca, Cárdenas de Dwyer, and Dueñas González were interviewed for the *Writing and Working for Change* project. These leaders include Victor Villanueva, Cecilia Rodríguez Milanés, Jaime Mejia, Cristina Kirklighter, Bobbi Houtchens, Mary Carmen Cruz, Damián Baca, Steven Alvarez, Cristina Ramirez, Aja Martinez, and Tracey Flores. While this is not the entire group of leaders, our criteria were to have a representation of Caucus leaders from the various decades who called the NCTE and/or the CCCC their home. Their voices are interwoven in these sections.

THE CAUCUS AS EL *CORAZÓN*

As part of this project, later Caucus leaders, long time members, and recent members were interviewed and asked how they remember the caucus, hence the idea of *corazón,* or heart, in the heading of this section. While these interviews do not fully represent every caucus leader, which was our original hope, their insights do cross the various decades in which the Caucus has existed. We also do not claim to have captured all the insights of long-term or new members. Still, collectively, we hope to have captured the spirit of the caucus. Indeed, many of those interviewed considered the Caucus "like home," as well as "a welcoming place to all scholars of color." Additionally, many chairs and members considered the Caucus a place of solace when compared to the annual conventions and even to their own doctoral programs in Rhetoric or English Education. While the Caucus felt like home, it was not a passive group. On the contrary, the Caucus was where members learned to discuss injustices and to take action. As evidenced in the interviews, many members of the Caucus were invited to participate, mentored to be leaders, and took leadership roles.

As far back as 1971, Dueñas González, recalls how excited she was to find a like-minded group of colleagues at the NCTE. In her words:

> The first time I met the members of the Chicano Teachers of English [it was] just "How excited I was!" It's just we were all singular in our institutions. I was the only Chicana in the entire department of English, which had 90 members at that time. In fact, in the early '70s there were hardly any women in the department. To be a Mexican American woman was like complete isolation. (Hernández, 2017)

Dueñas González perspective of being the singular Chicana within her home department also rang true for other leaders of CTE and, later, those in the Chicano Caucus, and in the Hispanic Caucus within the NCTE and CCCC.

Together collectively at the NCTE and CCCCs conferences, these Chicano scholars began to channel their tremendous energy to move the field of Chicano and Chicana Literature and Chicano and Chicana Studies forward. Cárdenas de Dwyer, Ortego y Gasca, and Dueñas González through their involvement in their small knit group became contributing scholars in the NCTE's program by providing some of first convention workshops on

Chicano literature. Below is the November 27, 1974 (8:30 a.m. to 9:45 a.m.) announcement for the convention discussion session:

A 10. Chicano Literature for the High School Student (Secondary)

Chair: Martha T. Davis, Phoenix Union High School System, Arizona

Associate Chair: Gilbert Garcia, Texas Lutheran College

Speakers: Carlota Cárdenas de Dwyer, University of Texas, "Chicano Lit: Materials and Methods"; and Roseann Dueñas de González, University of Arizona, "Se Habla Ingles" (NCTE, 1974)

As the heart of the Caucus, Cárdenas de Dwyer and Dueñas González were not only interested in presenting their work advocating for Latino and Latina literature and Chicano and Chicana students in public schools and colleges, they also expected the NCTE to be inclusive of Chicanos and Chicanas and Latinos and Latinas on the Executive Board and in the various committees. In the 1980s, when Cárdenas de Dwyer, Dueñas González, and Gutiérrez were Caucus leaders, Gutierrez remembers that while they were a small group, they were bold and would have their voices heard by attending the NCTE meetings. In a quote from her talk to the Latinx Caucus in 2016, Gutiérrez reminisces about the early Caucus meetings, where they discussed experienced injustices that resulted in actions, such as presenting them to the Executive Committee of the NCTE: "We would write demands and proposals and sign them from the Chicano Caucus, even though we were only three!"

Fast forward to the 1990s, while the Caucus remained small, its officers and members continued to create a welcoming spirit to new members. When Cecilia Rodríguez Milanés, a graduate student from Albany, New York, attended her first Caucus meeting in 1991, she noted Victor Villanueva's affability:

> I was very happy to find the Caucus.... There were only a handful of us. The leader was Victor Villanueva. Anybody who has ever met Victor Villanueva knows he's absolutely charming and totally welcoming. I felt really comfortable, and I thought there's a place for us, for me.... The Caucus really was like a refuge from a very White organization. It became a vital pivot on which my academic career service turned because I became involved in the organization and leadership almost right away. (Hernández, 2016c)

In the late 1990s, Bobbi Houtchens, a high-school English teacher from San Bernardino, California, and a former chair, noted that the Caucus was a safe haven from what seemed to be the large impersonal NCTE convention:

> I was a graduate student earning my M.A. degree with Barbara Flores in Bilingual Education. She encouraged me to present at the NCTE convention, and she introduced me to the Latinx Caucus, which is where I felt at home.... At the convention, I felt very isolated from everyone, and without Barbara Flores, I probably would not have gone back. She introduced me to the Caucus and to some outstanding leaders in education for Latinx students. (Hernandez, 2016e)

Not all scholars were invited by mentors or their graduate advisors in their home departments in Rhetoric and Composition or through the English Education programs such as was the case for Bobbi Houtchens. Latinx scholars came because the Caucus business meeting was announced in the NCTE and CCCCs conference program. They were attracted by the possibility of connecting with other Latinx scholars. Cristina Ramírez, a doctoral student at the University of Texas, El Paso, attended her first Caucus meeting at the 2007 NCTE conference, as she looked through the conference program. In her own words, Cristina recounted her initial experience with discovering the Caucus:

> As I looked through the conference program—as a newcomer, you go through every single page—I saw there was a Latinx Caucus. I had to go find out what it was about. I even missed dinner with my friends. Ever since then, I have been a member because I knew it was home for me. At the time, Victor [Villanueva], Cristina [Kirklighter], Octavio [Pimentel], Cecilia [Rodríguez Milanés], and Alejandro [Hidalgo] were the main people in charge of the Caucus. (Hernandez, 2016b)

Again, it was the welcoming spirit of the Caucus leaders and members at the Caucus meetings, such as Ramirez mentioned above, that attracted new scholars to join and to assist with the larger mission of networking and improving the education of Chicano and Chicana and Latino and Latina students in public schools and colleges. It was the combination of the Latino Caucus meetings in the program, conference venues with large Latino populations, and mentors in the home departments that encouraged new Latinx scholars to join and stay connected.

Through NCTE and CCCCs efforts to increase graduate students of color conference attendance, such as *Scholars for the Dream,* Latinx scholars were invited by Caucus leaders to attend meetings. This was the case for Aja Martínez in 2008. Martinez, a graduate student at the University of Arizona, noted that she joined the Caucus when she first attended a CCCC meeting as a *Scholar for the Dream*. Again, it was a Caucus member who took the initiative to invite Aja to the Caucus meeting.

> I attended the Scholars for the Dream special reception, and I was there by myself. I was heartbroken because none of the faculty from my program in Arizona attended. But it was Octavio Pimentel who invited me to the Latinx Caucus meeting on Friday. He said, "Come be with us" and "Come do this thing." When I attended, I was drawn to those who were already members. (Hernández, 2016a)

As a result, the Caucus played an important role in how emergent Latinx scholars began to see themselves within the fields of English Studies and Rhetoric and Composition, and within organizations such as NCTE and CCCC. As Damian Baca, an Associate Professor at the University of Arizona, noted:

> I think the role of the Latino Caucus in the CCCC has been incredibly important to me, and I would like to especially note the role of the Latino Caucus working with former NCTE employee Dr. Sandra Gibbs, who placed diversity at the forefront of all of the work we do—teaching, research, outreach, community engagement. (Garcia, 2017b)

> The reception at CCCC was fairly cold. I have been embraced by NCTE. I don't have training in English education. I don't try to pass myself off as acknowledged. But they have been overwhelmingly supportive, and the Latino Caucus, of course, through NCTE, has been a huge resource.

> As we pursue these goals, we are not alone, we are working parallel to other groups, other scholars, other teachers of color, who are also asking and demanding change. (Garcia, 2017b)

THE CAUCUS AS A PAN-ETHNIC GROUP

Aside from feeling that the Caucus was like home, Dueñas González and Cecilia Rodríguez Milanés also recalled that the Caucus was always pan-ethnic, a form of coalition building across ethnicities. Some Latinos and Latinas, especially Chicanos and Chicanas, identify with Native culture and having American Indian scholars attend Caucus meetings was understood as a welcoming gesture. Indeed, to feel connected with other scholars of color, Malea Powell and others attended the Latinx Caucus meetings before the American Indian Caucus was created in 1997 (Pinkert and Elder). In the 1980s, Dueñas González recalls two colleagues, Karen Begay and Lawson Fusao Inada, who were members of the Caucus:

> From the beginning, let's say in the 1980s, Karen Begay, who was a Navajo educator, was a regular member of the Caucus, and so was Lawson Fusao Inada, a famous Japanese American poet. They were both members of the Hispanic Caucus, because there was no Asian or Native American caucus to attend. Whenever we created a Rainbow Strand, Begay and Inada were, of course, major representatives of two of the four federally established minorities: Asian American, Native American, Latino American, and African American. They were very often chosen for representing their group: Lawson Inada for Asian American and Karen Begay for Native American. And they served incredibly well for many years. In fact, Lawson Inada used to give an incredibly wonderful presentation on what it was like on the day that the Japanese internment happened. (Hernández, 2017)

Asian American colleagues, such as Lawson Fusao Inada and Gail Okawa also became members in the Latinx Caucus by participating in the meetings and becoming involved in the Caucus activities. As part of the announcements section of Caucus Newsletter, Rodríguez Milanés announced Okawa's promotion to associate professor at Youngstown State University and her recent publications in *English Journal*, *"Re-Seeing our Professional Face(s)"* and her chapter titled "Removing Masks: Confronting Graceful Evasion and Bad Habits in a Graduate English Class" in Gilyard's *Race, Rhetoric, and Composition* (Okawa, 1998; Rodríguez Milanés, 1999).

Still Rodríguez Milanés also noticed that very few scholars and teachers of color attended the NCTE or CCCC conferences, which necessarily impacted the Caucus membership.

THE POWER OF THE CAUCUS

In the 1990s, as noted, when scholars of color felt unwelcome at the NCTE and CCCC conferences, the Caucus was perceived as a home for Latinos and

Latinas, Asian American, and American Indian scholars. During annual conferences of those two organizations, some of the White members expressed racist or ethnically insensitive remarks. The Caucus was a place where members of color could discuss specific incidents of insensitivity, create action plans to remedy them, and then meet with the NCTE and CCCC leadership. Cecilia Rodríguez Milanés described one of these incidents from the early 1990s:

> Renee [Moreno] was in the first class of the Scholars for the Dream, and there was a special session of the CCCC in San Diego [in 1993]. Renee was giving an important and poignant presentation, and the person who spoke after her was a White woman, who totally didn't hear a single word Renee said. Instead, she said all of this racist crap. "My Latino students are silent," she said. "They don't talk." And so, a bunch of us were, like, "Oh, my god! I can't believe she just said that." And there were about three or four of us, and one of the people with me was Gail Okawa, who was also one of the original members of the Latino Caucus. She's retired now, but she was from Youngstown, Ohio. Renee was insulted by this stupid woman in the way that she just dismissed her presentation, so we got up and walked out, because the audience was then piling on top of Renee. We got up and said, "This is intolerable, this is racist, and we're not going to stand for it." And then we stormed out.
>
> We then decided that we had to find Victor Villanueva to let him know about this inappropriate presentation. When the group found Victor, he said, "Okay, now you need to participate in the Caucus. This is a place where you can get your voice heard when you can express your concerns to the leadership." (Hernandez, 2016c)

Rodríguez Milanés further explained that many Caucus members were recruited in this way, which energized new members. Under Victor's leadership, this new group of Caucus members outlined the problem at the CCCC session and met with the leadership the next morning to discuss the racist comments that followed Renee's presentation.

In another example of Caucus leadership, in 1989, when Jaime Mejia was serving on the Executive Committee, he voiced his concern about increasing Latinx participation at the next CCCC conference. He describes his experience on the Executive Committee as follows:

I was the only Latino on the Executive Committee, and my voice rang through. We voted on a future site for CCCC, and the choices were Cleveland, New Orleans, and San Antonio. There was a case made for New Orleans and even Cleveland. But when I spoke up and said, "We need to go to San Antonio because it's a Mexican American community—we don't have enough Mexican Americans in CCCC—we need to go there and pick up more Latinos," that settled the argument, and we went to San Antonio. You know that was a key move to just draw more people in who were Latinos. And if I hadn't been on the Executive Committee arguing that case, I don't think we would have gone to San Antonio. I convinced them. I'm very proud of taking the CCCC to San Antonio. (Medina, 2016)

San Antonio in the late 1980s and 1990s reported a Hispanic population of 55% (U.S. Census Bureau, 1990). This example of holding a national conference illustrates how venues are key to including diverse groups of people to organizations.

Throughout the 1990s and 2000s, issues of Latino and Latina representation at the NCTE continued to surface, year after year. Mary Carmen Cruz, a former chair of the Caucus, identified several ways that she was mentored by the Caucus leadership—specifically, by Dueñas González and Gibbs—to speak up and help resolve issues. In 1995, five of the seventeen members of the *Involving People of Color in the Council Task Force* were dedicated Caucus leaders: Roseann Dueñas González, Victor Villanueva, Cecilia Rodríguez Milanés, Mary Carmen Cruz, and Aurelia Davila de Silva. In 1996, the Task Force submitted a report that affirmed the meaningful involvement of members of color within the NCTE.

Another committee that pushed the diversity, inclusion, and equity agenda forward was the Committee Against Racism and Bias in the Teaching of English. For many years, various members of the Caucus chaired the Committee Against Racism and Bias in the Teaching of English. From 1987 to 1992, Victor Villanueva, an active Caucus leader, was the chair of the committee and later a member of the committee (1993 to 1996). Later Caucus leaders who were also chairs of this committee included: Bobbi Ciriza Houtchens (2001), Mary Carmen Cruz (2002), and Maria Franquiz (2003–2005). These Caucus leaders were instrumental in carefully guiding this Committee Against Racism and Bias to be vigilant about identifying discrimination against Latinos and Latinas, African Americans, Asian Americans, and American Indians at the NCTE and CCCC conferences. While she was not the chair of this committee, Aurelia Davila de Silva, a very active Caucus member, also served on the Committee Against Racism and Bias in the Teaching of English between 1999–2001 and again between 2006–2008.

While the Task Force on Racism and Bias in the Teaching of English continued to exist after 2013, it had lost its focus and was no longer serving the needs of the students. In 2014 and 2015, the committee did not meet at all, because its members and chair could not decide on a meeting time. Fortunately, in 2016, two Caucus members, Iris Ruiz and Lorena German, joined the committee, and have helped return it to its original mission. The situation with the Task Force on Racism and Bias is a reoccurring theme for the work of the Caucus, that is, one step forward and two steps back. But as is shown, strong Chicana Caucus leaders, such as Ruiz and German, were able to push this committee forward after it had lost its leadership and continue its role of ensuring representation of scholars of color on the conference program.

THE POWER OF AN ALLY, THE NECESSITY OF CONTINUED PRESSURE

Sandra Gibbs, Director of Minority Group Affairs, created a welcoming environment for Latino and Latina Caucus members to become even more involved in the NCTE and CCCCs. Mary Carmen Cruz credits Gibbs for her own involvement in the NCTE. When Cruz had returned to teach in the Tucson Unified School District after being away from the NCTE for several years, she received a surprise phone call from Gibbs, inviting her to serve on the *Rainbow Strand* Planning Committee. In Cruz's words:

> Sandra Gibbs was our godmother and our *niña* [godmother]. She made sure that our voices were heard and made sure there was communication among the caucuses. She knew the history of NCTE and she was a powerful promoter of our involvement. She was involved in the Committee on Writing. People of color were also involved in the committees she was involved with. She spread the wealth and was involved in the main work of NCTE. (Hernandez, 2016e)

As Cruz notes, Gibbs did a whole lot more than just direct the caucuses. She was in charge of the NCTE's Writing Task Force, and any special professional programs, such as a research project by the National Council of Accreditation for Teacher Education, or NCATE (McCracken and Gibbs).

Gibbs' involvement goes back to 1972. When the NCTE Executive

Committee saw the need to facilitate the representation of the Black Caucus and Chicano Caucus leadership, the NCTE created a new Director of Minority Group Affairs and Special Projects position. Gibbs was hired for the express purpose of involving teachers of color within the organization to volunteer and to take leadership positions. From 1973 to 2004, Gibbs was the NCTE's liaison with Black and Chicano leaders, and later with American Indian and Asian Caucus leaders. For the thirty-one years she served the NCTE and CCCCs, Gibbs was central to the history of the Caucus. It was through Gibbs' efforts that many Caucus members became involved in the NCTE's section committees, task forces, and the Rainbow Strand Planning Committee. She was instrumental in involving Caucus members in the NCTE and CCCCs committees and initiatives, which is why the Caucus leaders remember her fondly as the godmother or the *madrina* of the Caucus.

When Gibbs was asked to leave the NCTE in 2004, there was a unified effort to bring her back. After the Caucus wrote fifty unsuccessful letters to have the NCTE reconsider its decision, a void emerged between the organization and the caucuses. However, Sandra Gibbs' legacy continued: Caucus leaders carried on by working across caucuses. At the conventions, the Black Caucus continued to be scheduled at the same time as the Latino Caucus and in close spatial proximity for the purpose of working side-by-side on issues. Cristina Kirklighter recalled this time:

> I became co-chair with Renee Moreno when Sandra Gibbs had already left. This was the moment when Caucus co-chairs realized our cross-caucus relationships needed to be strengthened to send out our collective voices to NCTE and CCCC. The approaching NCTE 2011 Centennial Celebration also brought us together as we worked to document our collective histories. . . The co-chairs at the time knew we had to create a strong voice together and work on many cross-caucus initiatives to fight the injustices of academia, NCTE, and beyond. (García, 2017)

While Gibbs is no longer with NCTE, she left a legacy of working together across all the identity Caucuses, of having Caucus members becoming involved in the larger NCTE and CCCCs organizations; and of sharing the wealth and creating new opportunities for involvement among its members in the caucuses.

CAUCUS LEADERS AND THE RAINBOW STRAND COMMITTEE (1987 TO PRESENT)

When the Task Force on Racism and Bias in the Teaching of English and the Minority Affairs Advisory Committee became actively involved in annual convention planning in 1987, they instituted the *Rainbow Strand*. The goal of the *Rainbow Strand*'s planners was to increase the involvement of Latino and Latina, Black, American Indian, and Asian scholars at each conference, since that continued to be an issue at the NCTE and CCCC. Our Caucus leaders were instrumental in creating the *Rainbow Strand* and its Planning Committee, whose focus was to provide an exchange of pedagogies relevant to culturally diverse students. Below is the Planning Committee's description of the rationale for the *Rainbow Strand*:

> Rainbow Strand sessions highlight issues and strategies related to enhancing the education of culturally and linguistically diverse students. Affirming the lives and literatures, literacies, and legacies of people across complex and multiple lines of difference is central to the mission of the Rainbow Strand. Thus, Rainbow Strand sessions represent the cultural and linguistic diversity of a nation, if not a globe, and thus affirm and explore, examine, and pay unique attention to historically underrepresented populations—specifically, Latinos. (NCTE, 2015a)

The Latinx Caucus and the Black Caucus were responsible for naming representatives to serve on the Rainbow Strand. Bobbi Ciriza Houtchens noted the need for the *Rainbow Strand* planners:

> Before the Rainbow Strand was instituted, virtually no sessions or workshops focused on affirming cultural and linguistic diversity that Latinos bring to classrooms. Instead, the national convention included sessions that had a deficit view of Latinos. For example, "Helping Latinos Improve Their Writing in Vocational Careers." (Hernandez, 2016e)

Cruz noted that it was Gibbs who called on Hispanic Caucus members to ensure their representation on the *Rainbow Strand* Planning Committee (Hernández, 2016d). The purpose was to give the Executive Committee and the section leaders a resource of experienced Latino and Latina and Black educators who could help improve the program for both White Language Arts teachers and Latino and Latina and Black educators who attended the conference and were seeking professional development. Cruz described the inclusion of the *Rainbow Strand* Planning Committee during the February conference planning days. At first, in 1987, the *Rainbow Strand* was met with resistance from the NCTE Planning Committee. In Cruz's words:

> Meeting with the NCTE Planning Committee was powerful. Initially, we would go into their planning sessions as working consultants by bringing our expertise of working with students of color. Usually, the Executive Committee and the section leaders and members were White. At first, they were intimidated that we were in the room, but because we had been mentored, we knew how to point things out without being confrontational. Being in the room, we were able to read body language, and we were skilled at reading the tone of the conversation. They didn't realize we were on the same team and that it was okay for the Rainbow Strand consultants to participate in this important endeavor. (Hernandez, 2016e)

By the end of the third and final planning day, the Caucus members had forged relationships with the Planning Committee, which translated into the Caucus members feeling vested in the organization and having contributed meaningfully to an improved convention program. The Caucus members also felt that attitudes had changed, with the NCTE officers now enlightened about issues important to the Caucus members. Again, in Cruz's words:

> The face-to-face meetings in February were powerful in raising the level of sensitivity of NCTE, including the NCTE staff. Because we interfaced with the staff, friendships and relationships developed, and we were able to move the organization along. (Hernández, 2016e)

That is in contrast to what happens today, now that the NCTE has reduced the number of Planning Committee members at headquarters, and with the convention program having gone digital. Cruz noted this difference:

> All you can build is acquaintanceships, and you can't build a level of trust. That has hurt NCTE and the Caucus. Alliances are built when you interact with others over three days. (Hernández, 2016e)

However, with much of the program now in digital format, the face-to-face convention planning has been reduced by the number of members involved. Cruz has described the current planning process as follows:

> What happens now is that the committee meets for two and a half days, not the three full days, and there is a smaller Planning Committee,

which consists of the Executive Committee, the chair of the different sections, elementary, middle, secondary, and college. Then there are one or two members from the Research Strand, one or two members of Rainbow Strand, someone from the LGBT Strand, so the number is reduced from a hundred Planning Committee members to maybe twenty people max. I was part of the new NCTE Planning Committee when we met in Florida. (Hernández, 2016e)

Unfortunately, the camaraderie has been lost that was built up between the NCTE and the Caucus when more Caucus members were involved over the three days. Now readers submit their scores digitally for each proposal before the Planning Committee meets. While the process has been streamlined, the relationships that had been forged in the 1990s were being lost in the 2000s with the new digital program process. As Cruz has noted:

> With the digital conference program, there are eight *Rainbow Strand* planners. There used to be twenty, when we met with Sandra. When these twenty people had a readout, Rainbow consultants read the final proposals; and when there were issues, we worked with chairs to discuss those issues and to help set the program. Rainbow Strand consultants and other conference planners came together to talk with each other. (Hernández, 2016e)

By 1995, when the Task Force met in Washington, D.C., for a three-day review, the Caucus members questioned why it seemed that the NCTE had lost its momentum in involving scholars of color. The Caucus members were involved in the Task Force chaired by Charlotte Brooks, with Sandra Gibbs as the NCTE liaison. Six Caucus leaders were instrumental: Roseann Dueñas González, Mary Carmen Cruz, Gail Okawa, Cecilia Rodríguez Milanés, Aurelia de Silva, and Victor Villanueva. During this meeting, they reviewed all the avenues for involving scholars of color at all levels of the organization. According to the report, an inconsistent process for involving people of color was identified as the main problem:

> People of color have been elected to various levels, and some have chaired task forces, committees, and commissions, but there are no set procedures to ensure consistent representation on the NCTE Executive Committee. Nor is there a person of color in a policy director role at headquarters. NCTE must build a plan to assure the continued and systematic involvement of people of color at all levels and in every facet of

its structure. The Task Force members, which included Caucus leaders, asked why the Council in 1995 is back to where it was twenty years ago.

- How can we stop the cycle?

- How can we consistently use the creativity and perspectives of people of color in the NCTE dialogue?

- How can we build upon the successful programs and strategies developed by people of color, that is, the Rainbow Strand, without having to reestablish them?

- Are the policies on involving people of color more "on paper" than systemically implemented? (NCTE, 1996)

Also, not too long in the distant past, anthologies and basal texts did not include Latino and Latina and Chicano and Chicana writers. The 1995 Committee Involving Scholars of Color brought awareness to the national office, so that English teachers could be inclusive and sensitive to culturally and linguistically diverse students.

CAPIROTADA—THE CAUCUS NEWSLETTER (1994–2008)

In 1994, three Caucus leaders—Alfredo Lujan, Cecilia Rodríguez Milanés, and Victor Villanueva—initiated a newsletter and called it *Capirotada* to continue networking among the Caucus scholars by recognizing members' contributions and milestones before and after each of the NCTE and CCCC conferences. *Capirotada* is the name of a bread pudding dish that is made during Lent in many different variations, depending on one's family and country of origin. In general, the bread pudding is made with ingredients that are at hand, such as nuts, cheese, dried fruit, and old bread, which are then flavored with a cinnamon-sugar syrup. The founders of the newsletter gave it that name as a metaphor for bringing together Latinos and Latinas at the NCTE and CCCC conferences to network for the betterment of their students. In other words, diversity was inherent in the very name of the newsletter.

The first issue of the newsletter, which was published in the summer of 1994, featured poetry, the Caucus's goals, a review of Victor Villanueva's new book (*Bootstraps*), and Rodríguez Milanés's promotion of the Hispanic Literary Heritage Reading, which paralleled the African American Read-In that began in 1970. In 1995, twenty-five years later, on the front page of the newsletter, Dueñas González encouraged Caucus members to become involved in NCTE committees and commissions, since she had already been an active member of the NCTE since 1971. She wrote that while she had seen overall progress in the integration of African Americans in the NCTE, she had seen little progress for Latinos and Latinas in the organization. Dueñas González attributed this to the nature of NCTE's work, which needs to be continuously carried out from year to year with a large network, while also noting the Black Caucus had a large membership, whereas the Latino Caucus had only a handful of members.

Furthermore, Dueñas González observed that many Latinos and Latinas who attended the NCTE or CCCC conferences tended to be loners who did not network through the Latino Caucus, unlike their African American colleagues in the Black Caucus.

Her article was also a call to involve many more Latino Caucus members within the NCTE/CCCC committees and commissions—a call that continues to resonate to this day. Dueñas González made the organizational structure of the NCTE transparent in order for Caucus members to move into Executive Committee positions, as Victor Villanueva, Kris Gutiérrez, Jaime Mejia, Mary Carmen Cruz, and Bobbi Houtchens had. Dueñas González wrote:

> NCTE's role in creating national language arts policy and influencing general educational policies is critical and one that needs our closest attention. To develop our voice, we have to work to empower ourselves with the National Council of Teachers of English. We have to be visible. We have to flourish in NCTE and the larger educational community. We have to collaborate with other groups and forge educational attitudes, approaches, and policies that will facilitate and enhance the education of Latino children. This is a leviathan but noble endeavor, and we all need to work synergistically with each other to carve a path. (González, 1995, p. 2)

For some Caucus members, such as Cárdenas de Dwyer, Dueñas González, Gutiérrez, Rodríguez Milanés, and Villanueva, service to NCTE and CCCC through the Caucus was key to their university careers. In Cecilia's words:

> Service to the [NCTE/CCCC] Caucus was a vital pivot for my academic career service. I became involved in the organization and in the Caucus leadership almost right away. Victor had been a co-chair for a long time [1988–1994], and he was ready to pass it along, and I then ended up doing it for fifteen years. (Hernandez, 2016c)

In the 1990s and into the 2000s, Rodríguez Milanés was the backbone of the Caucus. She not only served as chair and co-chair, but she was also the newsletter editor, publishing it twice a year from 1994 to 2008. During her tenure as newsletter editor, she invited many members to contribute poetry and articles on how they were advancing the education of Latino and Latina students in their local communities. According to Cecilia, the Caucus not only served as an important academic service organization, but also as one that allowed its members to expand their voice beyond their workplace to the national level within the profession.

THE CAUCUS AND THE ANTI-LATINO BACKLASH, 1998 TO 2012

Although Latinos and Latinas had won a number of civil rights in the 1960s in education as well as voting at the national level, there were a number of national anti-Latino initiatives between 1998 and 2005. In that period, a series of contentious anti-Spanish-Language and anti-Latino initiatives, cloaked under English-only initiatives, emerged publicly. This backlash began when Ron Unz, a businessman and unsuccessful California gubernatorial candidate, spearheaded four English-only initiatives that advocated a nativist ideology instead of bilingual education. Unz's first ballot initiative, in 1998 in California, was Proposition 227: English for the Children, which passed by a wide majority. His second initiative, Proposition 203, in 2000 in Arizona, also passed, eliminating bilingual education for many Latino students. During that 2000 ballot initiative in Arizona, several Caucus members drafted a sense of the house motion for the NCTE through the Caucus listserv, which read as follows:

> We support K-12 educational systems which acknowledge and respect students' home cultures and native languages by providing comprehensive dual-language programs—including listening, speaking, reading, writing, computing, and critical thinking skills—in students' first languages as well as in English to develop fully biliterate members of a multicultural U.S. society. (Milanés, 2000)

Unz's anti-Latino initiatives continued on the East Coast and in the Southwest. On November 5, 2002, Massachusetts voters passed his Question 2, which was an English-only initiative for public schools. However, on that same day, Colorado voters defeated Unz's English Language Education Initiative, or Amendment 31. In effect, the defeat in Colorado ended the blatant attacks on Latinos and Latinas and on bilingual education across the country, especially in the four states with the most Latino and Latina students, but great damage had already been done to the cause.

Against this anti-Latino national backlash, a group of Chicano and Chicana education activists began planning the Mexican American Studies program in Tucson, Arizona, which started with a few courses at the end of the 1990s and flourished by the 2000s into forty-three course offerings. The program, however, came under fire from White politicians, and was formally ended in 2012 by the Tucson school board, which voted to terminate the program after Governor Jan Brewer signed a bill to outlaw "resentment toward a race or class of people" and "courses designed primarily for pupils of a particular ethnic group or that advocated ethnic solidarity, instead of treating pupils as individuals" (Santistevan). In 2015, Iris Ruiz, along with other members of the Caucus, led the drafting of the NCTE/CCCC Position Statement in Support of Ethnic Studies Initiatives in K-12 Curricula:

> The National Council of Teachers of English (NCTE) and its members support the implementation of K–12 ethnic studies curricula nationwide. As a professional organization committed to professional development and the creation of innovative curricula, NCTE seeks to play an instrumental role in the developmental needs of ethnic studies teachers and institutional curricular development.
>
> NCTE also recognizes ethnic studies as a scholarly field that has always been invested in providing equal access to literacy, encouraging democratic principles, and promoting different ways of knowing—of producing and disseminating knowledge. (NCTE, 2017c)

Beyond the specifics of this resolution, however, what this effort demonstrates is that the Caucus, through the help of the chairs, has continued to forge ahead with initiatives and statements that promote a Latino and Latina agenda even with the bias and racism that Caucus leaders and scholars experience at the conferences, colleges, and within the country writ large.

CONCLUSION

This chapter traced the history of the Caucus through the interviews with Caucus leaders and relevant NCTE/CCCCs artifacts. As more members joined, the Caucus changed its name to become more inclusive; beginning with the Chicano Teachers of English in 1968, changing to the Hispanic

Caucus in the 1980s, to the Latino Caucus in 1994, and to how it is known today—the Latinx Caucus. Caucus leaders and members felt that the Caucus was the heart of the NCTE and the CCCCs. They also embraced scholars of color who did not have a specific Asian nor a Native American Caucus dedicated to their identity or issues. Furthermore, from the 1960s to the 1990s, the Caucus remained small, however, its chairs and members accomplished major goals, from presenting conference sessions on Chicano and Chicana literature as early as 1972, to publishing textbooks that included Latino and Latina literature, to fulfilling leadership roles on its Executive Committee and general CCCC and NCTE committees to represent Latino and Latina issues, and to assist the NCTE and CCCC with the many committees focused on diversity initiatives within the organization, such as the *Rainbow Strand*. In the mid 1990s to the mid 2000, Caucus co-chairs published the Caucus news *Capirotada* to continue the networking, camaraderie, and communication among its members; today that communication happens through the email Listserv. Caucus members also responded to societal anti-Latino rhetoric and policies (1998 to 2012) on English-only language policies and the termination of the Mexican American Studies program through motions and resolutions. Overall, while Caucus leaders and members experienced microaggressions and discrimination while serving the NCTE and CCCC, these same leaders and members forged ahead with having their voices heard in the NCTE and CCCC while publishing a vibrant Latino scholarship that in several cases broke new ground.

WORKS CITED

Cárdenas de Dwyer, Carlota, and Robert Hayden. *United States in Literature: Grade Eleven.* Scott Foresman, 1979.

Council Chronicle. "Writing and Working for Change Project: Recognizing the Collective Work of Teachers within and across Diverse Identities." *Council Chronicle,* vol. 21, 2011, pp. 14.

García, Romeo. Interview with Steven Alvarez. Writing and Working for Change project. 2016a, August 15. *Viva Nuestro Caucus: Rewriting the Forgotten Pages of Our Caucus.*

---. Interview with Damian Baca. Writing and Working for Change project. 2016b, October 1. *Viva Nuestro Caucus: Rewriting the Forgotten Pages of Our Caucus.*

---. Interview with Cristina Kirklighter. Writing and Working for Change project. 2016c, October 3. *Viva Nuestro Caucus: Rewriting the Forgotten Pages of Our Caucus.*

González, Roseann Dueñas. "Saludos." *Capirotada Newsletter,* vol. 2 no. 1, 1995, pp. 1–3.

---, editor. 2001. *Language Ideologies: Critical Perspectives on the Official English Movement,* vol. 2: *History, Theory, and Policy.* National Council of Teachers of English, 2001.

Gutiérrez, Kris. Remarks to the Latinx Caucus. E-mail sent to the members of the Latinx Caucus, 19 November, 2016. (Reproduced in the Appendix)

Hernández, Anita. Interview with Roseann Dueñas González. Writing and Working for Change project. February 7, 2017. *Viva Nuestro Caucus: Rewriting the Forgotten Pages of Our Caucus.*

---. Interview with Aja Martinez. Writing and Working for Change project, 2016a, July 12. *Viva Nuestro Caucus: Rewriting the Forgotten Pages of Our Caucus.*

---. Interview with Cristina Ramirez. Writing and Working for Change project. 2016b, August 3. *Viva Nuestro Caucus: Rewriting the Forgotten Pages of Our Caucus.*

---. Interview with Cecilia Rodríguez Milanés. Writing and Working for Change project. 2016c, August 17. *Viva Nuestro Caucus: Rewriting the Forgotten Pages of Our Caucus.*

---. Interview with Tracy Flores. Writing and Working for Change project. 2016d, October 15. *Viva Nuestro Caucus: Rewriting the Forgotten Pages of*

Our Caucus.

---. Interview with Bobbi Houtchens and Mary Carmen Cruz. Writing and Working for Change project. 2016e, December 13. *Viva Nuestro Caucus: Rewriting the Forgotten Pages of Our Caucus.*

Lujan, Alfredo. "Somos quien somos, ¿No?" *Capirotada Newsletter*, vol. 1, no. 1, 1994, pp. 1.

Martinez, Aja Y. "The American Way": Resisting the Empire of Force and Color-Blind Racism." *College English*, vol. 71, no. 6, pp. 584-595.

McCracken, H. Thomas, and Sandra E. Gibbs. *Final Report: NCTE/NCATE Research Project on the Assessment of the Preparation of Teachers of English Language Arts*, (2001, January). Available at http://www.ncte.org/library/NCTEFiles/Groups/CEE/NCATE/NPEAT -FinalReport.pdf/.

Medina, Cruz. Interview with Jaime Mejía. Writing and Working for Change project. 2016, May 10. *Viva Nuestro Caucus: Rewriting the Forgotten Pages of Our Caucus.*

Miller, James, et al. *United States in Literature: Grade Eleven.* Scott Foresman, 1982.

---, et al. *Question and Form in Literature: America Reads*, Medallion Edition. Scott Foresman, 1979.

National Council of Teachers of English (NCTE). Resolution on Preparing Teachers with Knowledge of the Literature of Minorities, 1972. Available at http://www2.ncte.org/statement/teachlitbyminorites/

---. *64th Annual Meeting Advance Conference Program, New Orleans, Louisiana*, (25–30 November, 1974). Available at http://www.ncte.org/library/NCTEFiles/Resources/Journals/CE/1974/0362-oct1974/CE0362Advance.pdf/.

---. Resolution on Multicultural Curriculum Materials. 1975. Available at http://www2.ncte.org/statement/multicultmaterials/

---. *For the Members: Prepared by Headquarters Staff*, December, 1977. Available at http://www.ncte.org/library/NCTEFiles/Resources/Journals/CE/1977/0394-dec1977/CE0394Members.pdf/.

---. Non-White Minorities in English and Language Arts Materials. 1978. Available at http://www2.ncte.org/statement/minoritiesinelamat/

---. How to Help Your Child Become a Better Writer (Spanish version). 1980a. Available at http://www2.ncte.org/statement/howtohelpspanish/

---. Resolution on the Responsibility of English Teachers in a Multilingual, Multicultural Society. 1980b. Available at http://www2.ncte.org/statement/multiculturalsociety/

---. *Report from the Task Force on Involving People of Color in the Council*, 1996. Available at http://www.ncte.org/library/NCTEFiles/Involved/Volunteer/Elections/Motions_Related_to_the_Report_on_Involving_People_of_Color.pdf/.

---. Supporting Linguistically and Culturally Diverse Learners in English Education, 2005. Available at http://www2.ncte.org/statement/diverse-learnersinee/

---. *Statement on Anti-Racism to Support Teaching and Learning*, 2007. Available at http://www2.ncte.org/statement/antiracisminteaching/

---. *About the Rainbow Strand in NCTE Advancement of People of Color Leadership Award Recipients*, 19–22 November, 2015a. Available at http://www.ncte.org/library/NCTEFiles/Groups/Caucuses/2015Diversity.pdf/.

---. *American Indian Caucus*, 20 November, 2015b. Available at http://www.ncte.org/caucus/amindian/.

---. *NCTE Position Statement in Support of Ethnic Studies Initiatives in K-12 Curricula*, 15 October 2015c. Available at http://www.ncte.org/positions/statements/ethnic-studies-k12-curr

---. *Latinx Caucus*, 2017a. Available at http://www.ncte.org/caucus/Latinx/

---. *NCTE Funds Teachers for the Dream Affiliate Award*, 2017b. Available at http://www.ncte.org/affiliates/awards/teacherdream/.

---. *NCTE Position Statements on Diversity*, 2017c. Available at http://www.ncte.org/positions/diversity/.

---. *The Committee Against Racism and Bias in the Teaching of English*, 2017d. Available at http://www.ncte.org/volunteer/Groups/Racismbiascom.

Okawa, Gail Y. Re-Seeing our Professional Face(s). *English Journal*, vol. 88, no. 2, 1998.

---. "Removing Masks: Confronting Graceful Evasion and Bad Habits in a Graduate English Class" In Keith Gilyard (Ed.) *Race, Rhetoric, and Composition*. Portsmouth, NH: Heinemann. 1998.

Pinkert, Laurie, and Cristyn Elder. *American Indian Caucus, Part 1: Writing and Working for Change Video Project*, 19 October, 2011. Available at https://www.youtube.com/watch?v=WdW2smlM1Konw&feature=feedu/.

Rodríguez Milanés, Cecilia. "Announcements and News." *Capirotada Newsletter*, vol. 4, no. 1 and 2, 1999, pp. 2.

---. "From the Editor." *Capirotada Newsletter*, vol. 5, no. 2, 2000, pp. 1–10.

Ruiz, Iris. Interview with Victor Villanueva. Writing and Working for

Change project, 2016, July 17. *Viva Nuestro Caucus: Rewriting the Forgotten Pages of Our Caucus.*

Santistevan, Ryan. *Mexican-American Studies Ban Back in Court.* Available at http://www.azcentral.com/story/news/local/arizona-education/2017/07/03/arizona-mexican-american-studies-ban-back-court-hb-2281/437781001/, 3 July, 2017.

U.S. Census. Texas—Race and Hispanic Origin for Selected Cities and Other Places: Earliest Census to 1990.

Villanueva, Victor. *Bootstraps: From an American Academic of Color.* National Council Teachers of English. 1993.

Young, Vershawn Ashanti and Aya Y. Martinez. *Code-Meshing as World English: Pedagogy, Policy, and Performance.* National Council Teachers of English. 2011.

CHAPTER EIGHT

We're Here to Stay: The Current State of the Caucus and Future Directions

Romeo García, Iris D. Ruiz, Anita Hernandez, and María Paz Carvajal Regidor

It has been 50 years since CTE was formed and established. The Caucus initially came together to bring to light the needs of Latino and Latina students, advocate for their representation in curricula, pedagogy, theory, as well as textbooks, and, finally, to gain representation and power within NCTE/CCCC. Much has changed in this time with regard to the Caucus and NCTE and CCCC as well as to the field of Composition and Rhetoric, in general. Yet, as we've attempted to illuminate in *Viva Nuestro Caucus*, the Caucus mission and goals have remained constant across leaders and the voices of its members have only become more significant and powerful. Indeed, the work of Latinx Caucus today rests upon a foundation created by the elders present throughout the pages of *Viva Nuestro Caucus*.

Viva Nuestro Caucus was never meant to be a full history of the Caucus. It was written from a sense of urgency to document and write a Caucus history. In part, this was in response to the centennial volume *Reading the Past, Writing the Future*. More importantly, though, it was written as a testament to the fact that "We've been here" and "we're here to stay." *Viva Nuestro Caucus* chronicled the early history of CTE within a historical and political context. *Viva Nuestro Caucus* also delved into how leaders who came after the first generation continued to forge new paths by being elected as officers of the NCTE and CCCC, chairing the organizations' committees, and publishing pioneering ideas in journals and books.

While we have tried to represent this important history, we recognize our work is just a beginning. As a Caucus and a field, we still need to record and amplify the work of figures such as Kris Gutierrez, Adela Licona, Alfredo Lujan, Isabel Baca, María Franquiz, Renee Moreno, and Aurelia Davila de Silva. And we hope others will build upon our admittedly limited history, collectively articulating important moments and themes not fully developed here. Indeed, while recognizing the shortcomings of this project, we made a collective decision to continue with the manuscript since we believe *Viva Nuestro Caucus* captures the essential objective—to document the Caucus has and continues to be present, in large part thanks to its leadership and members. The project in itself, we would argue, encourages and calls for a much larger project, which must be continued by other current and/or future members of the Caucus. We call upon other Caucus members to take up what hasn't been included in this volume and to continue writing and preserving the Caucus history.

And we would argue that important history is still being written as the Caucus responds to current events within and beyond the field. Even as we write *Viva Nuestro Caucus*, in the fall of 2017, the leadership of the CCCC Conference debated whether to host the conference in Kansas City, Missouri, amidst social and cultural tensions and conflicts, which were directly related to the passage of SB 43 in Missouri, the set location for the NCTE conference in November 2017 and CCCC in March 2018, and the resulting travel advisory issued by the NAACP. On August 3rd, James Chase Sanchez notified the Caucus through the listserv that the NAACP issued a travel advisory warning for the state of Missouri. He suggested that a joint statement be written to warn all ethnic caucuses of this advisory before traveling. We were particularly concerned with specific parts of the bill that made discrimination particularly hard to prove by placing the burden of proof on the plaintiff to claim that race discrimination serves as a "motivating" vs. "contributing" factor. We found this law quite troublesome being that it was passed in Missouri, a racially hostile state, as noted by the *Missouri NAACP* in their travel advisory issued to its members.

Given our socially activist history and mission, we felt that such a law was likely to affect the sense of well-being, respect, and equal protection and representation under the law of, not only Missouri residents, but also both NCTE and CCCC conferences attendees. As a result of this dissatisfaction with the conference location, on August 8th, Iris Ruiz, the current co-chair of the CCCC Latinx Caucus (and contributing author to this text) drafted a statement that would later become the *Joint Caucus Statement* that initially became a collaborative effort with Cruz Medina (current co-chair), Christina Cedillo (current vice-chair), and Karrieann Soto (current secretary). At this time, Cruz Medina decided that the motive of the statement would be the specific request to move conference locations out of safety concerns for members of color. We all agreed to this position, and with the help of Alexandria Lockett, from the Black Caucus, we drafted a letter that made some specific recommendations which were titled, "Options for Action." There were seventeen options for action. We, then, asked other Caucuses, such as the Black Caucus, the Asian/Asian American Caucus, and the American Indian Caucus, to sign the statement requesting a relocation of the conference. The statement reads in part:

> Given the concern expressed by many conference participants, regarding their safety and the moral ethical stance of NCTE as a professional organization, jointly, the Black, Latinx, American Indian, and Asian/Asian American Caucuses strongly suggest moving the locations of the 2017 NCTE and the 2018 CCCC conventions from St. Louis, MO and Kansas City, MO, respectively, to locations that are more inclusive of and safe for all of the NCTE and CCCC membership.

In addition to this request, we provided the following options for action:

- Select conference sites that are located in cities where political leaders (e.g. legislators) have rejected any discrimination and have pledged to continue to do so.

- Provide individual members with more ways to access data regarding how conference sites are selected--including vendors, contract information, and budgetary limitations and possibilities.

- Expand opportunities for representatives from the Caucuses and/or SIGs to directly participate in executive decisions about annual conference planning and execution.

- Offer more lobbying transparency, so that members can see NCTE's commitment to democratic principles.

- Provide an account of NCTE's relationship to NAACP and anti-hate organizations.

- Explain the role of NCTE's Political Action Committee. If there is not one, create one.

- Write a letter to the Missouri legislature/governor.

- Take safety precautions and share them widely with members.

- Consider more remote options.

- Organize a die-in or protest at the Missouri State House.

- Wear black and brown armbands at the conference to show solidarity with people of color.

- Consult local grassroots organizations and elders to get their input on developing resources for the members attending each conference, including HBCUs, American Indian cultural centers or studies programs, tribal colleges, and more.

- Create opportunities for members or the organization to donate money to the NAACP and/or local anti-hate organizations.

- Create and distribute a list of anti-hate and minority owned/friendly businesses at the conference site where members can dine, stay, or socialize.

- Offer members a list of safe/protected spaces including friendship centers, LGBTQ zones, etc.

- Invite anti-hate organizers and/or the NAACP to run a workshop or series of workshop on how to organize (and find funding to pay them appropriately for their labor).

Ultimately, the leadership of the CCCC decided to keep the conference in Kansas City, citing financial and economic implications. The leadership of the CCCC conference responded to the joint-caucus statement, and other statements issued, by announcing the creation of a new Task Force, entitled the *Task Force on Social Justice and Activism*, on September 12, 2017. The charges of the task force were:

- Provide the Program Chair with a prioritized list of ways to make this year's annual convention safer and more accessible for members and provide events and experiences for members to do appropriate social justice and activist work at the convention site.

- Help coordinate, design, and put into action the ideas, events, and experiences that the program chair approves from the prioritized list.

- Work with the local site committee on safety, accessibility, social justice, and activist ideas, events, and experiences.

The Latinx Caucus appointed two members—Romeo García and Victor Del Hierro—and one member from the Executive Committee—Aja Martinez to represent the interests of the Caucus and to serve on this new task force. Ultimately, given these events, the Caucus decided through a very close vote (54-46%) to boycott CCCC, 2018 in Missouri. However, the Caucus remained deeply committed to supporting its most vulnerable members, such at its junior faculty members and graduate students, so the leadership pledged to support any member that decided to attend and who might participate in the social justice and activist events that were organized by Asao Inoue (conference Chair) and The Task Force on Social Justice and Activism. In addition, in order to ensure our needs and the demands listed on the Joint Statement were met, the Caucus decided to hold its workshop virtually and boycott the Pre-Conference workshop, which has been an integral part of Latinx Caucus presence and community building. We are proud of the results of our activist efforts, for we understand that without action, there can be no enduring justice for our members.

We believe the actions not only speak to the historical commitments of the Caucus, but also prove that the Caucus is here to stay. We believe it demonstrates that its members will continue to advocate for representation and to shape the future direction for our professional organizations and the field.

FINAL THOUGHTS

Recovering our Caucus' history in *Viva Nuestro Caucus* has allowed us to learn how Caucus leaders participated in the life and structure of the NCTE and CCCC through work in the elementary, middle, secondary, and college sections, and on task forces and committees, including the Executive Committee. As the interviews in the volume demonstrated, Caucus chairs and members cherish their advocacy roles in the organization and are proud of the scholarly contributions they have made, some published by the NCTE and CCCC and some through other venues, about Latino and Latina cultural and educational issues. Their work has diversified the male-centric and Eurocentric views of teaching materials and of scholarship in our field. Furthermore, their efforts have improved the education of students across the nation by urging publishers of literary textbook anthologies to include Latino and Latina authors, thereby helping English teachers to diversify and their curricula and more accurately reflect the range of literature written in the United States.

It is the hope of the co-editors of *Viva Nuestro Caucus* that the history of the Caucus will serve as guideposts for future chairs and members to ponder and guide the Caucus's future. As we have learned from our past leaders, ensuring the continued success of the Caucus will likely require the involvement of its current members and a new generation of members in the structure of NCTE and CCCC and the cultivation of their ideas for new scholarship and their publication through NCTE and CCCC venues as well as outside these organizations. While we are thankful for the leadership models established by our founding members and previous leaders, we also acknowledge that a new generation of members will likely find themselves navigating new challenges and having to create new leaderships norms.

WORKS CITED

Alvarez, Steven. "Literacy." *Decolonizing Rhetoric and Composition Studies: New Latinx Keywords for Theory and Practice*. Iris D. Ruiz, Raúl Sanchez, eds. Palgrave MacMillan, 2016.

Baca, Damían. *Mestiz@ Scripts, Digital Migrations, and the Territories of Writing*. Palgrave MacMillan, 2008.

Flores, Tracey. "Breaking Silence and Amplifying Voices: Youths Writing and Performing Their Worlds." *Journal of Adolescent and Adult Literacy*, 2018, pp. 1-19.

Garcia de Mueller, Genevieve and Iris Ruiz. "Race, Silence, and Writing Program Administration." *Journal of the Council of Writing Program Administrators*. 40:2, 19-39, 2017.

Gutiérrez, Kris D. "Unpackaging Academic Discourse." *Discourse Processes*. 19: 21-37, 1995.

---, et al. "Rethinking Diversity: Hybridity and Hybrid Language Practices in the Third Space." *Mind, Culture, and Activity*, 6:4, 286-303, 2009.

Joint Caucus Statement Statement. Written and endorsed by the Latinx Caucus, the Black Caucus, the Asian/Asian American Caucus, and the American Indian Caucus. August 15, 2017.

Lindemann, Erika. (ed.). *Reading the Past, Writing the Future: A Century of American Literacy Education and the National Council of Teachers of English*. National Council of Teachers of English, 2010.

Martinez, Aja. "A Plea for Critical Race Theory Counterstory: Stock Story versus Counterstory Dialogues Concerning Alejandra's "Fit" in the Academy." *Composition Studies*. 42:2, 33-55, Fall 2014.

NCTE Position Statement in Support of Ethnic Studies Initiatives in K-12 (http://www2.ncte.org/statement/ethnic-studies-k12-curr/) DOA: 06-24-2018.

Ortego y Gasca, Philip. *Selective Mexican American Bibliography*. Border Regional Library Association, 1972.

Ramirez, Cristina. *Occupying Our Space. The Mestiza Rhetorics of Mexican Women Journalists and Activists, 1875–1942*. UA Press, 2015.

Romano. Susan. "Tlaltelolco: The Grammatical-Rhetorical Indios of Colonial Mexico." *College English*. 66:3, 257-278, 2004.

Ruiz, Iris D. *Reclaiming Composition for Chicano/as and other Ethnic Minorities: A Critical History and Pedagogy*. Palgrave MacMillan, 2016.

Villanueva, Victor. *Bootstraps: From an American Academic of Color*. National Council of Teachers of English, 1993.

---. "On the Rhetorics and Precedence of Racism." *College Composition and Communication*, 50:4, A Usable Past: CCC at 50: Part 2 645-661, 1999.

PART II
Experiences:
In Their Own Words

EXPERIENCES: IN THEIR OWN WORDS
Felipe de Ortego y Gasca

Based on Interview by Iris Ruiz and Anita Hernández
August 4, 2016

I did a Master's degree on *Hamlet* as a thesis, and then, when I went to the University of New Mexico in '66, my first year there as a doctoral student, I declared myself to do a dissertation on *Chaucer*. That was in my period, when I thought that I had to follow this white track. In 1969, the University of New Mexico established its first Chicano Studies program and director, and I was the only Chicano faculty in English, at that time, at the University of New Mexico. The director asked if I would organize a course in Mexican Art and Literature for the fall of '69, which I did. I had about 80 students. The course went over so well that it changed my life. At the beginning of 1970, I went to the Chair of the English department. I had already finished three chapters of my dissertation on Chaucer. I went to the English Department Chair, Joe Satterfield and said, "Joe, I want to change my dissertation topic." He thought I was crazy. Finally, he agreed, and I changed my dissertation topic from Chaucer to the book, the study that came out called *Backgrounds of Mexican American Literature*. The first in the field. It set me back one year, but I'm glad I did it.

The truth of the matter is that I didn't realize that I was doing any pioneering work. What I know is that growing up and my first years in academia, I just assumed that I was supposed to follow a particular path. That path, unfortunately now, on reflection, that path was an all-white path. It wasn't until 1966 that I really, thanks to Octavio Romano, who organized *El Grito* and the *Quinto Sol* Publications. It was in '66 when he really turned me around, and I became a Chicano. Up until that time, I had a grey flannel suit, and I thought that I was supposed to follow the track, the white track. Do you know who Richard Rodriguez is? Well, I think he and I are nemeses to each other. If it weren't for Romano, I might have been in the same camp as Rodriguez.

Romano was on the NMSU campus in 1966. His wife was from Las Cruces. He looked lost. I came out of the English building. He hailed me and wanted to know where he could get a cup of coffee. I directed him, and after that, we just established a long friendship. I became one of the *Quinto Sol* writers. It was a mixture [of academic and non-academic writing]. . . I'll tell ya' what's more important. In the first issue of *El Grito*, Octavio Romano published a manifesto, which I think explains it all. The emphasis there was that we should stop as Chicanos trying to get the white publishers, white publications to give us an opportunity. We should stop shuffling on our and cap in hand, and asking, begging for anything. He said, "We were the ones that had to determine what the parameters or the worth of the works that we wrote."

Up until '62, I was teaching at a high school in El Paso, and I was teaching French because there was no job for a Mexican-American, Chicano, or Latino in El Paso in 1962. They didn't believe that we spoke English and they didn't think we spoke very good Spanish either. El Paso was a really racist town, unfortunately. That's considering that we've always been at least 75 percent of the population. Today, we're 85 percent of the city. I started teaching English in 1964 at New Mexico State University, which is just down the road from us here. Of the six years that I was there, five of those years, I was the Associate Director of the Freshman Writing Program. In 1966, it was, I went ahead and joined the NCTE as a member and started going to their conferences. In 1968, I met Carlota Cárdenas and Jose Carrasco. We thought, well, we seem to be the only brown faces in the crowd. There were African-American members, but we were the only three Chicanos. The three of us decided that we would just go ahead and organize as a Chicano caucus, essentially.

[NCTE] really didn't know who we were. We were just beginning to articulate our identity. The Chicano Renaissance was just bubbling to the surface at the time. Even though we were small in numbers, three, it was important to us because, first of all, we felt that it was our responsibility to be present, to be part of "the other" in the organization of National Council of Teachers of English since there were so few of us. I'm not sure what the exact number might have been in 1968, when we first organized. All we knew was that we were the three of us, that we saw each other pretty regularly at these meetings. I guess, it's part of what the philosophy and commitment that grew out of the Chicano Movement. That we began, at that time, to realize, that we needed to be more assertive, aggressive, and more in your face with a lot of white people.

I'll tell ya' what began to change the character considerably was when—I thought his name was Hogan, or something like that, who was the executive director of NCTE—when he enabled creation of the NCTE Taskforce on Racism and Bias in the Teaching of English, that really spirited us considerably because four caucuses of NCTE joined hands in that effort - The Chicano Teachers, the Black Caucus, the Native American Caucus, and Asia/ Asian American Caucus. Ernece Kelly was running the Black Caucus. The Asian American Caucus was headed by Frank Chin—he was the playwright, who wrote *The Chickencoop Chinaman* that was produced on Broadway. Let's see. Frank Chin and Jeffrey Chan. Jeffrey Chan was then chair of Asian American studies at San Francisco. We met regularly then as the taskforce, while still maintaining our identity as caucuses.

In 1972, the Taskforce, when we finished our report, it was called "Searching for America." In 1972, we had a NCTE meeting in Las Vegas, Nevada. We were able to, by then, to get the number of Chicanos who had established book outlets for Chicano-material outlets. They brought their stuff to the Las Vegas conference in 1972. The Taskforce also invited the publishers, and presidents, and vice-presidents to attend that meeting, our task force meeting. We all met in a fairly decent room in a Las Vegas conference center. We locked the doors and then Mau Mau'd them. I don't know if you know that expression, the African Mau Maus. We threatened them. We cursed at them. We were really wild with them. They were scared shitless. I have to tell ya'. That began to move those publishers, at least, to consider the writers, who were represented by the four caucuses. That's when the Simon & Schuster, that's when they approached me to put together an anthology of Mexican American literature, which I did. This was called *We are Chicanos*. It was considered the first critical anthology of Mexican American literature. Now, there were anthologies before that. I wouldn't want to mislead you. *Quinto Sol* put out, perhaps, the first of the Chicano anthologies of literature, the anthology of Chicano literature. That was called *El Espejo*.

I think, what I would say probably the greatest disappointment was that we seemed to be unable to make any inroads in the white publications. Yeah....Of course, that was, I think, due to the fact that we were still so small a number of Chicanos at the time in English. Now, there were a number of Chicanos who were in Spanish, and who were getting published. Not at any greater rate, but in the *Journal of Spanish and Portuguese* that's still out. I guess, I hit a lucky streak because I wrote a number of critical pieces on major English and American writers that found a publishing home. I was doing relatively well. I think that is exemplified best by the fact that when I went in 1975 as a visiting professor at the University of Houston, I was on their graduate faculty, actually working with the English students, the students of English who were Ph.Ds. there. At the end of my first year there, the chair of the department, who was a Miltonist, he came up to me and told me, asked me if I'd be interested in staying on at the university permanently because the English faculty liked me. They had voted that they would make me an offer to stay. Then he added, he said, "And, Felipe, I want you to know that we're not asking you to stay because of any of that Chicano stuff you write."

In a day, where I am today, I'm not at all keen on whether I get published by a white magazine or a white journal, or not. Because I'm discovering that we have a great network now of Hispanic-Latino outlets. Like *Arte Publico Press* of Houston, like *Hispanic Vista*. There's at least 15 or 16 of these outlets that are available to us. Those essays or pieces that we get published, or posted in these Latino, Hispanic outlets, they are the same as publications for us. I've known Nick Kanellos since he was a graduate student in Spanish. He's the one who has run *Arte Publico Press* for many years now. As a consequence of initially the three of us, Carlota, Jose, and myself at NCTE, I think that we encouraged Nick Kanellos in his first efforts at publishing, at that time, publishing Chicanos and Puerto Ricans. His first publication was called the *Revista Chicano-Riqueña*. He's done a lot of good work, especially in looking for the forgotten pages of American literature.

We were very pugnacious, I have to tell you. I suppose, part of that pugnacity on my part was because I was a Marine during WWII. That tenacity or pugnaciousness, was invented by—well, I'm having a senior moment—by Octavio Romano. They were heady days, I have to tell you. We thought that we had a mission to perform, and I think that I like what's come out of it, frankly. I'm so impressed by the scholarship that I see now with Chicanos especially, but certainly overall Latino-Chicanos, the scholarship that I see coming out of the universities.

EXPERIENCES: IN THEIR OWN WORDS
Carlota Cárdenas de Dwyer

Working for Change Founders Panel Part 1: 1960s-1970s National Council of Teachers of English Centennial / Early History of the Latino/Chicano Caucus

"When I was your age…You were never my age."

—*The Year of the Dragon*, Frank Chin

If we were to turn the clock back about fifty years to 1962, step outside the door of this hotel, walk to Wabash Ave., and hop a bus to Old Town, there around a corner at 1660 North Hudson Ave. would be St. Michael's H.S. Peering into our 1962-time capsule, we would see an unrecognizably youthful, slim, naturally chestnut haired, eager, first year teacher called "Miss Cárdenas." She would be teaching her first of many/plus years of high school English—the curricular twin pillars of (1) school-room language, a hybrid species in itself and not to be confused with "language arts;" and (2) the eleventh-grade survey of American literature.

Naturally, like almost every other teacher of the time, I was teaching what I had been taught and what was in our textbooks of the early sixties—one book for grammar and mechanics, doggedly presenting every year the same nuts and bolts of parsing sentences in binary exercises, requiring students to choose one from a parentheses-bound pair, like an eye exam (Which is better, one or two?)—verb or verbal? subject or complement? who or whom? That's what passed for literacy, and, furthermore, we diagrammed sentences with chalk on a board of black slate; Paleolithic/Stone Age cave dwellers would have felt right at home!

American literature started in the fall right around the mid-1600s. All of the authors lived on the East Coast, with names like John Smith and William Bradford, a monochromatic procession of U.S. writers that slowly inched westward, I should say mid-westward, so after the holidays Earnest Hemingway and F. Scott Fitzgerald would appear, and by spring were joined by the likes of Willa Cather and John Steinbeck! Those were the days when in September we began our survey of so-called American literature lockstep in mid-seventeenth century Plymouth Colony and by June had rarely made it past 1940.

At that time to step into an English class was to enter a self-perpetuating, self-referencing world—the teacher, the textbooks, the curriculum, a veritable house of wax figures, all produced annually, like prototypes of an unyielding worldview, repeated but never renewed. The breadth and depth of our national literary reserves, if sketched by means of reverse engineering from this perspective, would be rather anemic. The reverend canon of U.S. literature, the bedrock of eleventh-grade English classes across the entire country, managed to grow without expanding its vision of the nation. By extension, one could view the NCTE as a microcosm of American culture for the first half of the twentieth century. It was a narrow path that wound its way through the materials and methods of our profession.

So, there I was, teaching my class in 1962 when a Black student raised her hand and asked, "Why don't we read something written by a Black author?" Good question I thought, but considering the practicalities, I responded by saying there was nothing in our textbook and we didn't have any other books in the bookroom, except for The Scarlet Letter. I had just read my first James Baldwin myself in a Great Books group, and wasn't sure I could actually bring it into my classroom. The moment passed. Now when I look back on those years in the early sixties, I realize that an unprecedented awareness was developing in classrooms—students understood that they no longer recognized themselves in their teachers or in their textbooks, and they would start to ask for change. Seeking to expand my own education, I left St. Michael's at the end of the next year and went to the University of Illinois in Urbana to begin a master's degree program in English.

For two years my foundation in American literature was strengthened and soon included such writers as Sylvia Plath and John Updike, more contemporary, perhaps, but certainly not what we would consider diverse today. In fact, you might say a funny thing happened to me on my way to that degree. I ended up learning German because at that time the University of Illinois did not accept Spanish to fulfill the graduate school foreign language requirement. They did not consider Spanish a "scholarly" language, and I had to choose either French or German. So German it was…

No surprise that in those days, I did not see the Mejicano/Latino culture, history, or language of my home and family in Chicago in anything I ever read or taught in an English classroom. Great writers have told us that "the past is never over," but from this time on, nothing would ever be the same in our professional lives. In fact, this point in the past—those early sixties—is still so long ago and different from today that I think of it as BC—Bill Gates and Steve Jobs were not yet ten years old and probably still playing with their Legos—so it was BC—before computers, before cell phones—even before Chicanos! Of course, I refer to Chicanos not as a population or an ethnicity but to Chicanos in particular and Latinos in general as a cultural constituency. However, by the time I finished that degree and took on a new teaching position in New York, a national spotlight was placed on Delano, California. César Chávez and his Chicano labor movement of 1965 instantly ignited a near explosion of social and cultural activity, propelling the sixties to an unprecedented level of ethnic self-awareness and literary creativity. Activist writers sounded a call that we all heard—north, south, east, west, it no longer mattered. From the fields of Delano to the barrio communities of Denver, Chicago, Detroit, and many, many more, it was a time of an outpouring of cultural and social expression. Writers of every genre—poetry, prose, drama—all appeared, adapting and creating their own texts and aesthetic as they went along. The voices of a few rose into a chorus of the many.

For those of us who were already trained and experienced in teaching English, for me, American literature in particular, the sounds and sights of these recently created works that my teaching colleagues in academia found so confounding, rang straight to my mind and heart like a familiar tune. I heard Melville's admonition to follow no more the authors of a foreign, European sensibility ("Hawthorne and His Mosses," 1850), I heard Emerson's invocation to capture the language of the common man ("Art and Criticism," 1859) and to conform to none other than one's self ("Self-Reliance," 1841). I heard Thoreau's impassioned plea to cease support of anything less than what was right and true to my own majority of one ("Civil Disobedience," 1849)—messages that had new cadence but were no longer distant nor far away.

More to the point, I recognized roots of early Greek drama in Luis Valdez's huelga oriented teatro campesino, and saw essentially no space between Walt Whitman's free verse of 1855 and that of Abelardo Delgado and other poetas of 1975 who re-liberated verse, challenging rather than cajoling, and inventing rather than imitating. Who could not embrace Antonio Mares of Bless Me, Ultima as a twentieth-century Huck Finn, torn by conflict and seeking renewal in the reconciliation of his heart with a voice only he heard. Who could require more footnotes than T.S. Eliot? What was so different?

It quickly became apparent to this emerging generation that our challenge would be threefold—the literature itself, criticism, and textbooks: 1) We ourselves would have to seek out and gather the literature, generated by the great upheaval of Chicano social activists and artists; (2) We would be the ones to write the criticism and pedagogy vitally necessary to accompany this recent literature. When I looked for critical analysis, here is what I found in my routine survey of critical literature. Robert Spiller first published his Literary History of the United States in 1946, with a copyright renewed up through 1974. I quote: The Spanish civilization of the Pacific coast was too thin in population, too indolent to make a concerted stand…Within a short time it underwent absorption into the cultural complex of the new West—along with southern New England, New England, Midwestern, European, and Oriental elements—while lending the mass some of the richness of its pigment (659).…That is what passed for criticism of the Hispanic tradition at the time… (3) We personally needed to make contact and persuade textbook publishers to change everything they were doing—this literature—historic and contemporary—needed to be transformed into curriculum with pedagogical support on a national level. For us it was not simply an issue of what to teach, but just as importantly, how to teach it. Contextualize it.

I soon realized that the first means of distribution for Chicano writers was the network of small publications in the numerous barrios scattered across the whole country. With my husband's support, I embarked on an excursion from New York that took me to Chicago, Detroit, Washington, and finally to Denver. I met with writers and visited community organizers and small publishers—I picked up manuscript papers and past issues from the floor in one barrio newspaper office because they had been raided by the police the night before, and everything was helter-skelter. One contact I met, said "Oh, you're looking for Chicano literature, give me a piece of paper and I'll write something for you here!" Before long, Chicano publishers were identified, and the first wave of contemporary literature became available. Our efforts converged, and a new canon was gradually accumulating, so when we received requests for teachable titles, we could say, "take this, and this, and now this."

Because we were still technologically in BC with no pdfs, no email, not even a fax; our tubes were not You, but Ipana or Colgate…almost all of our early work was done on our own, each in our own small patch of the universe. We traveled with paper copies, and the range of circulation frequently did not exceed the span of our arm's reach. Felipe Ortego in 1971 was just finishing the first dissertation on historical backgrounds of Mexican American literature, with a final chapter on emerging contemporary writers. Shortly before that, in 1969 when I applied to the doctoral program in English at SUNY Stony Brook, I indicated that I intended to write my dissertation on the contemporary Chicano literature I saw proliferating by the day. I was told that I would be accepted to the program, but that there was no SUNY faculty that could assist me with the dissertation.

Not discouraged by their lack of a qualified advisor, but moving forward, I assured SUNY that I would accept a current faculty member, Ruth Miller, specializing in African American literature, as my advisor. I assured them I would have no difficulty identifying appropriate resources on my own. Somehow, they acquiesced.

Just as my students in Chicago did not view themselves reflected in our classroom earlier, so I did not perceive myself or my culture represented in the first convention of the NCTE that I attended Milwaukee 1967. When I met many of the people on these Founder panels and in this room for the first time, we were not only strangers to each other but also estranged from the prevailing sensibility. It was not exactly a replay of "Dr. Livingston, I presume," but not really very far from that. We essentially spotted each other a mile away, just as Victor Villanueva writes about his Stanley/Livingston moment with Kris Gutierrez in Philadelphia, and the conversation and collaboration would begin.

Because we were geographically separated, we had to wait until a national NCTE convention, sometimes a 4Cs meeting, was scheduled, so we could meet in person. We were still in BC. Roseann González, Felipe Ortego, Jose Carrasco, and myself—along with several others predominantly hovering below the radar across the Southwest—were already working in concert.

The assassination of Martin Luther King in April 1968, right in the middle of a 4Cs meeting, was a major turning point for all of us in the NCTE. We were instantly activated, as we prepared to mobilize ourselves into taking meaningful steps to impel changes we knew could be delayed no longer. A fresh sense of urgency spurred us to organize ourselves into a vital coterie of change agents. Again, we had to move on multiple fronts—starting with our deep sense of affiliation and connection within the NCTE. The small group dialogue first initiated by a few kindred souls needed to be taken up by many and expanded to impact not only individual classrooms across the country but also the whole English teaching profession and textbook industry.

Evidence of this new attitude and purpose was shared across many fronts when various NCTE caucuses joined the Task Force on Racism and Bias and expressed ideas that had been simmering all along but had not been translated into a national agenda or defined rules of engagement. In 1970 *Searching for America*, published by the Task Force on Racism and Bias and the NCTE, articulated the problems—the gaps and distortions of the literary presence of whole generations (both past and present) of people of diverse cultures. The response was formidable—background became foreground, activist attitudes dictated agenda, and private knowledge was converted into every English teacher's arsenal of bibliographies and duplicated handouts of sample literature, ready for action in the classroom—purple ditto, black mimeo, eventually multi-hued photocopies—we covered the whole color wheel of printing history!

However, progress was not smooth or even without some rancor. In 1970 when Felipe Ortego submitted an essay on Chicano literature to *College English*, it was rejected. Ortego was advised that another essay on the subject had already been accepted. With the control that flows from nothing less than smoldering indignation, Felipe responded with a letter to the editor, published in a 1970 issue of *College English*. Citing our formation of a NCTE Chicano caucus, Felipe noted that the incident underscored our sense of urgency, pointing out that it was yet another painful example of "... the kinds of responses Chicano teachers of English have received from NCTE and its Anglo oriented publications" ("Huevos Con Chorizo: A Letter to Richard Ohmann," *College English*, 1970).

Nonetheless we persevered. The learning curve among the gathering personalities was quick if not instantaneous. Our energies were exerted in numerous, sometimes overlapping but never conflicting directions. During NCTE conventions we would meet in one of our own rooms, forming and performing as a de facto caucus even before we had the name. We would move furniture, slip off our shoes and sit on beds with calendars and program proposal forms in hand, to plot and strategize on how we could integrate our issues and resources into the next convention—from Las Vegas in 1971, where we had finally achieved a critical mass, we planned for Minneapolis in 1972, from there we planned Philadelphia in 1973. We outlined one- and two-day pre-convention workshops, we brought materials by the carton, we engaged not only scholars like Felipe Ortego, our first English Ph.D., but also boots (literally) on the ground poets, like Ricardo Sanchez in New Orleans

1974, and later Tino Villanueva in Boston, who spoke and read from their own works. The dots were slowly connecting—English teachers were emotionally electrified and asking for more and more materials to take back to their local multi-cultured students and schools.

Our network of contacts grew and grew—our panels of consultants similarly multiplied; we were teaching ourselves, as we were involving more and more teachers. From Montana Walking Bull Rickards, we learned to reject the generalizing overtones of terms like "Native American" in favor of more specific identities, such as Mohawk or Navajo. From Lawson Inada, we learned the bitter emotional toll a presidential Executive Order had on a population of American citizens who discovered the bitter limitations of their presumed equality. From Bill Cook we learned with dramatic underscoring about a perspective that had been earlier only suggested. And the pages kept adding up, and the connections were reinforced.

Emboldened by this powerful response, Roseann González and I instigated our own guerrilla actions, stealthily trolling through publishers' booths on the convention floor, innocently asking for the American literature textbook, and then causing tremors of shock and agitation when we provocatively identified the use of that label as deceptive because there were few or no writers of diversity represented. Rejecting the tactic of subtle sotto voce, we would cause heads to turn, and were quickly referred to a token editor, usually in a quiet corner, but no substantive follow-up was forthcoming.

Washington Square Press had published *We Are Chicanos* in 1973, and Houghton Mifflin *Chicano Voices* in 1975. However, U.S. literary anthologies remained the white elephant in the room year after year. It was not until the NCTE convention in Chicago 1976 that an editor from a major press signaled possible change in the conventional table of contents.

Even then the contact was less than congenial—after one of my own program presentations, among the clutch of teachers who approached afterward, asking for more materials and information, was a gentleman who questioned the "ethnic exclusivity" of publications like *Chicano Voices*. I responded that it was the sole avenue we had at the time to insert Chicano literature into the national curriculum. I said, somewhat peeved at the underlying criticism, that it was our only recourse until major publishers were open to adding minority literature to the ossified American literary anthology, and I didn't know of any publisher that was interested. What followed was both a totally unexpected shock and music to my ears. He said, "Scott Foresman is interested." And Scott Foresman was and with several of us participating, the next revised edition of their America Reads series was completely changed.

In 1979, teachers across the nation would finally be equipped to start the first days of eleventh-grade English class with the chronicles of Cabeza de Vaca along with those of John Smith, with the autobiographical account of W.E.B. Dubois accompanying that of Benjamin Franklin, and countless other works that finally mirrored the complexions and ethnicities of students and teachers in the classroom. Similarly, English teachers of diverse cultures and backgrounds were no longer limited to a peripheral presence but were welcome to join as effective participants and leaders in numerous NCTE committees, commissions, boards, and affiliates.

As the decade of the 70s ended, there was no question that the status quo of 1962 had changed. Was even more change needed? Clearly the answer is yes; and the decade of the 80s would be witness to even more progress than we had hoped for earlier. By 1984 Sandra Cisneros would immortalize her own corner of Chicago itself, as we say here, 1500 North on Campbell Avenue/Humboldt Park, in The House on Mango Street. However, as I imaginatively step out back on Wabash Ave. to take the return trip from the St. Michael's H.S. of the past and look around this room on this bright NCTE Centennial Saturday morning, I do not feel alone on this stage. I stand with Roseann González, Felipe Ortego, Kris Gutierrez, and numerous others from the past. We all join you today with more to celebrate than we might ever have anticipated. When someone invariably asks that familiar question, the answer rings with more truth than ever before, "…teach English, it's not only what we do, it's what we are (finally!)."

EXPERIENCES: IN THEIR OWN WORDS
Roseann Dueñas González

Based on Interview by Anita Hernández
February 7, 2017

I wanted to say, the first time I met the members of the Chicano Teachers group of English is just how excited I was! Because if anything is true, I think about all of us, it's just we were all singular in our institutions. I was the only Chicana in the entire department of English, which had 90 members at that time. In fact, in the early 70's, there was hardly any women in the department. To be a Mexican American woman was like complete isolation. The only reason that I was going to conferences, getting out there is, because I had an incredibly tremendous mentor who was responsible for hiring me. There is a funny story. He was my undergraduate major professor and then I went away and taught at Arizona State University. When I graduated with my Masters and then I was recruited back to U of A as a lecturer, I was recruited by him, who was a head of the program in Freshman Composition. So, because of him, I began going to the Arizona English Teachers Association and becoming a really active participant in our state affiliate of NCTE.

[It was when] I was President of the Arizona English Teachers Association and a brand-new lecturer (2 yrs.) at the University of Arizona where my mentor insisted that I attend the national NCTE conference, which was being held in Las Vegas that year. I attended a program sponsored by the Caucus or attended heavily by the NCTE Hispanic Caucus and met Carlota Cárdenas de Dwyer, Ortego y Gasca, and Ricardo Sanchez, the poet. I had already been teaching Chicano literature and was delighted to find a session on it and meeting all of these bright, informed, and exciting Latinos. The Caucus held a meeting that I was immediately invited to and then had a get together after dinner in someone's hotel room, where we sat and talked endlessly about Chicano literature, our institutional experiences, and NCTE, and our place in its development.

By that time, it was a little sizable group may be 8 to 10 people who had come to this session. . . I think I got recruited at that time into the Chicano Teachers of English and I became the Secretary of the group right away because they needed help. That was the beginning for me. I believe that was 1974. I became national Vice-Chair of the Chicano Teachers of English. In 1982 that little group came to an end. [And] it became the Hispanic Caucus. I believe that's the way it worked.

Joining the Caucus was the most exciting opportunity there was for me, which I would never pass up. The opportunity to meet other like-minded Latinos, who were at once, excited about Chicano literature and concerned about the inclusion and appropriate treatment of Latino students in the schools as well as about the inclusion of Latinos and themes surrounding Latino students in the schools in NCTE programs and projects, including publications, etc. The Caucus gave us a home inside of NCTE, gave us a voice in an otherwise "white" institution, seemingly indifferent at best or hostile towards the issues surrounding Latino students and Latino professors and lecturers, who were excluded in their own home institutions and at NCTE.

It must have been in early 80's [when we recruited Victor Villanueva] because there was hardly anyone. If we found someone who would even look like they might be somebody, we would reach out to them. Usually, we met people who came to our session. By that time there were always at least one session on Chicano literature. Sometimes, there was perhaps a session dedicated to teaching Hispanic students or something, though at that time the sessions were, you never knew, who was going to be speaking and what their point of view was, what kind of methodology they were trying to foster. We would go to those sessions, obviously to try find who had something good to say or a place where we could lend our voices or where we could find other people who were interested as we were. So, we used to do all kind of things to try to find people who had our same interest, because there were so few Latino and Latina educators that came to the conferences.

Regardless of race, you reached out to the people because you knew that they were interested in the very important project of bringing Chicano literature to either Chicano students themselves or to share with majority students. Whoever we found, we made quick friends with them. If they were Chicanos or other racial minority, we immediately invited them into the Chicano Teachers of English or Latino Caucus as that would be called later, Hispanic Caucus rather…. . . . .From the beginning, let's say in the 1980s, Karen Begay, who was a Navajo educator was a regular member of the Caucus and

Lawson Fusao Inada, a famous Asian American or Japanese American poet, was a member. They were both members of the Latino or Hispanic caucus, because they there was no caucus to attend for them.

Something really exciting is that, right from the beginning, the Hispanic Caucus used to have some input into the program, even before the *Rainbow* session began and that was one of the most inspiring and one of the most important things that we were able to do. Every year we were able to propose a program. Sometimes, we called it a symposium. The symposium was even different from the pre-convention workshop. This could be done during the convention, but it would be instead of just one program like an hour or two hours or three hours, it would be like an entire morning. We felt we were really blessed because we had four hours to be able to talk to teachers about, let's say, five or six important Chicano literature works and be able to get into how best to approach their teaching and what the major things of literature are in their work, something about the author and the context and the key, for teachers to bring this work to their students in the most efficacious way. That was something that I remember with lot of excitement in terms of giving us the opportunity to invite major authors. I believe major authors were even helped to attend by the NCTE. With the support of NCTE, we were able to bring major authors in Chicano literature to the attention of classroom teachers wherever NCTE might be held.

Those were really exciting days and exciting opportunities. That is what Latino Caucus was all about to ensure that the NCTE programs, activities, publications, and all of their projects have something to offer Latino students and a way to include Latino literature, cultural ideas into the curriculum for the good of Latino students and for the good of majority students who needed to be able to experience the literature, the ideas, and the thinking of the all members of American society.

Whenever, well this is getting into the future, whenever we created a *Rainbow Strand*, they were of course major representatives of the four federally established minorities: Asian American, Native American, Latino American, and African American. They were very often chosen for representing their group - Lawson Inada for Asian American and Karen Begay for Native American. And they served incredibly well for many years. In fact, Lawson Inada used to give an incredibly wonderful presentation on what it was like on the day that the Japanese internment was posted by the President and the faculty were given 24 hours to appear with one suitcase in their hand and go on to the internment camp. His family was a part of that, of course. He was a child at that time. He used to talk about that and he used to bring a poster and talk about his own poetry and other Asian American poets and writers on that subject. It was a powerful presentation and very often we were able to create pre-convention workshop on the subject where we had introducing Asian American, African American and Latino and Native American literature into the classroom. Here we had an entire day to work with teachers who were interested in doing that work to help them get to know major pieces of literature and methods and strategies by which to make them familiar to students and to help them with their understanding.

As the Caucus became the actual Caucus of the Council, you know, there were some formal relationships that were established, that were obviously to the benefit of the Caucus. Those relationships were to do with what information the Caucus was given by the Executive Council. The fact that we had a liaison to the Caucus who came from the Executive Committee to talk to us about major nominations coming up and other activities of the council that needed the Caucus' input. Of course, the major person who oversaw all of the liaisons' work was Dr. Sandra Gibbs, who I mentioned in my discussion in the paper that I gave you, who was the liaison between the caucuses and the Executive Council and, of course, she was a member of the NCTE staff. But it was her careful work that the caucuses were kept informed, were given a voice, not so much as in the days of *Rainbow Strand*, but certainly a formal way of having some input into council activities. Even if it was limited, it was something. That was, I think, was a very important reason for moving from the Chicano Teachers of English to the Hispanic Caucus, so that we would become a regular program participant. You know how there is always a place for the caucuses to meet and a place where new members can find that information and come to the meeting. All of that helped in perpetuating the important work that was begun by the Chicano Teachers of English.

First, I was Secretary and then I was national Vice-Chair. I am looking at an old copy of my data from 1974 to 1982. For some reason, I have 1982. I do not know what you have as the beginning of the actual Hispanic Caucus. We were in the same group. I believe the Chicano Teachers of English. One of the things we did was the kind of a newsletter that might have been continuing even though the establishment of the Hispanic Caucus. I am pretty sure that's how it was. I believe Hispanic Caucus began in 1979.

I mean you have to remember that we were excited when there was one session that was delegated to us. We were excited to have one session to work with or when we had this symposium, which did not happen very often, but it was once in a while, or when there was a pre-conference, you know, workshop, we were excited. But it wasn't until, well it was surely after *Searching for America*, as a result of *Searching for America*, people began looking at ways of incorporating minority literature into their language art textbooks. I don't know if you recall, but in those days, there were state adopted textbooks that were used in most high school classrooms. Carlota and I were both invited to participate in what became the most celebrated language art textbooks to incorporate minority literature in the Medallion series. It became one of the most adopted textbooks in the United States. I believe that it was as the result of all of the great works done, that has been done, on "Searching for America." I believe that it was in 1979.

Members were most interested in making sure NCTE was being inclusive of the issues, problems, and differences surrounding Latino students, in terms of cultural attitudes, interests, and curricula. They wanted to ensure that teaching Latino students was not diminished to teaching a remedial curriculum, which was often the case in the schools, and that encouraging students to share their cultural lifestyles in the classroom, along with their language, became a major tenet of NCTE. To further this goal, members were very aggressive about being included in NCTE programs, having representation on working committees and commissions of the Council in order to influence policy and to represent the needs and goals surrounding the proper education of Latino students and to integrate the teaching of Chicano literature, history, and culture in the Language Arts classroom elementary through college.

As Caucus chair, I and other Caucus members would take proposals to Executive Council, especially for special projects and major program proposals. These were tense times, as often Executive Council would not be particularly prone to our proposals. So, there were many behind the scenes meetings with sympathetic members of the Executive Committee whenever possible. One of the Latinx Caucus's greatest achievements was the creation and development of the *Rainbow Strand*, a proposal to the Executive Council to provide a mechanism at the yearly Convention planning meeting in which members of the four federally designated minorities would meet and review proposals for *Rainbow Strand* program for the following year's conference. This allowed direct input into the annual meeting program and an opportunity to assess the quality of papers, workshops, seminars, etc. with respect to appropriate methodology, materials, and techniques most suited to the development of the potential of students of color. The *Rainbow Strand* opened up a small, but important component of NCTE programs to the needs and learning interests of students of color. The interaction between other program planners and the *Rainbow Strand* group was tense at times, especially when program planners comprised NCTE members who were resentful of the "special" attention being shone on students and educators of color.

Throughout the time that I was an active member of the Caucus and when I was Chair, I found that there was always someone in the leadership or the Executive Secretary who was responsive to the Latino scholars and educators. The degree of response was always the problem, in that no one person governed all actions of NCTE, as these are distributed among the committees and commissions, as well as journal editors, etc. Therefore, response to Latino scholars and educators was uneven, depending on the issue, but for many years, that I would describe as the heyday of NCTE, when the *Rainbow Strand* was fully implemented, I would say that the response was quite good. I can't judge that now, but after what I believe to be the firing of Dr. Sandra Gibbs, I know that the strong leadership she provided was gone, and that it had a deleterious effect on the strength of the caucuses. I disagreed strongly with the decision to fire Dr. Sandra Gibbs and then the decision to not replace her with someone of equal strength, experience, and capacity, who knew the internal workings of the NCTE, CCCC, and other affiliate organizations, who could fill those giant shoes.

[The] NCTE and the NCTE membership was extremely fortunate to have among the NCTE staff Dr. Sandra Gibbs, an African American educator who was quite canny and very vigilant of NCTE actions in regard to students and educators of color. She carefully reviewed all commission and committee upcoming policies and projects to ensure that the needs and learning interests of students of color were taking into consideration. She made sure that the Black Caucus and the Chicano Caucus were kept informed of all of these issues, policies, and projects so that both of these important entities could have a voice in these large NCTE activities that would affect the lives of all students, including those of color. Therefore, even though her work was admired by many, many NCTE officers and members had great animosity towards her, and she finally fell victim to the decision to end her tenure with NCTE after many hard and fruitful years of service. I'm not sure that her diligence and vigilance has ever been replaced. Without the kind of information, she forthrightly provided the caucuses and all members of the NCTE and CCCC, it is doubtful that the Latino Caucus would ever regain the primary role it had in assuring that the needs of Latino and other limited and non-English students were met by NCTE.

[Throughout my career, I was also] was head of the CCCC English Second Language Composition Committee, and as such, was able to influence program content on the teaching of writing to English as a Second Language learners for many years; I was elected to the CCCC Executive Committee for four years, and was able to bring the viewpoints of Latino educators and needs of Latino and other ELL learners to the fore in the CCCC. In NCTE, I had many posts through the years, all of which allowed me to bring the viewpoint of Latino educators to the fore and the needs and requirements of Latino and other ELL learners to the center instead of the margins. For example, I was chair of the Commission on Language for, I believe, 8 years, and it was during this time that I published *Language Ideologies*, as a publication of that Commission on the English Language Amendment and other issues relating to the declaration of English as the official language of the U.S.. I was also the chair of a committee whose name I cannot remember which was entrusted with choosing one of the major speakers at the NCTE annual meeting. This allowed me help choose a speaker who was outside the mainstream of language arts, such as a sociologist, political scientist who could shed light on the sociocultural or sociopolitical issues that plagued students of color. This brought an exciting and very much needed viewpoint to the membership, which would not ordinarily be heard in an annual program.

[I would like NCTE, CCC, and its members to] remember that diversity requires diversity in the curriculum, so that students can see themselves in the pages of their books, so that they can see the world around them, and understand that they have the potential to be whatever they choose. This can only happen in an inclusive, open, diverse learning environment, where students feel welcome, where their language and cultures and lifestyles are valued, celebrated, and respected, where they feel joy in their everyday school experiences. The Latino Caucus can help NCTE in making these goals a reality in the classroom by having a strong input in the programs, publications, and activities of the Council. If not already done, bring back the *Rainbow Strand*.

EXPERIENCES: IN THEIR OWN WORDS
Victor Villanueva

Based on Interview by Iris Ruiz
July 17, 2016

I'm Victor Villanueva and I'm a Regents Professor and Director of the University Writing Program at Washington State University. I've been at Washington State University since 1995, prior to that I was at Northern Arizona University, prior to that I was in University of Missouri Kansas City, and prior to that I was a graduate student at the University of Washington, wow yeah. And I got to the Pacific Northwest by way of the army and ended up liking it here, so I have now, even though I was born and raised in Brooklyn, New York, I have lived in the Pacific Northwest for most of the last 15 years. Very much of a New Yorker left in this New Yorker except to people who are New Yorkers. They all hear a New Yorker, but I go to New York I'm way too slow for those people.

    The first time I went to CCCC's it was in fact in New York City, which was really interesting because I left there a decidedly poor Puerto Rican high school dropout and came back a completing graduate student, so that was way cool, kind of mind-boggling actually, but I was there because one of my mentors, my key mentor basically, Anne Ruggles Gere had put me on a panel as respondent, a panel that she was on with Anne Matsuhashi at the time This is how one does this career, and that's what my boss told me and she's been CCCC's chair and she's been NCTE president in her career, but so that's why I went to CCCC's the first time. I went to NCTE the first time because another mentor, William Irmscher, who had also been CCCC's chair and NCTE president, and, I think, the second editor, I think the second, maybe the third editor of CCC, and recommended me for a committee and it was an NCTE committee, the resolutions committee. So that's why I went off to NCTE and for a good chunk of my career I have attended both meetings. I stopped going to NCTE, I don't know about 10 years ago or so and I will probably do much less CCCC's from this point on also because I'm getting up there in age. I wasn't born with a white beard, so yeah, that's why.

[It's] a funny story [how I joined the caucus]. . . . I was looking for food; I was still a graduate student and that's what we do at the conferences. So, I was looking for food and this Latina, Kris Gutiérrez, kind of grabbed me by the collar. Actually, what she did was grab my name tag and told me to start looking around for others with Spanish names. . . . I was just going to do what I was told and, if you would have seen Kris Gutiérrez and . . . you would too. So, "Yes okay, yes ma'am." And so, as it turns out, we three then, Rosanne González and Kris Gutiérrez (and myself) had been doing a whole lot of Hispanic Caucus stuff, and in fact, were responsible for changing the name from Chicano Caucus, which is what it had been, to Hispanic Caucus and then later we changed it, and I can tell you that story if you ask, to Latino Caucus, because that was an interesting—that happened in '97 in Phoenix. So anyhow, so we met, the Latino Caucus had a meeting and the meeting was the three of us we were, we were it.

[At] the time there weren't too many Latinos to speak of and, I mean it's, this is very different nowadays. . . . So what was clear was that we are here we are a presence, whether we were recognized or not as a presence. So, it was clear that this needed to be done if only to have our voices heard, even though the voices at that point amounted to three of us. And, in fact, because there was only three of us, we extended the Latino Caucus in those days to other folks of color. The *Black Caucus* was already very highly well organized and well represented. It had even done a boycott at CCCCs, like maybe the second Cs that I had gone to about investment in South Africa, which at the time was still immersed in apartheid. So, they were a highly organized unit already, but there were no others. So, there were only the two Caucuses; Hispanic Caucus, Black Caucus. And so, since there were only the three of us, we became at that point the people of color not the Black Caucus. We called ourselves Hispanic Caucus and our major concern was that was us, gente, but we also had Susanne Banali, who was a Navajo, and Gail Ocala, who's still my friend. I'll be talking to her later today. It stayed that way until '98. In '98 point, Paul Matsuda insisted, asked, he was very courteous, he asked, he was incoming chair of the organization, and he asked if he could put together and have a space for an Asian Caucus. I think the American Indian, at that time it wasn't called American. It was called the American Indian Scholars and Intellectuals, and I think that began with somebody who had just been awarded the Scholars for the Dream that I was in charge of and, you won't recognize her name, it's Malea Powell.

I think that the role of the Caucus has remained steady, which is representation and voice within the organization and then within the profession at large. We are too readily dismissed as, still and all the way down to students, dismissed as the folks who have some sort of deficit, and our deficit is that we have abilities with more languages then the people who weren't power, which is no deficit at all. It's an asset that refuses to be recognized. So, at the time however, if we go back to 1981 or '82 when I first joined the Caucus, when we became the Caucus basically, what we wanted to do, and we ended up doing, was not only be a presence, but assure that we had a presence in these conferences, that we weren't dismissed or simply spoken about.

At some point, you'll probably end up talking to Renée Moreno and she can tell you that story [as well]. She was in the group of first ten Scholars for the Dream. Sue McLeod had proposed *Scholars for The Dream*. So even though nobody wants to know this in the history, a white woman actually proposed it, and it was because there was something similar that NCTE was doing already. The Executive Committee voted for it, Bill Cook was Chair. He assigned me at that point to start doing it and what we did was we sat in the lobby, we had all of these proposals for next year's CCCC's and we sat in the lobby and looked through all of these proposals from folks of color, that had to do with color and decided on the first ten. Renée was among those. So, it was highly informal. It became very very formal overtime, but at that time, it was just Bill Cook and me in one of those round couches that you see in hotels, just sitting in one of those things, and then talking about what we are reading and it included folks of color doing stereotypical stuff to you know but, that was pretty exciting, I don't remember what year Bill Cook, who's now dead, was Chair. . . . When she gave her panel presentation as a Scholar for the Dream, somebody else on her panel just started carrying on with the same old stereotypes about Latinos, which Renée lost her temper over. But even with our presence, even standing right there, the stereotypes continued. So, that was our job too—try to educate these educators about who the hell we are and with all our complexities and contradictions.

Okay, so let's talk about that there have been good sides to [the professional organizations]. At my very first CCCC's in 1981 or '82, I went to see Pat Mizel, who was a new young thing too. I went to see her because, she was not a big name yet, I went to see her because she was going to speak about Richard Rodriguez. At the panel, at the thing, she kind of singled me out and asked "Was I right?" She says, "Am I right?" to me. I just kind of said nothing. So, after the panel, she came up to me to ask why I said nothing. I said that I think he is crying too much in his beer and is too assimilationist, is that the word, to be very helpful for us. When she published that essay, which is something about what happens to basic writers or something like that, she footnoted and cited me, even though I was nobody and this was just the conversation at a panel. So, there was the respectful side, like that. And others not just Pat, I mean that I the reason I was there at all was because of people who took good care of me, like Anne Gere and Bill Irmscher, and others. Anne Feldman ended up being the local arrangements Chair for my CCCC's, so there were others.

The negative thing, the biggest negative thing that happened was, and this is, it is history it's going to irritate some folks who see it, but it is what happened. Miriam Chaplain, then as chair of CCCCs on the Executive Committee, proposed the *Rainbow Strand*. When she first proposed it, it died for lack of a second. In parliamentary procedures, somebody says something, makes a proposal, and it has to be seconded. If it doesn't get seconded, then it dies. There could be no conversation. So, it died for lack of a second with some of the great leaders of the organization refusing to take up the issue of having folks of color represents themselves in helping to put together the national conference. Now, Miriam was a smart cookie and at NCTE the Executive Committee, which meets twice, it meets right before the convention and then they have the time when the committee changes, when those who are stepping out step off and the new people come on board, they all meet again right after the convention after the convention. Miriam Chaplin proposed it again.

And this time it passed. Even though it passed, there was someone who said, I don't know who it is, it doesn't matter, that they didn't need any watch dogs, because, of course, they were so liberal and advanced. But our idea was never, and when we first got to Urbana, Roseann, in particular, got a lot of flak from the secondary section because their perception was that we were there to censor them, which was never the case. What we wanted to do was to respond if somebody said something foolish, like there was a panel that had a title "Do you have to be one to teach one?" It's a legitimate concern, but phrasing it that way is not legitimate. So okay, we're not going to censor it. We're not going to say "no" to it. We created another panel that responded to that notion. So, we saw what the tendencies were and, sometimes, those tendencies were decidedly, let's just say stereotyped, and we created new panels. So, at first, there was some hostility to our presence. At one point we were asked why, at Urbana, why we didn't eat lunch with the rest of the folks. While we all hung out together, the Black and Latino, the Rainbow folks.

And someone like me, I was in a decidedly white university, it's a little less so now, but it was at that time in the 90th percentile, about 96%, white, and, so, here I am finally around folks of color, who are all so intellectually interested in the same things I am, and I'm going to go talk to more white folks? I do that every day. It was good to be with them, but someone who was in a position of authority at that time said, "Why, we're just trying to do away with the sins of the past in demanding that we go and be with them during lunch?" So, you see, the good intentions, but not understanding that import of what they were saying. One of the members of the Black Caucus said "They are not our sins, so we shouldn't be punished for your sins, and we like hanging out together because this is our one opportunity."

[W]e had a champion, somebody who watched out for us at NCTE headquarters doggedly and, sometimes, even to the point of really aggravating people. That was Dr. Sandra Gibbs. I don't know the story and I will never know the story because the person who made that decision has died and he refused to tell me, but she was asked to retire. In other words, later in her career, she was essentially fired in that kind of respectful, to a respectful way, but fired even if you say asked to retire.

You see part of the reason why I ended up writing *Bootstraps* was because of these people that I met at CCCCs and NCTE, almost exclusively because of them. Because the intentions were always good, the real bigots are few and far between, but for all of the good intentions, there was also this phenomenal ignorance. So that, good heart, wrong thing. It happened a lot and I think it's still happens. I don't think, I know, it still happens. It's still happens. Their hearts are in the right place. They want us included. They do see us as a part of the organization, as part of the profession, as part of the teaching world. They see all of that. There isn't the hostility that we're seeing in local politics or national politics right now. We don't get that from the profession. But we have this phenomenal degree of ignorance that, despite the good intentions, ends up being bigoted in their effect. So, it's not bigotry by intention, but bigotry effect. . . .

So, what I wanted us to do, what I wanted to have recognized and I still don't think it is, is that we don't just do our kind. That's an unintentional bigotry that still there. That if it's a Latino, the Latino is speaking about Latino things and since the Latino is speaking about Latino things, we don't have any reason they're saying to go to that panel. I'm interested in other larger things, without recognizing that we do rhetoric, we do Shakespeare. I mean you know shit! We're American academics. Our heritage is Latino and it's a prideful heritage it's not one that we put into the background, we are proud of our heritage, we are proud of our abilities to move in more than one tongue, to move in more than one culture, but we are Americans and most of us have been subjected to American education. Why wouldn't we know all the same folks that the white folks know? And why wouldn't we be interested in those things as well? So that I think is a problem that continues, the degree to which we are ghettoized, intellectually ghettoized. "Latinos do Latino stuff." Now it's true for me now, but before I did that, I wanted to be recognized for what I could do with the Greeks and the Romans and all that stuff. Now man I'm legit, even by your definition of legit you know. And I think that is, I think, I still think that is the biggest, our biggest hurdle, the degree to which we are pigeonholed, ghettoized, and because of that and because its seen as an exclusive self-interest, we don't get enough of the folks who really need to hear us, hearing us. I mean I am sort of an exception to that but it wasn't easy and I have been at this game a very long time.

Here's a funny way to put that, and a couple of funny ways to put that. The book has done outrageously well. According to academia.edu, I have counted out, because I needed to for an annual review, 54 different countries that read and respond to that book [*Bootstraps*]. So, it's done really well. It's available in several languages and I get emails from folks from all over including—I mean you know when they come, when there are Latinos from Latin America I get it, but Italians like it, people from Scandinavia like it, which I really don't get it. But the one I really don't get was some person from Kuala Lumpur. I mean you know, why? You know it's cool. I'm proud of it. I'll brag about it when I write my annual review, but was like why? I've got a student coming; she'll start here this fall from Guam, who is a Filipino in Guam. So, she's a person of color in the Guamanian, who are people of color in the America. I mean, it's a very interesting thing. She's here to work with me because she knows my work in Guam and has said very flattering things that I can't say without sounding like I'm really arrogant, and I am, but I don't want to sound like it.

But here's the interesting thing. At first, there's this person who was a big shot at NCTE when the book first came out. She came up to me to tell me that she loved the book. She just started it and she loved the book. Well the book intentionally starts out very personal and then gets more and more theoretical as the book develops. I did that. But she hadn't finished the book, when she finished the book, she stopped talking to me for a long time. So, she liked the *pobrecito* stories right, which is what made Richard Rodriguez so damn famous too, *pobrecito*. But when we get onto the real politics that I'm not okay with all of this, and that are things, that's when things start to change. For the first few years, even though that book was phenomenally well received, I got two national awards for it. I mean the second award, I thought was a mistake. I got the letter, it was '95, I got the letter telling me I got the second award and I thought are you stupid? You already gave me the award and I didn't realize it was the second award. So even though it was well received and there were some who really wanted to talk about the politics, John Trimbur, Lester Faigley, they wanted to talk about what I'm talking about, not the *pobrecito* stories. But for the first for first five to six years maybe, everybody wanted to talk about the writing as opposed to what I had written. And even though I had a big enough ego to be flattered by that and was willing to talk about it, after a while it got on my nerves. I'm glad y'all think I'm a good writer, I'm glad you like the way I do this. How about what I said? And that took a while, that took a while before that became the issue. I had a student, I forget who and it's one of us, one person from the Latino Caucus, somebody you'll ask at CCCC's, but one of us had their students reading *Bootstraps* and writing me emails about it and one student asked me if I wrote poorly on purpose: "Did you write that on purpose?" Because I switch voices in this thing, he wasn't sophisticated enough yet to see that, but it looked like it was intentional so why the hell would I do that, you know, it would confuse everybody. Yeah anyways, so that's the answer. It's done really well and to the degree that there's been negatives, not really negatives, just more like ignoring. I never got a bad review of that book, not ever. Some of the reviews were better than others, but never a bad review, now I'm echoing.

EXPERIENCES: IN THEIR OWN WORDS
Cecilia Rodríguez Milanés

Based on the Interview by Anita Hernández, 17 August 2016

My doctoral program was very interdisciplinary, so I had specialization in composition and rhetoric theory, literary theory, African-American women writers, and my dissertation was actually a collection of short stories. So, it was really flexible and wonderful for me because I wanted to do everything. My professor thought that that was probably not a good idea, that I needed to focus because it would be harder for me to get tenure and promotion and so on and so forth. It might have been true but I also felt that if I had to focus on only one area, I would be very unhappy. So, personally it was more satisfying to me to be able to do composition theory, creative writing, multicultural literary stuff. When I started my career I basically was encouraged to join NCTE and CCCC from the beginning.

[So, to]_be to be honest, membership and participation in CCCC primarily was expected of all of us as composition rhetoric students at the State University of New York at Albany, where the professors in specializations in comp and rhetoric were Lil Brannon, Sino Block, and Steve North. My main area professor was Lil Brannon, so she basically said to us, she inculcated in in our minds, you must belong to the profession, you must participate in conferences. So CCCC was basically, okay you're a grad student now, you have to be a member of NCTE and CCCC.

[My] first experience with any Caucus was actually with the Black Caucus. I went to my first NCTE in Baltimore in 1988 or '87. I saw on the program that there was this Black Caucus and I was like "Wow! Okay." The reason why I wanted to attend is they had a writer and I can't remember if it was June Jordan or Jade Cortez. It was an African-American woman writer that I admired and I went to the meeting. It was a huge ballroom. I mean huge ballroom with almost all African-American educators and it was so impressive. They had a business meeting and then they had this writer. I thought

"Wow! This is amazing! This is so great." Then I realized "Oh! Wait. There's a Hispanic Caucus." So, I didn't go to that meeting because, of course, the caucuses are always booked against each other. So I felt a great sense of belonging, but also admiration for this organization. I guess the next year, I went to NCTE first. Then I got pregnant in '89 and I was supposed to present at the CCCC in 1990, but I was like eight months pregnant. I wasn't allowed to go, but I had my paper read by one of my classmates because all my classmates were going. That would have been 1990.

I must have gone to the first Hispanic Caucus meeting in 1991 possibly which might have been in Boston. My daughter was a baby and I took her with me. I went to every single CCCC from 1991 to 2010 so that's like 20 years. I was very happy to find the Caucus, but it was nothing like the Black Caucus. There was only a handful of us. The leader was Victor Villanueva and if anybody has ever met Victor, they know he's absolutely and utterly charming and totally welcoming. I felt really comfortable. I thought "Oh, there's a place for us."

I became involved in the organization and leadership almost right away. Victor had been the co-chair for a long time and he was ready to pass it along. I think he was actually Co-Chair for 15 years. I ended up doing it for 15 years also, which is a long time and it isn't right because you get burnt out and it's exhausting. So, when I joined one of my goals was to have the newsletter published twice a year with contributing contributions from Caucus members. I wanted to recruit more members. I wanted to get membership dues regularly organized. I think I accomplished all those things.

One of the things that I did as Caucus Co-Chair was that I tried to go to as many Caucus members' sessions as I could. At that time, there weren't that many of us. Sometimes I was just going to these sessions with the last name Martinez. I'm going to go to that session and I'm going to recruit that person. I would go to the sessions and basically invite them to come and go to our meeting. I would give them the Caucus newsletter *Capirotada* and I'd say "Hi! I'm Cecilia. We'd love to have you join the Caucus." This is one of the things that I figured out was that the personal touch is really important because the Caucus is always meant to me a warm inviting and welcoming place and that was regardless of what kind of scholarship you did. We had to have it. For me, it was a refuge and I wanted to make sure that it was a refuge for others.

Victor has always been a leader and it is because he's been around a long time and because he knows everybody. Victor was kind of a shining star example for us as someone who could navigate the publishing world within

NCTE, but even his book *Bootstraps* didn't come out like right away. I can't remember right now when that was published but we were a long time waiting for that book to be published. And it was a long time that it was by itself and there were no other books by Latino colleagues published by NCTE. Just look at the catalog. What books has NCTE published by Caucus colleagues? That's just a very easy search.

Victor's book was the only book by a Latino that was published by NCTE for many, many years. You're going to see a big gap before you get a book by Raul Sanchez or Cristina or anybody. The mentoring really has always been from colleagues and it is essential and extremely important and valuable because it always is done with love. Victor Villanueva has probably reviewed more manuscripts than like twenty-five people put together. He was always willing to read manuscripts whether they were essay manuscripts or book manuscripts. And this was under the table. This was not like NCTE sent the manuscript to Victor for him to review. No, this is us saying "Victor, will you please read this for me because I don't know if I'm making any sense?" And he would do it. Because it behooves him to have more of us published. I think that the books that were published, if you read the acknowledgments, almost all of them would say, "Victor Villanueva," "A shout out to Victor Villanueva because he helped birth it." So, he was helpful to me. I remember I was writing an article for an MLA book and I was trying to do some kind of cross-genre work and sort of making my way as I was doing it. He read it. I was so full of ah you know intimidation and nerves because I wasn't sure if I was doing this right and it was early in my career. He was just like "do what comes natural." That was like "Oh, I can do that." So yeah, Victor was super helpful. He helped others and if you look at those acknowledgment pages, you'll see, you'll see.

I think I did a lot of mentoring through the Caucus, especially of young emerging scholars and graduate students. One of the things that I also did was I brought undergraduates to the Caucus. We never had undergraduates come to conferences. I brought undergraduates to a lot of conferences. What's really ironic is that often there's more funding for undergraduate than there are for faculty members because there are the student unions. A lot of groups will fund students to do presentations and there's usually undergraduate research funds that will give money or departments will give money. But if it's for faculty, we're out of luck. That's why I often got students to present, co-present, on panels with me. That way it was initiating them into professional development. So that was one of the things that I did.

I also organized the first Latino Caucus workshop because, again, I thought we needed to do some mentoring. We needed to have a time outside of the Caucus meeting where we could review manuscripts, we could talk about dissertations, we could talk about the job search, we could talk about all the things that we need to do that we can't do in an hour meeting. So, I organized the first four workshops. The first one was in San Francisco, I think was 2005. Then I did the following ones. I think the last one I organized was the one in New Orleans. I always had co-organizers, but as the Caucus Co-Chair I did a lot of stuff on my own. I did a lot of nagging. I did a lot of phone calls and begging, "Come on, please help me do this. You need to join and do this." So, I did a lot of that. I kept in contact with people to encourage them to submit proposals. I reviewed proposals. I did a lot of things for the Caucus. Then I also served on committees and task force. I was on the Exemplar Committee. I was on the Scholars for the Dream Committee for several years. I was on the Nominating Committee for CCCC. I was on the Rainbow Strand Conference Planning Committee. I was on the College Section Nominating Committee. I was on the NCTE Election and HUD Section committee. I did a lot of work for NCTE throughout my years. But it was pretty good. Last year was my promotion year and national service is really important when you're going up for promotion. For Full professor and, to a lesser extent, Associate. Universities value research. Institutions, they're not going to value a lot of service, but the little that you do should be national.

I felt that within the Caucus I was able to, not just have my voice acknowledged and validated by the institution as far as the organization, but that it was a sort of communal and community voice. We could take our concerns to the leadership of NCTE and they would listen. They wouldn't necessarily act, but they would listen. At least I felt some progress, right? And we would often have sort of testy exchanges with the leadership because they had an idea about what the Caucus should be and should do and we had another idea because ultimately a Caucus is independent. It is not to be managed by the parent institution or organization that is NCTE for CCCC. It's like when I'm talking about it, NCTE is like the large umbrella and CCCC is under NCTE. I was on the task force when CCCC was investigating whether or not to break off, like to get a divorce, from NCTE and after like a two-year project, I think, there was just no way that could happen because we could not afford it. I need to remind people with this was investigated about 20 years or so ago and, maybe, it may be CCCC would be in a different position now, but one of the things that CCCC and NCTE have sometimes had happy relationships and some not so happy relationships. I think part of it is because CCCC is almost completely university and college affiliated members and NCTE is almost universally K through 12 colleagues. So that's a kind of a rub.

What I think might be a problem is that colleagues cannot depend on financial reimbursement for travel to the conference. A lot of networking happens at the conference. A lot of bonding and informal kind of negotiations happen at the conferences, both at NCTE and at CCCC. So, whether you are a K through 12 teacher who has a great idea about a book, but your principal won't even give you the days off to go to the convention or fund you to go to the convention. It's very discouraging. Universities and colleges are cutting, cutting, cutting and the humanities are usually the poorest of all disciplines. And so, at my University, I think we are going to get $450 and that has to cover everything. And you have to be presenting, you cannot just go to a conference for professional development. That's an ongoing issue that you can't really count on people returning year after year after year to the conference because they're not assured of funding. So, we'll meet some fantastic people one year and go "Oh! Wow! New colleagues!" Wonderful emerging scholars as emerging teachers. Then we lose them. They don't come back the next year because they haven't been funded. I think that one of the important things is maintaining this kind of contact through either an online a listserv or a website. I felt like the Latino Caucus newsletter (*Capirotada*) helped to keep people in touch. It was published twice a year. We had a Spring issue and a Fall issue. People would even make announcements, like "I had a baby" or "I was promoted" or "I have a publication out in press." There was usually poetry. There was usually a book or movie review. There was student writing that was included in it. There was always an editorial. There might be an issue that we wanted to raise to the membership. So, I know they're all archived because I had them archived and digitized.

I published *Capirotada* newsletters for more than 15 years. The first issue was put together by Alfredo Lujan, who was one of the leaders in the Caucus from way back. This is another thing that's like in the history that maybe some people don't know or remember, but the Hispanic Association for Colleges and Universities actually funded the printing and mailing of the first issue. And that was because of my friend, Lala Leena Martinez, was the president of HACU at that time, 1992 or 1993 and maybe even earlier, and, of course, nobody had any money. We didn't have any sponsorship or anything like that and it was a one-page two-sided folded little newsletter, but I asked Lala Leena to please help us with this and she paid it out of HACU's fund. She paid for the printing and for the mailing. She was the first Puerto Rican to be the president of HACU. After that I convinced my university, Indiana University of Pennsylvania, to pay for the paper, the copying, and the postage, but of course, we had to collect funds anyway. We had to collect membership dues so there was money to pay for the printing.

Every year at a conference, there was always some racist incident or two or three. Always, always, always. The Caucus traditionally is always held on Friday. It's usually the second day right and, by the second day, everybody's already pretty pissed off and frustrated. People would complain that nobody came to a session that was really important about race or about language. There would be snubs. There are two examples that I would give. I think you probably interviewed Renee Moreno already.

So, Renee was giving this really important presentation and the person who spoke after her was a white woman. She totally didn't hear a single word that Renee said. She also said all this racist crap and then called her students, "my Latino students" and said they are "always silent, they don't talk." A bunch of us were like "Oh my God, you believe, you just said that." There were about three or four of us and Gail Okawa was one of the people with me. We said *"que locura."* Gail was also one of the original members of the Latino Caucus; she's retired now, but she was at Youngstown, Ohio. She goes back even further than I do, and I would say you could interview her. She was even before Victor's time because she and Victor are contemporaries. She was on a lot of committees. She was on the Executive Committee.

Anyway, so Renee is just assaulted by this woman in the way that she just dismissed her presentation. We got up. We walked out because members of the audience were then piling on top of Renee. So, we just, like a bunch, got up and said "This is intolerable. This is racist. We're not going to stand for it." We stormed out. This was in San Diego, and, of course, the first thing we did was find Victor Villanueva and give him all the complaints. He says "Okay, good. You're mad. Now you need to participate in the Caucus. This is a place where you can get your voice heard. You can express your concerns to the leadership." That's what we did. A bunch of us did get recruited in that way. So that's how I became energized and invigorated.

The second example which was much more recent what that we had a person at NCTE who worked in Champaign, Urbana, who was our advocate. Her name was Dr. Sandra Gibbs. She would look out for us. She would let us know of any kind of legislation that they were considering or any rules they were going to change that would impact us, people of color not just the

African-American not just the Black Caucus, but the Latino Caucus. Sandra was basically fired. There were all kinds of very ugly things. We were furious. There were boycotts and letters. I say we actually sent a packet of 50 certified letters to the president of NCTE at that time, who was Kent Williamson, who has passed on, but Kent and nobody from NCTE even acknowledged our letters. They didn't even acknowledge them. So, we were just furious because Sandra didn't deserve to be treated that way and we didn't deserve to be treated that way either. That was another experience. There's always something going on. I think that the fact is we have to complain and protest and come and really make our issues known to them. They almost get kind of embarrassed and then they want to do the right thing, but they don't do the right thing to start with, they never do.

That's their modus operandi. They don't even think about it. Like what are we for if not to consult with you people at NCTE, to see that you do the right thing, but they don't. They don't consult us. They just say, "Oh here's this curriculum and it's going to be so good." And we're like, "Excuse me! You don't have any Latinos on this curriculum." We're supposed to be consulted. That was one of the things that we also complained about because it was 20 years ago when Bobbi and I were co-chairs and NCTE was trying to get the Caucus to become affiliated. This meant a legal relationship so that they would give us money. They would give us space on their server and blah blah blah blah blah, but it came with conditions.

There were these meetings that we were invited to with leadership at that time, Kathy Yancey, who was at FSU. She was the president of NCTE and she invited me, Bobbi, and people from the Asian American Caucus. There was this wonderful woman from the Black Caucus, but I can't remember her name, and I think Joyce Rain Anderson from the American Indian Caucus. They invited us to a meeting in Washington, D.C. to tell us why it would be such a good idea for the caucuses to be affiliated with NCTE. Kent Williamson was also present. He was the Executive Director at that time and he unfortunately missed this amazing history of the caucus and the Black Caucus. The woman from the Black Caucus gave a great history and he came in after the fact. We were like "Dude you should have been here to hear this. She talked about how Black scholars and educators didn't get couldn't get on the session, wouldn't be allowed in the hotels, I mean, like it was like civil rights issues from the get-go within this organization. Of course, you know African-Americans have been founding their own organizations for many years when MLA, for example, wasn't up to inviting African-Americans to propose sessions, so they had their own organizations called the CLA, the College Language Association, which continues to have conferences. CLA was started because MLA was exclusive. And so NCTE was the largest organization for teachers of English and Language Arts teachers. So, there were many African American teachers who wanted to be part of the national organization, but the organization was not really interested in them. So, they said, "Nope, we're going to we're going to make a change. So, their leadership really paved the way for the Latino Caucus, American Indian Caucus, Asian American Caucus, Queer Caucus. So, their history is really on what we are based on. We exist because they started it.

The other times when we make our voices known is after the conference when there is a meeting on Sunday morning with the chair of CCCC and the future chair CCCC. We basically call it Caucus concerns. The Caucus always sends a representative to this meeting on Sunday morning and we complain, we protest, and we tell them what went wrong, and how they should deal with it. So, I don't know if this still goes on, but I went to many of those meetings.

Scholars for the Dream is a wonderful thing that came out of these issues. We wanted to have more students of color and emerging scholars of color come to the conference, so it started out with a little bit of money. Then we got a little bit more money. Then more Scholars for the Dream were invited and now they have a network. That's really a really wonderful thing. There was a task force for the involvement of people of color and that was a great group. I remember Jackie Jones Royster was on that group. There were many people from the Black Caucus and Latino Caucus. We were we were fighting the good fight. You want us to get involved, then these are the ways to get us involved. They're like, "Oh hey, we'll just have this task force and that means you're involved." They want to recruit us to do stuff, but often it doesn't come with any resources. So, for example, to be the on the membership of the Executive Committee of CCCC. It's labor intensive because you have to go to NCTE and CCCC and usually there's another meeting, right? So, they only give you a little bit of money to travel and your university has to support you, right? If you want to help CCCC, your university has to give you a graduate student and they will pay for part of your travel for NCTE and CCCC and the workshops and so on and so forth. But your university has to give something, so your university has to say "Oh this is a good idea. We will help you to do this. It's a lot of work and it's a lot of travel. If you're teaching, this is something that, you know, there's a cost to your students, to your department, to your university.

In the past, NCTE offered grants to emerging teachers and I'm sure there continue to be mentoring initiatives and I think none of these things happen without us pushing. I think it's definitely a mixed bag. I think it depends on the leadership within NCTE administration and the presidential team. Who is chair of CCCC? Has this person exhibited a track record of working with educators of color? Is this person educatable? Because they don't necessarily have to have a track record, but they have to be willing to cooperate and to advocate. So, one of the things that I've seen year after year, many times, when you have president of NCTE that might be from the K through 12. You ask yourself, where do you teach? Where are your students? If the Latino demographic of the United States makes us the largest minority, the majority minority, and the majority minority is under the age of 18, those kids are in your classrooms. What are you doing to help those kids? What are your practices? What is your curriculum? What have you done to adjust to those students in your classes? And we're not just talking about Texas or Illinois or Florida, because you know we're everywhere. Two percent women of color faculty at University, two percent. It's still a wasteland.

It's like we cannot let up. We have to continuously make our concerns known right to the administration, call on the phone, network with the other Caucuses. That's another important issue. The Caucuses always work together in order to get stuff done, in order to make it known that we were going to stand for this issue. You know that the organization needed to be responsive to its members even if we are a minority of the membership. We're active members, yes.

[Therefore,] I think [cross-caucus work is] really important because we really need to work together. All the Caucuses should. We should know each other. Everybody should know who is the leader of the Asian American Caucus and who leads the American Indian Caucus, and who is the leadership of the Black Caucus. These are things that need to be remembered. We always work together. I went to one of their meetings once and also felt really silenced, but again, it depends on leadership, depends on what you know, who's there. Are they really wanting to hear us? Do they really want to hear us? Or they just want the color there, we can check that box off?

The story about the Caucus is that it is warm and has a welcoming vibe. It is what drew me and kept me returning to the Caucus and then taking on leadership and service. We were a family and families have new members all the time. The other thing that is important to note is that the Caucus was always Pan-ethnic. There were American Indian, Native American scholars, that participated with us as well as Asian-American. The Caucus was always Pan-ethnic because there were so few of the rest of us, scholars and teachers of color. It really was like a refuge from a very White organization and it did become kind of like a vital point on which my academic career and service turned.

Then there's some family members that are around a long time, right? But, you know, you try to keep the sense of somo familia. And, you know, families squabble all the time. So, I think the story about the Caucus, its sense and sensibility, is that we should be welcoming. It's part of our founding. The other part of our founding is that we're Pan-ethnic. It's never been exclusive. Our mission statement said "like-minded folks," it didn't say you have to have certain blood percentage. It said if you believe what we believe that students of color and particularly Latino students need to have their issues advocated for, join us. . . .

EXPERIENCES: IN THEIR OWN WORDS
Bobbie Houtchens and Mary Carmen Cruz

Based on Interview by Anita Hernández
December 13, 2016

Cruz: One of my professors, who was my mentor, pulled me in and she said you need to get involved in [CCCC] That was Roseann Dueñas González, co-founder of the Caucus. I was one of her students as an undergraduate and also one of her graduate students, when I graduated with my BA and then stayed on to work on MA degree. She said I need to start coming to the NCTE meetings and she would take me, so I became involved in the Caucus meetings. She knew her away around NCTE working with the presidents and the executive committees. She was advocating for issues and not just Latino Caucus issues, for all teachers of color, and for all students of color, issues of students who were culturally and linguistically underrepresented. I got to meet the folks she was working with. It was rewarding, eye-opening, enlightening, mind expanding, career developing. Rewarding and career developing. Then as a graduate student, I went to one or two CCCCs. The bulk of my experience was with NCTE. It was through her efforts that I became involved.

[Actually] she would let me sleep in her room and that was paid for. I paid for my own transportation and I paid for my own registration. There may have been a couple of times where the college may have paid for my registration. In all the years I have been involved in NCTE, I paid my own way, never reimbursed except for the time I was on the Executive Committee and that was paid for. I received per diem when I was on the secondary section.

Houtchens: My story is like Mary Carmen. I have been active in CABE [California Association for Bilingual Education) and Washington, D.C. area TESOL regional organizations and did presentations for CABE. As a graduate student again and earning my MA in bilingualism and biculturalism degree with Dr. Barbara Flores, she encouraged me to present at the NCTE. She introduced me to Latino Caucus leaders and members, which is where I felt at home. NCTE was overwhelming. People were not community-oriented as I was used to finding at CABE and at TESOL. I felt very isolated from everyone and without Barbara Flores I probably would not have gone back. She introduced me to the Caucus and to some outstanding leaders in education for Latino Students. Meeting Sandra Gibbs, who was the liaison for the Latino Caucus and to the Black Caucus, I was connected to amazing brilliant activist black women and men in the Black Caucus. That is where I found my home, it expanded my network. When I was weary to fight those battles in our own communities, I could always find renewal at the Latino Caucus and how Latino Caucus was involved in NCTE. I was not the only warrior. There were many people in front of me and behind me . . . The caucus made me a lot smarter, being with NCTE helped me understand . . . how different states had beliefs about kids, especially Latino kids and English learners. This gave me entry to NCTE that I would not have received by myself. It changed my life. The things I have done nationally, would not have been for the Latino Caucus.

Cruz: Thank you for summarizing, it's absolutely true. We gained an awareness of activism and advocacy at the national level. The entry way and finding our home in that large organization was through the Latino Caucus. It inspired us and spread our wings to work with other leaders.

Houtchens: I think the Latino Caucus gave me voice, more than just credibility, more than just strength and power. I don't know how to frame it. Once our names were connected to the Latino Caucus, people listened to us. It was like this is the fuse you are talking to, whether it is Mary Carmen or Bobbi, we got this explosive device behind us if you don't listen to us. Especially, in the positions we had chairs of the caucus that also put us in positions to be invited where our voices would be heard. For example, at every national convention, in the past, what would happen at the convention is that we leaders of the Latino Caucus and Black Caucus, we were asked to meet with certain members of the Executive Committee, president, outgoing president, and convention chair to talk about what was working at that particular convention. what we thought necessary changes for the next convention, how NCTE was coming up with initiative with language policy or had to do with recruitment of teachers, or with how the program looked. We were always invited to come and talk. Sometimes we were the ones that prompted the invitation. We were always there and we were listened to by them. It was a debriefing. We would meet with the caucus members in order to get a debriefing before we went to the meeting, to get a feeling about the convention. Members would tell us experiences they had had, other things they had noticed, which publishers were invited, about areas of instruction might not have been addressed, or if they had been addressed, they were not very sensitively addressed, like working with Latino urban kids. . .

Cruz: I was remembering when we went to the table, we were not just talking about issues that were affecting Latino youth, but we were talking about all students of color. One session where Native American literature and stereotypes within certain curriculum were discussed, but some of the examples to resolve this were stereotypes themselves. There were authors who never lived on a reservation, were not Indian themselves, who also were being promoted. We were bringing issues to the forefront to help make the other decision makers aware of what was going on. We were the voices. It was no longer Mary Carmen. It was no longer Bobbi. It went beyond us by working with our colleagues across the nation. The struggle and the challenges, as well as the resources and successes of our students and colleagues, that was what we could bring together and that was what the other NCTE leadership were hearing. We were bringing all of those powerful experiences collectively together. It was a unified voice. There she goes, go ask her what she thinks about this. What do think about this? How about joining us?

Cruz: I started going in the '80s and then I moved away to go to a small private college on an Indian Reservation in the state of Washington. I lost connection. I laugh because my mentor did not forget us. So, I lost connection with NCTE and I lost connection with my mentor because

I was busy doing other things. Then when I came back to Tucson, the year that I started working in the school districts, I got an invitation to do a presentation at NCTE. It came out of the blue. I knew who was inviting me. It was Roseann Gonzalez and Sandra Gibbs. I knew it was them because no one at NCTE knew me. I wasn't that involved at the time. Previous to that, I was a protégé following my mentors around and learning from them as much as I could. They had not given up. So, I went to give the presentation. Then I came back again and not sure how I found my way to the Caucus. Then a couple years later, I received a phone call from Sandra Gibbs. That phone call said "Mary Carmen, this is Sandra Gibbs." I was so delighted. You will hear about how instrumental Sandra was in our organization and in NCTE. Sandra did more a whole lot more than just the caucuses. She was in charge of writing scholarships for students, she was in charge of NCATE, and a lot of other initiatives. She was especially our godmother, our *nina*, she made sure that our voices were not just heard but that were paid attention to and she made sure there was communication with each other across the caucuses. We were united in our vision. She knew the history of the involvement of people of color and she knew the history of NCTE. She was a very powerful promoter of the Caucus. She invited me to become a member of the *Rainbow Strand* organizers. So, I became more involved in the organization.

Houtchens: Because she was on the committee on Writing, people of color were involved in the many committees she was involved with. It was a way that she spread the wealth and not to be segregated in the caucus work, but actually be involved in the main work of NCTE.

Cruz: I think that NCTE as an organization has policies and statements that talk about the rights of students to their own language, committed to recruiting teachers of color, being against racism and bias in the teaching of English, promoting involvement of minority involvement, looking at diverse and multicultural education. So, if those are the beliefs that an organization professes, then there should be evidence in the actions of the organization. So, as members of Latino Caucus, we also are concerned about the success of all our students because the organization exists to bring teachers together to promote professional development and to look at issues that affect students as well as our teachers.

As Latino Caucus members were very concerned about Latino students and Latino educators.

At the time when Bobbi and I were involved, those very issues came to be. For example, at time Bobbi and I were involved, those issues in terms recruiting people by headquarters, you could count the number of people of color in leadership positions at headquarters. It went back to the stock room. In terms of NCTE elections, again, it got to where we were making recommendations, that for example only persons of color are nominated on a regular basis for vice president. People of color were not being elected into the executive committee. I am talking about the presidency. Continually having regular meetings for people of color to be involved because as Bobbi said, that is a big convention. The smallest convention was 5,000 and the largest was 9,000. If you are a teacher of color, if you are a brand-new teacher, it is daunting. It can be confusing, especially if you are teacher of color who is trying to see where are others who have like interest.

It was one of the issues we wanted promoted in the organization. There was a program for Teachers for the Dream we wanted promoted for the organization. Looking at the program, how the program was not doing what it was supposed to be doing for professional development and help to enlighten our colleagues. I think those are four little issues. To make our we sessions stronger. We didn't see concerted efforts to make changes. NCTE making the same promises over and over no real change. Even in 2014, NCTE making the same promises but there was no real change.

Teachers for the Dream still exists now, but it has changed from when it started. It must have been 1995 or 1996. I am trying to remember the name of Black Caucus leader. He was a short black man, older man. Teachers for the Dream was his baby. He started Teachers for the Dream. It was started to promote initiatives that would encourage students of color to join the teaching profession. That was its mission. I had a feeling that it was the Black Caucus that got it started. There were private donations in the initial year and they gave out two 10,000 grants that were available to those who had a program for people of color to join the teaching profession. A lot of those who put in proposals were from universities. Sara was her first name and I think she taught at a college and she worked with 10 students. She was from the Carolinas. She was from the Black Caucus.

In 2000, we opened a new school. I was given a grant to start a program at my school. My idea was to start this tutoring club. I taught at an urban high school in San Bernardino. Most of my kids were Latinos and most of those were English learners and long-term English learners or newcomers. My idea was to start an after school tutoring group where I would teach kids to read a book aloud to elementary school children. They could choose to work at an elementary school near their homes in case they were bused. The elementary schools let out one hour after we let out so they could tutor the last hour of school. They went and made their own contacts, but had a letter of introduction from me. They had training on child development and had to anticipate development mental needs of the kids at the grade they were tutoring. Most went five days and read stories to little kids at the elementary schools by their house. Because it was by their house, many were tutoring their nieces and nephews and making their community a better place. It became a family thing.

Their job beyond reading to the kids and making their community in a better place, contributing to their community because there was not a lot of outlets. They had to carry the message to the little kids. The more time they spent they started to believe in the motto. it was like positive affirmation. I pulled in the students from the School of Education from CSSB and they worked as mentors and supervisors. I ended up with 200 students. It was so powerful. The principals thought it was wonderful to have these kids independently going. GS would pop in and out and monitor and collect data who was reading and what the books they were reading and bring back info to our club meetings to further develop their skills. The superintendent was so impressed that he said we need to connect this club to Future Teachers of America, which was a dead club in our group. The next year, he made an announcement every high school had to have a similar program to serve their community.

My school would start a teaching academy to take over what Teachers for the Dreams were doing. What I was able to do with the money I got from the money was to buy materials for the kids—books, T-shirts for PR, and publicize what they were doing. If they worked 100 hours tutoring, they earned a letter which was more beautiful than the athletic letter. They got recognition from the mayor. We went on two field trips that year. Most had not been 10 miles from where they were living. We left at 7:30am and visited University La Sierra, University of Redlands, Cal State SB and these kids were promised assistance in their applications. Came to LA to a museum, we go out to a real Chinese restaurant. Many had never gone to a restaurant with tablecloths and did not know how to function. It was part of what we had students experience, Russian food, including borscht. We'd go see a play where bilingual foundations for the arts had the actors come into the audience to talk with the kids. We went to see *Phantom of the Opera*. We went to see a symphony. The kids arrived to the school at midnight. I wanted them to come back to school the next day because I wanted them to talk about their whole experience.

The teaching academies are still going. The teaching academy has become a mentor for other academies in California. I received Edison funding, another one from the Gas Company and another three million from federal money. They used that money to start the teaching academies, that little initiative. This blossomed into something incredible. They took over my position when I retired. San Bernardino is putting out teachers of color, most of them bilingual. It is the gift that is still giving.

Cruz: That fund has evolved differently and you don't hear too much about it. When you go to the NCTE website, you can see that. It has changed quite a bit. Grants up to $750 and it goes to an affiliate. What they do is they submit a proposal that implements recruitment initiatives during the school year through the affiliate. A teacher cannot apply for it. The money is to recruit a teacher of color into your affiliates. This is for one teacher into the affiliate. The power has been reduced. It has been reduced.

Another thing that happened during our time was with the *Rainbow Strand*. NCTE used to bring to Urbana in February the Executive Committee and all members of the different steering committees, the elementary, the middle, the secondary, the college, as well as members of the research group. Then it would bring in members of the *Rainbow Strand* planning committee, who were members of each of the different section levels, to assist in reading proposals. We would read the proposals, two to three thousand proposals that were submitted in a given year. They were divided into the different section levels. The committees would read the proposals which would go into the program as *Rainbow Strands* planners. We kept an eye for those proposals, whether they were marked Rainbow or not if they met the criteria for *Rainbow Strand*. When we saw the proposals being accepted to be on the program, we would get together and discuss what else needed to be on the program to provide greater diversity. That was valuable. What was happening at the same time was those of us on the Rainbow strands were being mentored on issues of leadership, not just for the convention, so as we went back to our own schools and our own areas with leadership skills within the organization. We grew as professionals and we grew as leaders. We were invited to different meetings with other committees and commissions. This did not happen overnight. We requested that continued. . . .

Meeting at the *Rainbow Strand* planning was powerful. When we went to the leadership, the secondary sections, we would go into their planning sessions as working consultants and bring expertise of working with students of color. Traditionally those groups were white. Initially people were intimidated that we were in the room, but we had been mentored where there were ways to point that was not confrontational. Being in the room, we were able to read body language. We were skilled at reading the tone of the conversation that can't get in the digital. They didn't realize we were on the same team. It was okay. That face to face meeting in February was powerful to raising the level of sensitivity of NCTE and raised the sensitivity for NCTE staff. We interfaced with the staff, made friendships and relationships to move the organization along. . . .

Cruz: When we were face to face from 7am to 8pm, we were there with everyone. Living and breathing for three days and you build those relationships that was critical when the convention happens. Something happens when the caucuses that have room apart from each other. Placement was not most effective. We went right away. Here is what our needs. How can you help us before the event happened and for next time it would be the way? Relationships with students. Relationships is at the heart of working with colleagues. The two caucuses have rooms that are apart from each other. That has happened in the past and was not most effective. We went to staff and they were happy to help us rectify before the event. We create the relationships. Relationships are at the heart. of NCTE. . . .

It took years before they became more responsive. We build it, and it took years to become more responsive. Changed three times while we were there. Kent Williamson worked for the publication division and he ran the bookstore at the convention. I built the relationship with him and we already had a relationship. He became much more sensitive over the years. We talked to him along. When we started, they presented an outsider point of view of our kids and our literature. He became more open to doing that of bringing Latino and Black voices.

At the convention planning, keynote speakers are also decided. When we were first involved, the main keynote speakers are determined by the chair who is the incoming president, that person will ask others, people you are interested in, depending on your concern for many years influenced who you bring, Sections invited to suggest names, speakers of color who could help advance understanding to promote effective practices for all students. Often times they were. In more recent years and more brainstorming of speakers of Color to the consideration list and making it to speakers. Couple of years ago, Sonia Nazario, former LA times writer was the keynote speaker. Kathy Short brought her. I am seeing those change.

I was proud of the leadership of the Latino Caucus in using the avenues to reach out to each other and support each other, to promote each other, and help each other to grow. I am hoping that the Caucus will continue to be united again at not just at CCCCs but also at NCTE, what happens in one, will be integrated, and not separated. I want to encourage the Latino Caucus to keep doing what it is doing and finding those avenues. To continue knowing our history. When we don't know our history, then we are limited in how we go forward. Knowing the history of CCCC can give more power to what you are say, what the issues are that need to be addressed, and how we go about that change. . .

EXPERIENCES: IN THEIR OWN WORDS
Cristina Kirklighter

Based on Interview by Romeo García
October 3, 2017

In the early years when I joined the caucus and when it was a lot smaller (maybe 5-15 at most in our meetings), we seemed to have less of a voice in cross-caucus concerns. In contrast, the Black Caucus would fill up their rooms, and they had some powerful clout in caucus decisions, especially when Sandra Gibbs was at NCTE Headquarters. Sandra Gibbs though worked with all of us and would visit our meetings. It was good to have her at NCTE, but when she left, we all felt we had less of a voice at headquarters.

Gradually, the caucus started to grow as more Latinx graduate students entered Rhetoric and Composition. I became co-chair with Renee Moreno when Sandra Gibbs had already left. I believe this was the moment where caucus co-chairs realized our cross-caucus relationships needed to strengthen to send our collective voices to NCTE and CCCCs. The approaching NCTE 2011 Centennial Celebration also brought us together as we worked to document our collective histories [Writing and Working for Change].

We learned through these early histories how a small group of people of color, many as founders of our respective caucuses, worked together to make a difference not only at NCTE, but throughout our nation and world in literature, linguistics, creative writing, and community outreach. The NCTE *Searching for America* document where Asian American, African American, Chicano and Chicana, and Native American literature and creative writing leaders sent a strong message to this nation on how the literature our students read needed to include these group's writers. Later Geneva Smitherman and Roseann Dueñas Gonzalez and still later Victor Villanueva became the linguistic leaders. Reading these early histories and what our elders had done together I know had an impact on me and others.

So, we began coming together in force as co-caucus leaders, and it became much more difficult for others who ignored or downplayed our concerns to not hear us. Mila Fuller who worked with the caucuses at NCTE headquarters for a few years did help as she could, but her role was not as clearly defined as Sandra Gibbs. Co-chairs at that time knew we had to create a strong voice together and work on many cross-caucus initiatives to fight the injustices of academia, NCTE, and beyond. *Writing and Working for Change* cross-caucus initiatives was what I focused on the most and encouraging our cross-caucus members to present on the same panels and workshops. Even if our attendance is still small at these panels or roundtables, we're dialoguing with each other and learning more about how our scholarship, teaching, and community outreach intertwine. For the growing number of caucus members who have multiple identities and thus affiliations with more than one caucus, going to cross-caucus sessions, workshops, working on articles, books, multimedia, digital, and films together, convening together in casual settings, speak to these collective identities and make them feel at home with who they are.

[Before becoming co-chair of the caucus], I first served on a 4Cs committee while I was a doctoral student. Victor Villanueva was Chair then in 1998 and decided I should serve on the Ad Hoc Use of Student Writing in Composition Research Committee. I was the student representative on this committee, and the rest of the committee were made up of well-established scholars in this area. Victor knew I had just finished co-editing *Voices and Visions: Refiguring Ethnography in Composition* (Heinemann Boynton Cook 1997), and he thought I was a good choice. At that time, I was sure this committee would find out I was an imposter and didn't belong in academia. Back then, we were writing on a listserv (no Skype available then), so all they saw were my words until we eventually met up at 4Cs much later. Reflecting on this experience years later, I will say how these insecurities and imposter syndrome helped me. Before I pressed the send button on my e-mails, I spent hours researching the topic they were discussing and reading all their comments carefully. It was the best self-training I could have put myself through. I was determined to show them this Latinx could enter their conversations and had something valuable to say. I was determined not to be an imposter. As the only student on this committee, I also believed I was the spokesperson for students. Years later this spokesperson role prepared me to serve on other committees and leadership positions for my gente and others. At the end of serving on this committee, Paul Anderson as chair, told me how appreciative he was of my work on this committee and advocacy for students. I had joined the conversation as a valuable 4Cs committee member, and this was the foundation I needed for my future work at NCTE and CCCC.

I successfully entered committee conversations, and my next step with committee work was to learn the rules of NCTE/CCCC when I began serving on the Resolutions Committee. But, as I later discovered, it is not enough to learn the rules, but how others use these rules or bend these rules or do whatever else with these rules. The more committees you serve on, the better you become at gauging these rules and applying them for advocacy purposes and/or preventative measures. We've had leaders at NCTE/CCCC who have supported us, and we've had leaders who sought to derail and/or silence us. Knowing who does what and how they operate within these systems of rules is important. When you serve on a number of committees with them, you eventually can see what's coming around the corner and take appropriate measures. Both Renee and I had served on a number of committees, so we would confer together and confer with previous co-chairs and other caucus co-chairs to gauge certain situations that could hurt or help the caucuses. We seldom made decisions without conferring with others. I would say it is part of Latinx collective leadership for we are anything but silos. Also, you eventually figure out who are your allies and who are not after serving on a number of committees with them. With each committee I served on, I grew more confident and more outspoken. I figured out who to bring into certain conversations for collective purposes and who was out for their own self-interests or interests of their circle of friends.

Serving on a number of committees also demonstrates to the NCTE/CCCC leadership that you care for the organization. They may disagree with you, but they know you care, and this can gain you respect as a leader. They might say under their breath, "Oh no, what is she going to demand now" and, as Latinxs, we're used to making demands for justice over again and again until someone hears us, but that's okay. We persist because of all the injustices we've faced in our lives. We have no choice but to persist, and it is a quality that can serve us well. My last piece of advice on this matter is to serve on committees, not to alleviate insecurities or call attention to yourself. Proving yourself to others time and time again is way too exhausting. Validation comes within as I eventually learned. Serve because you want to make a difference and improve the lives of others. Others will see this in your leadership style and respect you for it.

I want to say how pleased to see so many caucus members at the last few caucus meetings. I want to thank many of caucus members who have continually encouraged and brought their graduate students to these meetings. This is how we grow through our mentoring efforts and networking. My first advice to new or young members is to become engaged with this caucus and its members. As a graduate student, I had a few good mentors at my university, such as Joe Moxley and Elizabeth Metzger, but I also had mentors within the caucus, such as Victor Villanueva, Gail Okawa, Cecilia Rodríguez Milanés, Mary Carmen Cruz, Bobbi Houtchens and, later, when I discovered them in my archival research of the Latinx Caucus, Felipe Ortega de Gasca, Carlota Cárdenas de Dwyer, and Roseann Dueñe Gonzalez. I also shortly later found mentors in the Black Caucus, such as Geneva Smitherman and James Hill. And, a little later found mentors in the Asian/Asian American Caucus and American Indian Caucus, such as Lu Ming Mao, Morris Young, Malea Powell, and Joyce Rain Anderson. When I was a junior faculty member, I found Steve Parks who later mentored me when I became editor of the journal, *Reflections*.

So, the number one piece of advice is to always search for mentors no matter what stage you're at in your academic career and beyond. And, most importantly, remember all the mentors that came before you entered academia. They'll keep you grounded and remind you who you are when you start thinking you're all that and more. Whatever you do, don't fall into the "I'm too big for my britches" syndrome, an old Southern saying my grandmother taught me. Academia can lure you into this syndrome with its almost Hollywood star worship of academic stars. If you feel you might be slipping into this syndrome, pay a visit to your *familia* and let them tell you who you really are. It works every time for me.

Mentors also come in the form of those you teach. I've learned more from my students than they have from me given my Freirean approach to teaching. Remember, their combined total of years out number yours, and they are a valuable source of your learning. When you become a senior leader in the caucus, remember how much undergraduate and graduate caucus leaders can teach you.

[As part of mentoring], I feel our gente's scholarship is very important to help them with getting jobs, promotion, awards, and building a community of scholarship affiliated with our scholars' work. It also helps scholars outside the caucus to understand what we value in scholarship and how it defines us. Years ago, we only had a few Rhetoric and Composition Latinx scholars and allies contributing to this body of scholarship. Then, as we grew, we had to push publishers to go beyond just publishing these few and encourage them to discover our increasing number of emerging scholars. This didn't work out too well and publishers kept asking the same gente to be authors, reviewers, awardee nominees, etc. While the junior gente and graduate students kept encountering publishing roadblocks, some of the established gente scholars had enough of this and took matters into their own hands by becoming editors/co-editors of special issues, books, journals, videos, films, etc. They also encouraged our gente to become reviewers and review the books of our gente. We must look out for each other if we want Latinxs in R&C to thrive in academia.

Although our number of publishing allies outside the caucus are increasing, we still have a ways to go. Before I became co-caucus chair, I co-edited the book collection, *Teaching Writing with Latino/as Students: Lessons Learned at Hispanic-Serving Institutions*. A few caucus members were in the book: Isabel Baca, Dora Ramírez-Dhoore, and Beatrice Méndez Newman. I knew that this book would resonate with our caucus members, especially Latinx students, because it was about their experiences even if they were not at an HSI at the time of the book's publication. It countered many of the deficit-driven perceptions aimed at them by faculty, administrators, students, and the deficit scholarship on Latinx students. It's important for Latinx students, many of whom began at community colleges, to see authors capturing their challenges and breakthroughs as writing students. Once when I was teaching a graduate class at Texas A&M Corpus-Christi, I asked students how many of them began in "developmental" or "basic" writing classes. All of the Latinxs in the class raised their hands, and there were many great Latinx writers in my classroom many of whom went on to get their PhDs and are now professors. So, editing these types of book, is more than just helping Latinx Caucus members get published. It's also about telling their stories for other students to read and educating professors on how to work with Latinx students.

Listening to Our Elders, co-edited with Samantha Blackmon and Steve Parks, was another book, but this one was for the caucuses and Disabilities Committee. Just as I have multiple identities that speak to caucuses and/or committees, so do other caucus members. Some members must sometimes choose which caucus and/or committee they will attend given we all meet at the same time at 4Cs. They especially needed to read a book with many of their historical caucus identities in it. I am especially happy to see the after the caucus program after the caucus meetings at 4Cs, and I believe it's driven by the newer generation of scholars, teachers, and activists. I'm pleased to have mentored through this book initiative and *Writing and Working for Change* this newer generation and so pleased how they work together now in panels, books, and other initiatives. This is our future, and we are anything but silo caucuses.

The third and final major project was when I took on the editorship of *Reflections: A Journal of Public Rhetoric, Civic Writing, and Service Learning*. I edited the journal for five years ending in the summer of 2017 after my retirement from academia. I was co-chair of the caucus for two and a half of those years. *Reflections* is a small independent journal in Rhetoric and Composition, but this suited me fine. There was less politics, and I enjoyed working with our small staff, Wilma Harvey, Jess Pauszek, and Tobi Jacobi. Steve Parks did a good job of mentoring me as the previous editor, and I thank him for that. My list of reviewers became populated with cross-caucus and committee members, and I made sure at least some of the special issues focused on a diversity of issues (Latino/a, African American (reprint), Disabilities, and Veterans). Caucuses found our journal to be friendly to book reviews from their authors, so this was another opportunity. The Fall 2013 special issue co-edited with Isabel Baca focused on Latinos/as in Public Rhetoric, Civic Writing, and Service Learning. This special issue had many submissions and acceptances from our caucus members, some of whom published for the first time. It's what many of us do in the caucus, so the high submission rate from the caucus wasn't surprising. For the last seven years, the 4Cs Latinx Caucus has been one of the few caucuses and committees to reach out to the conference's local communities and ask them to present at our workshops. I enjoyed working with Steve Alvarez, Damian Baca, and Kendall Leon organizing these outreaches while I was co-chair, and I love to see how it continued with Iris Ruiz and Raúl Sánchez. If we're committed to community outreach as many caucus members are, we have to walk the walk. The most rewarding part of promoting scholarship in the caucus was to watch as these scholars grew in confidence and began mentoring others. The cycle of giving is what's so important, not your legacy.

My mother taught me early on in life to take pride in who I am. She would often tell me "You are no better than anyone else and no one is better than you." I believe this was passed on to her as well. Later, as a graduate student, I had a fascination with autobiographical writings and the personal essay. What courage it took for some of these writers to be candid with who they were or are. They were my mentors too. As I was growing up with biracial parents, they never encouraged me to select one identity even though society at that time and still to this day pressures biracial children to be one or the other. They made me feel I had a strong foundation in the cultures they came from. Victor Villanueva, whose children come from similar cultural backgrounds as me, once told me he could see how open I was about my identities, and I took that as a compliment. But not all are so lucky as I later discovered, especially when I became a teacher. I did notice as I candidly talked about my identities, students and eventually caucus members would confide in me about certain identity challenges they faced. I was happy to listen and some chose to be more open and others did not. It's everyone's choice to what level they wish to open up, but those who are open know they have particular roles to play as teachers, mentors, mothers, etc. I came from a middle-class background with a father who was a successful engineer, and I know what privileges I had growing up. Later in life when I discovered I had a disability (ADHD), I decided to be open and tell my university, my students, and wrote about it in the journal I edited, *Reflections: A Journal of Public Rhetoric, Civic Writing, and Service Learning.* I was then able to mentor more students who had disabilities and wished to confide in me. More recently, I've become much more aware of my Mayan ancestors and their ways that I now know I've always strongly identified with. As I grow older, I've come to celebrate and welcome all these identities and the opportunities it affords me to connect and possibly mentor others. Each has an impact on my leadership style, and I appreciate what these identities have done for me and others. Sometimes, it's challenging living with all of these identities, but it has opened up so many cross-identifications with others. I would have it no other way.

EXPERIENCES: IN THEIR OWN WORDS
Damian Baca

Based on Interview by Romeo García
October 1, 2016

I joined the Latino Caucus and the C's in 2000. It was the C's Minneapolis Convention. I was a graduate student in the Master's program at Northern Arizona University. I am aware I am not first-generation that there are several who have come before me in the organization. But as a graduate student getting a Master's degree at Northern Arizona University in Flagstaff, I was feeling very much like first generation in that I was the first Latino to attend the Rhetoric for Masters programs which was new, with the intent of eventually earning the Ph.D. and moving on into the office of the professoriate. I was the first Latino that the faculty that I was working with in the graduate program, I guess you can describe it as first contact. It was not their first contact with Latinos, there were a number of Latinos as custodial staff at the University, the cafeteria was well staffed with Latinos. But having a Latino show up in class interested in a Masters degree in Rhetoric and Composition for the purposes of obtaining a Ph.D. in Rhetoric and Composition, that was very new for the faculty that I was working with.

Also problematic was growing up in New Mexico having Spanglish as my first language, having acclimated to standardized American English at a fairly early age, there wasn't much for faculty to do for me regarding, you know, fixing me linguistically. And that was another challenge for the faculty. And then also being *güero*, being *güerito* from New Mexico, being a light skinned Mexican I did not conform to the conventional stereotypical expectations of an ethnographic encounter with Mexicans. It was very much first contact and I felt very much like first generation.

[My] goal was to get myself into a Ph.D. program that would allow me for options after. As a first-generation college student and as first-generation graduate student, first in my family to earn a college degree, first in my family to go on to graduate school, I had quite a bit of catch up to do in learning from a few faculty in my undergraduate degree in Texas about peer institutions, about feeder schools, about national rankings. Learning about those institutional hierarchies was very informative. And, also looking at the labor practices, the hiring practices, and particular in English departments, which is not all that encouraging. I did recognize early on that as a young punk kid from New Mexico that if I had any intentions of returning to New Mexico and returning to this part of the world that actually heading outward and getting a Ph.D. far beyond my own regional sense of place, that that may enable a possibility of returning somewhere close—close to home. I ended up finding myself at Syracuse where again though I am not a first generation that is in the Caucus, I am first generation in that I was the first student of color that was in the Syracuse CCR Program—Composition and Cultural Rhetoric program. Again, at that moment of first contact, I was a great ethnographic disappointment.

Coming to the CCCC was only further alienating and it was the Latino Caucus that I discovered fairly quickly was my institutional home, my emotional home, a place of support, and a sense of belonging. Of course, this is under Ceci Milanés (the Latino Caucus chair). I was interested in language because I know you've asked about the interest in Rhetoric and Composition, so I was interested in language and identity formation, historical memory, and also the physical corporeal act of writing. It was alarming to me that the majority of the sources that were used to inform Rhetoric and Composition came primarily from Colonial-centric, Euro-centric, North Atlantic Western civilizations that really had very little beyond a 200-year history. It was thinking of the field primarily through the Enlightenment. Yes, Rhetoric and Composition studies the Greeks, but they study them through Hegel. We are really learning very little about the Greeks of the 4th century BCE in the ancient Mediterranean. We are learning more about Hegel and Hegelian visions of the intellectual kidnapping of ancient Greece as a cradle of Western Civilization. That myth. We were being asked all of us, regardless of where we came from in the classroom in the graduate level, we were being asked to take on the skin and the mentality of Euro-Centrism. So, on one hand I was interested in Rhetoric and Composition, but on the other hand the lenses that the field continues to use I felt to be highly damaging and destructive. I think the role of the Latino Caucus in the CCCC's has been incredibly important to me and I would like to especially note the role of the Latino Caucus working with former NCTE employee Dr. Sandra Gibbs who placed diversity of the forefront of all of the work we do—teaching, research, outreach, community engagement. And, a recognition that as we pursue these goals that we are not alone, that we are working parallel to other groups, other scholars, other teachers of color, who are also asking and demanding change. And, so it was Sandra Gibbs who was a very important point person for us for the Latino caucus in our interactions and correspondence with the other Caucuses of color, the co-chairs and the chair of the other caucuses of color.

It is interesting about the vision of the Latino caucus under the time of Ceci Milanés because her work comes to the world of language and text through the lens of creative writing and poetry. Her work has been a huge inspiration to me. I have always read it and engaged it as clearly as rhetoric. This can tell us much about rhetorical theory and reveals much about composition and composing strategies and the craft of writing. Ceci's work has always been stretching beyond disciplinary borders, but I was aware at the same time that the field of Rhetoric and Composition did not take her work into account and so it was very clear to me that the policed borders of what counts as rhetoric and composition and what does not. Those borders are still heavily policed even as the field claims itself as a transdisciplinary field. I do not think we have really reached that and I am not sure this intellectual work has earned that designation.

Ceci's work has broadened my horizon and I think it was very important to me. When we think about her vision of coming, again crossing borders and conventional borders, we can ask the question of who is Latino, what counts as Latino and Latina, who is in and who is out. The Latino Caucus under Ceci, and I know this even before her, had a fluidity, and I believe it still does, of accommodating, of welcoming, of including people of who actually may not be Latino and Latina. I am thinking Gail Okawa would have been one figure that comes to mind. Other members of the Latino Caucus who have been part of our community who may or may not identified with this subjectivity of the marker of Latino and Latina, so Ceci's vision was very important. I hope that the Latino Caucus will continue to be embracing those fluid categories and thinking across conventional barriers for solidarity.

Under Ceci, we continued to grow, our numbers continued to grow. They are not the numbers we see now. I am thinking of the numbers at the Latino Caucus at the CCCC in Houston in 2016, this past April. That would have to be the largest Caucus meeting I have seen and that is in a ten-year period of time. At least twelve or more years. There is significant growth beyond what we have seen. There have been years at NCTE, ten years ago,

I went to one Latino Caucus meeting in Minneapolis at NCTE and there was only four of us in the room. There was more Latinos at the convention that year, but they were also spread in multiple directions. Not everyone can get to those meeting. It is a challenge. Sometimes, some years our numbers would be very small. I think we are moving beyond that. The days of the Latino Caucus coming and being able to count those in attendance on one or two hands, I think we have exhausted that era and we've moved on, we've moved beyond on. There are many of us, it is in every state and in every region of the country.

One of the first things that I noticed that was a great disappointment to me at CCCC are panels that would presumably be celebrating diversity. You would see one scholar would be a prominent, one of the few prominent voices of African American rhetorical traditions, she would be there. Next to her you would have a scholar that would do Asian American rhetoric and Asian American rhetorical traditions, again one of a very small number of people, she would be there. The next presenter she would be presenting on disability, still a small circulation of scholars which is growing. And then the fourth member would be someone who is taken from literature and someone taken from another field and speak for and represent Latina and Latino rhetorical traditions. On the one hand that could be seen as a strength, but if we look at hiring practices and if we look carefully at the pipeline that actually speaks to a significant systemic problem and that is that the under-representations of Latinos and under-representations of Latina scholars in particular, women of Mexican American descent, women of Puerto Rican descent, there are very few women even today, right now in 2016. If we were to count the number of scholars in Rhetoric and Composition who are Latina, who have tenure, we are talking about people, I would probably count them on one hand right now, we are talking about a very few. I observed this at the very beginning, that if you are looking for a Latino or Latina that does scholarship in rhetoric and composition who is publishing for other scholars in Rhetoric and Composition on Latina and Latino Rhetoric and Latina and Latino Composition Practices then the CCCC is not the place to go. It is not the place for you. What I noticed I could only describe as absence, erasure, and no significant or sustained attempt to fix that situation, to tend to that, and to promote change.

The Caucus has been well aware of that sense of dread, those moments of hopelessness. I think it was important for us to be able to go even when we were in smaller number, to attend the Latino Caucus and to be able to share those moments with each other. As well as planning ahead, planning for the future, and thinking not simply what is the next step, but thinking two to three steps out how do we want to see ourselves begin making change and affecting everlasting change in the field, in the discipline.

It is very interesting about my own relationship with the C's, because some of my work as you know does touch on questions of Rhetorical history and historiography, although I really would not describe my work as necessarily rhetorical historiography, although it certainly touches on that and certainly speak into the Euro-Centric limit of what passes itself off as history of rhetoric in our field. I do not see that the field has been all that responsive. For example, in *Mestizo Scripts Digital Migrations in the Territories of Writing*, I am attempting to retell the story of Rhetoric and Writing as technologies that emerge not in Athens, because archeologists and historians will confirm that is not where writing begins. I was telling the story of Rhetoric and Writing as they emerged in the Valley of Mexico, which is not something you can do really in the expansiveness of a single book, but there was an ambitious attempt to engage in this sort of hermeneutic reconstruction with direct implications for the studying and teaching and the practicing of writing today. The reception at the CCCC was actually fairly cold, oddly enough. I have been embraced by NCTE. I will be the first to acknowledge I don't have training in English education, I don't try to pass myself off as something I am not, but, they have been overwhelmingly supportive and in the Latino Caucus, of course, through NCTE has been a huge resource of support. Also, NCTE's Cultivating New Voices (CNV) for scholars of color mentorship program has been incredibly helpful to me. I was part of the cohort of 2004 to 2006. Being able to work with other scholars in the field, I was the only one of my cohort, this would be significant to this conversation, that was a graduate student at the time. I was the only graduate student in Rhetoric and Composition. All of my colleagues in my cohort were coming from the school of education or were focusing on English education and that is important I think to note. Being involved in NCTE CNV scholars of color has been helpful.

I think one of the most significant developments that comes to mind would have been under Cristina Kirklighter and this was when NCTE lost Dr. Sandra Gibbs. This could have been 2006 or 2007 or right around that period of time. There was no transparency. We did not know what was happening nor were we able to really get much information, but we wanted to make sure that we communicated to the Executive Committee that we were concerned. Cristina Kirklighter and I drafted a letter to the Executive Committee encouraging them, strongly encouraging them, to reconsider their decision to release, to let her go, after around 20 years of service to the organization. I don't know the name of the letter I will have to check with Cristina Kirklighter, but we should be able to track that down.

Sandra Gibbs had worked with NCTE, I believe, for about 20 years. She was, in network theory, what we would describe as a hub. She was the connector between the Latino Caucus, the Black Caucus, and the Asian American Caucus. She was the connector across caucuses of color and caucuses of difference. She was someone that we relied on heavily. She would come and we would see her doing caucus meetings at CCCC. She'd share with us very brief necessary information about proposals that the Black Caucus was considering, for example, and which we could consider supporting. This was prior to Executive meetings. It was good for us to know ahead of time what our fellow peers and colleagues and good friends in our other Caucuses are interested in supporting so we would have the opportunity to lend our support, to explore possibilities of displaying solidarity. It was a very important position. When she was let go, I believe she was up for retirement in a couple of years, a year or two, and, so, she was let go prior to retirement. We do not have the whole story, but we were concerned and we wanted to make sure that the Executive Committee understood our concerns. There was no attempt to replace Sandra Gibbs. There was no replacement. We were at a great loss.

I drafted the letter with Cristina Kirklighter and we mobilized the Latino community and many letters were sent. We wrote one and co-wrote one of them. I know the Black Caucus also was sending letters to the Executive Committee at that time. We wanted to communicate to the Executive Committee the importance of Sandra Gibbs. We wanted to make sure this was made visible to them, that they understood the key role Sandra Gibbs played in bringing in issues of diversity to the table to be taken very seriously. Other caucuses likewise were interested in questions of race, writing, rhetoric, diversity, multilingualism and questions of representations on Executive Committees, questions of representations on editorial boards. The conversations we are still having today. Sandra Gibbs was the connector. We were able to communicate through her between caucuses. We wanted to make sure that the Executive Committee knew the value and the importance of her work. We felt the way in which she was fired from her job was a problem. Again, we do not know why, but this was someone who was incredibly important to us and we were not hearing from NCTE and the CCCC that they were aware, that was not clear. There were other caucuses in participation, so we could describe it as a cross-caucus initiative. I do not have the hard numbers. But, it was a moment that stands out in my mind that was a cross-caucus initiative.

One of the things I will add is this past April 2016 in Houston at the CCCC, there was the after-Caucus mixer. This is something I do not know who is responsible for making that happen, but I do know there has been a push to make this happen for several years. I have been calling for it for almost a decade. It started with a question, Sandra Gibbs was still with us at the time, it started with a question, couldn't the meeting rooms be next to each other, be adjacent to each other, place them nearby. Don't segregate and put us into silo spaces far from each other at 6 pm and 7pm at night. The halls are empty and you are looking for some room several floors up. That is isolation. Do not do that. Instead take all the Caucuses, especially the Caucuses of Color, organize meeting rooms next to each other with the possibility of making some sort of connection after those meetings. In my mind that was actually a very minimal request. We weren't asking for something else other than the reservation of room assignments. It was actually a fairly modest request, but it took years of asking.

I remember several years ago there was a proposal that went up, I am not going to remember the name, offering financial assistance to teachers and professors and instructors who were employed at tribal colleges providing financial travel support to the C's for Tribal College employees. That initiative came up, it was proposed by Scott Lyons, one of the few indigenous scholars of Rhetoric and Composition and that went through, I believe it was unanimous. There was cross-caucus support to ensure we are supporting those teachers and instructors who are dedicated at teaching tribal colleges. There are virtually no representations in our academic journals or conferences that would account for the pedagogies, the research, the life experiences of educators at our tribal colleges. Scott Lyons is the one who spearheaded that and there was a pronounced support from members of the Latino Caucus for that.

I think there is an understandable situation where the Caucuses can become siloed and segregated and there is some space where we need to meet in our own groups to discuss the immediate pressing of needs of our own communities. We need to have that space. At the same time, there are shared concerns, they might not be identical, so I am not interested in flattening difference, but I think there are connections across differences and there are shared concerns that we can collaborate on, that we can work together on. My perception that there has been a bit of siloing and unfortunate segregation between the Caucuses of Color. I'd like to see that changed. I do think that the Latino Caucus is in a great position. There is an advantage we have, precisely because we have a very fluid identity, a fluid Caucus identity, and even the mission statement that we have had throughout the years, going back to Ceci Milanés, the mission statement was actually never really targeting Latino and Latina scholars. The mission statement, the original mission statement under Ceci, targeted scholars who were committed to matters of Latina and Latino composition and committed to Latina and Latino contributions to rhetoric and rhetorical theory regardless of one background. It has always been rather inclusive and I'd like to see it continue to move forward in working with other caucuses in that inclusive spirit.

I think there is a great deal of ambiguity when I think about how the CCCC or NCTE has been responsive to Latino and Latina scholars and educators. I see that it has largely not been. I think that one year that stands out that we can find a clear exception to that is the year of the CCCC under Adam Banks. We can flip through the program schedule and there is a very clear effort to make sure that some of the most prominent voices in the Latino Caucus are featured not just in the program in concurrent sessions, but they are speaking as featured speakers. Featured speakers and in keynote events, that is incredibly important. We actually did see a kind of diversity at that point that had been unprecedented. It is not unprecedented outside. There is an incredible amount of diversity in our schools, in our neighborhoods, but stepping into the CCCC that is where you see an erasure. Under Adam Banks we do see a significant shift. Whether or not we have been able to mirror that in the two years past of the CCCC, I am uncertain. I think we still have a ways to go. I'd like to make sure that the C's is moving in that direction.

When we talk about what the organization has done or has not done, keep in mind that we are talking about an organization that has had only one Latino male as program chair, Victor Villanueva, and that was before my time, it might have been as early as 1999, when Victor Villanueva was serving as program chair. There has been no Latina ever in the entire history of the organization and no Latina or Latino before or since Victor. It is very easy to point to a kind of tokenizing that we see in the field. It is time for the field to shed that tokenism and begin to move forward.

The Caucus has a great history of inclusivity and alliance building and solidarity. I'd like to make sure that it continues to do that, alliance building across Latina and Latino subjectivities and experiences. For me, writing *Mestizo Scripts* was coming from a very specific Northern New Mexico perspectives and that one book simply could not account for all of the subjectivities and the histories and memories and rhetorical practices of Latina and Latino populations. No single book can do that. That is beyond the bounds of possibilities. But, it is one contribution to the question of if there is such a thing as Latina and Latino rhetoric that could not be fully articulated and accounted for and explained by Greco-Roman concepts, re-imagined through the lens of Enlightenment thinkers such as Hegel. If there is such a thing, which of course we know to be true, but if academics were to recognize that, as such, that argument would not be made in a single book. It would be made in a multitude of dissertations and books across generations and across time. So, one book is not enough. The very few other book-length works that have contributed to our understanding of Latino and Indigenous rhetorical traditions, I could probably count all of the books on one hand coming from Rhetoric and Composition. It is important for us to be thinking of alliance building across subjectivities. Even the idea of Mexican subjectivity. We are talking about a wide canvas of life experiences. I think there is a way of continuing to foster alliance building across our cultural differences, across our experiences, and then moving that and continue to move beyond to look at Afro Latino and looking at African American Black solidarity movements. I think the time is ripe for this kind of crosstalk that we need to continue moving forward.

Mestizo Scripts is a highly controversial book and people hate it. That is simply where we are at. Maybe there are other ways I could have written it to make it more accessible. I could have asked, please accommodate our difference. There could have been many more gentle and diluted calls for change that could have made it accessible, made it less demanding on the reader, I guess. But, there are so few books one could turn to if they wanted to know the story of writing as it emerges in Egypt, well there are books that you need to turn to like archaeology. Or, what about the great painted book traditions of the Valley of Mexico, well you are not going to turn to Rhetoric and Composition for that. You would turn to art history, that will give you that. What if you wanted to know the development of Sanskrit coming out of the Indus Valley several generations ago in what is now the border of Pakistan and India. You are not going to find that in Rhetoric and Composition. They are not interested in that. But at the same time, they are claiming to be interested in that, because the field wants to say that Rhetoric and Composition, and the future of writing, must be multi-modal and must be multilingual, but it is precisely multi-modal and multilingual contributions to the field of writing that the field has systematically erased out of our histories, which is why we go to Greece. I would characterize both NCTE and CCCC as primarily unresponsive.

I do not know about the vision of what the field thinks of when they think of Mexican American. They certainly do not think of me. I am aware that I am not going to be a stereotypical representation while simultaneously understanding that it is precisely the light skinned, those of us in the Mexican American community and in the Latino community that are light skinned, that will have it better off in higher education and easier than our dark-skinned brothers and sisters. But the vision of Mexican American in both the C's and NCTE seems to be someone who has arrived recently, who is in desperately need of linguistic salvation that can only come from the National Council of Teachers of English. The literacy salvation narrative, the linguistic salvation narrative, it is still that progress narrative, which is very much still part of the humanities and social sciences, it is embedded there. And, Ralph Cintron in the last *Octalog*, in the *III Octalog*, addressed this barely and he is absolutely right. We need to continue to rethink this progress narrative. They are positioning Mexican Americans as someone who has arrived recently and Mexican American also seems to be associated with manual labor not with the flowery arts of written communication. It is associated with manual labor, with custodians, food services, and being caught in cycles of low literacy. That model is still the dominant one in the field. I think the salvation and progress narrative has to do with attainment of standardized American English, that is part of it. We could go beyond it. We have those who have followed in the tradition of Freire and there is a liberatory pedagogy that goes only so far. It is liberatory pedagogy as being able to mirror the political sentiments of one's professor - and others have made that argument far better than I am right now—I think there is a fairly reductive and damaging view of the progress narrative. It is literacy as the cure all. Literacy is standardized American English, alphabetic literacy, literacy will lead the people into civilization. That was the earlier argument. It will lead people into salvation, also an earlier argument. That the rhetoric of modernity is still very much caught in that, the vocabulary words can shift, your diction can shift, you can change it at the sentence level, but the theoretical grounding is still there and still present.

I think we are better as a Caucus, we are in a better position now to respond to the narrative of salvation. I am thinking about Iris Ruiz and some of her work, *Reclaiming Composition for Chicanos/as and other Ethnic Minorities* and the co-edited collection she did with Raúl Sánchez, *Decolonizing Rhetoric and Composition Studies: New Latinx Keywords for Theory and Pedagogy*, published with Palgrave MacMillan. I think when we take that scholarship into account, we are actually in a far better place to offer a counter strike in response, a much healthier response to those very easy and, you know, paternalizing salvation narratives. I do not see us as being doomed to necessarily complicit in that language. I suspect that the scholars who have come before us had fewer options available to them than we do now.

I would say the story of the Latino Caucus is one of inclusivity and solidarity building. That is its strength. That we are inclusive of a wide range of differences within the Latino and Latino canvas. That we are not threatened by the differences. That we actually see that as a strength and that even the marker, this identity marker of Latina and Latino and Latinx, that multiplicity and the difference is not something to be erased under those mantels. Instead those markers can be used as connectors across great difference.

Doesn't publication itself suggest sort of an editing out of difference? I am thinking about just very, very simple things working with my own publications with *Mestizo Scripts* and following that up with *Rhetoric of the Americas*, it is a fairly conventional practice that any word or phrase or expression that is not in English will appear in your book italicized. We can go back. Ghere has been a debate about Gloria Anzaldua's *Borderlands/La Frontera* because, of course, as she engaged in her multilingual-codeswitching and code entanglements and those linguistic innovations blurring those borders, that if you are taking something that is not English and italicizing it you are actually emphasizing difference. You are not bridging across difference. You are making the difference more evident and apparent to the reader. This is standard publication strategy. I faced it with my own two books and it was not a battle I was willing to fight. I fought other battles. There is some degree of complicity in some of our publications and maybe in the future we might be able to collectively work toward changing and making significant changes.

I think the most important thing for us to be thinking about now is how we can continue the fight for inclusivity and solidarity building. There is too much at stake for us to squabble or to fight unnecessary fights with each other. There is a time to engage in horizontal critique I guess you could say. But, we are also thinking collectively about the vertical, we are critiquing up and not across. We are at a point where I think we can continue our focus on critiquing up while working together in inclusivity and solidarity-building and that can look like different things. Sometimes, I think, I might be thinking of something very simple like how we engage each other on the Latino Caucus listserv, how we are communicating with each other on the listserv. Email, I think, is not actually a great tool for solidarity building. That is a terribly unpopular thing to say because we want to think about the creation of community in digital environments. But, I am arguing, that if we are looking at email that is actually not that helpful. I am thinking specifically about academics and how they use email. It has not been that healthy. I think maybe we need to pause when we are thinking about how we are using it as a tool. Which is more important to be right all the time and argumentative or to exist in coalition with others?

EXPERIENCES: IN THEIR OWN WORDS
Steven Alvarez

Based on Interview by Romeo García
August 15, 2016

My name is Steven Alvarez. I am originally from Safford, Arizona, a small town in Southeast Arizona. I'm now an Assistant Professor in Writing and Rhetoric Digital Studies at St. John's University, though my first job was at the University of Kentucky. My research focuses mostly on language and literacy practices of Mexican immigrants, more specifically branching into homework practices, bilingual practices, and, now, starting to go into more food and tacos

I've been with the caucus, I guess, since about 2012. When I attended my first attended C's, I had this job already accepted at Kentucky in the same year I was *Scholar for the Dream*, presenting for the first time at C's. It is little of a weird situation. [CCCC] was new to me, I couldn't even articulate what it was, what the structure of the organization was, what this meant for my career, and how important both the publications are and building a network. It was new to me. I guess what I noticed was that I was coming in as an outsider and also that being Latino may or may not have contributed to that. I did notice it was pretty white organization. That goes without saying. That was something I was already use to coming out of an English program.

I don't know why I felt like an outsider. In the beginning, I could not really say it was even, if anything, about whiteness, but more about just learning how the organization was functioning really, just as I was going through it pretty suddenly. What I was looking for was people who, more or less, had maybe gone through some of these hoops before.

As soon as I went to my first C's, I found the Caucus. I found people who were supportive and were really just able to give me some guidance I really did not have in graduate school. That was the first one for C's, but ever since C's I've been involved in different capacities. With NCTE beginning, I believe, in 2014. That is when I started to speaking to older people in the organization, but specifically to older folks in the Caucus that had reached out to me.

I think it was on the program. You get the book and I was going through the book and it was some of the pre-conference. I think it was a pre-conference in the afternoon. I saw a Latino workshop and I just signed up for it. It is funny because I guess I saw Latino and I was like, "Alright let's check it out." I was like, "I didn't see too many others, so this must be where they hang out. "That is where I met folks such as Aja Martinez for the very first time. Cristina Kirklighter was running it at that time.

Typically, this was something I would have ordinarily done anyway. Seek out groups for Latinos. I think maybe it was something I didn't think about exploring as a professional or even what it meant to be or have a community. But I did see there was an identity that intersects with some of my own interests and also even my research, so I thought, let's go, maybe trying to work with people. It turned out to be that it was really a lot more mixture of junior faculty and other students, plenty cool. But I think probably not knowing anybody and seeing that I saw "Latino" in the workshop title, I thought this could be a welcoming space.

I had never experienced [a workshop at CCCCs] before. It was all very new. Come to find out through people who were on it, it was basically the same routine that was happening over and over every year. That it was sort of just a small informal roundtable, sort of informally people making complaints about the job market, maybe about different encounters of racism, on the programs, and different things like that. Stuff that was just new to me. For me, it was interesting because I had never really been around Latinos and Latinas in graduate school, at least not in English studies, so that was cool. People who were also serious about teaching. That was pretty fun. I think as I learn more about the program and the Caucus, I could see with different eyes, but the first time it was pretty cool to see so many people.

[For instance, I noticed] Isabel Baca was presenting on community service learning kind of research, bilingual communities, working where she was located. Then also Octavio was pretty cool. I remember Cristina Kirklighter was showing a book she was editing and spoke about how the Caucus came together for the project. And, then we went over the history, I did not know a lot, so it was all very new. Then meeting people who just got jobs and we were talking about the market. I gave my experience with that. I remember at the same time, Aja had just got a job, so she was able to talk about her going on the market and I had very similar experiences. It was pretty cool, because it was informal, but also it was giving us a professionalization. It gave me some sense that this was an important space. People who know each other. How that worked in my research I think I was already coming in doing stuff with community, so I saw that this was building community in a different kind of way. I could see that my research could be valued.

I guess in some ways it got me to think about who is reading my scholarship, especially, I think as we are collecting our own citations of each other. It got me think about we are not being heard even in terms of conference proposals. A lot of the sort of checks in play. To really keep the organization on its toes, to really have an organized voice of dissent, along with the Black Caucus, it kind of puts our issues that affect us into context and to have our voices be represented in the leadership capacities. On the one hand, I think that is more about the administration of organization and how that ties our scholarship is really the channels. Once you get inside the organization, it does not even matter if you are not a great scholar, being part of the organization opens up channels to be heard more and to have an active voice in the ways things are run. I think somebody I admire that has come through the Caucus is Juan Guerra and what he has done, giving back to some of the younger scholars especially through NCTE. His research has dealt with teaching and giving back to younger members as a mentor. I think if anything, it is looking at some of those folks who have been able to bridge those research interests and some of their activism has been pretty inspiring.

I have grown to see a lot more that the [the caucus has also] been a publication network and also publication assistance from older folks who have gone through some of these hoops with newer folks coming at grad school, graduate students. It has always been there. Somebody, for example, like Jaime Mejia has given me a lot of help and a lot of feedback and a lot of introductions to publishers. It has been very helpful to have colleagues who are not obliged to share the information, but who really want to share the information to help us to succeed. That also happens, I think, with even graduate students who are further along the line with graduate students. It seems very helpful in the sense that people are willing to share some of that knowledge. Unfortunately, I really never had this in my program. I wish I would have been part of the Caucus earlier because it would have helped me a lot going into being a professor, but as a young professor it was definitely very helpful. That is where I got to meet a lot of colleagues across the country who were also able to speak about similar things that they experience as junior faculty.

I would like to think that with the Caucus, we push back on what could easily be conversations that get pushed off as being overly politically correct or being too touchy about certain things. But I would say, for example, like at the last NCTE when the Black Caucus and the Latino Caucus teamed up to speak out about a few issues that were related, to see that kind of stuff happen is interesting, because it actually pushes back on the organization. I think there is a long way to go and I think, probably, if anything, we are seeing more people get elected to positions which is pretty cool. The fact is the organization is changing, but, if anything, it gives us a space to strategize as community and to support each other. I think, if anything, we are getting better at playing the game, especially as more members become part of the institution and learn how the game functions, how it has been excluding us for many years.

There are some issues where I get a sense of further intersections involving different caucuses, even to the point of meeting times and meeting times that conflict. And maybe some people have made the argument about the silos that don't communicate. We have to see really the caucuses having at least one collective that is part of a larger network. We have interests we share. There is also the shared interest of social justice across Caucuses regardless. If anything, it is important only because the issues that affect Latinos and Latinas are unique. Not only for our research, but also for who we are as members of the organization and the future of the organization. Coming back to students of the classrooms and the change of demographics of students in the country. Our voices and our research matter.

There is no doubt . . . that, especially during times, such as the political situation we are in now, the dehumanizing rhetoric of immigrants, the connection with charter schools, that [the Latino voice has been marginalized]. You get this flipped individual sense that failure is your own fault and success is your own fault as well. Looking away from some of the social contextual issues that affect students and create inequality, I think this happens at all levels, especially for many of us who are Ph.D. students who become professors. The odds have been highly stacked. It is not that any of us are supremely special, we just have different opportunities. But, also remember, we need to give back and be aware of the communities around us. We make an impact both as teachers but also as just voices to speak about some of these inequalities which other people do not always experience.

I can give the example of Jaime Mejia and even Cristina Kirklighter [as examples of strong caucus leadership]. Cristina especially, because she was chair of the Caucus when I first started. Her and Renee Moreno. But someone I got to know better was Juan Guerra, partly because of CNV, Cultivating New Voices, which several other members of our Caucus have gone through the pairing up an advanced graduate student or junior faculty with a seasoned mentor. Juan was in charge of this and many of the people who have passed through this program have gone into administrative positions in the organization. It really has been an important program, huge, in terms of diversifying the organization. I saw that happening in NCTE. For CCCCs, I started seeing more a turn towards community when we started doing our workshops. What I really started to see was people coming together and accessing and researching the history who were just incredible about doing things like newsletters. Just doing a lot of work to keep people connected. So, it was really cool especially when I started doing a little bit of the history. The different people who really stepped up. When I first came into it, the people who reached out to me were Jaime, Cristina, and Juan. But it could have been a different time or any number of people who would have been there.

[Recently, I served as co-chair.] Basically, my understanding was that Cristina was going to step away and there was not time for an election. I was provided the opportunity to be the interim co-chair. I said okay. We want to make sure, I said, we have an election in terms of an organization choosing who would do this. At the same time, I think Renee passed leadership on as well. I am not sure at that time who it was. I am not sure if it was Tracey or Sandra or together. I think it might have been Tracey first, then Sandra, and then they became co-chair. For a little while, I hung around Sandra and Tracey and we would have these conversations on the vision of the organization. But I stepped aside because the bad spirit of tenure and writing a book. And Raul was interested, so actually at that time I was just putting it up in the air for anyone who wanted to take on the position. Since it was already a co-chair on one side, we did co-chair on the other. So, we did a general election. I guess I did my job as an interim. I do regret that as Cristina was moving on, there were no folks who were senior scholars who wanted to step up and take the position. There were several of us as junior scholars who were a few years in. Aja specifically said we can do it together. I said, I could learn, but really no one decided to step up and take the leadership, someone with tenure basically. I said I would take it on, but it was more like until someone who knows what is going on will take it on. At that time, I think Tracey and Sandra had interesting things going on with re-writing some of the guidelines.

The story would have, like any other story, its ups and downs. I do not want to say the hero is a villain. Everyone's a hero. It has different personalities. And like any organization, there have been clashes and outlooks or ideologies, especially from people who study argumentation, lots of debates. But, I think it's all for the best. It keeps the organization going forward. We are starting to see more collaboration between NCTE and CCCCs, which is important because, I think, we will be only one of the caucuses, beside the Black Caucus, that has that kind of collaboration. This is important because that will connect us further with K to 12. It is a cool moment especially with so many people who are coming up as Ph.D. students that are finding jobs and becoming part of the organization. It seems really exciting. For a long time, it was always Victor Villanueva, now there are more voices and people being recognized. Not even Latino and Latina scholars, major voices in the field.

It is important for others to know who we are. If they remember us at all, that is perfect. If anything, they can remember that this was a group of scholars who organized themselves who had a vision, a shared vision, to give back to each other. So much of this work can be isolated and there can be a lot of back fighting and competition even amongst really good friends. The Caucus has been cool because it breaks down those smoke screens. We do not always see that competition, but more importantly, it helps us see opportunities to help each other. People publishing together, doing books, collaborations, research, writing. I mean, we are seeing more of that happen. I think the way we are using social media is a lot more savvy than other caucus groups. It is cool to see where we are going.

I really didn't know a lot of the history until the interim position where I worked with Tracey and Sandra, when we were trying to find the newsletters. So, we found all the letters from the 60s and it was "wow." There were like recipes, poems, various accomplishments, people's birthdays. It was pretty cool. She had done this basically once a month or every couple of months. It was mass mail, folded. But just the amount of time, she took to do this, it was important to keep people together. Tracey and Sandra archived a lot of them and saved them as PDF's. Seeing them was cool because it showed me from the very beginning, it was a smaller group of people with the same interest. For me, especially, we have our different get-togethers and we see how the rooms are getting bigger and bigger. It is cool to see the community grow. It is even more important to start thinking of the kind of diversity of

Latino and Latinx we need to learn amongst ourselves. A lot of more cool debates about what the identity means and, especially moving into the future, the direction we want to see the organization move.

[It] was always about community. I remember Kirklighter talking about buena gente, it was always about people, good people. I think for me it was always a sense that it was up to the collective to make it what it was or what it is. I didn't know a lot about the history, but, of course, at different times, there have been different leaders that have come and gone. The organization changes with leadership as well. As far as I know it has always been about a group of people who are basically are all volunteers.

EXPERIENCES: IN THEIR OWN WORDS
Cristina Ramírez

Based on Interview by Anita Hernández
August 3, 2016
http://youtu.be/FuXszgSaZcU

This turns out to be my 22nd year teaching. I started teaching in the middle schools and high schools in El Paso. Twelve years into my career, I went into the Rhetoric and Composition at UTEP. My research interest as a graduate student had been into the feminist historical recovery of Mexican women journalist and activists. In recovery work, feminist historiography. I remember having a phone conversation with Victor. He had suggested that he be on my dissertation committee. He ended up not being in my dissertation committee because it was overwhelming to have 4 people on my committee as a graduate student, but I felt his support from afar. A dissertation chair told me that if Victor was in my committee, later in my career, he could not serve as a letter writer for promotion in tenure. Then I moved to Tucson and I was just going up for tenure. I started in August 2011.

I just authored, *Occupying Our Space: The Meztiza Rhetoric of Mexican Women Journalists and Activist*s published by the University of Arizona Press. Jacqueline John Royster wrote my forward. I was very deliberate about choosing these women because it showed a coalition, a representation from an African-American, and Andrea Lunsford, who represents the roots of feminist recovery work, and Cristina Kirklighter, a major player, advocate, and leader in the Latino Caucus for a long time. It was book- ended very nicely. I was very strategic because I wanted a coalition coalescing with the scholarship. I did not want this to be only for Latino (a) voices. I could have asked Victor Villanueva to write my forward, but I wanted an African-American scholar to do that. Jacqueline and Andrea are in the coalition of Feminist Scholars. I am active in the coalition and in the Latino caucus.

I didn't get involved with the C's and NCTE [or the Latino Caucus] until I started with my graduate work. As a public-school teacher, I did not know that much about the C's or NCTE, but as a graduate student I was introduced to this conference. As a doctoral student, the first time I attended the C's conference was in San Francisco. As I looked through the conference program as a newcomer, you go through every single page. I saw that there was a Latino Caucus. I missed dinner with my friends that got upset with me. I don't know what it is about, but I am going to find out. The main people I remember that time are Victor, Cristina Kirklighter, Octavio. I remember. Cecilia and Alejandra Hidalgo were there. Those were the main people I remember attending the first caucus. This goes back to 2007 or 2008, almost 9 years now. Ever since then, I have been a member because I knew it was home for me. Attending Cs and being welcomed in the Latino Caucus was formidable me as a scholar knowing that my research and my voice had a place.

They were encouraging us to find our voices as Latinos and Latinas; these research projects focused on the pedagogy of Latinos and Latinas, and the recovery of these voices. We need to get our voices up there. I knew that my project will take off and I had a support base for my project. [Also, my university, University Texas - El Paso] did not in the least question my project in recovering the voices of "mujeres Mejicanas." They saw the gap between the historically Anglo voice and the emerging African-American discipline. They felt that my research was going to feel that gap. I knew it was important and necessary. I remember Victor told us to publish, and, since then, there has been a proliferation of publications from the Latino (a) community in the C's and NCTE. [For instance,] Octavio co-edited a book that received an outstanding award as well as my book, *Occupying Our Space: The Meztiza Rhetoric of Mexican Women Journalists and Activists*, that won the Feminist Coalition Outstanding Book Award. We are starting to see our work being recognized. Victor won a prize many years ago, but we are starting to see our work being recognized.

[The caucus also responded to issues with CCCC's, issues of representation.] Raúl Sánchez, Octavio Pimentel, Victor Villanueva, Cristina Kirklighter, and Iris Ruiz responded by taking these concerns to the board meetings the next day. Issues with representation within the caucus have remained. (Ruiz is now one of the co-directors). One of the ways they have shifted dealing with these issues is by getting people on ballot and review boards for the conference. Jaime Mejia and Octavio Pimentel have been long-time reviewers. But we have been getting more people on the ballot. Also, in the conference at San Antonio, people commented (disparaging comments) about what they heard. They were being reported at the Latino Caucus meeting. It was taken up by the leaders, like Victor and Cristina. I have not been involved personally, but I know these issues have been always taken up at the board meetings. A combination of those complaints came at the conference in Tampa, where Adam Banks was the organizer; in that conference we felt we were seen. It was the tweeting, the positioning of our presentations at certain times. We felt we were heard. For the first time he had ribbons made for the Latino caucus.

The story I [would tell] about the caucus is that of an emerging voice of traditionally marginalized voices within a very traditional Anglo organization. The voices have been heard and their histories count by persistent activism, research, and outreach. The way I want them to remember is that the Latino Caucus is a "familia" and you can call on them for help. They have been advocates. When something cool happens, they blast something on the Latino Caucus page. It is nice!

EXPERIENCES: IN THEIR OWN WORDS
Aja Martinez

Based on Interview by Anita Hernández
July 21, 2016
https://www.youtube.com/watch?v=c3DtTvkPgnU

I am originally from Arizona. I went to the University of Arizona where I got my degree in Rhetoric and Composition. I had my first job after the Ph.D. at Binghamton University. It is one of the SUNY universities in upstate New York. I have just recently been hired by Syracuse University's newly titled Department of Writing Studies, Rhetoric, and Composition. We have a graduate program in Composition and Cultural Rhetoric. I am excited to get started. I have gone to both [NCTE and CCCC], primarily CCCC because of my teaching and research in college spaces. My first time at NCTE was to promote an edited collection I did with Vershawn Young. The second time I went, I was elected to the Nominating Committee, so I went to complete my service and also to participate in the Cultural Celebration that the Latino Caucus and Black Caucus put on.

    I remember my first year in graduate school, my first year in Rhetoric and Composition, I was coming out of with an undergraduate degree in Anthropology and I was accepted into the Ph.D. at Arizona, into a new program at Arizona called Rhetoric and the Teaching of English. I remember during the spring semester, it was like a ghost town, everyone disappeared for a weekend in March or April. Classes were cancelled. I didn't know what happened. No one had clued me on the fact that CCCC was that weekend and everyone left. I didn't know what CCCCs was. That was the year it was in New York City. When everyone came back that was part of my miseducation, part of my lack of knowing how to navigate professional conferences that I was supposed to be participating in. The following Fall, I was encouraged to submit to CCCC because it was made clear to me that is what we do.

We are participants in this conference. Everyone should be submitting and attending. I did get accepted. I was also encouraged to apply to the *Scholars for the Dream*. I did that as well. I was awarded the *Scholars for the Dream*, which made it a big possibility for me to attend that following spring in New Orleans. That was in 2008. That was the year that I met some prominent elders in the Latino Caucus, like Jaime Mejia, in particular, and everyone who was associated with him at Texas State, San Marcos. Because of the *Scholars for the Dream*, I was there at the reception. I was able to meet other people from the other caucuses and that became my home and community in the overall organization.

That year was my second year in grad school. I was already feeling a bit of displacement in my own program at Arizona. When I got to CCCCs that year, in panels but also in the Caucus meeting I attended, I started hearing people voicing similar issues at the graduate and professional level. So, I realized "I am not alone." [I heard from] people who have been through various stages. Some people were beginning in their graduate programs, other were early career or later career, like Dr. Villanueva. That was comforting. . . . that happened [was that] in all the *Scholars for the Dream*, fanfare happening, the opening session, and having special designated session that the *Scholars for the Dream* present at and having the reception, none of the faculty from Arizona attended any of it. They ignored the whole thing. I remember feeling very hurt, personally hurt - whether it was personal on their part or not. It was Jaime Mejia and Octavio Pimentel who attended my panel, that then took me into their arms. They said "We are excited for you. Congratulations! Come be with us." They noticed I was at this reception and I was by myself. I didn't know anyone. I didn't have faculty attending to be excited for me. They noticed I was there by myself at the reception. They were that for me. They were the ones that, after the reception, said our meetings happen on Friday, come do this thing. I would have not known otherwise. That was a big part of how I became involved, I was getting drawn in by people who were already members.

One that is closest to my heart that happened right in the middle of my graduate education was the ban on ethnic schools in Arizona. Mostly it was close to my heart because it was one of the schools banned, that was teaching it, the teachers were in the high school I attended. I noticed that it was one of the issues that was paid attention to in Atlanta. It was a national issue that there was space made for one of the educators, Carlos Acosta, to come and relate the issues legislatively to the entire Caucus. Our leadership at the time, Cristina and Renee, took that to the CCCCs board and up to the NCTE level. Since then, that started the ball rolling for part of what happened this past year, our resolution and our statement on Ethnic Studies that we did in cooperation with other caucuses. I feel like that is something I have seen the Caucus take serious leadership on and talk to the upper levels, that our organization as a whole is speaking on a national level about something like Ethnic Studies resolution of 2015 (NCTE, 2015c http://www2.ncte.org/statement/ethnic-studies-k12-curr/).

I think access to the [national] organization has always been a big concern. [It means] . . . representation on the program and in the awards, in the many different avenues that happen both through conference recognition to access to elected roles and leadership positions. Our leadership has continued to work on that issue. What I take on in my own work, now as a more advanced person in the Caucus because I was a participant for a few years, is to tap the social media angle of representation, making sure that the media programs are announcing not just who are members are, what we are doing, our accomplishments, our publications, but things that may be small passing exams, small things like that. What we are doing? I have tried to be the person who continues the representation. Something that is important to me, because of the way I joined the Caucus, is to make our CCCC Chairs aware of who are the new Latinos attending CCCC. Making sure that there is an email that says we exist, "Come be with us on Friday and the other events we are having." There have been more Latinos, like me, who are coming up that is creating a critical mass, so the recruitment has been a major concern for the Caucus.

All you have to look at is the group picture every year it is taken. The first year I attended it was in a pretty big ballroom, but a small circle of gente. In the past few years, we had slightly smaller rooms, but less space because the large number of people. We can't do a circle because there are too many people. It is a great story about a testament to that growth. But two years ago, in Indianapolis, I went to request the Latinx ribbon tags. It was the first year we had the tags for Latino Caucus badges. Adams Banks was in charge and he was thinking about these things. He thinks about things like that. Once again, representation. We like to show that we exist. We are walking around and, for other Latinos who would see the blue badge, [would] see we exist. I went to request a stack of them, so I could go to the next meeting and distribute them to anyone who didn't have one. The woman at the registration counter for CCCC, when I asked her for forty for that year, which was an underestimate at that, said "Oh are there that many of you?" It was rude and it was racist. "Yes, there are and there are more. We didn't have enough ribbons."

[It] seems small. It is in terms of representation. "We exist." "We are part of this in an important way." The first year was the year Adam Banks was involved in the leadership of running CCCC. That was Indianapolis in 2013. That was the first moment that I saw that it was available to us. The year after that it, this year in Houston, they ran out of the Latinx Caucus ribbons that are taped to our badges by 8am Thursday morning. It was really bad. The conference had just started. People brought the issue up. I brought up the issue with senior members, like Keith Gilyard, and that this was important to us. I did not know what to say to the Chair. The entire conference. What the difference has been between Adam Banks and other chairs is that he thinks about representation. He honors that he thinks about it before we have to complain. We didn't know we could have something like that. Now that we expect it, it has to be something that we insist on. Adam set a precedent. He did that. It is something that seems small, but it is big at the end of the day. To run out on the first day made me think that none had been ordered. We were using the ones from the past conference.

My earliest memories are the transfer of leadership from Ceci to Renee and Cristina. That was cool to me to see women being the leaders of the Caucus. That made me feel like that this is a good organization I am joining. I remember just hearing about *Rainbow Strand*. To know what that means, how that has developed has been an interesting story to me. I remember also meeting some of the people who became my mentors to me, like Jaime Mejia and Victor Villanueva, in particular, who have both been instrumental in my publishing career, applying for jobs, and the giving advice. Those are my earliest memories of having a space that has now become for me, especially for a year which I'm less enthusiastic about participating for different political reasons that have come up. That gives me something to come back to. It is like family reunion, an academic family reunion, and coming to see everyone and catch up. There are probably new members who are feeling the way that I got to CCCC for the first time and can really use someone like myself to bring them into the fold and be there for them.

I [also wonder about] how inclusive are our publications beyond the special issues, which comes up every year. The representation of our work in the publications is what I think drives the stage 1 reviewers, in particular, and what they are thinking is important in the field at that moment. If they are not seeing our work published by the organization, they may be putting our scholarship on the backburner that may germinate at the conference. This is what happens. It sparks at the conference and then it turns into publication of scholarship. So that is one thing. As a chair, Adam Banks brought that up in his chair's address and that makes people uncomfortable, by saying that it is true that beyond special editions or special issues that our work is too sparsely featured. Representation there, then, influences the reviewers to accept work.

The other thing, when the work is there, when it is accepted, I notice our works seem to be slotted at the same time. So, if people are interested in the work that is concerned with Latino issues, they have to choose and pick between two panels that are competing for audiences. Take some of the work that two of our members Sara and Steven Alvarez, a married couple, their panels are pretty consistently put in the same time slot. These are people who are related, they have to pick and choose. They can't go to each other's sessions. Their times slots have been unfortunate. That has been unfortunate. I know Joyce Carter in her chair in Houston mentioned if you can think of an app I want to hear about it. Wouldn't it be cool if there was some sort of matrix or a technology or an app, that could space things out that is more conscious of the fact that there are few of us and we shouldn't be at the same time slot. There has to be some sort of mathematical way to do this. We have a chair calling for this kind of thing. Let's call back to her and say what can we do? Is there an app that can help us do something about this? I have been hearing about it since my first year at CCCCs and up to this year. This is something that hasn't improved.

[This topic also relates to mentorship.] The first home for my publishing was *College English* and it was special issue in *College English* that was edited by Damian Baca on Latino issues. Helpful. Because Victor became interested in my work early on, he took it upon himself to mentor me through a lot of the publications. I rarely submit anything without passing it by him first. My second major publication was through NCTE as a press with Vershawn Young. It was called *Code Meshing as World English,* our edited collection, an NCTE book. I think what I liked about publishing with NCTE, a book in this case, was I got to know the process early on. I was still a graduate student when I did this project with Vershawn. He as a mentor, part of the Black Caucus, at that moment, said to me, "Do you want to do this?" Not knowing what I was getting into, I said. "Alright, Let's do it." It was at Louisville. He had me approach Kurt Austin of NCTE. Propose the book to him and to see what happens. The rest is history. We have a book. I got to know the stages of being a co-editor of an edited collection. I learned that with NCTE as a press. Helpful. The mentorship has been helpful, particularly a project through the Black Caucus and the Latino Caucus. It was important. It was imperative because I wasn't getting that mentorship necessarily from my faculty at Arizona. To have people from these other Caucuses that I would not have met, had I not been involved in CCCC, that was something that made my career what it is, at this point.

There have been different conversations and efforts toward to strengthen the mentorship role. There has been a thread in the most recent listserv conversation about what our mentorship should look like, especially since our membership because we have grown so much. Some of it has been organic, people getting to know each other and who get along fine. Something more structured could definitely be needed at this time because of the sheer number of people who aren't going to pick up someone and put them under their wing. Especially when it comes to publishing because the other side of journals and the presses being more inclusive our work is that our work needs to be proposed. Walking through and teaching our members what those steps are, the navigation strategies, to put a proposal together, to get the work out there in good shape, that is the other side of the mentorship. Jaime Mejia has been instrumental to those of us he mentors to make sure it is in tip top shape. He tells us the truth about our work. It hurts. It is an important type of mentorship because he is going to tell us the things when ignorant or arrogant reviewers will tell us the same thing. Best if it comes from him to get those things in order then send it out. To have something structured in place would be great.

This is related to one of the other questions about who I have interacted with from the other caucuses. I have mentioned Adam Banks a few times because he is one of my mentors. Through having his mentorship, my name has become part of the names of people passing on when he was in leadership chair position. There are a few of us who he mentored in a writing group. I think getting the recognition of somebody who is going to pass your name along is where it starts. The networking is tantamount because then you participate in something and your name is out there. You are on a committee like deciding on the best dissertation, the other committee was the best article, the kind of things that are not elected positions, then you start working with people who you may not have interacted yet. They get to know your name and they put your name forward. I was on the ballot for the nominating committee. Now I am on the ballot for the Executive Committee. Which is great.

What is not so great is that I am in direct competition with another good friend, Cruz Medina, and the way they put it to us is if we weren't in direct competition, there would be no Latinos. That needs to be fixed. I don't have the answer. But also, the word is out that I like mentoring. I am interested in mentoring others, so now I am part of the Welcoming Committee and that is a new position and that is a two-year commitment. It boiled down to they became aware of me and passed my name along and through participating in other things. It is who you know.

It dials back to what I started with say, it's about giving; the aspect of giving *un abrazo* that you need when you are new and don't know anybody. You don't even know if it is even a field or if it is a good fit. You might be getting the message from your home organization, which I was getting, that you don't fit and you are someone that doesn't belong. So, to get to a conference and to see people who somewhat look like you and some that do not. It is about Latinidad and learning about the different directions people are coming from, whether it is culturally or the heritage or the type of work that you do. Feeling that there is a place for you especially in this huge conference of both NCTE and CCCC. There are going to be people there that will be supportive and look out for you, especially now with social media. You can keep in touch with them through the whole year. Let them know what you are up to. People can keep tabs on you. What I started to do was checking in on people. "Hey, how are you doing? Did you get a job this year? If not, I heard of this." Sending those sorts of messages. Keeping track of each other. That is the story to me about the Caucus—that there is a place, there is a home for people who feel displacement in so many aspects, in their career, and in this crazy country. There is a place for us in our work and people interested in our work. That is the other aspect of the Caucus, that we have not been exclusive to people who just identify as Latinos, but are inclusive of those who are doing work that benefit our youth and our students and us as professionals. There are people who have heart and work out there. People are not turned away becoming part of who we are from our group, who we are, just because they are not the right heritage or ethnic makeup.

EXPERIENCES: IN THEIR OWN WORDS
Tracey Flores

Based on Interview by Anita Hernández
October 15, 2016

I only attend NCTE. My first NCTE convention was in 2010 in Orlando . . . I was in Orlando and I attended the convention at the same time as the National Writing Project. I was invited by the National Writing Project to share work that I was doing with my second-grade students and their families in my school and in a bilingual writing workshop. That was the day before and NCTE was later. I was in Orlando for the very first time for the same convention. I was excited to be there. I remember as an undergraduate our professors did a lot with NCTE and I always said one day I would like to present my work and meet people. I never thought that I could be sharing it on the national level in that space. When I was there, I did not know anyone from my university. I saw Mary Carmen Cruz, earlier that year like in September and she was the Arizona English Teachers Associate. It was the local affiliate of NCTE. She was presenting with a teacher. I had seen her at the conference. She invited me to the Caucus meeting. I wasn't sure about attending the Caucus meeting. I had not planned on going to the Caucus meeting. The more I thought I about, I thought it would be good for me to attend the Caucus meeting. When I went there Mary Carmen Cruz was there. You were there. José Montelongo was there. Bobbi Houtchens was there. At the same time, they were doing the interviews of elders of the caucuses. I remember that Dr. Hill was there. Sandra from the Black Caucus was interviewing him. At that moment, I felt it was special space. The intergenerational project. It felt really good. I remember meeting Dr. Hill and him being around at the Caucus. It felt very special and very important. I was happy I had attended.

From my earliest memories, it was a lot of the leadership Bobbi Houtchens, Cristina Kirklighter, and Renee Moreno. Cristina was the more vocal voice of the Caucus. Also, Mary Carmen Cruz, even though she was not one of the co-chairs, but she had that historic memory. Her work throughout was important and as we move forward we need to call on this memory. Because when I came in 2010, there were conversations about concerns and there are still concerns. [For instance,] my earliest memories were always [that] we talked a lot about representation, historically the underrepresentation in the convention and the leadership roles and also at the national office level. As I continue to stay active and as one of the co-chairs, I continue to see those trends manifest as we have new leadership at the national office. For instances, we no longer have Dr. Mila Fuller, who we used to work with. As I stayed active, I interacted more with the Black Caucus and had conversations with the leadership. I am noticing the same trends. That is part of why Adam Banks resigned from his post and the protest of these types of occurrences. I remember hearing a lot about of the fact that the program with *Rainbow Strand* needed to be continued looked at and revitalized, that making sure we were staying true to the *Rainbow Strand* goals which was supposed to be not replicating deficit views of people of color from different backgrounds. This was an issue among us (the caucuses). We need to think about how we can make people aware of what *Rainbow Strand* is supposed to be. Sometimes I think that people think that it is just LGBTQ issues, but that is not true. We have to make sure we have certain topics covered, for instances there are rarely any presentations on Native American education issues, on language, on how can we get these important issues of teacher education on panels.

[I also remember] Iris and Raul helped, and this happened more in the CCCCs side, [a] resolution for ethnic studies. Lots of folks at CCCCs helped draft resolutions. Iris and Raul drafted a document that is now a resolution on the importance of ethnic studies and there was even a couple of blogs. We met with Dale, talked with him about the different sections. We drafted an important document, especially important in Arizona and all that is happening here. It was a complete process - we got signatures and then it was voted. (NCTE's position statement in support of ethnic studies initiatives in K-12 curricula can be found at: http://www2.ncte.org/statement/ethnic-studies-k12-curr/.)

I would say there is a lack of transparency and there are communication failures at times. I know that everyone is very busy, but I feel those things are important, especially when we voice our concerns. It is important that we are communicated with as well as how things are being communicated and how things are being handled. Yes, that directly impacts our Caucuses and our memberships and our concerns. One thing that I have seen just happened last year. We had a meeting with the Black Caucus leadership and our leadership, very late night, about our letter of our demands. I thought that it was a positive direction. However, I also thought it was more or less damage control so there was not a big spectacle, that we did not interrupt the conference in ways that people would start to ask questions. They caught wind of a possible die in or protest and I think from there that is when the damage control started. They met with us and we gave them a list of demands, then agreed to apologize for moving Adam Bank's photo. There was one thing we wanted them to do the next morning and I believe it had to do with Adam Banks. So, in the presidential address, she did mention about people's feelings being hurt and since they mentioned some of those things, we did not have the protest. Then afterwards, there was a timeline and following through. There has been a breakdown.

I want people to know that the Caucus has come a long way from its origins. Even though there are things we are working on to get our business side going, we want to have more organization. The main objective is to come together to advocate for issues of concerns for all of us. This is a space that is inclusive of everyone, their concerns, and their needs. We are working really hard to continue to open up space for the next generation of scholars and educators and teachers. I am still very privileged to be in this space as a leader. As I look behind me, I see all the of the people who have paved the way before me. I don't take it lightly because I know that without them, I would not be here. While I honor their legacy and while I pave the way for the next group of scholars, I hope to leave the organization better than when it was handed over to us.

PART III
Results: Work and Works Achieved

EDUCATION RESEARCH ASSOCIATES
Box 12403, El Paso, Texas 79912

Now available from Education Research Associates:

P114. PROBLEMS AND STRATEGIES IN TEACHING THE LANGUAGE ARTS TO SPANISH SPEAKING MEXICAN AMERICAN CHILDREN
By Carl L. Rosen and Philip D. Ortego

P163. THE LINGUISTIC IMPERATIVE IN TEACHING ENGLISH TO SPEAKERS OF OTHER LANGUAGES
By Philip D. Ortego

R412. PERSPECTIVES IN LANGUAGE, CULTURE, AND BEHAVIOR
By Philip D. Ortego

R175. SOME CULTURAL IMPLICATIONS OF A MEXICAN AMERICAN BORDER DIALECT OF AMERICAN ENGLISH
By Philip D. Ortego

R212. SCHOOLS FOR MEXICAN AMERICANS: BETWEEN TWO CULTURES
By Philip D. Ortego

R391. LANGUAGE AND READING PROBLEMS OF SPANISH SPEAKING CHILDREN IN THE SOUTHWEST
By Carl L. Rosen and Philip D. Ortego

R468. WHICH SOUTHWESTERN LITERATURE AND CULTURE IN THE ENGLISH CLASSROOM?
By Philip D. Ortego

To order please check quantity below:

Qty		Amount	Qty		
____	P114 @ 1.75 ea	_____	____	R212 @ .35 ea	_____
____	P163 @ 2.25 ea	_____	____	R391 @ 1.45 ea	_____
____	R412 @ .60 ea	_____	____	R468 @ .25 ea	_____
____	R175 @ .50 ea	_____		TOTAL	_____

Please add 50¢ postage on all orders. Minimum order $3.00. All orders prepaid only.

Ship to: Name (Please print) _____

Address _____

City _____ State _____ ZIP _____

Annotated Caucus Archive

María Paz Carvajal Regidor, Romeo García, and Anita Hernández

Image 1: Education Research Associates List of Publications by Philip Ortego. Ortego published extensively on issues regarding Latinos and Latinas even though publishing on these topics was not always easy. NCTE/Racism and Bias Task Force File (TFRB), 1968-80, Materials on Mexican-Americans Minority publishers Readings on Racism, 1968-72. Record Series 15/73/08, box 2. University of Illinois Archives, University of Illinois at Urbana-Champaign, Urbana, IL.

Images 2 and 3: Letter from Charlotte (Carlota) Cárdenas Dwyer to Nancy Prichard Regarding TFRB Work. In this letter, Dwyer reassures Nancy Prichard that she wishes to continue working for the TFRB and outlines her goals for the next few months. 7 October 1970. NCTE / Racism and Bias Task Force File, 1968-80, Correspondence Materials on American Indians. Record Series 15/73/8, box 1. University of Illinois Archives, University of Illinois at Urbana-Champaign, Urbana, IL.

34 Michael Drive
Old Bethpage, Long Island
New York 11804
7 October 1970

Mrs. Nancy S. Prichard
National Council of Teachers of English
508 South Sixth Street
Champaign, Illinois

Dear Nancy:

I am very pleased to continue working for the Task Force on Racism and Bias in the Teaching of English. I feel greatly satisfied with the spirit of intensity that Ernece Kelly maintains during all our encounters and hope to continue contributing to the productive output of the Task Force. I have discussed the following points with Ernece and will be working along these lines during the next few months.

1. As soon as I receive the final draft of the criteria on texts, I will translate it into Spanish. I would like NCTE to duplicate a complete set (both languages stapled together) with NCTE Task Force identification clearly indicated on top of each page.

2. I am working with the Chicago based "Mexican-American Council on Education" and hope to function as a liaison between this group and our own. I would like to bring one hundred copies of the above set to the January convention of this Council.

3. I am working with Ernece on a ninety-minute program which will be presented at our open meeting on Thanksgiving Day in Atlanta. I hope to present a variation of this program to the above group in January.

4. I have talked to Darwin Turner regarding his Committee on Minority Literature. Some work is being done in the New York-Puerto Rican area but nothing as extensive nor intensive as my project so far. I am scheduled to meet with his Committee in Atlanta. Darwin was especially pleased to hear of my contact with the Mexican-American group in Chicago.

   Since Darwin's group only meets at conventions, it is possible that I could also work with his group without over-extending myself.

5. I spoke with Toni Morrison at Random House and was advised to write a "Prospectus" of my project which is now, more appropriately, referred to as a "Brown Anthology." I will send all concerned copies of this when completed.

That's about it for now. I hope I have explained everything clearly. Things are moving quickly and new ideas pop up constantly. Will try to stick to these major points, however, for the next few months.

Thank you, Nancy, for all your help and personal consideration. I'm looking forward to seeing everyone soon--even if it is over a Thanksgiving turkey.

Sincerely,

C. Cardenas Dwyer

cc: Ernece Kelly

Image 3

Image 4: Recommendations for Future Operations of the Task Force on Racism and Bias. November 1970. This document provides important insight into the early work and goals of the TFRB and shows that Ernece Kelly submitted Charlotte (Carlota) Dwyer's name for permanent membership. NCTE Commissions, Committees, and Task Forces. NCTE/Racism and Bias Task Force File, 1968-80, Ad Hoc, 1977-78-Excellence, 1984. Record Series 15/73/08, box 12. University of Illinois Archives, University of Illinois at Urbana-Champaign, Urbana, IL.

Images 5 and 6: Invitation to TFRB Membership from Ernece Kelly to Philip Ortego. 27 January 1971. In this letter, Ernece Kelly invites Ortego to participate in the TFRB and explains in depth the goals of the TFRB following the publication of the "Criteria for Teaching Materials in Reading and Literature." NCTE / Racism and Bias Task Force File, 1968-80 Correspondence Materials on American Indians. Record Series 15/73/8, box 1. University of Illinois Archives, University of Illinois at Urbana-Champaign, Urbana, IL.

Images 7 and 8: Acceptance Letter from Ortego to Ernece Kelly. 7 February 1971. In this letter, Philip Ortego accepts Ernece Kelly's invitation to join the TFRB and highlights how his own interests might drive the TFRB forward. NCTE / Racism and Bias Task Force File, 1968-80 Correspondence Materials on American Indians. Record Series 15/73/8, box 1. University of Illinois Archives, University of Illinois at Urbana-Champaign, Urbana, IL.

Images 9 and 10: Acceptance Letter from Joe Carrasco to Ernece Kelly. 15 February 1971. In this letter, Joe Carrasco accepts his TFRB membership invitation from Ernece Kelly and expresses concern over being able to acquire funding to attend CCCC. NCTE / Racism and Bias Task Force File, 1968-80 Correspondence Materials on American Indians. Record Series 15/73/8, box 1. University of Illinois Archives, University of Illinois at Urbana-Champaign, Urbana, IL.

Images 11 and 12: Philip Ortego TFRB Acceptance File. 2 March 1971. This file contains Ortego's official acceptance of TFRB membership and provides details of where he worked at the time he joined the TFRB. NCTE / Racism and Bias Task Force File, 1968-80, Correspondence Materials on American Indians. Record Series 15/73/8, box 1. University of Illinois Archives, University of Illinois at Urbana-Champaign, Urbana, IL.

Agenda Item: XI.H.c
November 1970

Recommendations for Future Operations of the Task Force on
Racism and Bias

Membership and Calendar of Meetings: Last November, when the Executive Committee approved the creation of the Task Force, the number of permanent members was set at from 5 to 7. At that time, too, the Executive Committee asked that the names of all members appointed to the Task Force be submitted to them for prior approval. To this moment, Miss Kelly has not submitted any names because she has wanted to size up prospective members, either by talking to them extensively or by inviting them to a meeting on an ad hoc basis, before extending a firm invitation. However, she would now like to submit the name of Charlotte Dwyer for permanent membership.

She also had in mind two types of membership on the Task Force--permanent members who would be expected to attend all meetings; and an advisory group who could be called upon when their special competence is needed. For this latter group she would like to propose the names of Janet Emig (University of Lethbridge) and Gabriel Cordova (San Jose City College).

In all, Miss Kelly would like colored minority group members in this proportion: 2 blacks, 1 Mexican-American, 1 American Indian.

Future meetings: Setting up a calendar of future meetings for the Task Force was discussed with Miss Kelly in Chicago. She would like to hold meetings in March (probably at CCCC), early June, and early October 1971, and in her invitations to prospective members will mention these meetings as part of their commitment.

Because those who have participated in the Task Force meetings so far are more interested in and knowledgeable about literature than in language/linguistics, or testing, the Executive Secretary suggests that it might be worth while to consider creating either sub-Task Forces or parallel Task Forces to consider these fields. A further suggestion is that writing the criteria or guidelines for language/linguistics might be a task for the Commission on Language; alternatively, the Commission on Language might monitor the writing of such criteria, perhaps through a liaison person to the Task Force.

Miss Kelly has been in correspondence with Elisabeth McPherson, program chairman for the CCCC annual meeting, and has proposed a meeting which will bring together publishers' representatives and minority group individuals. The purposes will be (a) to discuss the kinds of materials minority group members wish to see in print or back in print, (b) to encourage minority group members to write, or encourage others to write, some of the desired materials, and (c) to offer an occasion for publishers and minority group members to meet and a forum for exchange of ideas.

January 27, 1971
Page Two

Please reply to:

Assistant Professor, English
Loop City College
64 East Lake Street
Chicago, Illinois 60601

January 27, 1971

Mr. Phillip Ortego
English Department
New Mexico State University
Las Crusas, New Mexico

Dear Mr. Ortego:

A year ago the National Council of Teachers of English approved creation of a Task Force on Racism and Bias in the Teaching of English. One of the concrete results of the work of the small membership of the Task Force is the enclosed "Criteria for Teaching Materials in Reading and Literature."

We want and need to expand the membership of the Task Force to include others who are interested in fighting against racism in this particular area. So far, the core members are Black and Chicano. I'm writing to ascertain if you would be willing to work with us for a period of at least two years.

We have already committed ourselves to some projects for 1971. However, that doesn't mean that their focus can't be shifted or that new projects can't be undertaken. This year, for example, we will be examining the problems which non-white students face in such national tests as the SAT and ACT. What steps we take to affect change after our investigation and discussions is up to the resources, vision and collective direction of the Task Force members--within the broad limits imposed upon us by our working within the context of the NCTE.

A second major project will be our development of critiques of the most popular American literature anthologies for their treatment of literature and literary history materials. The essays will, if we meet our deadline, be published by NCTE and available for distribution in November, 1971. You may be familiar with the book, Textbooks and the American Indian, a 1970 publication of the American Indian Historical Society. It will serve, more or less, as our model for the NCTE publication.

Briefly, other projects include: discussion of feasible follow-up activities for those persons and groups which have received the "Criteria"; drafting of letters to accompany the "Criteria" when sent to department chairmen and to textbook publishers--those letters will, by the way, include recommendations for operationalizing that document; and, lastly, translating the "Criteria"

January 27, 1971
Page Two

into Spanish to facilitate its usage among bilingual groups concerned with bias in English education.

Again, I don't want to make it appear that our activities are absolutely firm. But I do want to provide a clear idea of what kinds of things we are about.

The Task Force has meetings planned for the following dates in 1971:

March 27-29 (Cincinnati, Ohio at the CCCC conference)
May 21-22 (tentative) (Champaign, Illinois at NCTE headquarters)
October 1-3 (Same as above)
November 25-27 (Las Vegas, Nevada at the NCTE convention)

Because of the many other activities going on at the annual conferences, our work there is largely limited to sharing information and assessing progress on current projects, whereas our meetings at NCTE headquarters are not in competition with other activities. At them we discuss, work on small group projects and plan activities. Generally, we work 5-6 hours each day we meet. All expenses for these meetings are paid for by NCTE. On the other hand, we hope that you would be attending the annual conferences anyway, and so your expenses would be taken care of by your own institution.

Our Task Force is comprised of two groups: the core-group which is made up only of urban minority persons is most responsible for work and decisions. It is this group I am asking you to join. However, there is an advisory group which is larger, includes whites, and only joins our meetings at the annual conventions indicated above. These persons contribute ideas regularly, but help with implementation only occasionally.

If your other comments are such that you could not be a member of the core-group, would you join the larger advisory group? If that participation is precluded, but you are interested in work of the Task Force would you recommend someone to us?

Please let me know at your earliest convenience whether or not you can join us. I hope that you can. Also, if you have any questions or comments, please address them to me.

                              Sincerely,

                              Ernece B. Kelly
                              Chairman, Task Force on Racism
                              and Bias in the Teaching of English

EBK:rjg

The University of Texas at El Paso

February 7, 1971

Department of English

Ernece B. Kelly
Chairman, Task Force on Racism
  and Bias in the Teaching of English
Department of English
Loop City College
64 East Lake Street
Chicago, Illinois 60601

Dear Professor Kelly:

Thank you for your letter of the 27th last, and for inviting me to participate as a member of the core-group in NCTE's Task Force on Racism and Bias in the Teaching of English.

I accept with pleasure, for indeed the question of racism and bias in the teaching of English is a professional issue of great important to me and other Chicano English teachers. Sad to say that literary historians and anthologies have not yet caught up with us.

By spring I hope to complete my study on Backgrounds of Mexican American Literature and to find a prospective publisher. I mention this only to indicate my concern for the fact that Mexican American literature is but another aspect of American literature which has been neglected. American lit textbooks, like Norton, for example, focus only on the literature of the Atlantic frontier and of Anglo American writers. This is thus one area I'd be very much interested in exploring with the Task Force.

We're making some headway here in El Paso this year. A group of English teachers, known as the El Paso Articulation Committee, has been working since September on creating a 9-week unit on Mexican American literature which will plug into the Junior year of American lit. Since I'm the only Chicano in the English department at UTEP I've been working closely with the group as "consultant." But the effort is nominal at the moment considering the fact that there are few Chicanos teaching English in the El Paso Public Schools.

Since receipt of your letter I've been making plans to get with the Chairman of our English department and to establish new criteria for our selection of American literature texts, one which will reflect the multiethnic composition of the United States. Perhaps if we indicate to publishers our intent to seek such texts, they'll undertake revising their present practices. A ver?

Again, thank you for considering me as a member of the NCTE Task Force. Unfortunately, I won't be able to make the March meeting at Cincinnati, but I'll be in Chicago April 19-21 for an HEW conference. Would it be possible to chat then?

Image 7

- 2 -

In the meantime, I'd appreciate receiving any information and materials which you're all working on or which you think might be of interest to me in terms of the goals being pursued by the Task Force.

Sincerely,

Philip N. Ortego

Philip D. Ortego
Executive Director
Chicano Affairs Program
and Assistant Professor of English

PDO:rs

Image 8

Joe A. Carrasco
2313 Hart Avenue
Santa Clara, California 95050

February 15, 1971

Ernece B. Kelly
Assistant Professor, English
Loop City College
64 East Lake Street
Chicago, Illinois 60601

Dear Mrs. Kelly,

I am writing in response to your letter of January 27, 1971, inquiring as to my interest and possible participation in the National Teachers of English, <u>Task Force on Racism and Bias in the Teaching of English</u>. My answer to your request is affirmative. I think that the purpose and goal of your task-force is to be commended and that it will hopefully gain the support of everyone.

In accepting membership on this task force, I understand that I am expressing a willingness and commitment to participate for a minimum period of two years. It should be mentioned however, that I, like many of you, am often very busy, and would have to anticipate that there might at times arise a conflict of schedule between a task force meeting and a serious local issue. If a conflict of this sort were ever to arise, I would feel it necessary to remain at home and work toward helping to resolve the problems that might be confronting us locally. Hopefully, this situation will not create a problem for me or the task force.

Because I am presently teaching in a new and struggling department (Mexican American Graduate Studies Department), here at San Jose State College, it is doubtful that I will be able to have the department incur the cost of travel to the annual C.C.C.C. conference to be held on March 27-29 in Cincinnati. M.A.G.S. is presently striving to utilize all its financial efforts into staffing and the creation of a strong quality program. Needless to say, the institutions of higher learning are not always generous in the funding of new, although innovative programs.

Image 9

Although any attempt may be futile, I will make an effort to get the financial support from my department and San Jose State College.

Until I have the opportunity to meet you and the other task force members, I will await further correspondence from you.

Sincerely,

Joe C. Carrasco

Joe A. Carrasco
Assistant Professor

Hughes Note he's in El Paso — not Las Cruces — MAR - 8 1971

I accept the invitation to serve as a member of the NCTE Committee on Task Force on Racism and Bias in the Teaching of English

Name __PHILIP D. ORTEGO__

Title: Mr. Mrs. Miss Prof. (Dr.)
(Circle)

Position __Executive Director Chicano Affairs Program__

School __University of Texas at El Paso__

Location __El Paso, Texas 79999__

(Please return with the Identification Form for NCTE Records to Robert F. Hogan, Executive Secretary, 508 South Sixth Street, Champaign, Illinois 61820.)

NCTE:

Unless requested otherwise, NCTE will inform your superior administrative officer and local newspapers of this appointment. Please indicate below the person(s) or place(s) to whom this information should be sent:

Name __President Joseph R. Smiley__

Title __President__

Address __UTEP__
__El Paso, Texas 79999__

Newspaper __El Paso Times / Herald-Post__

Address __El Paso, Texas__

Image 11

Please fill out in full and return immediately to the Executive Secretary, NCTE, 508 South Sixth Street, Champaign, Illinois 61820

IDENTIFICATION FORM FOR NCTE RECORDS

Personal Name: PHILIP D. ORTEGO
(Print exactly as you wish it to appear in NCTE Directories; include abbreviations for clerical orders.)

Title to Go with Personal Name: Mr.   Mrs.   Miss   Prof.   (Dr.)   Sister   Brother   Father   The Reverend   Rabbi   Other _____
(Circle the title which you want to precede your name in NCTE correspondence.)

Academic or Business Title: Executive Director, Chicano Affairs Program
(E.g., Teacher of English; Professor of English; Chairman, Dept. of English; Superintendent of Schools; Supervisor of Language Arts.)

Academic Department or Division: Chicano Affairs Program
(E.g., Department of English; Department of Comparative Literature; College of Education; Division of Humanities.)

School or Firm: University of Texas at El Paso
(E.g., Classical High School; University of Utah; Appleton-Century-Crofts.)

Address or School of Firm: El Paso, Texas 79999
(Street)   (City)   (State)   (Zip Code)

Mailing Address You Prefer If Different From Address Above: _____
(Street or Building, etc.)
(City)   (State)   (Zip Code)

Is this address for your home? office? other?
(Circle correct answer and fill in if "other.")

Date: March 2, 1971   **Signature:** Philip D. Ortego

Image 12

Images 13 and 14: Charlotte Cárdenas Dwyer TFRB Acceptance File. 10 March 1971. This is Dwyer's official acceptance of the TFRB membership and provides a sense of how early in her career Dwyer was involved with NCTE initiatives; she was still a graduate student when she joined the TFRB. NCTE / Racism and Bias Task Force File, 1968-80, Correspondence Materials on American Indians. Record Series 15/73/8, box 1. University of Illinois Archives, University of Illinois at Urbana-Champaign, Urbana, IL.

Images 15, 16, 17 and 18: "Schools for Mexican-Americans: Between Two Cultures" by Philip D. Ortego in *Saturday Review*. 17 April 1971. This short article is a good example of the type of writing Ortego was engaged in during the same time he was a part of the CTE and the TFRB. It provides a short history of Chicanos and Mexican Americans in the US and explains some of the issues these students face in educational settings. NCTE/Racism and Bias Task Force File, 1968-80, Materials on Mexican-Americans Minority publishers Readings on Racism, 1968-72. Series Number 15/73/08, box 2. University of Illinois Archives, University of Illinois at Urbana-Champaign, Urbana, IL.

Images 19, 20 and 21: Letter from Ernece Kelly to TFRB Core and Advisory Group Members Regarding May 1971 Meeting and TFRB Projects. 28 May 1971. In this letter, Ernece Kelly summarizes developments in the work of the TFRB following a two-day meeting in Urbana. The letter shows the depth of involvement by members of the TFRB and their range of interests and goals. NCTE / Racism and Bias Task Force File, 1968-80, Correspondence Materials on American Indians. Record Series 15/73/8, box 1. University of Illinois Archives, University of Illinois at Urbana-Champaign, Urbana, IL.

I accept the invitation to serve as a member of the NCTE Committee on Task Force on Racism and Bias in the Teaching of English

Name Charlotte Cardenas Dwyer

Title: Mr. (Mrs.) Miss Prof. Dr.
(Circle)

Position Graduate Student (doctoral candidate)

School State University of New York, Stony Brook

Location Stony Brook, L.I., New York

(Please return with the Identification Form for NCTE Records to Robert F. Hogan, Executive Secretary, 508 South Sixth Street, Champaign, Illinois 61820.)

NCTE:

Unless requested otherwise, NCTE will inform your superior administrative officer and local newspapers of this appointment. Please indicate below the person(s) or place(s) to whom this information should be sent:

Name_____

Title_____

Address_____

Newspaper_____

Address_____

Image 13

Please fill out in full and return immediately to the Executive Secretary, NCTE, 508 South Sixth Street, Champaign, Illinois 61820.

IDENTIFICATION FORM FOR NCTE RECORDS

Personal Name: C. Cárdenas Dwyer
(Print exactly as you wish it to appear in NCTE Directories; include abbreviations for clerical orders.)

Title to Go with Personal Name: Mr. (Mrs.) Miss Prof. Dr. Sister Brother Father The Reverend Rabbi Other_____
(Circle the title which you want to precede your name in NCTE correspondence.)

Academic or Business Title: Doctoral candidate, SUNY
(E.g., Teacher of English; Professor of English; Chairman, Dept. of English; Superintendent of Schools; Supervisor of Language Arts.)

Academic Department or Division: English Department
(E.g., Department of English; Department of Comparative Literature; College of Education; Division of Humanities.)

School or Firm: State University of New York at Stony Brook
(E.g., Classical High School; University of Utah; Appleton-Century-Crofts.)

Address or School of Firm: _____
(Street)

Stony Brook,   New York   11790
(City)   (State)   (Zip Code)

Mailing Address You Prefer If Different From Address Above: 34 Michael Drive
(Street or Building, etc.)

Old Bethpage, L.I.   New York   11804
(City)   (State)   (Zip Code)

Is this address for your (home) office? other?_____
(Circle correct answer and fill in, if "other.")

Date: 10 March 1971   Signature: _____
                           C. Cárdenas Dwyer (Mrs.)

Image 14

Schools for Mexican-Americans:
BETWEEN TWO CULTURES

by PHILIP D. ORTEGO

—Marcia Keegan, Photo Trends

Reprinted with permission of the author and Saturday Review from the April 17, 1971 issue.

Copyright 1971 Saturday Review, Inc.

They were here before the Conquistadores, before the Puritans, before the Pennsylvania Dutch, before the Irish of Boston or the Italians of New York or the Poles of Chicago. Despite the overlay of Spanish culture, Mexican-Americans are essentially descendants of the great Mayan and Aztec civilizations, the children of Montezuma. The face of Mexico even today is an Indian face. The pyramids of Teotihuacán seem more impressive than the elegant facade of Chapultepec Castle. The legend of Ixtacíhuatl fascinates more than do the exploits of Cortez. Although Spanish influences are everywhere visible in Mexico, it is the Indian character of the people that is more obvious. Yet, only in recent years has Indian blood rather than Spanish blood become a source of national Mexican pride. To be a Mexican today is to be a member of *la raza*, the race of Montezuma's children.

Yet, within the boundaries of the United States, Mexican-Americans are still struggling to overcome not only the linguistic disadvantage of speaking a foreign language but the disadvantage of visibility—of looking like a Mexican. In the Southwest—Texas, New Mexico, Colorado, Arizona, and California—where approximately eight million Chicanos live, they subsist on levels of survival exceedingly below national norms. Eighty per cent live in predominantly urban environments, ranging from the megalopolis of Los Angeles—where more than a fifth of the Mexican-Americans reside—to such small urban centers as Las Cruces, New Mexico, with a population of about 55,000, half of whom are Mexican-Americans. Throughout the region, they suffer the ills of discrimination in education, housing, and employment—ills that established the patterns of poverty of the *barrios* and *colonias*, the Mexican ghettos of the Southwest. Few non-Southwesterners realize, for instance, that brown Americans, like black Americans, were segregated in the schools in California until 1947 and in Texas schools until 1948. This prejudice, this discrimination, many Mexican-Americans argue, stem from the 1848 Treaty of Guadalupe Hidalgo, a treaty that identified those who came with the conquered lands of the Southwest as a defeated people, a treaty that usurped their territorial rights and turned them into strangers in their own land. Those who came later, in the great migration of the early 1900s, have been equally victimized by the

PHILIP D. ORTEGO is executive director of the Chicano Affairs Program and assistant professor of English at the University of Texas at El Paso.

SR/APRIL 17, 1971

can-American War.

The consequence in recent years has been the formation of the Alianza in New Mexico led by the fiery Reies Lopez Tijerina, who—though he may never succeed in his quixotic mission to recover the lands for the present claimants—nevertheless has elevated the social and political consciousness of many Mexican-Americans to the point of demanding reformation of the socio-economic structure that has kept them subordinated these many years. In California, César Chavez has mobilized the grape pickers; and in Colorado, Corky Gonzalez has infused the Mexican-Americans with the spirit of protest.

Nevertheless, at the moment what continues to characterize Mexican-Americans in the Southwest is the fact that most of them have a limited and inadequate education. The educational statistics on Mexican-Americans are shocking. Their dropout rate is more than two times the national average, and estimates of the average number of school years completed by Mexican-Americans (7.1 years) are significantly below figures for black children (9.0 years) or Anglo children (12.1 years). In Texas, 39 per cent of the Mexican-Americans have less than a fifth-grade education, and Mexican-Americans twenty-five years of age or older have as little as 4.8 years of schooling. Almost half of the Chicanos in Texas essentially are still functional illiterates.

In fact, many Mexican-American youngsters never get to the first grade. In Texas, only about one-third of the five- and six-year-old Chicanos are enrolled in school, and of those, four out of five fall two grades behind their Anglo classmates by the time they reach fifth grade. In California, more than 50 per cent of Mexican-American high school students drop out between grades ten and eleven. Less than half enrolled on the seven campuses of the University of California are Mexican-Americans, although they constitute more than 14 per cent of the public school population of the state.

The high dropout rate cannot be blamed on a lack of emphasis on education in the home. A 1968 study by James Anderson and Dwight Johnson points out that "there appears to be little difference between Mexican-American families and other families with respect to the amount of emphasis on education that the child experiences in his home." Moreover, "these children experience the same high degree of encouragement and assistance at home as do their classmates." The inescapable conclusion is that the academic failures of many Mexican-American youngsters are the result of inadequate school programs rather than the consequence of low achievement or aspiration levels of their families.

The issues in Mexican-American education are formidable, but they have thus far been approached simplistically. To begin with, existing education programs (with the exception of pilot or experimental model programs) make no allowance for the fact that many Mexican-American children come to school either a) knowing a fair amount of English but being psychologically reluctant to use it, b) knowing little English, or else c) knowing only Spanish. Thus, from the start, Chicano children are burdened with the disadvantage of being unable to deal with the national language. In many states, English is prescribed by law as the official language of instruction, and Mexican-American students are expressly forbidden to speak Spanish on the rationale that by speaking English the student will learn English.

Traditionally these children are herded into schools where the proceedings are conducted in a language they don't pected to learn all the standard subjects, including reading. Usually their teachers are Anglo-Americans who are not bilingual and who therefore cannot communicate to their charges the learning content of first grade. First grade, then, can become a traumatic experience in which the teacher, with little or no facility in Spanish and untrained in language theory and analysis, attempts to create enough English fluency in the pupils to begin the required instructional materials.

Just as this "come and get it" approach to the common curriculum fails to deal with the fundamental educational problems of Mexican-Americans, so too does the more recent approach of preparing the child before he must enter school. Projects such as Head Start, Follow Through, and other pre-school compensatory educational programs suffer from the assumption that all Spanish-speaking pre-schoolers who are recipients of such programs—short- or long-term, well-designed or inefficient—will be fluent in English and able to deal with a traditional curriculum. Six months of pre-school alone is hardly enough time to overcome the disadvantage.

Thus, Mexican-American children arrive at the schoolhouse door with educational needs their Anglo, non-Spanish-speaking teachers are woefully unable to meet. As a result, Spanish-speaking children are often relegated to classes for the mentally retarded, simply because many teachers, wittingly or unwittingly, equate linguistic disadvantage with intellectual deficiency. The percentage of Mexican-American children classified with inferior IQs is two-and-a-half times their ratio to the general population. In California alone, Mexican-Americans account for more than 40 per cent of the so-called mentally retarded.

Until recently, most educators ac-

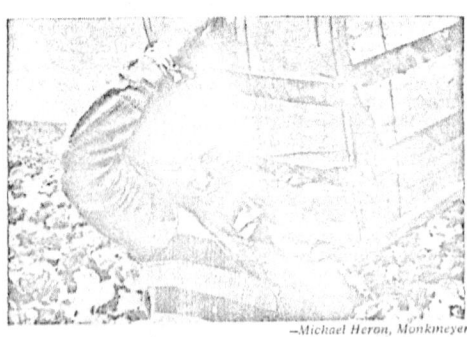
—Michael Heron, Monkmeyer

—Jim Seymour, Pix

The daily life of young Mexican-Americans contrasts sharply with the Anglo culture of the schools, and the Chicano student must frequently repudiate his cultural identity or perish in the educational process.

—*George W. Gardner*

The development of Chicano education must come "from Chicanos themselves."

cepted the results of IQ tests—whether Stanford-Binet, Otis, or SCAT—as accurate measurements of the intellectual capacity of Spanish-speaking Americans, despite the fact that all these tests are given in English and their culture content is biased toward middle-class Anglo-America. Only in the last few years have educators become aware that the right instruments are lacking for measuring intelligence and the achievement potential of Mexican-Americans, although as long ago as 1935 Herschel T. Manuel had pointed out the deficiencies of the Stanford-Binet. Today most enlightened educators acknowledge the relationship between the amount of retardation and the extent to which intelligence tests require a knowledge of English.

In 1968, as a result of severe criticism from the Association of Mexican-American Educators, the California State Board of Education created a special advisory committee to investigate charges that IQ tests seriously hinder some children—especially minority children—in achieving normal educational goals. The findings of the committee are startling. Mexican-American children, classified as mentally retarded after IQ tests in English, did remarkably better on tests in Spanish. Some of the children tested had had "a retarding influence." After re-testing, one Mexican-American student showed an improvement of twenty-eight points, while the group's average rose thirteen points, from seventy to eighty-three. The report of the committee asserts that Mexican-American students apparently are placed in remedial or special classes "solely on their ability to function in what is a foreign language."

But the issues cannot be reduced to language alone, for language is only one manifestation of the ethnic bias of the school culture. To imagine such courses as "Speech X" (Corrective Instruction in English Pronunciation) as a palliative or form of remediation for the linguistic ills of Mexican-Americans is to treat the symptoms rather than the malady, for the malady is a social one, and not one of grammar or pronunciation.

The teacher, as the central figure in the dynamics of social relations in educational institutions, needs to fully comprehend the nature of language and its psycho-social function in human beings, especially children. He needs to understand, for example, that when Chicano children are punished for breaking "no Spanish" rules, they are being reprimanded for the crime of speaking the only language they know. They are being pressed into thinking of their language as "wrong" and "inferior," and the more this continues the more they become hostile, resentful, and alienated from society, from their families, and even from themselves. Thus, the Spanish-speaking child who encounters stern and imposing prohibitions against using his language not only is traumatized by a conflict he does not readily understand but is forced into a position of repudiating his cultural identity or else of perishing within the educational process.

Only recently have "no Spanish" rules been challenged by Mexican-Americans in such cities as San Antonio and El Paso, but only after actual or threatened Mexican-American student uprisings. In 1969 the proposed action on the part of the National Education Association to decertify one El Paso high school if it continued its rule of prohibiting Spanish helped resolve the issue there in favor of the Spanish-speaking student population of the city.

Although the "no Spanish" rules are slowly being eliminated, the Anglo-dominated educational systems of the Southwest still tend to culturally and assimilate quickly into Anglo culture or face economic and financial deprivation when they are adults. In effect, this is like telling the Mexican-American child that there is something wrong in being a Mexican-American. And though Spanish may no longer be prohibited on some school grounds, José (Joe) has become more self-conscious of his Spanish and is more and more withdrawn. Not only has he been made to feel marginal in Anglo-American society because of his lack of English, but he is made to feel equally marginal in his Spanish-speaking environment. To eliminate such identity crises, not only must teachers of Mexican-Americans become more aware of the Mexican-American's heritage and culture, but they must rid themselves of outmoded concepts about language. As Harold Howe, former U.S. Commissioner of Education, put it, "It is time we stopped wasting [our linguistic resources] and instead enabled youngsters to move back and forth from one language to another without any sense of difficulty or strangeness."

What is needed is a new breed of teacher, according to Dr. Miguel Montes, member of the California State Board of Education, "sensitive to the many and diverse problems of Mexican-American youth." Yet, in most of the schools of education, few if any Mexican-Americans are on the teaching faculties, and considering the high dropout rate of elementary and secondary students, it is little wonder that there are so few Mexican-Americans in colleges and universities. Recent studies point out that only 2 per cent of the California State College population is Mexican-American, and of these, less than half of 1 per cent goes on to graduate. For example, of the 12,000 students at San Jose State College in 1968, only 1,200 were Mexican-Americans. At UCLA, there were only 300 Chicano students in 1968 out of a student population of 25,000. In New Mexico, despite the fact that Mexican-Americans comprise almost half the state's population, less than 8 per cent of them attend the state universities and colleges.

In his testimony before the Senate Subcommittee on Executive Reorganization of the Government Operations Committee, Vicente T. Ximenes, a member of the Equal Employment Opportunity Commission and former chairman of the Interagency for Mexican-American Affairs, pointed out that Mexican-Americans in the Southwest

1969, only 600 Spanish-surnamed students were graduated in the spring of 1969. Mr. Ximenes identified the schools as UCLA, the University of Colorado at Boulder, the University of Texas at Austin, and the Universities of Arizona and New Mexico, pointing out that the total enrollment of Spanish-surnamed students in these institutions was only 3,370.

In California, the Chicano Movement advocates outright elimination of *all* entrance requirements for Mexican-Americans and the establishment of a Chicano studies program that is more pragmatically attuned to the needs of the Mexican-American community. One Chicano cites the lack of relevance on college campuses as a major cause for the very limited enrollment of Chicanos. Students from predominantly *barrio* and *colonia* backgrounds enter the almost exclusively middle-class, Anglo-American environment of colleges and universities to their own detriment and eventual alienation.

Like the blacks, more and more Mexican-Americans are beginning to reject the assimilationist concepts of American education. Most Mexican-Americans see the need for the bilingual-bicultural school as the most pressing issue in Mexican-American education, and one of the most challenging. According to Armando Rodriquez, chief of the Mexican-American Affairs Unit of the U.S. Office of Education, "the rise in cultural militancy among young Chicanos is directly related to the schools' appalling ignorance about the Mexican-American and his role in American democracy."

A first step toward correcting the situation was the Bilingual Education Act of 1968. Essentially, the act provides for the development of programs designed to meet the special educational needs of children of limited-English-speaking ability in schools having a high concentration of such children. The scope of the act includes pre-service training for teachers, teacher-aides, and counselors, and takes in early childhood education, adult education, reinstatement and retention programs for dropouts, and vocational training programs for people of limited English proficiency.

Essentially, bilingual-bicultural education aims to teach the non-English-speaking (or limited-English-speaking) child in his first language, while introducing him to the target language (via foreign language instruction methods) in small, regulated doses at first, then in increasingly larger time units until Rodriquez pointed out, "We spend millions of dollars to encourage school children to learn a foreign language and at the same time frown upon Mexican-American children speaking Spanish in school. . . . Bilingualism must come to be accepted as a blessing—not a problem. It must be cultivated, not neglected."

The Bilingual Act also provides for teaching Mexican-Americans about the history and culture of their language. For example, Mexican-American children will learn about the history of Mexico and how it relates to their present situation as Mexican-Americans. American literature courses are to be revised to include the chronicles of the Spanish Southwest as part of the lit-

erary heritage of Mexican-Americans. In the primary grades, Dick-and-Jane-type readers are replaced by figures Mexican-American children can readily identify with and relate to.

Unfortunately, the practice differs from the goals, for bilingual-bicultural education exists at the moment only in a handful of programs throughout the country. Last year, EPDA (Education Professions Development Act) programs tapped teachers for training in bilingual-bicultural education, but the ratio of Mexican-American teachers selected has been meager. In such projects as Head Start, the thrust of the teaching is still on preparing the child for the English curriculum of the primary schools. And in those few schools hosting bilingual programs, more of the educational material relates to middle-class Anglo-America than to the realities of Mexican-American life. Instead of works in Spanish by and about Mexicans or Mexican-Americans, Anglo-American works in Spanish translation are used.

Moreover, many of the teachers who are tapped into EPDA and other bilingual training programs are barely conversant in Spanish. Many are simply piling on the band wagon. When they go back to their schools, they effect little or no change in their teaching styles despite their training. Even on the staffs of many EPDA institutes, one finds at best only token Mexican-American educators or workers. Of course, the directors of these institutes primarily are Anglos.

Consequently, the only viable alternative, many Mexican-American educators feel, lies in creating special Such programs are being establish in numerous public schools and leges in California, Arizona, New M ico, Colorado, and Texas, with m coming into being regularly as Chic educators create distinct kinds of lo state, and national organizations the improvement of Mexican-Ameri education. The National Council Chicano Studies and the Natio Council for Mexican-American Edu tion are two such organizations t bring the collective efforts of Chic educators to bear on the problem Mexican-American education.

The improvement of Mexican-Am can education from kindergarten college has become the watchword MECHA (Movimiento Estudiantil C cano de Aztlan), the national C cano student organization, which pricked the consciences of educati al administrations with the strateg of "confrontactics." At the Univers of Texas at El Paso, MECHA created a model program for Chic education, which is reinforced by Chicano activities component pro ing tutorial assistance and counsel for Chicano students who require s help. But the heart of the program in La Mesa Directiva, an advise board to the president of the univ sity, composed of a tripartite consti ency: Chicano community, Chic faculty, and Chicano students. Th the development of Chicano educat comes from Chicanos themselves. next step is to create such advise boards in the public schools.

Mexican-American educators see education of Mexican-American c dren as involving a coalition of number of groups, but especially community and the school. Mexic American parents must be involv in the educational decisions affec their children. The monocultural of school boards must yield to new enlightenment; more Me Americans must, out of necessit come members of the school b in order to effect the necessary ch in Mexican-American education. canos insist that Mexican-Ame must, if necessary, take the schoo of the hands of those who are acad cally suppressing them. The time looking upon the Mexican-American the poor, uneducated, tortilla-cat peon who is a victim of some f stemming from Quetzalcoatl's dis preval is over. Montezuma's child are descendants of a proud race. Chicanos of *la raza* will no longer patient. They are insisting on act now.

28 May 1971

To: Task Force on Racism, Core and Advisory Group Members

From: Ernece B. Kelly, Director

We just completed a two-day meeting in Urbana. Rather than repeating the items, I've enclosed a copy of the original agenda. But, by way of correction, James Hill's report on testing was replaced by conversations with Leo Kneer, editor-in-chief of secondary English at Scott, Foresman.

Briefly, I feel that these were the more important developments growing out of our meeting:

I   Extensive evaluation of the meeting between minority group members and publishers sponsored by the Task Force and held at the CCCC Conference in Cincinnati. This led to planning for a meeting at the next annual conferences of NCTE and CCCC which would have some of the same goals, but tighter structure and broadened participation.

II   Detailed planning for the structure of the June 5-12th textbook review project at which 15 or so American literature anthologies will be reviewed using the Task Force Criteria. (I've enclosed a description of that project)

III   Discussion of the complexity of the proposition that the Task Force membership work to influence the procedures whereby texts are selected in states using state-wide selection procedures.
      a. As a pilot project, Marianna Davis of Benedict College and an advisory member of the Task Force is going to work with the South Carolina Council toward the end of influencing members of the textbook selection committee in that state. This is a long-range project and you will be kept informed of its progress.

Image 19

IV Discussion of the kinds of materials used with Spanish speaking students in English-as-a-second-language classes. Mrs. Sylvia Herrera-Fox, who is director of ASPIRA in Chicago, a group working with Puerto Rican drop-outs, and who was acting as substitute for a core member of the Task Force, will be working toward development of improved materials with the hoped-for cooperation of the OEO agency, Training of Teacher Trainers.

V Discussion of Gabe Cordova's suggestion that the Task Force have its own letterhead stationery and that one of its first uses, in substantial numbers, be for the recruitment of Chicanos to NCTE membership. This idea was approved and we expect to have such stationery around September 1st.

The group and individual projects I've described indicate that our interests and energies are now moving in three levels of education: elementary, secondary and college. Ambitious, given the relatively small number of persons active with the Task Force, but certainly achievable given the demonstrated creativity and commitment of our membership.

I wanted you to know what was happening, but also want to enlist your help. Item I, the meeting between minority group persons and publishers planned for November presupposes that attending that meeting will be individuals, knowledgeable about certain facets of the publishing business, who are sympathetic to the difficulties minority persons face in getting published and the difficulties of integrating minority materials into textbooks generally.

What names can you send me of persons who fit that description? Please don't hesitate to provide your own name if you're fairly certain at this point that you'll be at NCTE in November. I've enclosed a postcard for your convenience. Would you jot down the names and addresses of individuals so that we can contact them as early as possible about participating in this program?

Briefly, the format will be small round-table discussions with each one dealing with a specific aspect of publishing, such as hiring; integrating texts, and minority presses. We anticipate having three key persons at each round-table: a representative from the publishing industry, a person knowledgeable about publishing who is sympathetic to the problems of minority

Image 20

exposure, and a member of the Task Force. If you don't think that you fit the second description, would you volunteer to come to the meeting in the capacity of a Task Force member?

Too, I will need Task Force personnel to volunteer <u>at least</u> one hour of their time during the NCTE Convention to sit at the Task Force booth which will be located among the exhibition booths of publishers. We're hoping to get students to assist us in this, but will need you to answer questions teachers might raise about implementation of the Criteria, projects and plans of the Task Force and so on. Again, would you drop me a note at your earliest convenience to let me know if you can help out in this matter.

I hope I haven't overwhelmed you with words. I'd appreciate getting any responses to any of the projects we're launching. Our next meeting is October 1-3rd in Urbana and it would be helpful for me to have as much feedback as possible to bring to that meeting.

EBK:pg

Enclosures

Image 22: Letter from Carlota Cárdenas de Dwyer (?) to Esther Hamon regarding Mexican-American readings and Bibliographies. 16 November 1971. This letter, likely written by Carlota Cárdenas de Dwyer, shows that the bibliographies that members of the TFRB and CTE put together were helpful resources for teachers looking for readings by and about Mexican Americans. NCTE / Racism and Bias Task Force File, 1968-80, Correspondence Materials on American Indians. Record Series 15/73/8, box 1. University of Illinois Archives, University of Illinois at Urbana-Champaign, Urbana, IL.

Image 23: Agenda for Meeting of NCTE Task Force for Racism and Bias in the Teaching of English. 25 November, 1971. This agenda for a TFRB meeting shows some of the projects and concerns of the task force, including efforts to attract Chicano and Native American participants to NCTE. NCTE / Racism and Bias Task Force File, 1968-80, Correspondence Materials on American Indians. Record Series number 15/73/8, box 1. University of Illinois Archives, University of Illinois at Urbana-Champaign, Urbana, IL.

Image 24: Letter from Carlotta Cárdenas Dwyer to James T. Lape regarding the Minneapolis Convention and the CTE. This letter by Carlota Cárdenas Dwyer mentions that the Chicano Teachers of English (CTE) is in the process of becoming an NCTE affiliate and provided us with the inspiration for the title of this book. 5 January 1972. NCTE / Racism and Bias Task Force File, 1968-80, Correspondence Materials on American Indians. Record Series number 15/73/8, box 1. University of Illinois Archives, University of Illinois at Urbana-Champaign, Urbana, IL.

November 16, 1971

Mrs. Esther Hamon
1426 South 20th Street
Lincoln, Nebraska   68502

Dear Esther:

How very nice to hear from you and know that you will be at Las Vegas. And even though there will be a great deal of rushing around at the convention, certainly we can have a few moments quiet conversation.

In answer to your request for information about Mexican-American readings, I'm afraid I can send you very little, especially for younger students, but perhaps some of the sources I name will be more fruitful.

First of all, I am enclosing two different bibliographies—the selected bibliography and supplement which I put together for the Council, and a list of books about Mexican-Americans which has marginal notes by Philip Ortego, a member of the NCTE Task Force on Racism and Bias in the Teaching of English. The bibliography I did very much needs to be updated, not only because so much material has come out in the last 18 months, but especially because the Mexican-American section (among others) is so thin. I keep saying I will get around to revising the list, but so far have not found the time.

A new and very extensive bibliography on all areas of Mexican-American lives and culture is <u>Bibliografia de Aztlan: An Annotated Chicano Bibliography</u>, available from Centrol de Estudios Chicanos Publications, 5876 Hardy Avenue, San Diego, California 92115. Single copies are $3.95, and they do offer discounts for bulk sales to educational institutions. Again, the list is not strong in books for younger readers, but it would certainly be a valuable resource to have on hand.

Image 22

Agenda for meeting of
NCTE Task Force on Racism and Bias in the Teaching of English

Thursday, November 25, 1971
1:00 - 5:00 p.m.
Las Vegas Convention Center
Meeting Room #5

I. Reports

Task Force project in cooperation with South Carolina Council of Teachers of English: Mrs. Mariana Davis

Evaluation of effort to attract Chicano participants to NCTE: Mrs. Charlotte Dwyer

Progress report on meeting of publishers and minority group members: James Hill

Evaluation of effort to attract Native American participants to NCTE and to inform tribal leaders about NCTE and Task Force activities: Dr. Montana Rickards

Progress of the sub-committee to review existent materials on racism in English instructional materials or procedures: a representative of the sub-committee.

II. Discussion of

Journal advertisement project;

Original charges to the Task Force;

Feasibility of development of minority skills bank and minority journal listing.

III. Work project to write final draft of questionnarie to be sent to those who have received copies of Searching for America.

34 Michael Drive
Old Bethpage, L.I.
New York 11804
5 January 1972

Mr. James T. Lape
Lexington High School
251 Waltham Street
Lexington, Mass. 02173

Dear Mr. Lape:

Although I can well understand the pressures to which you must be subject in planning the NCTE national convention in 1972, I find it impossible to produce detailed plans and appropriate personnel within the next few days. As members of the NCTE Task Force on Racism and Bias, Dr. Ortego and I would be willing to assume responsibility in further planning of this aspect of the convention program if we were given more time. I am sure those persons I have already suggested could supply you with additional names and ideas. Perhaps those who rather ably recruited Chicanos to participate in Las Vegas might be consulted.

We are in the process of establishing the Chicano Teachers of English as an affiliate of the NCTE and hope one of its functions would be to collect a bank of resource people, such as you now need. Unfortunately this goal has yet to be realized.

I would like to assist you as much as possible. Time, however, seems to be the problem. After the wonderful progress made by Chicanos in NCTE, as evidenced by our participation in Las Vegas and in the forthcoming 4 C's meeting in Boston, it would be a terrible disappointment to us if Minneapolis were a step backward rather than a leap forward.

Viva Nuestras Causas!

Charlotte

C. Cárdenas Dwyer

cc: P. Ortego

34 Michael Drive
Old Bethpage, Long Island
New York 11804
8 May 1972

Prof. William Stafford
English Department
Lewis And Clark College
Portland, Oregon

Dear Prof. Stafford:

I am a Chicana and a member of the NCTE Task Force on Racism and Bias in the Teaching of English. One of our goals is to promote minority participation in the NCTE.

Nancy Prichard has informed me that you administer the Poets Festival at the national conventions. I would like to recommend one of our outstanding Chicano poets for your consideration. His name is Ricardo Sanchez and his most recent publication is a collection of his works entitled <u>Canto Y Grito Mi Liberacion</u> (Mictla Publications, Inc., P.O. Box 601, El Paso, Texas 79944). A knowledge of Spanish is not mandatory to appreciate this work.

Since the NCTE has pledged to promote all aspects of American literature, it seems especially important for us to insure a truly representative variety of writers in an official program, such as the Poets Festival. I personally am willing to do whatever I can to assist you in this effort. Do not hesitate to request further information or assistance.

Viva!

C. Cardenas Dwyer

cc: Nancy Prichard

Image 25: Letter from Carlota Cárdenas Dwyer to William Stafford Recommending Ricardo Sanchez for the Poets Festival. 8 May 1972. This letter demonstrates some of the strategies members of the TFRB and CTE worked toward including Chicanos and Chicanas and Latinos and Latinas in NCTE conventions. In this case, Carlota Cárdenas Dwyer wrote to William Stafford recommending a particular Chicano poet for his consideration in including him in the Poets Festival. NCTE / Racism and Bias Task Force File, 1968-80, Correspondence Materials on American Indians. Record Series number 15/73/8, box 1. University of Illinois Archives, University of Illinois at Urbana-Champaign, Urbana, IL.

Image 26: Letter from Philip Ortego to Nancy Pritchard Regarding CTE Finances. 7 December 1972. This letter by Philip Ortego shows that the Poets Festival Committee did not invite Ricardo Sanchez to read his work, instead the Chicano Teachers of English (CTE) invited him and worked hard to ensure that he received financial assistance for attending. NCTE / Racism and Bias Task Force File, 1968-80 Correspondence Materials on American Indians. Record Series 15/73/8, box 1. University of Illinois Archives, University of Illinois at Urbana-Champaign, Urbana, IL.

Image 27: Front Page of Philip D. Ortego's *Selective Mexican American Bibliography*. 1972 (?). This bibliography, compiled by Philip Ortego is one of the first of its kind. It was meant to highlight some of the existing literature by Mexican Americans and to serve as a way to encourage the inclusion of Latino and Latina and Chicano and Chicana literature in teaching materials. NCTE / Racism and Bias Task Force File, 1968-80, Books and Pamphlets on Spanish-American Literature and Literature of the American Indian. Record Series 15/73/08, box 5. University of Illinois Archives, University of Illinois at Urbana-Champaign, Urbana, IL.

METROPOLITAN STATE COLLEGE
250 WEST FOURTEENTH AVENUE
DENVER, COLORADO 80204

OFFICE OF THE **PRESIDENT**

December 7, 1972

Ms. Nancy Pritchard
Assistant Executive Secretary
National Council of Teachers of English
1111 Kenyon Road
Urbana, Illinois

Dear Nancy:

As always, it was pleasant seeing you at the NCTE convention. I wish there had been more time to chat. Perhaps at the 4 C's.

The $500 NCTE allocated to the Chicano Teachers of English for improving Chicano representation at NCTE activities will help us for the 4 C's conference in New Orleans. Minneapolis was tough for us without local contacts. But New Orleans is a lot closer to Aztlan.

We'll be better able to handle getting Chicanos to the 4 C's meeting if the NCTE allocation were given to us directly for disbursal to Chicanos interested in going to New Orleans.

In order to get one of our Chicano poets to Minneapolis for our presentation we had assumed we could utilize some of the NCTE allocation. Ricardo Sanchez is a struggling poet who could not afford to go to Minneapolis without assistance. His presentation was the highpoint of our meeting. If we can pay his expenses out of the NCTE allocation, the Chicano Teachers of English will take care of an honorarium for his help in making our program a success and in giving us all the psychological boost of having one of our finest Chicano poets present. We were sorry the Poet's Festival Committee did not see fit to have a Chicano poet as part of its program.

Abrazos,

Philip D. Ortego, Ph.D.
Assistant to the President

PDO/cb

PHONE: AREA CODE 303/292-5190

Sample TASK FORCE ON RACISM AND BIAS

SELECTIVE MEXICAN AMERICAN BIBLIOGRAPHY

by
Philip D. Ortego

Border Regional Library Association

February 2, 1973

Dr. Philip D. Ortego
Assistant to the President
Metropolitan State College
250 West Fourteenth Avenue
Denver, Colorado 80204

Dear Phil:

This is in answer to your December letter about financial support for bringing Ricardo Sanchez to the Minneapolis convention. I apologize for the delay in getting back to you on this.

If you have talked with Charlotte about the money voted by the NCTE Executive Committee to the Chicano Caucus, you will know that it was specifically allocated from the NCTE budget for bringing Chicanos to the Minneapolis convention. Therefore it cannot be used for the CCCC meeting in New Orleans. Although CCCC is part of NCTE, the two groups have separate budgets and separate Executive Committees which determine how those budgets shall be appropriated.

However, since it turned out to be so difficult to get a sizable number of Chicanos to Minneapolis under the program that Charlotte worked out, so the $500 could not be used for that, Bob Hogan has decided that we can stretch the provisions of the allocation a bit and use $252 of it to reimburse Mr. Sanchez for his expenses.

I listened to the tape of the Chicano literature session and Mr. Sanchez' presentation must have been a dynamic one in person—he comes over as a very exciting speaker on the recording.

If you will let me know whether to send his check to you or directly to him, we will get it off right away. If directly to him, I will need an address where it will be sure to reach him.

I haven't heard from anyone what the results of the Minneapolis Chicano Caucus meeting were in regard to the question of becoming an NCTE affiliate. Now that the NCTE constitution may be changed to provide for "assemblies," this may add a whole new dimension to the discussion. Maybe we can talk about this at New Orleans.

See you then.

Sincerely,

Nancy S. Prichard
Assistant Executive Secretary

NSP:bh3

cc: C. Cardenas Dwyer

Image 28

Image 28: Letter from Nancy Prichard to Philip Ortego Regarding Chicano Caucus Finances. 2 February 1973. In this letter Nancy Prichard explains to Philip Ortego why money from the NCTE budget can't be used for the CCC convention. After months of discussions, Prichard tells Ortego that they will be able to provide some support for Ricardo Sanchez for his attendance and reading at the Chicano Caucus. NCTE / Racism and Bias Task Force File, 1968-80, Correspondence Materials on American Indians. Record Series 15/73/8, box 1. University of Illinois Archives, University of Illinois at Urbana-Champaign, Urbana, IL.

Image 29: Counteracting Racism and Sexism in Classrooms Agenda. NCTE Convention program for November 22, 1977. Session with Carlota Cardenas Dwyer presenting on Chicano language and literature with other colleagues presenting on Asian American, Black, and Puerto Rican language and literature. University of Illinois Archives, University of Illinois at Urbana-Champaign, Urbana, IL.

Image 30: NCTE's Latino Caucus Newsletter *Capirotada* Vol. 1, No. 1, Summer 1994 sent to Caucus members from the Caucus leadership Alfredo Celedon Lujan Cecilia Rodríguez Milanés. The newsletter includes the article *Somos Quien Somos* where Alfredo Lujan chronicles the name change of the Caucus to Latino Caucus. It also includes Abrazos by Victor Villanueva, a call to Caucus members to join the college section (CCCC) and to send in a nomination for this committee; a review of *Botas (Bootstraps: From an American Academic of Color)*, and an Excerpt of a Letter by Cecilia Rodríguez Milanés dated January 2, 1994 in which she proposes a Hispanic/Latino(a) Heritage Reading for October.

Image 31: NCTE's Latino Caucus Newsletter *Capirotada* Vol. 2, No. 1, Fall 1995 sent to Caucus members from Caucus editors and chairs. This newsletter includes an article, En Esta Salida by Alfredo Celedon Lujan, in which he provides an overview the newsletter. Included is "el Hoyo" y la Olla, an excerpt by Mario Suarez (1947) published in the Arizona Quarterly. In Saludos, Roseann Dueñas González provides an overview of her participation in NCTE over the past 22 years and makes a call to Caucus members to become involved in Sections, Assemblies, Committees, and Commissions within NCTE and encourages members to interact with the Executive officers and NCTE staff.

The National Council of Teachers of English
1111 KENYON ROAD, URBANA, ILLINOIS 61801

TUESDAY, NOVEMBER 22, 1977

W.4 COUNTERACTING RACISM AND SEXISM IN CLASSROOMS

Cochairs: Ernece B. Kelly, Equal Educational Opportunity Project, Chicago, Ill.
Lallie Coy, Triton College, River Grove, Ill.
Velez Wilson, New Orleans Public Schools
Bradford Chambers, Council on Interracial Books for Children

9:00a.m.	Welcome and explanation of Grafitti Exercise
9:15a.m.	Psychological Effects of Racism Ernece B. Kelly, Chair, Task Force on Racism and Bias
9:30a.m.	Psychological Effects of Sexism Lallie Coy, Chair, Women's Committee
9:45-11:15a.m.	Small group discussions: How to Counteract Racist and Sexist Stereotypes in Language, Literature and Teacher Behavior Asian-American Lang./Lit. Jeannie Chin, Council on Interracial Books for Children Black Lang./Lit. Bill Cook, Dartmouth College, and Jane Hornburger, Boston University Chicano Lang./Lit. Carlota Cardenas de Dwyer, University of Texas-Austin

Image 29

Capirotada

**NCTE's Latino Caucus Newsletter
Volume I, Number 1
Summer, 1994**

Abrazos
por Victor Villanueva, Jr.
Northern Arizona University

In over eight years of active participation within NCTE, I have seen a great deal of progress when it comes to people of color, including *nosotros: la gente, Raza, Portorros, Cubanos, Hispanos: Latinos.* There has been the kind of progress within NCTE that I would wish for the country in general. But progress doesn't mean there still isn't work to be done. *No lo tenemos hecho.* It would be nice to see a *Latino* as NCTE president. It's been too long since a *Latino* has served on NCTE's College Section Steering Committee — with its four-year term, responsibility for several national public forums, and a part in general NCTE policy — a very critical committee.

Y yo, I got elected to something *que pienso es importante:* the Nominating Committee of the College Section Steering Committee. *"Chevere,"* pensé, "ahora lo *tenemos hecho."* But the job — at least my particular agenda within it — became more difficult than I had thought it would be: there were fewer active NCTE *Latinos* affiliated with the college section than I had thought (subscribers to *College English* or *College Composition and Communication*).

There's work to be done for our profession, for people of color in our profession and in our classrooms, work to be done for *Latinos.* And I have found that NCTE is my best place to get a good deal of that work done.

If you work within the colleges, please get active. Let Mildred Melendez or me know who you are and that you're interested. Send in proposals for NCTE panels. *Abrazos:* there's work to be done. We can get a good deal of it done within NCTE.

¿Donde está tu abuela?

The no name one, *la Prieta,* the one who charmed
    el gallego (or *el vasco*)
¿Donde estás? Are you buried next to him? in that
    gorgeous, monstrous cemetery in Havana?
Who kept your keepsakes? What of your legacy?
¿Donde estás? Did you leave me anything but the
    wild seed of imagination? The desire
    to recover you? The ability to recreate you?
Would you own me, *abuela?*

-- Cecilia Rodriguez Milanés
Indiana University of Pennsylvania

Somos Quien Somos, ¿No?
por Alfredo Celedon Lujan
Pojoaque Middle School, New Mexico

¿Quién somos? This question has come to mind each time I've attended the Latino Caucus meetings. *Fuí a las juntas en* Atlanta, Seattle, y Pittsburgh for obvious reasons: I saw the meeting advertised in the *Convention Preview,* and I was curious to know what *Latinos* are doing within NCTE. I hadn't been at meetings before because I had always gone to the convention primarily to attend the concurrent sessions. I was never there when the meeting was held. Things change.

In '89 I was invited to join the Assembly of Rural

Volume II, Number 1 — Semi-annual

Capirotada
The Latino Caucus Newsletter

En Esta Salida

Queridos, readers of *Capirotada:* for many years we talked about having a newsletter in the Latino Caucus. It has finally come to be. This is the second issue. The first two issues are the *abuelitos* of future *Capirotadas,* the written voice of the **Latino Caucus.** Our goal is to make this a semi-annual publication with contributions coming from many of you. Regretfully I must say that for the moment I take leave of my duties as editor. I am swamped with teaching and coaching responsibilities. *Ya saben:* how it goes in public education, *"saz y saz."* De todos modos, *Capirotada* is alive and well. *Doctora* Cecilia Rodriguez Milanés will be editing future issues. We look forward to the *evolución de nuestra voz.*

In this issue:

-- *"Saludos,"* a timely feature article by *Doctora* Roseann Dueñas González, urges Latinos and Latinas to become active in NCTE and the caucus.

-- *"'El Hoyo' y la Olla"* is my title, given to an excerpt from a series of stories written by *Mario Suárez* for the *Arizona Quarterly* in the 1940's. It is recycled from Volume I, Number 1 to pay tribute once again to Mr. Suárez' metaphor. Thanks to the insight of MaryCarmen Cruz, we have borrowed the metaphor to title of our newsletter.

-- *"Bienvenidos, Hispanic Literary Heritage Reading,"* by *Doctora* Cecilia Rodriguez Milanés is also recycled from the first issue. Read this, and read "Hispanic" texts.

Bueno ... enjoy.

Hasta luego,
Alfredo Celedon Lujan

SALUDOS
por Roseann Dueñas González

After twenty-two years of active participation in the National Council of Teachers of English, I have seen overall progress in the involvement of people of color in NCTE, but disappointingly little progress for Latinos/Hispanos in comparison to our African American colleagues. Twenty-two years represents almost a quarter of a century; yet for many years, we were barely able to keep a status quo of Latino participants. Those we did have were often driven away by lack of commitment on NCTE's part to involve them significantly in the leadership. Others went on to professional organizations such as MLA and NABE, organizations they felt met their professional and political needs more directly. Still others did not make it in academia because of the overt and institutionalized racism they had to confront and because of our society's general lack of commitment to inclusion.

Others had positions that were so tenuous and pay scales that were so noncompetitive, that they did not have the stability necessary to carry through a commitment from year to year to attend to the constant work that it takes to build presence in a huge organization like NCTE.

However, some of the fault lay with Hispanics/Latinos who did not understand the power of a united front -- of the strength in numbers. Chicanos, Puertoriqueños, Cubanos, Central Americans ... Hispanos/Latinos, unlike our African American counterparts, tended to be loners in their exploration of NCTE and the national educational policy issues in which NCTE engages. They did not realize the strength of networking with other Latinos and people of color. The leaders of the Hispanic Caucus have for many years admired the steady, united work of the Black Caucus and the many significant gains made by the combined academic and political expertise of that group.

We have made some inroads, but it is incumbent on us to begin the serious work of educating NCTE and all its commissions, committees, journals, and other constituents about us -- the Hispanic/Latinos of the United States, which represent the fastest growing minority ... projected to be the largest minority population in the United States by 2025! Our population has grown immensely in the past decade and now constitutes 10% of the total U.S. population. It is the fastest growing school-age population in the United States. Yet our students have the highest rate of attrition, score the lowest on all standardized achievement tests (whether they be valid measures or not), and are most egregiously under represented in colleges amd universities. We are a tiny 3% of the elementary and secondary school teacher cadre, and we are too few to even make a percentage among faculties at colleges and universities.

NCTE's role in creating national language arts policy and influencing general educational policies is critical and one that merits our closest attention. To develop our voice, we have to work to empower ourselves within the National Council of Teachers of English. We have to be visible. We have to flourish in NCTE and the larger educational community. We have to collaborate with other groups and forge educational attitudes, approaches, and policies that will facilitate and enhance the education of

Please see **"Saludos," P. 2**

Volume II, Number 1*

Capirotada

The Latino Caucus Newsletter

*this was the number listed on the newsletter distributed at NCTE in San Diego; we're using it again for continuity's sake since this is actually the third newsletter we've printed to date. Next issue, which we hope you will help us write (SEND US STUFF!), will be Volume II, Number 2; we hope to distribute these at NCTE in Chicago.

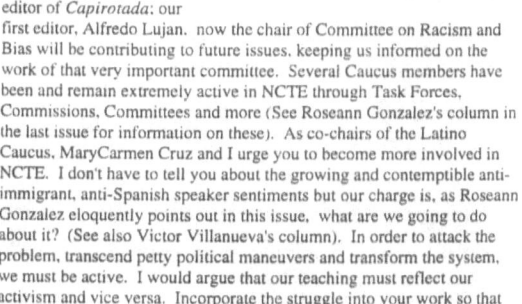

In this issue:

*editor's column
* Roseann Dueñas Gonzales--"Notes from the Arizona Underground"
*Luise Connal Rodriguez reviews Mike Rose's book (title)
*Reports on three sessions from San Deigo's conference
*poems by Maria de Jesus Estrada and Louise Connal Rodriguez
*MaryCarmen Cruz's column
*notes from Victor Villanueva

From the Editor:

It is my pleasure to greet you as I begin my tenure as editor of *Capirotada*; our first editor, Alfredo Lujan, now the chair of Committee on Racism and Bias will be contributing to future issues, keeping us informed on the work of that very important committee. Several Caucus members have been and remain extremely active in NCTE through Task Forces, Commissions, Committees and more (See Roseann Gonzalez's column in the last issue for information on these). As co-chairs of the Latino Caucus, MaryCarmen Cruz and I urge you to become more involved in NCTE. I don't have to tell you about the growing and contemptible anti-immigrant, anti-Spanish speaker sentiments but our charge is, as Roseann Gonzalez eloquently points out in this issue, what are we going to do about it? (See also Victor Villanueva's column). In order to attack the problem, transcend petty political maneuvers and transform the system, we must be active. I would argue that our teaching must reflect our activism and vice versa. Incorporate the struggle into your work so that your students, colleagues, community members, friends and family, understand the significance of the danger and work together for change. If we are to survive and thrive into the next century, we must act now! Make no mistake, Latinos are under attack and we must respond and react.

This issue was put together very quickly but efficiently with the help of an IUP workstudy student, Shawna France, without whom I could not have endured--mil gracias. I'd also like to thank all the contributors to this issue. And a grateful acknowledgement goes to my Dean at IUP, Brenda Carter, who considers my work to NCTE and the Caucus to be valuable. To all you would-be contributors, send us your reviews, columns or letters to the editor, poems, calls to arms, battle strategies, whatever! This newsletter is yours; make your voices heard. Tell us what you want to read/know.

Two items of business: if you have not paid Latino Caucus dues this academic year, please remit these to me at the address below (1 for full time teachers/instructors; for grad students; for undergrads, or send whatever you can afford). We use that money to pay for copying and mailing expenses etc. Finally, please do whatever you can to coordinate a Hispanic Literary Heritage Reading at your school or in your community during the month of October (Hispanic Heritage month in many states) this year. See my columns on how to run one of these events in the last two issues (or for more information including a sample bibliography, call me or email me). At the NCTE convention in Chicago, the Caucus will host "Hispanic Heritage Reading" (#L14), a session to provide information and share success stories--please bring us your own. One of goals is to make this a national event on the scale of the Black Caucus African American Read-In held every February. There is no set way to organize an event; the only stipulations are, 1) run the event any date in October, and, 2) read/recite/share Hispanic, Latino, Latin American, Spanish Literature etc.--in Spanish, English or both--we want to celebrate our rich, complex and beautiful literature.

Cecilia Rodríguez Milanés
cmilanes@grove.iup.edu
(412) 357-4940 or 22661.

address: IUP, English Dept.
110 Leonard Hall
Indiana, PA 15705

Image 32: NCTE's Latino Caucus Newsletter *Capirotada* Vol. 2, No. 2, Spring 1996 sent to Caucus members from Caucus editors and chairs. This newsletter includes an article by Maria-Cristina Kirklighter, in which she proposes a Caucus compositionalists Listserv. Included is an excerpt from a letter by Maria de Jesus Estrada about the Marcha en Washington, where she notes that gay individuals were acknowledged and given the right to speak on stage. In *California Craziness* Bobbie Ciriza Houtchens critiques Proposition 209 the anti-affirmative action law. Amanda Espinosa-Aguilar writes about her perspective about the 1996 NCTE Summer Institute for Teachers of Literature. The newsletter includes three poems, one by Jeanett Castellanos, Maria de Jesus Estrada, and one by Cecilia Rodríguez Milanés.

Image 33: *Capirotada.* NCTE's Latino Caucus Newsletter Vol. 7, No. 1, December 2001. This newsletter includes the ed: Gail Okawa writes about a special pan-ethnic program featuring the former Scholars for the Dream award recipients; An excerpt from the Listserv Raul Sanchez On Identify by Cecilia Rodríguez Milanés reviews Peter Ripley's book *Conversations with Cuba.* The announcement section features the accomplishments of Caucus members in 2001.

Image 34: *Capirotada.* NCTE's Latino Caucus Newsletter Vol. 10, No. 2, March 2005. This newsletter chronicles the awards and good news about Caucus members and the CCC Conference featured sessions, 2004 and 2005. The two featured essays include: Latina Writers as mentors by Ivonne Lamazres and female Mexican American film directors and Latina identity films by Victoria Mosher. The newsletter concludes with a book review of *More than Black: Afro-Cubans in Tampa* by Cecilia Rodríguez Milanés.

Image 35: *Capirotada.* NCTE's Latino Caucus Newsletter Vol. 12, Issue 2, March 2007. This newsletter Renee Moreno highlights Sandra Gibbs' legacy to the Caucus. Cecilia Rodríguez Milanés reviews *Mama Fela's Girl, along with the* the awards and good news about Caucus members. The newsletter concludes with a poem by Itzi Meztili, Raza, Child of the Morn. This is the last paper issue of Capirotada as Cecilia goes on sabbatical and there is an effort to put the newsletter online.

CAPIROTADA

The NCTE Latino Caucus Newsletter

December 2001
Volume 7, Issue 1

Memorial statue in Cementerio Colón, Havana, Cuba

In This Issue

Editor's Column 1
Student Writing 2
Cultivating Voices 2
Scholars for the Dream 3
On Identity 3
Book Review 6
Announcements 6
At NCTE 7
Renewal Form 8

From the Editor:

On September 10, 2001, my baby dropped in my womb, but on September 11, he changed his mind. Who could blame him? The world was a totally different place from one day to the next. On the 10th, the World Trade Center was still standing tall; planes weren't used as weapons, thousands of people in the US hadn't died in an all out assault against us. On the 10th, my baby would have been born into a world where "we" weren't at war, where we were still blithely untouched by international terrorism. On the 11th, I felt the life inside me hold still, move back up and away from my pelvis. I couldn't stop looking at the media images of the twin towers being hit, on fire, collapsing, crushing thousands of lives. The baby held still, and I had nightmares about my beloved city, the buildings I watched being built that served as beacons home. I couldn't stop thinking about the destruction, the death, the dangers; the baby was quiet, sitting high, staying put. For the next month, first Anthrax scares, then images of the US bombing Afghanistan plagued my mind. On October 14, I was admitted to the hospital to have a baby, whether or not he wanted to be born—and he didn't. Victor Enrique Milanés was delivered via C-section; we could argue about which method is more violent, but the end result, the first breaths and cries of a baby were heard. And he was welcomed, and he is beloved and we, his family, pitied him the world we gave him.

The world we teachers now inhabit includes a country at war against an entity—terrorism, but in practice, we are warring against one of the world's poorest countries. Our students, no matter how young or old, no matter how sophisticated or jaded, are affected by the images of devastation and sound bytes of caustic rhetoric. I believe that teachers today are in an unusually precarious situation if their curriculum includes critical thinking. As a tenured university professor, I have enjoyed the sanctuary of academic freedom, and part of my pedagogy is to entertain and utter provocative statements regarding our culture, history and politics. I am not so comfortable these days doing what I normally do; I am made to feel like a traitor questioning US policies, especially in the Mideast. My students are not expressing much tolerance these days; they aren't getting much of it modeled around them. Teachers spend important time with students; we have always known our impact on young lives. What are we supposed to teach during wartime? Are we doing our students a disservice if we point out hypocrisies? Shall we follow and lead blindly in the interests of the nationalistic status quo? It is good to know that at the annual convention this year, NCTE resolved to "continue to support literature and writing instruction as a means for understanding loss, anger, war, and difference; language study as a vehicle for understanding conflict, propaganda, and democratic discourse; and critical literacy as an instrument essential to an informed citizenship and global understanding." I hope that we all can teach justice and I pray for the sake of my newborn son and everyone that the world will change again, not back in time but forward, to a time when we are all responsible for peace.

MARCH 2005
VOLUME 10, ISSUE 2

Capirotada
The Latino Caucus Newsletter

From the Editor
Cecilia Rodríguez Milanés

INSIDE THIS ISSUE:

Announcements and Congratulations	2
Contact Information	2
Essay: "The Communal Effort of Creation: Latina Writers as Mentors"	3
CCCC Conference Highlights	4-5
Book Review: *More Than Black: Afro-Cubans in Tampa*	6
Film Review: *Real Women Have Curves* and *How the Garcia Girls Spent Their Summer*	6
Poem: "Working in *Mi País, Supermarket*"	7
Latino Caucus Renewal Form	8

Recently I heard Laura Bush announce on NPR that the administration was going to initiate a new "focus on boys" in education and mentoring. Her interest in the subject, she said, stemmed from what she and others felt was a "distressing" number of boys failing school, involved in gang activity and ending up incarcerated. While her motivation may seem noble and worthy, this is how I read it. "Those damn feminists have made too many gains and have forced us to spend too much time and resources on girls, and as a consequence, boys are getting the short end of the stick." I literally screamed in my car when I heard Laura Bush, in this propaganda interview, outline her plan to "focus on boys."

I am reminded of a catchy bumper sticker—"if you're not angry, you're not paying attention." I like to think that I'm not the only one paying attention, but obviously many more aren't giving the results of last fall's "election" a second glance—I live in Florida and my Latino husband was one of many individuals I personally know who was not allowed to vote, just for your information

What, progressive educators, are we to make of the push of "No Child Left Behind" in secondary schools when this "act" wasn't funded at the elementary school level? How is it that the government can hold the public schools accountable when no leader in the Bush administration is ever held accountable for obvious gross negligence, deceit, and more? What kind of confidence does Torture Czar Alberto Gonzalez—our newly crowned Attorney General--inspire in Latina/os? Do we think young girls should look up to Secretary of (the lying) State Condeleeza Rice?

Teachers are de facto role models—we often spend more time with students then their families do. What did professors say/teach in response to the University of North Texas's conservative student group's "Catch an Alien" day activity? Did high school teachers across America discuss the recent Knight Foundation's survey of 8,000 students regarding the First Amendment? Did they talk about the attitudes these students expressed regarding the "need for more censorship in journalism" as being directly related to the Bush presidency's imperious rhetoric and The PATRIOT Act? I believe that we teachers need to address these and other assaults on American values; we may be America's last hope.

MARCH 2007
VOLUME 12, ISSUE 2

Capirotada

The Latino Caucus Newsletter

Caucus Concerns

From the Editor:
Cecilia Rodríguez Milanés

INSIDE THIS ISSUE:

Announcements and Congratulations	2
Contact Information	2
Book Review: *Mama Fela's Girls*	3
Essay On Sandra Gibbs	4-5
CCCC Highlights	6
Poetry	7
Latino Caucus Renewal Form	8

On behalf of the members of the NCTE Latino Caucus, Bobbi Ciriza Houtchens and I wrote to the NCTE Executive Director, the presidential team and to the members of the NCTE Executive Committee stating our deep concerns regarding the Council's treatment of Dr. Sandra Gibbs specifically and people of color in general. Below is a brief excerpt:

> We have, it is true, been troubled of late at the lessening influence of people of color within the organization, perhaps most visible in the quality of sessions and the number of sessions within the Rainbow Strand. We were dismayed that our presence would no longer affect program planning to the degree it once had, thanks in great measure to the work of Dr. Gibbs at headquarters. But this last move underscores the degree to which NCTE is no longer committed to advancing the presence of people of color and our concerns. To put it quite succinctly, the members of the Latino/a Caucus are shocked at the treatment of our champion at NCTE and all that it represents. We are amazed that NCTE has not publicly addressed the abysmal void about to be created.

To date, neither Bobbi nor I have received any response to our letter (which went to 19 individuals). We urge members of the Caucus to write directly to Executive Director Kent Williamson, President Joanne Yatvin et al* in order to request more information about how NCTE plans on addressing our concerns, to express your own concerns or relate your own experiences at NCTE and/or CCCC. Caucus member Renee Moreno shared her letter with us included here on pages 4 and 5.

The process of making Capirotada accessible online is moving forward. Assistant Editor Adele Richardson and I had some training on scanning the newsletter for archival quality use from the UCF librarian in charge of digitizing materials. We hope to write a grant to pay Adele for her work later this semester. We'll keep you up to date on when the project is completed.

Finally, I want to announce that I will be taking a full year's sabbatical effective this summer. I plan on attending CCCC next year and perhaps NCTE this year but I will be passing on the primary editing duties to my colleague here at UCF and Caucus member Ivonne Lamazares. Adele Richardson will continue to work on the newsletter next year but under Ivonne's supervision. Caucus membership business should continue as usual with dues coming to UCF. Address updates should go directly to Adele and I remain on the listserve but please note that I will not be regularly on email so any urgent questions should go to Bobbi and/or Adele or Ivonne. As you can imagine, I am thrilled to be able to focus my time and energy on professional renewal, research and writing.

I will enjoy the break and continue contributing in other ways.

*For NCTE executives' mailing addresses, contact me at cmilanes@pegasus.cc.ucf.edu

Selected List of Caucus Members' Publications

The following list of publications was started by caucus members a few years ago via a Google Document, which all members could update. The goal was to have a centralized location where we could keep track of members' publications. Due to its relative newness and to the fact that it is maintained as Google Document and circulated periodically on the Caucus' listserv, it is an incomplete list and tends to highlight more recent scholarship. Yet, we think it's a nice expansion to the history of the caucus since it demonstrates that Caucus members are publishing widely across the field.

Alvarez, Nancy, et al. "Agency, Liberation and Intersectionality Among Latina Scholars: Narratives From a Cross-Institutional Writing Collective." *Praxis: A Writing Center Journal*, vol. 14, no. 1, 2016, pp. 9–14.

Alvarez, Nancy. "On Letting the Brown Bodies Speak (and Write)" in *Out in the Center: Public Controversies and Private Struggles,* edited by Harry Denny. Logan, UT: Utah State University Press, 2019.

Alvarez, Nancy. "On Longing and Belonging: Latinas in the Writing Center" in *Bordered Writers: Lessons Learned at Hispanic-Serving Institution,* edited by Isabel Baca, Yndalecio Isaac Hinojosa, and Susan Wolff Murphy. Albany, NY: SUNY (forthcoming 2019)

Alvarez, Sara P. et al. "On Multimodal Composing." *Kairos: A Journal of Rhetoric, Technology, and Pedagogy*, vol. 21, no. 2, 2017.

Alvarez, Sara P., Suresh Canagarajah, Eunjeong Lee, Jerry Won Lee, and Shakil Rabbi. "Translingual Practice, Ethnic Identities, and Voice in Writing." In *Crossing Divides: Exploring Translingual Writing Pedagogies and Programs,* edited by Bruce Horner and Laura Tetreault. Utah State University Press, 2017, pp. 31—47.

Alvarez, Sara P. "Composition Rhetoric's Translingual Turn: Multilingual Approaches to Writing." Rev. of *Reworking English in Rhetoric and Composition: Global Interrogations, Local Interventions*, edited by Bruce Horner and Karen Kopelson. *Internationals Journal of the Sociology of Language* vol. 241, no. 1, 2016.

Alvarez, Steven. "Statement." *Journal of Basic Writing*, vol. 31, no. 2 2012, 32-56.

Alvarez, Steven. "Life." *Readings in Language Studies*, edited by Paul Miller Chamness, John Louis Watzke, and Miguel Mantero. Vol. 3. Grandville, MI: International Society of Language Studies, 2012, pp.151-173.

Alvarez, Steven. "Translanguaging Tareas: Emergent Bilingual Youth Language Brokering Homework in Immigrant Families." *Language Arts*, vol. 91 no.5 2014, pp. 326-339.

Alvarez, Steven, and Sara P. Alvarez. "The translingual biblioteca: A Case Study of a Latin American Ethnolinguistic Community Library in the *Nuevo* US South." *Pedagogies of Resistance and Self-Determination*, special issue of *Equity and Excellence in Education*. vol. 49, no. 4, 2016, pp. 403-413.

Arellano, Sonia. "A Maker Project: Writing about Material Culture." *Blog Carnival 8*. Digital Rhetoric Collaborative, 24 March 2016.

Baca, Damián and Ellen Cushman, editors. *Landmark Essays on Rhetorics of Difference*. New York: Routledge, 2018.

Baca, Damián and Iris Ruiz. "Decolonial Options and Writing Studies." *Composition Studies*, vol. 45 no.2, 2017, pp. 226-229.

Baca, Damián and Victor Villanueva, editors. *Rhetorics of the Americas: 3114 BCE to 2012 CE* (Studies of the Americas Series). New York: Palgrave Macmillan, 2010.

Baca, Damián. *Mestiz@ Scripts, Digital Migrations, and the Territories of Writing* (New Concepts in Latino American Cultures Series). New York: Palgrave Macmillan, 2008.

Baca, Damián. "Rethinking Composition, 500 Years Later." Special edition on Working English in Rhetoric and Composition: Global-Local Contexts, Commitments, Consequences. *JAC* 29:1/2 (2009): 229-242.

Baca, Damián. "The Chicano Codex: Writing against Historical and Pedagogical Colonization." Special Edition in Writing, Rhetoric, and Latinidad. *College English*, vol. 71, no. 6 2009, pp. 564-583.

Baca, Damián. "te-ixtli: the 'Other Face' of the Américas." *Rhetorics of the Americas: 3114 BCE to 2012 CE*, edited by Damián Baca and Victor Villanueva. New York: Palgrave Macmillan, 2010, pp. 1-20.

Baca, Damián. "Rhetoric, Interrupted: La Malinche and Nepantlisma." *Rhetorics of the Americas: 3114 BCE to 2012 CE,* edited by Damián Baca and Victor Villanueva. New York: Palgrave Macmillan, 2010, pp. 197-216.

Baca, Damián and Victor Villanueva, editors. Special Edition in Writing, Rhetoric, and Latinidad. *College English*, vol. 71, no. 6, 2009.

Baca, Isabel. "English, Español, or los Dos." In *Bordered Writers: Lessons Learned at Hispanic-Serving Institutions,* edited by Isabel Baca, Yndalecio Isaac Hinojosa, and Susan Wolff Murphy. Albany, NY: SUNY (forthcoming 2019).

Baca, Isabel. "The Value of Internships in a College Education." In *High Impact Practices in Community Settings: Strategies for Student Success in Higher Education,* edited by Guillermina Gina Nunez-Mchiri and Azuri L. Gonzalez. Kendall Hunt Publishing. (forthcoming 2019).

Baca, Isabel, Yndalecio Isaac Hinojosa, and Susan Wolff Murphy, editors. *Bordered Writers: Latinx Identities and Literacy Practices at Hispanic Serving Institutions.* Albany, NY: SUNY, 2019.

Baca, Isabel. "The Writing Classroom Meets Community Literacy Needs." In *Community Engagement Best Practices across the Disciplines,* edited by Heather Evans. Rowman & Littlefield, 2017.

Baca, Isabel, Laura Gonzales, and Victor Del Hierro. "Editors' Introduction: Community Resistance, Justice, and Sustainability in the Face of Political Adversity." *Reflections: A Journal of Public Rhetoric, Civic Writing, and Service Learning.* Special Issue, Digital, fall 2017.

Baca, Isabel. "Finding the Right Partners for Service-Learning Courses." *Service-Learning and Civic Engagement: A Sourcebook,* edited by Omobolade Delano-Oriaran, Marguerite Parks, and Suzanne Fondrie. Los Angeles, CA: SAGE, 2015, pp. 155-164.

Baca, Isabel and Juan Arturo Muro. "The Hook-Up: College Writers and Nonprofits Building Relationships." In *Adding to the Conversation on Service-Learning in Composition: Taking a Closer Look,* edited by Susan Garza. Southlake, TX: Fountainhead Press, 2013, pp. 41-65.

Baca, Isabel, editor. *Service-learning and Writing: Paving the Way for Literacy(ies)through Community Engagement.* Leiden, The Netherlands and Boston, MA: BRILL Publishers, 2012.

Baca, Isabel, editor. *Borders.* Southlake, TX: Fountainhead Press, 2011.

Baca, Isabel and Cristina Kirklighter. "Editors' Introduction." *Reflections: Public Rhetoric, Civic Writing, and Service Learning,* special issue, vol. 3 no.1, 2013, pp. 1-12.

Baca, Isabel and Cristina Kirklighter. "Interview with Roseann Dueñas Gonzalez."*Reflections: Public Rhetoric, Civic Writing, and Service Learning*, special issue, vol. 13 no. 1 (Fall 2013), pp.13-51.

Baca, Isabel. "Una Mujer Partida." *Reflections: Public Rhetoric, Civic Writing, and Service Learning*, special issue, vol. 13 no.1, 2013, pp. 100-101.

Baca, Isabel and Joana Owens. "Editors' Introduction: Opening the Doors to Service-Learning in the Humanities." *Interdisciplinary Humanities*, vol. 29 no.3, 2012 pp. 3-7.

Baca, Isabel. "Exploring Diversity, Borders, and Student Identities: A Bilingual Service-Learning Workplace Writing Approach." *Reflections: Public Rhetoric, Civic Writing, and Service Learning*, vol. 6, no. 1, 2007, pp. 139-149.

Baca, Isabel and Elaine Fredericksen. "Bilingual Students in the Composition Classroom: Paving the Way to Biliteracy." *Open Words: Access and English Studies*, vol. 2, no.2, 2008, pp. 24-42.

Baca, Isabel. "It's All in the Attitude—the Language Attitude." *Teaching Writing with Latino/a Students: Lessons Learned at Hispanic Serving Institutions*, edited by Cristina Kirklighter, et al.. New York: SUNY Press, 2007, pp. 145-168.

Blythe, Stuart and Laura Gonzales. Coordination and Transfer across the Metagenre of Secondary Research. *College Composition and Communication*, vol. 67, no. 4, 2016, pp. 607.

Burdge, Hilary, Zami T. Hyemingway, and Adela C. Licona. Research Brief: "Gender Nonconforming Youth: Gender Disparities, School Push Out, and the School-to-Prison Pipeline." GSA Network, 2014.

Burdge, Hilary, Adela C. Licona, and Zami T. Hyemingway. Research Brief: "LGBTQ Youth of Color: Gender Disparities, School Push Out, and the School-to-Prison Pipeline." GSA Network, 2014.

Caraballo, Limarys, S. Genao, and A. Lipnevich. "Expanding Communities of Practice: Collaboration and Mentoring in Educational Leadership and Teacher Education". *Purposeful Teaching and Learning in Diverse Contexts: Implications for Access, Equity and Achievement*, edited by D. Hucks, Y. Sealey-Ruiz, S.C. Carothers, V. Showunmi & C. Lewis, New York, NY: Information Age. (In Press).

Caraballo, Limarys, Lozenski, B., Lyiscott, J., and Morrell, E. YPAR and Critical Epistemologies: Rethinking Education Research. *Review of Research in Education*, vol. 41. No. 1, 2017, pp. 311-336.

Caraballo, Limarys. Border-crossing Chespirito: El Chavo del 8 meets Pepito in Exile. In *"Fue Sin Querer Queriendo": Resonances of El Chavo del 8 in Latin American Childhood, Schooling, and Societies,* edited by D. Friedrich & E. Colmenares. London, UK: Bloomsbury Academic, 2017, pp. 87-110.

Caraballo, Limarys and E. Rahman. Visible Teaching, (in)visible teacher: An Educator's Journey as a Muslim Woman. *English Journal,* vol. 106, no. 2, 2016. 47–53.

Caraballo, Limarys. Students' Critical Meta-Awareness in a Figured World of Achievement: Toward a Culturally Sustaining Stance in Curriculum, Pedagogy, and Research. *Urban Education,* vol.52, no. 5, 2016, pp. 585-609.

Caraballo, Limarys. (2014). The Student as Assemblage of Success: Constructing Multiple Identities amidst Classed, Gendered, and Raced Discourses of Achievement. *Curriculum and Teaching Dialogue,* 16(1-2), 103-123.

Caraballo, Limarys. &, M. Hill. "Curriculum-in-Action: Cultivating Literacy, Community, and Creativity in Urban Contexts." *English Leadership Quarterly,* vol. 37, no. 1, 2014, pp. 5-11.

Caraballo, Limarys. "'Where I'm from is a Place Divided': Negotiating Multiple Selves in Academia and Beyond. *Polymath: An Interdisciplinary Arts and Sciences Journal,* vol. 4, no. 2, 2014, pp. 10-15.

Caraballo, Limarys. "Identities-in-Practice in a Figured World of Achievement: Toward Curriculum and Pedagogies of Hope." *Journal of Curriculum Theorizing,* vol., 28, no, 2, 2012, pp. 43-59.

Caraballo, Limarys. "Theorizing Identities in a 'Just(ly)' Contested Terrain: Practice Theories of Identity Amid Critical-Poststructural Debates on Achievement and Curriculum." *Journal of Curriculum & Pedagogy,* vol. 8, no. 2, 2011, pp. 155-177.

Caraballo, Limarys. "Interest Convergence in Intergroup Education and Beyond: Rethinking Agendas in Multicultural Education." *International Journal of Multicultural Education,* vol. 11, no 1, 2009, pp. 1-15.

Carter, Marcia, Hernández, Anita, & Richison, Jeannine. I*nteractive Student Notebooks for English Learners,* Portsmouth, NH: Heinemann. (2009).

Carter, R.T., Oyler, C. J., McIntosh-Allen, K., Schlessinger, S., & Caraballo, L. "First Steps in Understanding Diversity Climates in Educational Institutions." *Teachers College Record,* 2014.

Cortez, José. "Of Exterior and Exception: Latin American Rhetoric, Subalternity, and the Politics of Cultural Difference." *Philosophy & Rhetoric.* Vol. 51, No. 2, 2018, pp 124-150.(Forthcoming 2017).

Cortez, José. "History." *Decolonizing Rhetoric and Composition Studies: New Latinx Keywords for Theory and Pedagogy*, edited by Iris Ruiz and Raúl Sánchez. New York: Palgrave, 2016, pp. 49-62.

Cortez, Josè, and Romeo García. "In Preparation for Alterity: The Absolute Limit of Latinx Writing." *CCC*. Forthcoming.

Crabtree, Robbin D., David Alan Sapp, and Adela C. Licona, editors. *Feminist Pedagogy: Looking Back to Move Forward*. Johns Hopkins University Press, 2009.

Robert Eddy and Victor Villanueva. *A Language and Power Anthology: Representations of Race in a "Post-Racist"Era*. Provo: Utah State UP, 2014.

Fields, Amanda., Londie Martin, Adela C. Licona, and Elizabeth H Tilley. "Performing Urgency: Slamming & Spitting as Critical and Creative Response to State Crisis." *Kairos: A Journal of Rhetoric, Technology, and Pedagogy*, vol. 20, no. 1, 2015.

García de Müeller, Genevieve. "Digital Dreams: The Rhetorical Power of Online Resources for DREAM Act Activists." *Linguistically Diverse Immigrant and Resident Writers*, edited by Todd Ruecker and Christine Ortmeier-Hooper, Routledge, 2016.

García de Müeller, Genevieve and Brian Hendrickson. "Inviting Students to Determine for Themselves What It Means to Write Across the Disciplines." *The WAC Journal*. vol. 27, 2016, pp. 74-93.

García, Romeo, and Jose Cortez. "The Trace of a Mark that Scatters: The Anthropoi and the Rhetoric of Decoloniality." *RSQ*, Forthcoming.

García, Romeo. "Settler Colonial Archives and a Decolonial Option." *Constellations: A Cultural Rhetorics Publishing Space*. Forthcoming.

García, Romeo and Yndalecio Hinojosa. "Resistance: Embodied Narratives, Anti-Racist Agendas, and Compassionate Pedagogy." *On Teacher Neutrality: Praxis, Politics, and Performativity*, edited by Daniel Richards. Utah State University Press. Forthcoming.

García, Romeo, Wonderful Faison, and Anna Trevino. "White Benevolence: Why that Supa-Save-a-Savage Rhetoric Ain't Getting It." *White Benevolence: Deconstructing Whiteness in the Writing Center*, edited by Wonderful Faison and Frankie Condon. Utah State University Press. Forthcoming.

García, Romeo, and Douglas Kern. "We Do/Don't Have that Problem Here." *White Benevolence: Deconstructing Whiteness in the Writing Center*, edited by Wonderful Faison and Frankie Condon. Utah State University Press. Forthcoming.

García, Romeo, and Damián Baca. R*hetorics Elsewhere and Otherwise: Contested Modernities, Decolonial Visions.* Studies in Writing and Rhetoric, 2019.

García, Romeo. "Haunt(ed/ing) Genealogies and Literacies" *Reflections: A Journal of Community-Engaged Writing and Rhetoric,* vol. 19, no. 1, 2019, pp. 230-252.

García, Romeo. "The Predicament of 'Being There': Conflict and Emotional Labor." *Navigating Challenges in Qualitative Educational Research,* edited by Todd Ruecker and Vanessa Svihla. Routledge, 2019, pp. 67-79.

García, Romeo, and Beatrice Mendez Newman. "Teaching with Border Writers: Reconstructing Narratives of Difference, Mobility, Translingualism, and Hybridity." *Teaching Writing with Bordered Writers: Lessons Learned at Hispanic-Serving Institutions,* edited by Isabel Baca, Yndalecio Hinojosa, and Susan Wolff Murphy. SUNY Press, 2019, pp. 125-146.

García, Romeo, Joanne, Claudia, and Christie Toth. "'Work' As Taking and Making Place." *Journal of College Literacy and Learning,* vol. 45, 2019, pp. 104-106.

García, Romeo. "Corrido-ing State Violence." *Journal of Multimodal Rhetorics,* vol. 2, no. 2, 2018, pp. 51-69.

García, Romeo. "Creating Presence from Absence and Sound from Silence." *Community Literacy Journal,* vol. 13, no. 1, 2018, pp. 7-15.

García, Romeo. "Unmaking Gringo-Centers." *The Writing Center Journal,* vol.36, no. 1, 2017, pp. 29-60.

García, Romeo. "On the Cusp of Invisibility: Opportunities and Possibilities of Literacy Narratives." *Open Words,* 2017. n.p.

García, Romeo. Book Review of Tropic Tendencies: Rhetoric, Popular Culture, and the Anglophone Caribbean. *Reflections: A Journal of Public Rhetoric, Civic Writing, and Service Learning,* vol. 17, no. 1, 2017, pp. 199-205.

García, Romeo. Book Review of *Reclaiming Poch@ Pop: Examining the Rhetoric of Cultural Deficiency. Rhetoric Society Quarterly.* vol. 45, no. 4, 2015, pp. 387-391.

García, Romeo. Book Review of *Refiguring Rhetorical Education: Women Teaching African American, Native American, and Chicano/a Students, 1865-1911. Enculturation: A Journal of Rhetoric, Writing, and Culture.* vol. 20, 2015. n.p.

Gonzales, Laura. Multimodality, Translingualism, and Rhetorical Genre Studies. *Composition Forum,* vol. 31, 2015.

Gonzales, Laura, and Rebecca Zantjer. Translation as a User-Localization

Practice. *Technical Communication*, vol. 62, no. 4, 2015, pp. 271-284.

González, Roseann Dueñas, editor. *Language Ideologies: Critical Perspectives on the Official English Movement*, vol. 2: *History, Theory, and Policy*. Urbana, IL: National Council of Teachers of English, 2001.

Guiseppe Getto, Leon, Kendall and Jessica Rivait. "Helping To Build Better Networks: Service-Learning Partnerships as Distributed Knowledge Work." *Reflections: Public Rhetoric, Civic Writing and Service Learning*, vol. 13, no. 2, 2014, pp. 71-95.

Gurl, Theresa, Limarys Caraballo, Leslee Grey, John H. Gunn, David Gerwin, and Héfer Bembenutty, H. *Performance Assessment, Policy, Privatization, and Professionalization: Affordances and Constraints for Teacher Education Programs*. Rotterdam, The Netherlands: *Springer*, 2016.

Gutíerrez, Laura, Christina B. Hanhardt, Miranda Joseph, Adela C. Licona, and Sandra K. Soto. "Nativism, Normativity, and Neoliberalism in Arizona: Challenges Inside and Outside the Classroom," *Transformations*, special issue on Teaching Sex, vol. 21, no. 2, 2011, pp. 123-148.

Hernández, Anita., José Montelongo, and Roberta Herter. Crossing Linguistic Borders in the Classroom: Moving beyond English-only to Tap Rich Linguistic Resources. *Crossing Borders, Drawing Boundaries: The Rhetoric of Lines Across America*, edited by Barbara Couture & Patricia Wojahn, Logan, UT: University Utah Press, 2016, pp. 93-110.

Hidalgo, Alexandra. *Cámara Retórica: A Feminist Filmmaking Methodology for Rhetoric and Composition*. Logan, UT: Computers and Composition Digital P/Utah State UP, 2017.

Hidalgo, Alexandra. "A Feminist Approach to Social Media" (with Katie Grimes). *Kairos: A Journal of Rhetoric, Technology, and Pedagogy*, vol. 12, no. 2, 2017.

Hidalgo, Alexandra. "Alto Precio: Love, Loss, and Rebellion in Raising Bilingual Children." *Technoculture: an Online Journal of Technology in Society* vol. 6, 2016.

Hidalgo, Alexandra. "Vanishing Fronteras: A Call for Documentary Filmmaking in Cultural Rhetorics (con la ayuda de Anzaldúa)." *Enculturation: a Journal of Rhetoric, Writing, and Culture*, vol. 21, 2016.

Hidalgo, Alexandra. *Teta* (Documentary, 25 minutes, 2017). I tell the story of nursing my youngest son from birth to weaning him at 22 months.

Hidalgo, Alexandra. *William and Santiago Simultaneous* (Documentary, 5 minutes, 2016). A look at how different yet also similar the first year in two brothers' lives can be.

Hidalgo, Alexandra. *Vanishing Borders* (Documentary, 90 minutes, 2014). A documentary about four immigrant women living in New York City and transforming their communities with their work.

Hidalgo, Alexandra. *PERFECT: A Conversation with the Venezuelan Middle Class About Female Beauty and Breast Implants* (Documentary, 25 minutes, 2009). Featuring interviews with 13 middle-class Venezuelan women and men discussing the prevalence of breast implant surgery in their motherland.

Hidalgo, Alexandra. *A Visual Argument for Ethnic Studies* (Video Essay, 2 minutes, 2016). Featured on *Literacy & NCTE*.

Hidalgo, Alexandra. *Latin@s Taking Action* (Documentary, 5 minutes, 2016). Featured on *Literacy & NCTE*.

Hidalgo, Alexandra. *Lifting as We Climb: The Coalition of Women Scholars in the History of Rhetoric and Composition 25 Years and Beyond* (Documentary, 20 minutes, 2014). Published in *Peitho*.

Hidalgo, Alexandra. *The Underside of Dracula: Community and Masculinity in Pinball* (Documentary, 20 minutes, 2013). Published in *Itineration*.

Hidalgo, Alexandra. *#FavWomanFilmmaker Monday Video* (Promo Video, 5 minutes, 2015). Featured on *IndieWire, NPR and others*.

Hidalgo, Alexandra. *Cecilia Rodríguez Milanés Reading Barbie* (Documentary, 12 minutes, 2015).

Hidalgo, Alexandra. *A Mother's Cinematic Peregrinations* (Video Essay, 5 minutes, 2015). Featured on *Raising Films*.

Hidalgo, Alexandra and Kendall Leon. "Rhetoric, Multimedia Technology, and the Service-Learning Classroom." *Interdisciplinary Humanities*, 2012, pp. 41-55.

Hidalgo, Alexandra. "National Identity, Normalization, and Equilibrium: The Rhetoric of Breast Implants in Venezuela." *Enculturation: a Journal of Rhetoric, Writing and Culture*, vol. 13, 2012.

Hidalgo, Alexandra. "Unstoppable Force: Maternal Power and Feminism in the Harry Potter Series and its Film Adaptations." *Hermione Granger Saves the World: Essays on the Feminist Heroine of Hogwarts*, edited by Christopher Bell. Jefferson: McFarland, 2012, pp. 66-86.

Hidalgo, Alexandra. "Bare Life, Bridges, and Nodes: Race in the Twilight Saga and its Film Adaptations." *Genre, Reception, and Adaptation in the Twilight Series*, edited by Anne Morey. Surrey: Ashgate, 2012, pp. 79-94.

Hidalgo, Alexandra. "Group Work and Autonomy: Empowering the Working-Class Student." *Open Words: Access and English Studies*, vol. 2 no.2, 2008, pp. 3-23.

Hinojosa, Yndalecio Isaac. "The 'Complex Holism' of Broken Bodies: Anzaldúian Heuristics Re-constructing and Re-imagining Identities for Healing and Cultivating Hope." *Community Action for Social Justice*, edited by Victor Del Hierro, Isabel Baca, and Laura Gonzales Parlor Press, (forthcoming 2019).

Hinojosa, Yndalecio Isaac. "The Coyolxauhqui Imperative in Developing Comunidad-Situated Writing Curricula at Hispanic-Serving Institutions." *El Mundo Zurdo 6: Selected Works from the 2015 Meeting of the Society for the Study of Gloria Anzaldúa*, edited by Sara Ramirez, Larissa M. Mercado- López, and Sonia Saldívar-Hull,. San Francisco, California: Aunt Lute Books, 2018.

Hinojosa, Yndalecio Isaac and Candace de León-Zepeda. "Rhetorical Tools in Chicanx Thought: Political and Ethnic Inquiry for Composition Classrooms." *Bordered Writers: Latinx Identities and Literacy Practices at Hispanic Serving Institutions*. Eds. Isabel Baca, Yndalecio Isaac Hinojosa, and Susan Wolff Murphy. Albany, NY: SUNY, 2019: 77–103.

Hinojosa, Yndalecio Isaac and Candace Zepeda. "The Coyolxauhqui Imperative in Developing Comunidad-Situated Writing Curricula at Hispanic-Serving Institutions." *El Mundo Zurdo 6: Selected Works from the 2015 Meeting of the Society for the Study of Gloria Anzaldúa*. Eds. Sara Ramirez, Larissa M. Mercado-Lopez, and Sonia Saldívar-Hull. San Francisco, California: Aunt Lute Books, 2018: 57–71.

Houtchens, Bobbi Ciriza. "Teachers for the Dream." English *Journal*, vol. 86, no. 4, 1997. pp 64–66.

Hutchinson, Les. "Writing to Have no Face: The Queer Orientation of Anonymity in Twitter". *Social writing/Social media: Pedagogy, presentation, and publics*, edited by D. M. Walls and S. Vie. WAC Clearinghouse Perspectives on Writing book series/Parlor Press, 2017.

Johnson, Lucy A.. "Contending with Multimodality as a (Material) Process." *The Journal of Multimodal Rhetorics*, vol. 2, no. 1, Spring 2018, pp. 13-27.

Johnson, Lucy A.. Video Book Review of *Cámara Retórica: Feminist Filmmaking Methodology for Rhetoric and Composition*. Alexandra Hidalgo. Logan, UT: Computers and Composition Digital Press/Utah State UP, 2017. in *Peitho: Journal of the Coalition of Feminist Scholars in the History of Rhetoric & Composition*, vol. 20, no. 2. Spring/Summer 2018, pp. 406-411.

Johnson, Lucy A.. "Human vs. Machine: Tracking Political Discourse Using Voyant." Blog Carnival: Teaching Digital Rhetoric After the Election. *Sweetland Digital Rhetoric Collaborative*, 2017.

Johnson, Lucy A.. Book Review of Digital Rhetoric: Theory, Method, Practice. Doug Eyman. Ann Arbor, MI: University of Michigan Press, 2015. in *Enculturation: A Journal of Rhetoric, Writing, and Culture*, vol. 23 no.1, 2016.

Johnson, Lucy A. and Kristin L. Arola. "Tracing the Turn: The Rise of Multimodal Composition in the U.S." *Res Rhetorica*, no.1, 2016.

Leon, Kendall and Stacey Pigg. "Conocimiento as a Path to Ethos: Gloria Anzaldúa as Networked Theorist." *Women's Ethos: Intersections of Rhetorics and Feminisms*, edited by Rebecca Jones, Nancy Myers, and Kathleen Ryan. Southern Illinois University Press, 2016.

Leon, Kendall. "Chicanas Making Change: Institutional Rhetoric and the Comisión Femenil Mexicana Nacional." *Reflections: Public Rhetoric, Civic Writing and Service Learning*, vol. 13, no. 1, 2013, pp. 165-194.

Leon, Kendall. "*La Hermandad* and Chicanas Organizing: The Community Rhetoric of the *Comisión Femenil Mexicana Nacional Organization. Community Literacy Journal*, vol. 7, no. 2, 2013.

Leon, Kendall and Tom Sura. "We Don't Need Any More Brochures": Rethinking Deliverables in Service-Learning Curricula." *Writing Program Administration*, vol. 36 no.2, 2013.

Leon, Kendall, Stacey Pigg and Martine Courant Rife. "Researching to Professionalize, not Professionalizing to Research: Understanding the WIDE Effect. *Rewriting Success in Rhetoric and Composition Careers*, edited by Barbara Couture & Patricia Wojahn, Lauer Series in Rhetoric and Composition, Anderson, SC: Parlor Press, 2012, pp. 254-277.

Leon, Kendall, Jim Ridolfo, Martine Rife, Amy Diehl, Jeffery Grabill, Doug Walls, and Stacey Pigg. "Stories of Collaboration and Graduate Student Professionalization in a Digital Humanities Research Center." *Collaborative Approaches to the Digital in English Studies*, Laura McGrath, Computers and Composition Digital Press/Utah State University Press, 2011, pp. 113-140.

Leon, Kendall and Stacey Pigg. "Graduate Students Professionalizing in Digital Time/Space: A View from 'Down Below.'" *Computers and Composition*, vol. 28, 2011, pp 3-13.

Licona, Adela C. and Sandra Soto. "HB 2281: Key Points, Political Implication, and Local Mobilizations." *Encyclopedia of Latino/as in Politics, Social Movements, and Law*, edited by Suzanne Oboler and Deena González. Oxford University Press, 2016.

Licona, Adela C., and Karma Chávez. "Relational Literacies and their Coalitional Possibilities," *Peitho: The Journal of the Coalition of Women Scholars* in the *History of Rhetoric and Composition*, vol. 8. no 1, 2015, 96-107.

Licona, Adela C., and Karma Chávez. "Queer and Now." Queer and Now Special Issue of *The Writing Instructor*, 2015.

Licona, Adela C., and Marta Maria Maldonado. "The Social Production of Latin@ Visibilities and Invisibilities: Geographies of Power in Small Town America." *Antipode*, vol. 46, no 2, 2014.

Licona, Adela C., and Stephen T. Russell. "Transdisciplinary & Community Literacies: Shifting Discourses & Practices Through New Paradigms of Public Scholarship & Action-Oriented Research." *Special Issue Community Literacy Journal*, vol. 8 no. 1, 2013, pp. 1-7.

Licona, Adela C., and J. Sarah Gonzales. "Education. Connection. Action., ECA: Reporting on ECA as a Frame for Community Arts-Based Inquiry, Action-Oriented Teaching and Research, and Multi-Perspectival Knowledges," *Community Literacy Journal*, edited by Adela C. Licona and Stephen T. Russell, vol. 8. no. 1, 2013 (Selected for publication in *The Best of the Independent Rhetoric & Composition Journals* 2014).

Licona, Adela C. *Zines In Third Space: Radical Cooperation and Borderlands Rhetoric*. SUNY Press, 2012.

Maldonado, Marta Maria, and Adela Licona C. "Re-thinking Integration as Reciprocal Process: Implications for Research and Practice." *Journal of Latino-Latin American Studies*, vol. 2 no. 4, 2007, pp. 128-143.

Martinez, Aja Y.. "A Personal Reflection on Chican@ Language and Identity in the US-Mexico Borderlands: English Language Hydra as Past and Present Imperialism." *Why English? Confronting the Hydra*, edited by Vaughan Rapatahana, Robert Phillipson, Pauline Bunce, and Ruanni Tupas. Bristol: Multilingual Matters, 2016, pp. 211-219.

Martinez, Aja Y.. "A Plea for Critical Race Theory Counterstory: Stock Story versus Counterstory: Dialogues Concerning Alejandra's 'Fit' in the Academy." *Performing Anti-Racist Pedagogy in Rhetoric, Writing, and Communication*, edited by Frankie Condon and Vershawn Ashanti Young. Anderson: Parlor Press, 2015.

Martinez, Aja Y.. "Critical Race Theory: Its Origins, History, and Importance to the Discourses and Rhetorics of Race." *Frame—Journal of Literary Studies*, vol. 27 no. 2, 2014. pp. 9-27.

Martinez, Aja Y.. "A Plea for Critical Race Theory Counterstory: Stock Story versus Counterstory Dialogues Concerning Alejandra's 'Fit' in the Academy." *Composition Studies*, vol. 42 no. 2, 2014, pp. 33-55.

Martinez, Aja Y.. "Critical Race Theory Counterstory as Allegory: A Rhetorical Trope to Raise Awareness About Arizona's Ban on Ethnic Studies." *Across the Disciplines*, 2013.

Martinez, Aja Y.. "'The American Way': Resisting the Empire of Force and Colorblind Racism." *College English*, vol. 71, no. 6, 2009, pp. 584-595.

Medina, Cruz. "Identity, Decolonialism, and Digital Archives." *Composition Studies*, vol. 45, no. 2, 2017 (forthcoming).

Medina, Cruz and Octavio Pimentel, editors). *Racial Shorthand: Coded Discrimination Contested in Social Media*. Computers and Composition Digital Press, 2018.

Medina, Cruz. "Day of the Dead: Decolonial Expressions in Pop de los Muertos." *The Routledge Companion to Latina/o Pop Culture*, edited by Frederick Aldama. Oxfordshire: Routledge, 2016, pp. 370-380.

Medina, Cruz. "Poch@: Latin@ Blogs in the Decolonial Archives." *Rhetorics of Decolonization: Keywords for Theory and Pedagogy*, edited by Iris Ruiz and Raúl Sánchez. Palgrave MacMillan, 2016, pp. 93-108.

Medina, Cruz and Aja Y. Martinez. "Contexts of Lived Realities in SB 1070 Arizona." *Present Tense: A Journal of Rhetoric in Society*, vol. 4 no. 2, 2015, pp.1-8.

Medina, Cruz. *Reclaiming Poch@ Pop: Examining the Rhetoric of Cultural Deficiency* (Latino Pop Culture Series). New York: Palgrave Macmillan, 2015.

Medina, Cruz. "Teaching Jimmy Santiago Baca." *Latino/a Literature in the Classroom: 21st Century Approaches to Teaching*, edited by Frederick Aldama. Oxfordshire: Routledge, 2015, pp. 271-274.

Medina, Cruz. "Tweeting Collaborative Identity: Race, ICTs and Performing *Latinidad*." *Communicating Race, Ethnicity, and Identity in Technical Communication*, edited by Miriam Williamson and Octavio Pimentel. Amityville: Baywood Publishing, 2014, pp. 63-86.

Medina, Cruz. "(Who Discovered) America: Ozomatli and the Mestiz@ Rhetoric of Hip Hop." *Alter/Nativas: Latin American Cultural Studies Journal*, vol. 2. 2014.

Medina, Cruz. "The Family Profession." *College Communication and Composition*, vol. 65, no.1, 2013, pp. 34-36.

Medina, Cruz. "Nuestros Refranes: Culturally Relevant Writing in Tucson High Schools." *Reflections: A Journal of Public Rhetoric, Civic Writing, and Service Learning*, vol. 12 no. 3, 2013, pp. 52-79.

Mejia, Jaime Armin. "Bridging Rhetoric and Composition Studies with Chicano and Chicana Studies: a Turn to Critical Pedagogy." *Latino/a Discourses: On Language, Identity & Literacy Education*, edited by Michelle

Kells, Valerie M. Balester, and Victor Villanueva. Portsmouth, NH: Boynton/Cook Publishers/Heinemann, 2004, pp. 40-56.

Miller, James, Roseann Dueñas Gonzalez, and Michael Miller. *United States in Literature: America Reads,* Medallion Edition. Glenview, IL: Scott Foresman, 1982.

Moreland, Casie and Keith D. Miller. "The Triumph of Whiteness: Dual Credit Courses and Hierarchical Racism in Texas." *Haunting Whiteness: Rhetorics of Whiteness in a 'Post-Racial' Era,* edited by Tammie Kennedy, Joyce Middleton, and Krista Ratcliffe. Carbondale: Southern Illinois UP, 2016, pp. 182-194.

Moreland, Casie. "Chasing Transparency: Using Disparate Impact Analysis to Assess the (In)Accessibility of Dual Enrollment Composition." *Writing Assessment, Social Justice, and the Advancement of Opportunity,* edited by Mya Poe, Asao Inoue, and Norbert Elliot. (Forthcoming).

Naynaha, Siskanna, and Wendy Olson. "Learning Communities in the New University." *Linked Courses for General Education and Integrative Learning: A Guide for Faculty and Administrators.* Sterling, VA: Stylus, 2013, pp.151-68.

Naynaha, Siskanna. "Que(e)rying Capital: Toward a Xicanista Rhetoric." *Panini: NSU Studies in Language and Literature,* vol. 4, 2006-2007.

Ortego y Gasca, Felipe. "Reflections on Chicanos and the Teaching of American Literature," 2001.

Ortego y Gasca, Philip D.. "Reflections On The 'Chicano Renaissance.'" *Camino Real: Estudios De Las Hispanidades Norteamericanas,* vol. 1, no. 1, 2009, pp. 117-133. MLA International Bibliography.

Ortego y Gasca, Philip D., and Arnoldo De León, editors. *The Tejano Yearbook,* 1519-1978: A Selective Chronicle of the Hispanic Presence in Texas, Carvel, 1978.

Ortego y Gasca, Philip D. *We are Chicanos: An Anthology of Mexican-American Literature,* Washington Square Press, 1973.

Ortego, Philip D., and Jose A. Carrasco. "Chicanos and American Literature." *Searching for America,* edited by Ernece B. Kelly, The National Council of Teachers of English, 1972, pp. 78-94.

Parks, Steve, Brian Bailie, Romeo García, Adela Licona, Kate Navickas, David Blakesley. *The Best of the Independent Rhetoric and Composition Journals 2015.* Parlor Press, 2017.

Pimentel, Octavio. *Historias de Éxito within Mexican Communities: Silenced Voices.* Palgrave Macmillan, 2015.

Pimentel, Octavio, Charise Pimentel, and John Dean. "The Myth of the Colorblind Composition Classroom: White Instructors Confront White Privilege in Their Classrooms." *Performing Anti-Racist Pedagogy in Rhetoric, Writing, and Communication*, edited by Frankie Condon and Vershawn Ashanti Young, WAC Clearing House and Parlor Press, 2015.

Pimentel, Octavio and Katie Gutierrez. "Taqueros, Luchadores, y los Brits: U.S. Racial Rhetoric, and its Global Influence." *Race, Ethnicity, and Technical Communication for the Baywood Technical Communication Series*, edited by Miriam F. Williams, and Octavio Pimentel. *Race, Ethnicity, and Technical Communication*. New York: Baywood Publishing Press, 2014, pp. 7-99.

Pimentel, Octavio. "Learning to Write in Writing Centers: The Racial Experiences of Two Mexican Students." *English in Texas*, vol. 44 no. 2, 2014, pp. 34-39.

Pimentel, Octavio. "El Dia de Los Muertos." *Encyclopedia of Latino Culture: From Calaveras to Quinceañera*, edited by Charles Tatum, Santa Barbara, CA: ABC-CLIO-Greenwood, 2014.

Pimentel, Octavio. "The Changing Demographics of the United States: Rethinking the Academic Experience of English Language Learners." *The Council Chronicle*, vol.23 no.1, 2013, pp. 27-28.

Pimentel, Octavio. "An Invitation to a Too-Long Postponed: Race and Composition." *Reflections: A Journal of Writing, Community Literacy, and Service Learning*, vol. 12 no. 2, 2013, pp.90-104.

Pimentel, Octavio and Miriam Williams. "Introduction: Race Ethnicity and Technical Communication." *Race, Ethnicity, and Technical Communication: Examining Multicultural Issues within the United States. Special issue of Journal of Business and Technical Communication*, vol. 26 no. 3, 2012, pp. 271-277.

Pimentel, Octavio and Miriam Williams, editors. *Race, Ethnicity, and Technical Communication: Examining Multicultural Issues within the United States.* Special issue of *Journal of Business and Technical Communication*, vol. 26, no. 3, 2012.

Pimentel, Octavio. *"Mi Pobre Güerito." Teaching Bilingual/Bicultural Children: Teachers Talk About Language and Learning*, edited by Lourdes Diaz Soto and Haroon Kharem. New York: Peter Lang, 2010, pp. 73-78.

Pimentel, Octavio. "Disrupting Discourse: Introducing Mexicano Immigrant Success Stories." *Reflections: A Journal of Writing, Community Literacy, and Service Learning*, vol. 8, no. 2, 2009, pp. 171-196.

Pimentel, Octavio, and Paul Velázquez. "*Shrek 2*: An Appraisal of Mainstream

Animation's Influence on Identity Construction between African American and Latinas/os." *Journal of Latinos in Education*, vol. 8, no. 1, 2009, pp. 5-21.

Pimentel, Octavio, Charise Pimentel, Lourdes Diaz Soto, and Luis Urrieta, Jr. "The Dual Language Dualism: ¿Quiénes Ganan?" *Texas Association for Bilingual Education (TABE) Journal*, vol. 10, no.1, 2008, pp. 200-223; 15 July 2010.

Pimentel, Octavio, Jennifer Ramirez Johnson, and Charise Pimentel. "Writing New Mexico White: A Critical Analysis of Early Representations of New Mexico in Technical Writing." *Journal of Business and Technical Communication*, vol. 22 no.2, 2008, pp. 211-236.

Pimentel, Octavio and Charise Pimentel. "Coalition Pedagogy: Building Bonds Between Instructors and Students of Color." *Included in English Studies: Learning Climates That Cultivate Racial and Ethnic Diversity*, edited by Victor Villanueva and Shelli B. Fowler. Washington DC: American Association of Higher Education, 2002, pp. 115-124.

Powell, Malea, Stacey Pigg, Kendall Leon and Angela Haas. "Rhetoric." *Encyclopedia of Library and Information Sciences*, edited by M. Bates, M.N. Maack and M. Drake. London: Taylor & Francis/CRC Press.

Ramírez, Cristina D. & Jessica Enoch. *Mestiza Rhetorics: Anthology of Mexicana Activism in the Spanish-Language Press, 1887-1922*. Carbondale: Southern Illinois University Press. Forthcoming, 2019.

Ramírez, Cristina D. *Occupying Our Space: The Mestiza Rhetorics of Mexican Women Journalists and Activists, 1875-1942*. Tucson, University of Arizona Press: 2015.

Ramos, Santos F. "Building a Culture of Solidarity: Racial Discourse, Black LivesMatter, and Indigenous Social Justice." *Enculturation*, Special Issue: Cultural Rhetorics, vol. 21, 2016.

Ramos, Santos F. and Angélica De Jesús. "Xicano Indigeneity and State Violence: A Visual/Textual Dialogue." *Present Tense: a Journal of Rhetoric in Society*, Special issue on Race, Rhetoric and the State, vol. 5 no. 2, 2015.

Ramos, Santos F. "Digital is Dead: Techno-Seduction at the Colonial Difference, From Zapatismo to Occupy Wall Street" in *Identity and Leadership in Virtual Communities: Establishing Credibility and Influence*, edited by Joe Essid and Dona Hickey. Hershey, PA: IGI Global, 2014, pp. 220-236.

Ribero, Ana Milena. ""In Lak'Ech (You Are My Other Me):" Mestizaje as a Rhetorical Tool that Achieves Identification and Consubstantiality." *Arizona Journal of Interdisciplinary Studies*, vol. 2, 2013, pp. 22-41.

Richison, Jeannine, Hernández, Anita., & Carter, Marcha. *Text Sets: Scaffolding Core Literature for Secondary Students.* Portsmouth, NH: Heinemann. (2006).

Ruiz, Iris. *Reclaiming Composition Studies for Chicanos/as and other Ethnic Minorities: A Critical History and Pedagogy.* New York: Palgrave, 2016.

Ruiz, Iris, and Raúl Sánchez, editors. *Decolonizing Rhetoric and Composition Studies: New Latinx Keywords for Theory and Pedagogy.* New York: Palgrave, 2016..

Ruiz, Iris, and Raúl Sánchez, editors. "Race" *Decolonizing Rhetoric and Composition Studies: New Latinx Keywords for Theory and Pedagogy.* New York: Palgrave, 2016, 3-15.

Ruiz, Iris, and Raúl Sánchez, editors. "Introduction". *Decolonizing Rhetoric and Composition Studies: New Latinx Keywords for Theory and Pedagogy.* New York: Palgrave, 2016, pp. Xiii-xx.

Ruiz, Iris. "La Indigina: Risky Identity Politics and Decolonial Agency as Indigenous Consciousness" *As Us.* CreateSpace Independent Publishing Platform, 2015.

Ruiz, Iris, Alexandra Hidalgo and Christina Cedillo. "NCTE Position Statement in support of Ethnic Studies for K-12 Curricula," 2015.

Ruiz, Iris. Book Review of *Presumed Incompetent* in: *Reflections: A Journal of Writing, Service Learning and Community Literacy,* vol. 14, 2014.

Ruiz, Iris D., and Damían Baca. "Decolonial Options in Writing Studies." *Composition Studies,* vol. 45 no. 2, 2017.

Ruiz, Iris D. and Genevieve García de Müeller. "Race, Silence, and Writing Program Administration: A qualitative study of U.S. College Writing Programs." *WPA Journal,* vol. 40, no 1, 2017.

Ruiz, Iris D.. "A Decolonial Conference Review: Meditations on Inclusivity and 4 C's in Portland, Oregon." *Latino Rebels.* March 29, 2017.

Sanchez, James Chase. "Recirculating our Racism: Public Memory and Folklore in East Texas." *Lone Star Rhetoric: Methods of Rhetorical Placemaking,* edited by Casey Boyle and Jenny Rice. Southern Illinois University Press, 2018.

Sanchez, James Chase, and Kristen Moore. "Reappropriating Public Memory: Racism, Resistance and Erasure of the Confederate Defenders of Charleston Monument." *Present Tense,* vol. 5, no.2, 2015.

Sanchez, James Chase. "Postulating a Stereotype: A Rhetorical View of Chinese Immigration in *East of Eden.*" *Steinbeck Review,* vol. 9, no. 2, 2012, pp. 39-52.

Sanchez, James Chase, and Tyler Branson. "The Role of Composition Programs in De-Normalizing Whiteness in the University: Programmatic

Approaches to Racial Pedagogies." *WPA*, vol. 39. No. 2, 2016, pp. 47-52.

Sánchez, Raúl. "Writing." *Decolonizing Rhetoric and Composition Studies: New Latinx Keywords for Theory and Pedagogy*, edited by Iris Ruiz and Raúl Sánchez. New York: Palgrave, 2016, pp. 77-90.

Sánchez, Raúl. "Theory Building for Writing Studies." *WPA: Writing Program Administration*, vol. 39, 2015, pp. 141-157.

Sánchez, Raúl. "In Terms of Writing As Such." *Ecology, Writing Theory, and New Media: Writing Ecology*, edited by Sidney I. Dobrin. New York: Routledge, 2012 pp. 24-33.

Sánchez, Raúl. "Outside the Text: Retheorizing Empiricism and Identity." *College English*, vol. 74, 2012, pp. 234-246.

Sánchez, Raúl. "First, A Word." *Beyond Postprocess*, edited by Sidney I. Dobrin, J.A. Rice, and Michael Vastola. Logan, UT: Utah State UP, 2011, pp. 183-194.

Serna, Elias. "The Eagle Meets the Seagull: The Critical, Kairotic and Public Rhetoric of Raza Studies Now in Los Angeles." *Reflections: A Journal of Public Rhetoric, Civic Writing, and Service Learning,* vol. 12 no.3, 2013, pp. 80-93.

Serna, Elias. "Tempest, Arizona: Criminal Epistemologies and the Rhetorical Possibilities of Raza Studies." *The Urban Review*, vol. 45, no. 1, 2013, pp. 41-57.

Smitherman Geneva and Victor Villanueva. *Language Diversity in the Classroom: From Intention to Practice.* Carbondale, IL: Southern Illinois University Press, 2003.

Soven, Margot, Dolores Lehr, Siskanna Naynaha, and Wendy Olson, editors. *Linked Courses for General Education and Integrative Learning: A Guide for Faculty and Administrators.* Sterling, VA: Stylus, 2013.

Villanueva, Victor. "Calling a White a White." *Rhetorics of Whiteness: Postracial Hauntings in Popular Culture, Social Media, and Education*, edited by Tammie M. Kennedy, Joyce Irene Middleton, and Krista Ratcliffe, Provo: Utah State UP, 2017, pp. 253-254.

Villanueva, Victor. "'I am Two Parts': Collective Subjectivity and the Leader of Academics and the Othered." *College English*, vol. 79, no. 5, 2017, pp. 482-494.

Villanueva, Victor. "Metonymic Borders and Our Sense of Nation." *Crossing Borders, Drawing Boundaries: The Rhetoric of Lines Across America*, edited by Barbara Couture and Patricia Wojahn, Provo: Utah State UP, 2016, pp. 29-42.

Villanueva, Victor. "Subversive Complicity and Basic Writing Across the Curriculum," *Journal of Basic Writing,* vol. 32, no.1, 2013.

Villanueva, Victor and Kristin Arola. *Cross-Talk in Comp Theory: A Graduate Reader,* 3rd edition. Urbana: NCTE (1997, 2003), 2011.

Villanueva, Victor. "Of Ideologies, Economies, and Cultures: Three Meditations on the Arizona Border." *Present Tense: A Journal of Rhetoric in Society,* vol. 1, no. 2, 2011.

Villanueva, Victor. "Rhetoric, Racism, and the Remaking of Knowledge Making in Composition." *The Changing of Knowledge in Composition: Contemporary Perspectives,* edited by Lance Massey and Richard Gebhart. Provo: Utah State UP, 2011.

Villanueva, Victor. "Colonial Memory and the Crime of Rhetoric." *College English,* vol. 71, no.6, 2009, pp. 630-638.

Villanueva, Victor. "Blind: Talking about the New Racism." *Writing Center Journal,* vol. 26. no.1, 2009, pp. 3-19.

Villanueva, Victor. "The Student of Color and Contrastive Rhetoric." *Finding Pathways to Success In School: Culturally Responsive Teaching,* edited by Etta R. Hollins and Eileen I. Oliver, Mahwah, NJ: Erlbaum, 1999, pp. 107-123.

Villanueva, Victor. *Bootstraps: From an American Academic of Color.* Urbana: NCTE, 1993.

Whitney, Justin G. "The 2010 Citizens Clean Elections Voter Education Guide: Constructing the "Illegal Immigrant" in the Arizona Voter." *Journal of Technical Writing and Communication,* vol. 43, no.4, 2013, pp. 437-455.

Williams, Miriam and Pimentel, Octavio, editors. *Communicating Race, Ethnicity, and Identity in Technical Communication.* New York: Baywood Press, 2014.

Williams, Miriam F. and Octavio Pimentel, editors. *Race, Ethnicity, and Technical Communication: Examining Multicultural Issues within the United States.* Special Issue of Journal of Business and Technical Communication, vol. 26, no. 3, 2012.

Williams, Miriam F. and Octavio Pimentel. "Introduction: Race Ethnicity and Technical Communication." *Race, Ethnicity, and Technical Communication: Examining Multicultural Issues within the United States.* Special Issue of Journal of Business and Technical Communication, vol.26 no 3 2012, pp. 271-276.

Young, Vershawn Ashanti and Aja Y. Martinez, editors. *Code-meshing as World English: Policy, Pedagogy, and Performance.* Urbana, IL: National Council of Teachers of English, 2011.

Young, Vershawn Ashanti and Aja Y. Martinez, with Julie Anne Naviaux. "Code-meshing as World English Introduction." *Code-meshing as World English: Policy, Pedagogy, and Performance.* Urbana, IL: National Council of Teachers of English, 2011.

Zepeda, Candace. "QUEST First-Year Writing Program: Our Lady of the Lake University." *Working Writing Programs: A Reference of Innovations, Issues, and Opportunities: WPA Program Profiles Collection,* edited by Byrna SIegel Finer. Utah State: University Press, 2016.

Zepeda, Candace. "Chicana Feminism." *Decolonizing Rhetoric and Composition Studies: New Latinx Keywords for Theory and Pedagogy,* edited by Iris Ruiz and Raúl Sánchez. New York: Palgrave, 2016, pp. 137-152.

APPENDIX
Complete Interview Transcripts

In what follows, are a series of interviews conducted with members of the Latinx Caucus by the editorial team. While not all chairs have been interviewed, we the editors believe it is important to include those interviews we were able to conduct. There is no particular arrangement for how the interviews unfold. However, each interview is guided by a series of questions that begins on a personal level, transitions to questions that have the interviewees discuss the importance of the Caucus, and concludes with any insight that the interviewee would like to share that had not been covered already in the interview. The purpose of these interviews was to bring to the forefront the voices of various leaders of the Caucus throughout the years in both the NCTE and CCCCs. The following Caucus chairs and members were interviewed: Victor Villanueva, Cecilia Rodríguez Milanés, Jaime Armin Mejía, Cristina Kirklighter, Damian Baca, Steven Alvarez, Cristina Ramirez, and Aja Y. Martinez. In some cases, where the interview emerged from the Working and Writing for Change project, the link to the youtube.com video is included.

While some of the interviews were edited for and used in chapters and others were drawn upon for specific examples throughout *Viva Nuestro Caucus*, we felt it important to provide the full transcripts. Our rationale is that the full interviews provide a rich source of issues and insights that transcend the specific scope of this book, offering important research avenues for members of the caucus and the field in general.

VICTOR VILLANUEVA
Interview by Iris Ruiz
July 17, 2016
https://www.youtube.com/watch?v=LdHWGpAEFM8&t=77s

Iris Ruiz: Hello, I'm Dr. Iris Ruiz and I am the current co-chair of the NCTE CCCC Latino Caucus. I'm here today to interview Dr. Victor Villanueva from Washington State University. We're going to be performing an interview that's going to contribute to the current Latino Caucus historiography projects. We'll be going through an interview with Victor Villanueva and I'll be asking him 11 questions. First, I'd like to give Dr. Villanueva the opportunity to introduce himself.

Victor Villanueva: Hi, I'm Victor Villanueva and I'm a Regent's Professor and Director of the University Writing Program at Washington State University. I've been at Washington State University since 1995, prior to that I was at Northern Arizona University, prior to that I was in University of Missouri, Kansas City, and prior to that I was a graduate student at the University of Washington, wow yeah. And I got to the Pacific Northwest by way of the army and ended up liking it here, so I have now, even though I was born and raised in Brooklyn, New York, I have lived in the Pacific Northwest for most of the last 15 years. Very much of a New Yorker left in this New Yorker except to people who are New Yorkers. They all hear a New Yorker, but I go to New York I'm way too slow for those people.

Ruiz: You kind of assimilated a little bit to that area

Villanueva: That's a dangerous word, but yeah.

Ruiz: Yeah, I know I know bad word, maybe it'll come up in our conversation why. Ok, well cool that's a great area and thank you for agreeing to do this project with us today. Your voice is still very important, and your opinion and your experience, so thank you for giving us your time.

Villanueva: Thank you for saying all that.

Ruiz: All right so let's go ahead and get started. Just with a basic question, is when and why did you choose to attend C's and/or NCTE?

Villanueva: Now, it's an "and." The first time I went to four C's it was in fact in New York City, which was really interesting because I left there a decidedly poor Puerto Rican high school dropout and came back a completing graduate student, so that was way cool, kind of mind-boggling actually, but I was there because one of my mentors, my key mentor basically, Anne Ruggles Gere had put me on a panel as respondent, a panel that she was on with Anne Matsuhashi at the time. She's the end Feldman now and Melanie Sperling—and so this is how one does this career, and that's what my boss told me and she's been CCCC's chair and she's been NCTE president in her career, but so that's why I went to CCCC's the first time. I went to NCTE the first time because another mentor, William Irmscher, who had also been CCCC's chair and NCTE president, and, I think, the second editor, I think the second, maybe the third editor of CCC's, and recommended me for a committee and it was an NCTE committee, the resolutions committee. So that's why I went off to NCTE and for a good chunk of my career I have attended both meetings. I stopped going to NCTE, I don't know about 10 years ago or so and I will probably do much less CCCC's from this point on also because I'm getting up there in age. I wasn't born with a white beard, so yeah, that's why.

Ruiz: Why did you decide to join the Caucus? Who was involved and what did you sense was the importance of the Caucus for others? What were your goals? What has been the role of the Caucus in your career? I know that's a multi-faceted question so we'll just start off with why you decided to join the Caucus and who was involved.

Villanueva: Yeah well, well, that's a funny story, I was, and you know the thing is, I'm not sure whether it was for CCCCs or NCTE but when I stop to think about it, but somewhere along the way, we were in the Midwest someplace, maybe Minneapolis, I don't remember. I was looking for food; I was still a graduate student and that's what we do at the conferences. So, I was looking for food and this Latina, Chris Gutiérrez, kind of grabbed me by the collar. Actually what she did was grab my name tag and told me to start looking around for others with

Spanish names. I had no, I was just going to do what I was told and, if you would have seen Kris Gutiérrez and were a man, you would too. So, "Yes okay, yes ma'am." And so, as it turns out, we three then, Rosanne González and Kris Gutiérrez (and myself) had been doing a whole lot of Hispanic Caucus stuff, and in fact, were responsible for changing the name from Chicano Caucus, which is what it had been, to Hispanic Caucus and then later we changed it, and I can tell you that story if you ask, to Latino Caucus, because that was an interesting—that happened in 97 in Phoenix. So anyhow, so we met, the Latino Caucus had a meeting and the meeting was the three of us we were, we were it. So, did I think about—Ok what was the second half what was the second question.

Ruiz: Basically, so that's how you got involved and what did you sense was the importance of the Caucus for yourself and for others?

Villanueva: Well at the time there weren't too many Latinos to speak of and, I mean it's, this is very different nowadays and if....So what was clear was that we are here we are a presence, whether we were recognized or not as a presence. So, it was clear that this needed to be done if only to have our voices heard, even though the voices at that point amounted to three of us. And, in fact, because there was only three of us, we extended the Latino Caucus in those days to other folks of color. The *Black Caucus* was already very highly well organized and well represented. It had even done a boycott at CCCCs, like maybe the second Cs that I had gone to about investment in south Africa, which at the time was still immersed in apartheid. So, they were a highly organized unit already, but there were no others. So there were only the two Caucuses; Hispanic Caucus, Black Caucus. And so, since there were only the three of us, we became at that point the people of color not the Black Caucus. We called ourselves Hispanic Caucus and our major concern was that was us, gente, but we also had Susanne Banali, who was a Navajo, and Gail Ocala, who's still my friend. I'll be talking to her later today. It stayed that way until '98. In '98 point, Paul Matsuda insisted, asked, he was very courteous, he asked, he was incoming chair of the organization, and he asked if he could put together and have a space for an Asian Caucus. I think the American Indian, at that time it wasn't called American. It was called the American Indian scholars and intellectuals, and I think that began with somebody who had just been awarded the Scholars for the Dream that I was in charge of and, you won't recognize her name, it's Malea Powell.

Ruiz: No

Villanueva: So anyway, it was clear that our presence, and you know in the terms of Latinos and I'll slow down, at that particular time, the single most known Latino in our business was Richard Rodriguez and that was a problem. Now you know, I grew to like him overtime, but overtime he changed his story, his story changed and he came out that he was gay. Suddenly you knew that the big concerns he had with family was probably not about speaking damned English. But at the time it was, what is it? *Hunger of Memory* and he was a keynote speaker at NCTE Annual Convention - there's a great story there too. Jamie Mejia joined in a couple of years later when he was a graduate student working with Andrea Lunsford in Ohio. I don't remember what year that, that was probably, I'm going to say that happened in '95 or '96 that Jamie joined in, but before it was just a handful of us and that's that. Some stories to tell.

Ruiz: Ok, thank you. Let's see you so I want to make sure we finish that particular question, what do you think your goals were in being part of the Caucus and what has been the role of the Caucus in your career?

Villanueva: Well I think that the role of the Caucus has remained steady, which is representation and voice within the organization and then within the profession at large. We are too readily dismissed as, still and all the way down to students, dismissed as the folks who have some sort of deficit, and our deficit is that we have abilities with more languages then the people who weren't power, which is no deficit at all. It's an asset that refuses to be recognized. So, at the time however, if we go back to 1981 or 82 when I first joined the Caucus, when we became the Caucus basically, what we wanted to do, and we ended up doing, was not only be a presence, but assure that we had a presence in these conferences, that we weren't dismissed or simply spoken about. At some point, you'll probably end up talking to Renée Moreno and she can tell you that story. It's one of the very first. She was in the group of first ten

Scholars for the Dream. I'm going to tell you the story right now, even though she'll tell you the story too. When she gave her panel presentation as a Scholar for the Dream, somebody else on her panel just started carrying on with the same old stereotypes about Latinos, which Renée lost your temper over. But even with our presence, even standing right there, the stereotypes continued. So, that was our job too - try to educate these educators about who the hell we are and with all our complexities and contradictions. That ends up beginning, I don't remember what year, but Miriam Chaplain gets, it starts the Rainbow, the Rainbow Strand and that was a, let's just say, a troublesome beginning at Urbana. Just with people not being sure...(I don't know if you're there anymore, because you froze on the screen).

Ruiz: All right thank you, so was that like you said around in the 90's when you remember Renee's panel?

Villanueva: Renée's panel well, you'd have to, the way to find that out is to go back to William F. Cook as chair for C's.

Ruiz: Oh, ok.

Villanueva: And because what happened at the Executive Committee—I was a liaison on the committee, there used to be, people from the executive committee would be liaisons with the officers and they were the first two ever were, Wendy Bishop, who died some years back, and me - Sue McLeod, who ended up being my boss at CCCCs, I mean at WSU in the 90s, Sue McLeod had proposed *Scholars for The Dream*. So even though nobody wants to know this in the history, a white women actually proposed it, and it was because there was something similar that NCTE was doing already. The Executive Committee voted for it, Bill Cook was Chair. He assigned me at that point to start doing it and what we did was we sat in the lobby, we had all of these proposals for next year's CCCC's and we sat in the lobby and looked through all of these proposals from folks of color, that had to do with color and decided on the first ten. Renée was among those. So, it was highly informal. It became very very formal overtime, but at that time, it was just Bill Cook and me in one of those round couches that you see in hotels, just sitting in one of those things, and then talking about what we are reading and it included folks of color doing stereotypical stuff to you know but, that was pretty exciting, I don't remember what year Bill Cook, who's now dead, was Chair.

Ruiz: Okay we'll find him, we'll definitely find him. Okay thank you, I think you answered some of the third question already in terms of what you had witnessed. You can always expand on stuff because you have a lot of stories to share, so no problem at all. But maybe you can think of some of the issues that you witnessed from those organizations, CCCCs and NCTE, such as marginalization of other Latinos/Latinas or marginalization of research or publishing? So, if you witnessed anything like that or do you want to speak on those issues as they relate to both organizations.

Villanueva: Well, you know, it was less about publishing because there weren't that many of us out there. I mean over at the NCTE side there was, Puertoriqueña, I don't remember her name, I don't remember her name. There was Maria Franquiz y Dwyer, something de Dwyer

Ruiz: Carlotta?

Villanueva: Carlota, yeah. But they taught, they spoke mainly about—and Kris Gutiérrez herself, although she was still a graduate student, when she was in charge of the Hispanic Caucus and so was I. So, here's the thing, that, you know, Kris Gutiérrez was in Bilingual Ed. The other two were doing elementary or secondary school stuff and CCCCs. Rosanne González is a linguist.

Iris Ruiz: Okay.

Villanueva: So, in the CCCC's realm, the number of Latinos is the person you are looking at, I was it. Did I have trouble getting published? No, I didn't know how to publish, I was still a graduate student. My first essay came out in well my (breaks out) had to do with writing as a process of something. My first political essay, okay, that's a story, it was a about Richard Rodriguez. I was in NCTE and he was the Keynote Speaker. He just quite infuriated me because -and that evening talking about it with Jamie Mejia and Rosann González, Kris Gutiérrez, what was her name, Aurelia de Silva - we were sitting in a circle talking about it - I didn't understand they were telling me to shut up, but they kept saying

"Why don't you publish it?," That's code, I now know that that's code, "Why don't you publish it," meaning I'm sick of hearing this thing, go write it. So, we did.

Okay, so let's talk about that there have been good sides to [the professional organizations]. At my very first CCCC's in 1981 or '82, I went to see Pat Mizel, who was a new young thing too. I went to see her because, she was not a big name yet, I went to see her because she was going to speak about Richard Rodriguez. At the panel, at the thing, she kind of singled me out and asked "Was I right?" She says, "Am I right?" to me. I just kind of said nothing. So after the panel, she came up to me to ask why I said nothing. I said that I think he is crying too much in his beer and is too assimilationist, is that the word, to be very helpful for us. When she published that essay, which is something about what happens to basic writers or something like that, she footnoted and cited me, even though I was nobody and this was just the conversation at a panel. So, there was the respectful side, like that. And others not just Pat, I mean that I the reason I was there at all was because of people who took good care of me, like Anne Gere and Bill Irmscher, and others. Anne Feldman ended up being the local arrangements Chair for my CCCC's, so there were others.

The negative thing, the biggest negative thing that happened was, and this is, it is history it's going to irritate some folks who see it, but it is what happened. Miriam Chaplain, then as chair of CCCCs on the Executive Committee, proposed the Rainbow Strand. When she first proposed it, it died for lack of a second. In parliamentary procedures, somebody says something, makes a proposal, and it has to be seconded. If it doesn't get seconded, then it dies. There could be no conversation. So, it died for lack of a second with some of the great leaders of the organization refusing to take up the issue of having folks of color represents themselves in helping to put together the national conference. Now, Mariam was a smart cookie and at NCTE the Executive Committee, which meets twice, it meets right before the convention and then they have the time when the committee changes, when those who are stepping out step off and the new people come on board, they all meet again right after the convention after the convention. Mary Chaplin proposed it again.

Ruiz: Oh, that was smart.

Villanueva: And this time it passed. Even though it passed, there was someone who said, I don't know who it is, it doesn't matter, that they didn't need any watch dogs, because, of course, they were so liberal and advanced. But our idea was never, and when we first got to Urbana, Rosann, in particular, got a lot of flak from the secondary section because their perception was that we were there to censor them, which was never the case. What we wanted to do was to respond if somebody said something foolish, like there was a panel that had a title "Do you have to be one to teach one?" It's a legitimate concern, but phrasing it that way is not legitimate. So okay, we're not going to censor it. We're not going to say "no" to it. We created another panel that responded to that notion. So, we saw what the tendencies were and, sometimes, those tendencies were decidedly, let's just say stereotyped, and we created new panels. So, at first, there was some hostility to our presence. At one point we were asked why, at Urbana, why we didn't eat lunch with the rest of the folks. While we all hung out together, the Black and Latino, the Rainbow folks. And someone like me, I was in a decidedly white university, it's a little less so now, but it was at that time in the 90 percentile, about 96%, white, and, so, here I am finally around folks of color, who are all so intellectually interested in the same things I am, and I'm going to go talk to more white folks? I do that every day. It was good to be with them, but someone who was in a position of authority at that time said, "Why, we're just trying to do away with the sins of the past in demanding that we go and be with them during lunch?". So, you see, the good intentions, but not understanding that import of what they were saying. One of the members of the Black Caucus said "They are not our sins, so we shouldn't be punished for your sins, and we like hanging out together because this is our one opportunity."

So, there are all kinds of stories that early on, much of that until very recently had started to dissipate. There was, we had a champion, somebody who watched out for us at NCTE headquarters doggedly and, sometimes, even to the point of really aggravating people. That was Dr. Sandra Gibbs. I don't know the story and I will never know the story because the person who made that decision has died and he refused to tell me, but she was asked to retire. In other words, later in her career, she was essentially fired in that kind of respectful, to a respectful way, but fired even if you say asked to retire.

So, I don't know, publications? No, because we didn't exist. I mean we, Richard Rodriguez wasn't one of us, he wasn't an academic at all. Mike Rose did a beautiful job of speaking for us, but he was still speaking for us, it wasn't us speaking, you know, and the others, who were part of the group, were not Comp people. And it's, you know, I've been at this now 35 years and it's only recently that I realize that I am probably the first Latino Comp guy, I mean, which is kind of funny since we've been here for a little while, like even before the British got here.

Ruiz: Yeah, we were here for quite a while.

Villanueva: Yeah. And those you know, a few elections ago, they said "Oh we've just discovered the Latinos." No dammit, we've been here all along. We were here before you. We were talking to the Indians when you were still in England and Germany. You guys, we are not new, we've been here.

Ruiz: Yeah.

Villanueva: And rhet and comp has this American thing because, of course, there are many many Latino rhetoricians. So, somebody had proposed something and, it's like, they forgot that all of Latin America also teaches rhetoric. So we are not the first. We're not it, but we're talking about the in the U.S. So, U.S., the fields of rhetoric and comp, CCCCs, Cristina Kirklighter will actually know, but I think I'm it, and she has done the history. So, there were many people who were involved in Hispanic Caucus and the Chicano Caucus, almost all of NCTE, with the exception of Kris Gutiérrez and Rosanne González, neither of them are rhet comp people.

Ruiz: That makes sense they were associated.

Villanueva: You asked about the disciplines yeah? Rosanne González is a linguist. What she did was, she looked at the linguistics of translators in Federal, in Federal court, what the translators do, and she was doing mainly Navajo and Latinos in Spanish, but as a linguist. Kris Gutiérrez is probably one of the biggest names right now in bilingual education at the elementary school level, but again it's not comp.

Ruiz: What positive or negative actions have you experienced?

Villanueva: Well, I've already told the story of exclusion, and that was basically, the exclusion was being proposed by the Chair of CCCCs at the time. Yeah, she became president of NCTE later. Among those who took part in not bringing us in, there also leaders within CCCC's, I'm thinking of one in particular, but I don't want to name them. Now in terms of inclusion, now Rosanne put out a lot of personal money for this, but we used to have, I don't know if they still have it at NCTE, the "Black Caucus and Hispanic Caucus" presents. It was a major show and it included, the first one I ever went to included, Tish Hinojosa, as big a Mexican American poet as you could have in those days, and we had some music. The year that I was CCCC Chair, I brought in some Bomba and Plena players from the Puerto Rican Cultural Center in Chicago, which there's a funny story there too, because I said we would have salsa and Jackie Biddle ran around saying "I forgot to tell her to order the tortilla." Different salsa.

Ruiz: That's different, very different.

Villanueva: It's cool. It's cool, you know. What the hell. How was she supposed to know? But she found a mistake I had made, "You forgot to tell me." No I didn't forget to tell you nothing man, we were just going to go out and have fun. I have seen more. You see part of the reason why I ended up writing *Bootstraps* was because of these people that I met at CCCCs and NCTE, almost exclusively because of them. Because the intentions were always good, the real bigots are few and far between, but for all of the good intentions, there was also this phenomenal ignorance. So that, good heart, wrong thing. It happened a lot and I think it's still happens. I don't think, I know, it still happens. It's still happens. Their hearts are in the right place. They want us included. They do see us as a part of the organization, as part of the profession, as part of the teaching world. They see all of that. There isn't the hostility that we're seeing in local politics or national politics right now. We don't get that from the profession. But we have this phenomenal degree of ignorance that, despite the good intentions, ends up being bigoted in their effect. So, it's not bigotry by intention, but bigotry effect. One of the biggest problems we have is that, and it was something I always wanted to address long ago, when I was chair of the Latino Caucus, which I did that, I was head of Latino, I don't know a long time, nine years maybe, and then Ceci took it over after me.

And it's kind of funny we've had a Cuban involved a lot. So, what I wanted us to do, what I wanted to have recognized and I still don't think it is, is that we don't just do our kind. That's an unintentional bigotry that still there. That if it's a Latino, the Latino is speaking about Latino things and since the Latino is speaking about Latino things, we don't have any reason they're saying to go to that panel. I'm interested in other larger things, without recognizing that we do rhetoric, we do Shakespeare. I mean you know shit! We're American academics. Our heritage is Latino and it's a prideful heritage it's not one that we put into the background, we are proud of our heritage, we are proud of our abilities to move in more than one tongue, to move in more than one culture, but we are Americans and most of us have been subjected to American education. Why wouldn't we know all the same folks that the white folks know? And why wouldn't we be interested in those things as well? So that I think is a problem that continues, the degree to which we are ghettoized, intellectually ghettoized. "Latinos do Latino stuff." Now it's true for me now, but before I did that, I wanted to be recognized for what I could do with the Greeks and the Romans and all that stuff. Now man I'm legit, even by your definition of legit you know. And I think that is, I think, I still think that is the biggest, our biggest hurdle, the degree to which we are pigeonholed, ghettoized, and because of that and because its seen as an exclusive self-interest, we don't get enough of the folks who really need to hear us, hearing us. I mean I am sort of an exception to that but it wasn't easy and I have been at this game a very long time.

Ruiz: Do you want to comment further?

Villanueva: Here's a funny way to put that, and a couple of funny ways to put that. The book has done outrageously well. According to academia. edu, I have counted out, because I needed to for an annual review, 54 different countries that read and respond to that book [Bootstraps]. So, it's done really well. It's available in several languages and I get emails from folks from all over including—I mean you know when they come, when there are Latinos from Latin America I get it, but Italians like it, people from Scandinavia like it, which I really don't get it. But the one I really don't get was some person from Kuala Lumpur. I mean you know, why? You know it's cool. I'm proud of it. I'll brag about it when I write my annual review, but was like why? I've got a student coming; she'll start here this fall from Guam, who is a Filipina in Guam. So, she's a person of color in the Guamanian, who are people of color in the America. I mean, it's a very interesting thing. She's here to work with me because she knows my work in Guam and has said very flattering things that I can't say without sounding like I'm really arrogant, and I am, but I don't want to sound like it.

But here's the interesting thing. At first, there's this person who was a big shot at NCTE when the book first came out. She came up to me to tell me that she loved the book. She just started it and she loved the book. Well the book intentionally starts out very personal and then gets more and more theoretical as the book develops. I did that. But she hadn't finished the book, when she finished the book, she stopped talking to me for a long time. So she liked the *pobrecito*stories right, which is what made Richard Rodriguez so damn famous too, *pobrecito*. But when we get onto the real politics that I'm not okay with all of this, and that are things, that's when things start to change. For the first few years, even though that book was phenomenally well received, I got two national awards for it. I mean the second award, I thought was a mistake. I got the letter, it was 95, I got the letter telling me I got the second award and I thought are you stupid? You already gave me the award and I didn't realize it was the second award. So even though it was well received and there were some who really wanted to talk about the politics, John Trimbur, Lester Faigley they wanted to talk about what I'm talking about, not the *pobrecito*stories. But for the first for first five to six years maybe, everybody wanted to talk about the writing as opposed to what I had written. And even though I had a big enough ego to be flattered by that and was willing to talk about it, after a while it got on my nerves. I'm glad y'all think I'm a good writer, I'm glad you like the way I do this. How about what I said? And that took a while, that took a while before that became the issue. I had a student, I forget who and it's one of us, one person from the Latino Caucus, somebody you'll ask at CCCC's, but one of us had their students reading *Bootstraps* and writing me emails about it and one student asked me if I wrote poorly on purpose: "Did you write that on purpose?" Because I switch voices in this thing, he wasn't sophisticated enough yet to see that, but it looked like it was intentional so why the hell would I do that, you know, it would confuse everybody. Yeah anyways, so that's the answer. It's done really well and to the degree that there's been negative's, not really negatives, just more like ignoring. I never got a bad review of that book, not ever. Some of the reviews were better than others, but never a bad review, now I'm echoing.

Ruiz: Go ahead and continue our wonderful conversation. It's very interesting. Okay, let's see where we left off—and thank you for all that information about *Bootstraps* I know everybody who watches this video is really going to appreciate all of that information, everybody loves that book—but I think where we left off was talking a little bit about publishing. I know you definitely have more to talk about besides *Bootstraps*. The second, or the next question, does deal with publications it says: "How helpful has the CCCCs or NCTE, or colleagues in the Latino Caucus, been in your publishing, your articles, book chapters, or books? And what kind of mentoring has there been or not been?"

Villanueva: Well, okay, that's a matter of generations. Since I'm the oldest mother here—you know there I was—I got encouragement from Roseann González, but she didn't know our business, so no. It's not anyone's fault. It's that the numbers weren't there yet. And so, it's been kind of the reverse where I've helped out a lot of our folks and many others and it's what I enjoy doing. In terms of NCTE and CCCC's, I'm not sure why, but you know back when *Bootstraps* was first proposed, there was some resistance to it by the Editorial Board, but the Editorial Board also included Keith Gillyard and I think he had more to do with convincing the Editorial Board to go with Bootstraps than anyone. Then he was chair of C's right after I was, I mean we worked together for a while too, he's a phenomenally smart man but, I just realized what I just said. Not because he supported *Bootstraps*, because he just is a smart man. At the time that I propose Bootstraps, the Editor for NCTE was

Michael Spooner. He has been a support, and I even thanked him at one point, he said "No we both took advantage of it," but he has been a great supporter of my work ever since. We've got a quarter century working together now. He did *Bootstraps*. Ge was the one who first took up *Crosstalk*. The latest book I have with Bob Eddie on language and power reader, I couldn't remember the damn name, isn't that nice? It's such a nice problem, so many books I can't remember their titles. So, you know, I got support, a lot of great support from the NCTE people and even still to this day, even as they have changed over the years. The second edition of *Crosstalk* came out because, I'm trying to think of her name, can't think of her name, but she was associate editor and she asked me if I would do *Son of Crosstalk*, so that was the second edition and a chance to take care of some negative criticism's that I had gotten, which were well-founded. The third edition was another story, I did the third edition to help out a faculty member that I think is a wonderful person and because, rest her soul, Susan Miller's book, the book struck me as a phenomenal reference book, but a lousy book for teaching. So I thought, okay, we'll have to do a third edition of *Crosstalk* and so that's why that came out. But what was missing in the first two editions was stuff having to do with computers and you know at a certain point in your career you say, here I stop, I don't learn another new thing, and you know I'm reading a new body of theory for an article I am writing right now, but it's within the kinds of things I want to talk about, which is being Latino and being a leader in the organization. I'm actually writing an article about that, and the rhetorics of it and it's got me through this theory from a guy named Jose Morizo Dominguez.

Ruiz: Ok, thank you so much, and thank you for this interview and it'll be posted. Well it's going to be posted on our Google+ page, and it's going to be posted on YouTube, and it's also going to be included in the project when it's all said and done. So, thank you so much for your time.

CECILIA RODRÍGUEZ MILANÉS
Interview by Anita Hernández
August 17, 2016
http://youtu.be/VQqPG3JcVLA

Anita Hernández: Thank you for being here and let's start by having you tell us about yourself.

Cecilia Rodríguez Milanés: My doctoral program was very interdisciplinary, so I had specialization in composition and rhetoric theory, literary theory, African-American women writers, and my dissertation was actually a collection of short stories. So, it was really flexible and wonderful for me because I wanted to do everything. My professor thought that that was probably not a good idea, that I needed to focus because it would be harder for me to get tenure and promotion and so on and so forth. It might have been true but I also felt that if I had to focus on only one area, I would be very unhappy. So, personally it was more satisfying to me to be able to do composition theory, creative writing, multicultural literary stuff. When I started my career I basically was encouraged to join NCTE and CCCC from the beginning. I also teach at the University of Central Florida in Orlando and I've been here 17 years. I was just promoted to full professor. It took a long time. Long time. So you see some of the issues with being very interdisciplinary. I'm on sabbatical this year and I have two projects. My major project is working on a novel, revising a novel, getting it ready for circulation. I also started a memoir. I finished an essay that I sent off to a non-fiction editor about three weeks ago, so I'm hoping to hear soon. I'm at the beginning of my sabbatical and am looking forward to getting some good writing done. But my daughter just had a baby so that's another project. If she needs me I will go to her. She's in Chicago. She's actually, a medical anthropology doctoral student.

Hernández: Why did you choose to attend CCCC and NCTE?

Milanés: Well, to be to be honest, membership and participation in CCCC primarily was expected of all of us as composition rhetoric students at the State University of New York at Albany, where the professors in specializations in comp and rhetoric were Lil Brannon, Sino Block, and Steve North. My main area professor was Lil Brannon, so she basically said to us, she inculcated in in our minds you must belong to the profession, you must participate in conferences. So CCCC was basically, okay you're a grad student now, you have to be a member of NCTE and CCCC.

Hernández: Why did you decide to join the Caucus? Who was involved? And what did you sense was the importance of the Caucus for others? I notice that you attended both CCCC and NCTE.

Milanés: Right. It was one Caucus. There are members attending the CCCC and there are members attending the NCTE convention and some occasionally attend both. So, my first experience with any Caucus was actually with the Black Caucus. I went to my first NCTE in Baltimore in 1988 or 87. I saw on the program that there was this Black Caucus and I was like "Wow! Okay." The reason why I wanted to attend is they had a writer and I can't remember if it was June Jordan or Jade Cortez. It was an African-American woman writer that I admired and I went to the meeting. It was a huge ballroom. I mean huge ballroom with almost all African-American educators and it was so impressive. They had a business meeting and then they had this writer. I thought "Wow! This is amazing! This is so great." Then I realized "Oh! Wait. There's a Hispanic Caucus." So I didn't go to that meeting because, of course, the caucuses are always booked against each other. So I felt a great sense of belonging, but also admiration for this organization. I guess the next year, I went to NCTE first. Then I got pregnant in 89 and I was supposed to present at the CCCC in 1990, but I was like eight months pregnant. I wasn't allowed to go, but I had my paper read by one of my classmates because all my classmates were going. That would have been 1990.

I must have gone to the first Hispanic Caucus meeting in 1991 possibly which might have been in Boston. My daughter was a baby and I took her with me. I went to every single CCCC from 1991 to 2010 so that's like 20 years. I was very happy to find the Caucus, but it was nothing like the Black Caucus. There was only a handful of us. The leader was Victor Villanueva and if anybody has ever met Victor, they know he's absolutely and utterly charming and totally welcoming. I felt really comfortable. I thought "Oh, there's a place for us."

The other thing that is important to note is that the Caucus was always Pan-ethnic. There were American Indian, Native American scholars, that participated with us as well as Asian-American. The Caucus was always Pan-ethnic because there were so few of the rest of us, scholars and teachers of color. It really was like a refuge from a very White organization and it did become kind of like a vital point on which my academic career and service turned.

I became involved in the organization and leadership almost right away. Victor had been the co-chair for a long time and he was ready to pass it along. I think he was actually Co-Chair for 15 years. I ended up doing it for 15 years also, which is a long time and it isn't right because you get burnt out and it's exhausting. So, when I joined one of my goals was to have the newsletter published twice a year with contributing contributions from Caucus members. I wanted to recruit more members. I wanted to get membership dues regularly organized. I think I accomplished all those things.

Hernández: What were your goals?

Milanés: I felt that within the Caucus I was able to, not just have my voice acknowledged and validated by the institution as far as the organization, but that it was a sort of communal and community voice. We could take our concerns to the leadership of NCTE and they would listen. They wouldn't necessarily act, but they would listen. At least I felt some progress, right? And we would often have sort of testy exchanges with the leadership because they had an idea about what the Caucus should be and should do and we had another idea because ultimately a Caucus is independent. It is not to be managed by the parent institution or organization that is NCTE for CCCC. It's like when I'm talking about it, NCTE is like the large umbrella and CCCC is under NCTE. I was on the task force when CCCC was investigating whether or not to break off, like to get a divorce, from NCTE and after like a two-year project, I think, there was just no way that could happen because we could not afford it. I need to remind people with this was investigated about 20 years or so ago and, maybe, it may be CCCC would be in a different position now, but one of the things that CCCC and NCTE have sometimes had happy relationships and some not so happy relationships. I think part of it is because CCCC is almost completely university and college affiliated members and NCTE is almost universally K through 12 colleagues. So that's a kind of a rub.

Hernández: What were some of the issues that you witnessed or observed at the CCCC or NCTE as you participated almost 20 years? How do you remember the Caucus responding and who were some of the leaders that took such an initiative?

Milanés: Well, Victor has always been a leader and it is because he's been around a long time and because he knows everybody. Victor was kind of a shining star example for us as someone who could navigate the publishing world within NCTE, but even his book *Bootstraps* didn't come out like right away. I can't remember right now when that was published but we were a long time waiting for that book to be published. And it was a long time that it was by itself and there were no other books by Latino colleagues published by NCTE.

Hernández: Okay.

Milanés: Just look at the catalog. What books has NCTE published by Caucus colleagues? That's just a very easy search. What I think might be a problem is that colleagues cannot depend on financial reimbursement for travel to the conference. A lot of networking happens at the conference. A lot of bonding and informal kind of negotiations happen at the conferences, both at NCTE and at CCCC. So, whether you are a K through 12 teacher who has a great idea about a book, but your principal won't even give you the days off to go to the convention or fund you to go to the convention. It's very discouraging. Universities and colleges are cutting, cutting, cutting and the humanities are usually the poorest of all disciplines. And so, at my University, I think we are going to get $450 and that has to cover everything. And you have to be presenting, you cannot just go to a conference for professional development. That's an ongoing issue that you can't really count on people returning year after year after year to the conference because they're not assured of funding. So, we'll meet some fantastic people one year and go "Oh! Wow! New colleagues!" Wonderful emerging scholars as emerging teachers. Then we lose them. They don't come back the next year because they haven't been funded. I think that one of the important things is maintaining this kind of contact through either an online a listserv or a website. I felt like the Latino Caucus newsletter (*Capirotada*) helped to keep people in touch. It was published twice a year. We had a Spring issue and a Fall issue. People would even make announcements, like "I had a baby" or "I was promoted" or "I have a publication out in press." There was usually poetry. There was usually a book or movie review. There was student writing that was included in it. There was always an editorial. There might be an issue that we wanted to raise to the membership. So, I know they're all archived because I had them archived and digitized. I think it is important to connect to [the Working and Writing for Change]. There is a history and it's written.

Hernández: Any issues that you noticed while you were a CCCC? Any marginalization of Latino research? You've touched a little bit about that because of the *Capirotada* newsletters that you published.

Milanés: Yes. I published *Capirotada* newsletters for more than 15 years. The first issue was put together by Alfredo Lujan, who was one of the leaders in the Caucus from way back. This is another thing that's like in the history that maybe some people don't know or remember, but the Hispanic Association for Colleges and Universities actually funded the printing and mailing of the first issue. And that was because of my friend, Lala Leena Martinez, was the president of HACU at that time, 1992 or 1993 and maybe even earlier, and, of course, nobody had any money. We didn't have any sponsorship or anything like that and it was a one-page two-sided folded little newsletter, but I asked Lala Leena to please help us with this and she paid it out of HACU's fund. She paid for the printing and for the mailing. She was the first Puerto Rican to be the president of HACU.

After that I convinced my university, Indiana University of Pennsylvania, to pay for the paper, the copying, and the postage, but of course, we had to collect funds anyway. We had to collect membership dues so there was money to pay for the printing.

Hernández: And what about the issues that came up while you were the chair of the Latino Caucus?

Milanés: Every year at a conference, there was always some racist incident or two or three. Always, always, always. The Caucus traditionally is always held on Friday. It's usually the second day right and, by the second day, everybody's already pretty pissed off and frustrated. People would complain that nobody came to a session that was really important about race or about language. There would be snubs. There are two examples that I would give. I think you probably interviewed Renee Moreno already.

So, Renee was giving this really important presentation and the person who spoke after her was a white woman. She totally didn't hear a single word that Renee said. She also said all this racist crap and then called her students, my Latino students" and said they are "always silent, they don't talk." A bunch of us were like "Oh my God, you believe, you just said that." There were about three or four of us and Gail Okawa was one of the people with me. We said "*que locura.*" Gail was also one of the original members of the Latino Caucus; she's retired now, but she was at Youngstown, Ohio. She goes back even further than I do, and I would say you could interview her. She was even before Victor's time because she and Victor are contemporaries. She was on a lot of committees. She was on the executive committee.

Anyway, so Renee is just assaulted by this woman in the way that she just dismissed her presentation. We got up. We walked out because members of the audience were then piling on top of Renee. So we just, like a bunch, got up and said "This is intolerable. This is racist. We're not going to stand for it." We stormed out.

This was in San Diego, and, of course, the first thing we did was find Victor Villanueva and give him all the complaints. He says "Okay, good. You're mad. Now you need to participate in the Caucus. This is a place where you can get your voice heard. You can express your concerns to the leadership." That's what we did. A bunch of us did get recruited in that way. So that's how I became energized and invigorated.

The second example which was much more recent what that we had a person at NCTE who worked in Champaign, Urbana, who was our advocate. Her name was Dr. Sandra Gibbs. She would look out for us. She would let us know of any kind of legislation that they were considering or any rules they were going to change that would impact us, people of color not just the African-American not just the Black Caucus, but the Latino Caucus. Sandra was basically fired. There was all kinds of very ugly things. We were furious. There were boycotts and letters. I say we actually sent a packet of 50 certified letters to the president of NCTE at that time, who was Kent Williamson, who has passed on, but Kent and nobody from NCTE even acknowledged our letters. They didn't even acknowledge them. So, we were just furious because Sandra didn't deserve to be treated that way and we didn't deserve to be treated that way either. That was another experience. There's always something going on. I think that the fact is we have to complain and protest and come and really make our issues known to them. They almost get kind of embarrassed and then they want to do the right thing, but they don't do the right thing to start with, they never do.

That's their modus operandi. They don't even think about it. Like what are we for if not to consult with you people at NCTE, to see that you do the right thing, but they don't. They don't consult us. They just say, "Oh here's this curriculum and it's going to be so good." And we're like, "Excuse me! You don't have any Latinos on this curriculum." We're supposed to be consulted. That was one of the things that we also complained about because it was 20 years ago when Bobbi and I were co-chairs and NCTE was trying to get the Caucus to become affiliated. This meant a legal relationship so that they would give us money. They would give us space on their server and blah blah blah blah blah, but it came with conditions.

There were these meetings that we were invited to with leadership at that time, Kathy Yancey, who was at FSU. She was the president of NCTE and she invited me, Bobbi, and people from the Asian American Caucus. There was this wonderful woman from the Black Caucus, but I can't remember her name, and I think Joyce Rain Anderson from the American Indian Caucus. They invited us to a meeting in Washington, D.C. to tell us why it would be such a good idea for the caucuses to be affiliated with NCTE. Kent Williamson was also present. He was the Executive Director at that time and he unfortunately missed this amazing history of the caucus and the Black Caucus. The woman from the Black Caucus gave a great history and he came in after the fact. We were like "Dude you should have been here to hear this. She talked about how Black scholars and educators didn't get couldn't get on the session, wouldn't be allowed in the hotels, I mean, like it was like civil rights issues from the get-go within this organization. Of course, you know African-Americans have been founding their own organizations for many years when MLA, for example, wasn't up to inviting African-Americans to propose sessions, so they had their own organizations called the CLA, the College Language Association, which continues to have conferences. CLA was started because MLA was exclusive. And so NCTE was the largest organization for teachers of English and Language Arts teachers. So there were many African American teachers who wanted to be part of the national organization, but the organization was not really interested in them. So they said, "Nope, we're going to we're going to make a change. So their leadership really paved the way for the Latino Caucus, American Indian Caucus, Asian American Caucus, Queer Caucus. So their history is really on what we are based on. We exist because they started it.

So, there's always issues of marginalization. The other times when we make our voices known is after the conference when there is a meeting on Sunday morning with the chair of CCCC and the future chair CCCC. We basically call it Caucus concerns. The Caucus always sends a representative to this meeting on Sunday morning and we complain, we protest, and we tell them what went wrong, and how they should deal with it. So, I don't know if this still goes on, but I went to many of those meetings.

Hernández: What are some of your earliest memories of the Caucus interacting with others and the kinds of discussions, resolutions, and projects that transpired? Any projects that may have come out from the Scholars for the Dream?

Milanés: Scholars for the Dream is a wonderful thing that came out of these issues. We wanted to have more students of color and emerging scholars of color come to the conference, so it started out with a little bit of money. Then we got a little bit more money. Then more Scholars for the Dream were invited and now they have a network. That's really a really wonderful thing. There was a task force for the involvement of people of color and that was a great group. I remember Jackie Jones Royster was on that group. There was many people from the Black Caucus and Latino Caucus. We were fighting the good fight. You want us to get involved, then these are the ways to get us involved. They're like, "Oh hey, we'll just have this task force and that means you're involved." They want to recruit us to do stuff, but often it doesn't come with any resources. So, for example, to be the on the membership of the Executive Committee of CCCC. It's labor intensive because you have to go to NCTE and CCCC and usually there's another meeting, right? So, they only give you a little bit of money to travel and your university has to support you, right? If you want to help CCCC, your university has to give you a graduate student and they will pay for part of your travel for NCTE and CCCC and the workshops and so on and so forth. But your university has to give something, so your university has to say "Oh this is a good idea. We will help you to do this. It's a lot of work and it's a lot of travel. If you're teaching, this is something that, you know, there's a cost to your students, to your department, to your university.

In the past, NCTE offered grants to emerging teachers and I'm sure there continue to be mentoring initiatives and I think none of these things happen without us pushing. I think it's definitely a mixed bag. I think it depends on the leadership within NCTE administration and the presidential team. Who is chair of CCCC? Has this person exhibited a track record of working with educators of color? Is this person educatable? Because they don't necessarily have to have a track record, but they have to be willing to cooperate and to advocate. So one of the things that I've seen year after year, many times, when you have president of NCTE that might be from the K through 12. You ask yourself, where do you teach? Where are your students? If the Latino demographic of the United States makes us the largest minority, the majority minority, and the majority minority is under the age of 18, those kids are in your classrooms. What are you doing to help those kids? What are your practices? What is your curriculum? What have you done to adjust to those students in your classes? And we're not just talking about Texas or Illinois or Florida, because you know we're everywhere. Two percent women of color faculty at University, two percent. It's still a wasteland.

Hernández: How have you observed the CCCCs or NCTE be responsive to Latino scholars and educators? What actions has that organization taken that you've seen, whether you agree or disagree?

Milanés: It's a like we cannot let up. We have to continuously make our concerns known right to the administration, call on the phone, network with the other Caucuses. That's another important issue. The Caucuses always work together in order to get stuff done, in order to make it known that we were going to stand for this issue. You know that the organization needed to be responsive to its members even if we are a minority of the membership. We're active members, yes.

Hernández: How helpful has the CCCCs, NCTE, colleagues and the Latino Caucus been in your publishing? And what kind of mentoring has there been or not been for you and for others

Milanés: Victor's book was the only book by a Latino that was published by NCTE for many many years. You're going to see a big gap before you get a book by Raul Sanchez or Cristina or anybody. The mentoring really has always been from colleagues and it is essential and extremely important and valuable because it always is done with love. Victor Villanueva has probably reviewed more manuscripts than like twenty-five people put together. He was always willing to read manuscripts whether they were essay manuscripts or book manuscripts. And this was under the table. This was not like NCTE sent the manuscript to Victor for him to review. No, this is us saying "Victor, will you please read this for me because I don't know if I'm making any sense?" And he would do it. Because it behooves him to have more of us published. I think that the books that were published, if you read the acknowledgments, almost all of them would say, "Victor Villanueva," "A shout out to Victor Villanueva because he helped birth it." So he was helpful to me. I remember I was writing an article for an MLA book and I was trying to do some kind of cross-genre work and sort of making my way as I was doing it. He read it. I was so full of ah you know intimidation and nerves because

I wasn't sure if I was doing this right and it was early in my career. He was just like "do what comes natural." That was like "Oh, I can do that." So yeah, Victor was super helpful. He helped others and if you look at those acknowledgment pages, you'll see, you'll see.

Hernández: What was your role in mentoring others?

Milanés: I think I did a lot of mentoring through the Caucus, especially of young emerging scholars and graduate students. One of the things that I also did was I brought undergraduates to the Caucus. We never had undergraduates come to conferences. I brought undergraduates to a lot of conferences. What's really ironic is that often there's more funding for undergraduate than there are for faculty members because there are the student unions. A lot of groups will fund students to do presentations and there's usually undergraduate research funds that will give money or departments will give money. But if it's for faculty, we're out of luck. That's why I often got students to present, co-present, on panels with me. That way it was initiating them into professional development. So that was one of the things that I did.

I also organized the first Latino Caucus workshop because, again, I thought we needed to do some mentoring. We needed to have a time outside of the Caucus meeting where we could review manuscripts, we could talk about dissertations, we could talk about the job search, we could talk about all the things that we need to do that we can't do in an hour meeting.

So, I organized the first four workshops. The first one was in San Francisco, I think was 2005. Then I did the following ones. I think the last one I organized was the one in New Orleans. I always had co-organizers, but as the Caucus Co-Chair I did a lot of stuff on my own. I did a lot of nagging. I did a lot of phone calls and begging, "Come on, please help me do this. You need to join and do this." So, I did a lot of that. I kept in contact with people to encourage them to submit proposals. I reviewed proposals. I did a lot of things for the Caucus. Then I also served on committees and task force. I was on the Exemplar Committee. I was on the Scholars for the Dream Committee for several years.

I was on the Nominating Committee for CCCC. I was on the Rainbow Strand Conference Planning Committee. I was on the College Section Nominating Committee. I was on the NCTE Election and HUD Section committee. I did a lot of work for NCTE throughout my years. But it was pretty good. Last year was my promotion year and national service is really important when you're going up for promotion. For Full professor and, to a lesser extent, Associate. Universities value research. Institutions, they're not going to value a lot of service, but the little that you do should be national.

Hernández: What roles have you undertaken within the CCCC? What kind of benefits have you witnessed from such experiences? You have talked about the Task Forces and the Latino mentoring sessions.

Milanés: Right. I think it's always good to meet people and network, so when you're on these committees, you do meet people that you wouldn't ordinarily bump into. So, in that way, you learn more about the organization, learn more about how other universities function. I think that service is a way to really learn how stuff works, how things get done. I was the director of women's studies at this university and at my former university and I learned a lot. I learned a lot by doing that.

Hernández: What is the story you would like to tell about the Caucus? And how would you like others to remember the Caucus now you've told a couple of stories?

Milanés: The story about the Caucus is that it is warm and has a welcoming vibe. It is what drew me and kept me returning to the Caucus and then taking on leadership and service. We were a family and families have new members all the time.

One of the things that I did as Caucus Co-Chair was that I tried to go to as many Caucus members' sessions as I could. At that time, there weren't that many of us. Sometimes I was just going to these sessions with the last name Martinez. I'm going to go to that session and I'm going to recruit that person. I would go to the sessions and basically invite them to come and go to our meeting. I would give them the Caucus newsletter *Capirotada* and I'd say "Hi! I'm Cecilia. We'd love to have you join the Caucus." This is one of the things that I figured out was that the personal touch is really important because the Caucus is always meant to me a warm inviting and welcoming place and that was regardless of what kind of scholarship you did. We had to have it. For me, it was a refuge and I wanted to make sure that it was a refuge for others.

Then there's some family members that are around a long time, right? But, you know, you try to keep the sense of somo familia. And, you know, families squabble all the time. So I think the story about the Caucus, its sense and sensibility, is that we should be welcoming. It's part of our founding. The other part of our founding is that we're Pan-ethnic. It's never been exclusive. Our mission statement said "like-minded folks," it didn't say you have to have certain blood percentage. It said if you believe what we believe that students of color and particularly Latino students need to have their issues advocated for, join us. . . .

I went to that Caucus meeting in Las Vegas and I felt very unwelcomed. I felt like I was a stranger. I knew people in the room, but there were more new folks than there were returning folks. I am not asking anybody to pay homage to me or anything like that, I'm just saying, "Wow, there is no welcoming vibe here. "Because I could be a stranger and if I walk into the Caucus meeting as a stranger, you should welcome me. So, I left feeling very disconcerted. Right?

That's another thing that you do too because that actually that was one of the issues of Las Vegas, that they booked a session to honor Victor Villanueva against a featured session that I was on, so we couldn't attend each other's sessions. We had a big ballroom for my thing and there was like I don't know 15 people. And of the 15 people, there were you know 10 that were old folks from the Caucus or maybe not even that many. So that was really like, "Wow, what happened?" Yet at the Caucus meeting it was a lot of people. There was like maybe 30 people and like I said most of them were new young faces and that's wonderful, that is super super important, but I think that the thing that needs to be remembered in the history of the Caucus is that the place is a place of refuge and warmth, and even if I don't agree with your ideological theories of Education, we should we should get along. If I'm not from Arizona you should get along with me, if I'm not from Texas or

California. That's one of the things that I think should be remembered about the Caucus. It was it was always a place of warmth and refuge.

Hernández: We have come to the last question. Was there a question I did not ask that I should have asked?

Milanés: I think that when you when you interview people that have been involved in the Caucus for a long time, you should probably ask them what their cross-caucus work.

Hernández: Yes. Great idea.

Milanés: I think that's really important because we really need to work together. All the Caucasus should. We should know each other. Everybody should know who is the leader of the Asian American Caucus and who leads the American Indian Caucus, and who is the leadership of the Black Caucus. These are things that need to be remembered. We always work together. I went to one of their meeting once and also felt really silenced, but again, it depends on leadership, depends on what you know, who's there. Are they really wanting to hear us? Do they really want to hear us? Or they just want the color there, we can check that box off?

Well, I would also say that your university or college or Department, some of them are more willing to help you than others. When I came to this school, to the University of Central Florida, they actually put in my contract that they would pay me to go to CCCC as long as I was the co-chair. So, they gave me 500 dollars to use to travel to go to CCCC, to run the Caucus, to do the business meeting, and do all those things. They started an account at the University, where I can deposit the dues. They paid for the printing and the and the mailing. They gave me a graduate student. So, like that was under one chair but then we had financial issues and we lost all that help. So, you know that's another thing that it varies, it really varies. I do also believe that the Caucus should always have a Co-Chair leadership, someone who represents the NCTE group, NCTE K-12 that goes to that meeting, and there's should be somebody who's the co-chair from CCCC ,that goes to that meeting. So, the Caucus is always a presence at both conferences.

I mean I taught high school just for a year and I taught K-6 for a couple of years and I can't imagine going to any conferences. I can't imagine it. It's only when you become a university professor or college teacher, where you can think, "Oh okay. I think I could do this." Luckily some people get support from their colleges, their deans, and, most of the time, you know, you have to scrape by and pay your own way.

I appreciate your interest in my perspective, and I miss my Caucus colleagues, I do. I guess it was 2009 or 2010, I decided that I was going to sort of pull away from CCCCs because I was doing a lot of creative writing. CCCCs used to have a big creative writing group and they don't do it anymore. They used to have like a Special Interest Group of creative writers. Now I go to AWP (Association of Writers and Writing Programs), which is almost always around the same time as CCCC. I've been going to for AWP for the last five years or so.

Hernández: Cecilia, it was really a pleasure to interview you. Thank you so much!

JAIME ARMIN MEJÍA
Interview by Cruz Medina
May 10, 2016

I was first introduced to Jaime Armin Mejia in San Francisco, at the 2010 CCCC, when I received the Scholars for the Dream award. My presentation advocated for integrating pre-Columbian tropes into first-year writing pedagogy. I became better acquainted with Jaime when Octavio Pimentel orchestrated a pre-doctoral fellowship at Jaime and Octavio's institution, Texas State University-San Marcos, during the summer of 2011. In San Marcos, Jaime took me out for breakfast at his favorite restaurant for breakfast tacos (a distinctly Tex-Mex/Tejano delicacy). After breakfast, I saw Jaime's commitment to his Master's students firsthand as we went to several shops, stores, and specialty outlets before deciding on a very thoughtful and elegant leather satchel for his student who had successfully defended her thesis. I later learned that this was not a unique display of his generosity, but one case in a pattern of thoughtful gifts that included a pair of boots (a *Tejano* through and through), and a laptop computer for another student who had completed her MA and continued on for her PhD.

Since my time in Texas, Jaime has remained one of the greatest sources of generous and insightful feedback for my writing and for the writing of those who solicit the attention of his sharp, editorial eye. His feedback might not be suitable for those with a thin skin, but it always comes from a caring place that encourages you to put your best writing into the world. In the several years I've known Jaime, I've become more and more impressed by his span of influence and depth of knowledge about the field, as well as his commitment to the CCCCs and Latino caucus communities.

Cruz Medina: When was your first College Composition and Communication Conference (4Cs)?

Jaime Armin Mejía: My first Cs was '89 in Seattle, which meant that in '88 I submitted a proposal.

Medina: Were you still in grad school at the time?

Mejía: It must have been my third year. That was the year that Andrea Lunsford came to town and that might have been the year that I got associated with her. I imagine she might have helped me produce the panel proposal, and I think she was Program Chair [of 4Cs that year].

Medina: So, did you submit as a panel or an individual presentation?

Mejía: I think I was an individual paper proposal. This is where it gets curious—Lunsford comes to my panel in Seattle and she sits in the front row—she was very supportive and she helped produce the paper proposal. But I want to say at this point that she was either Program Chair, which means she delivered the keynote that year, or she organized the conference that year. I forget. But, of course, I didn't know anything about 4Cs. I didn't know that Thursday morning there was an opening plenary for the chairs to deliver their speech because I did not hear her. I remember that that year or the next year the three Cs [*College Composition and Communication*] journal published her chair's address and I remember that chair's address because she mentions linguine in it. But in any case, what I'm suggesting here is that...

Medina: There's some invisible mentorship going on, on her part?

Mejía: There was that, yeah.

Medina: As a graduate student, you probably didn't know what a vital role she was playing.

Mejía: I didn't know a lot of things. But I remember at that conference, Kenneth Burke was there and he was wearing Converse tennis shoes. A lot of people, especially grad students, were hovering around him. Wayne Booth was always there. I mean, I remember seeing Wayne Booth on more than one occasion. He came to Ohio State to deliver a talk. Of course, I studied Wayne Booth my first year at Ohio State in graduate seminar, in a class where I studied both Wayne Booth and Kenneth Burke. But you have to understand that Kenneth Burke at that time in 1989 was probably like eighty-nine or ninety years old.

Medina: And he's wearing Converse tennis shoes.

Mejía: And they told me in his session that he was not lucid. That's what I heard.

Medina: So, who were the first Chican@s that you ended up meeting?

Mejía: Well, you know what was interesting in Seattle, there were these tutors from the University of Washington and they attended my session. And I don't know that they were Mexican American. I remember one in particular; her name was Donna and she worked with Gail Okawa who I think was the director of the tutors. And she and a couple other tutors who attended my session came up to me and started talking to me. They were local yokels; they were from Seattle. They worked at the University of Washington as tutors.

Medina: They just happened to see your name on the program and thought they come by your panel?

Mejía: I don't know how they did, but the thing is they took me out to eat, and then they took me out to a really cool coffee shop-bookstore in Seattle. They drove me around and we went down to the wharf. They took me to a small, tiny hole-in-the-wall Mexican restaurant. In other words, I got treated royally by these tutors who were teaching and working and probably studying at the University of Washington who were minorities. I remember Donna was Native American and maybe Mexican. And Donna and I stayed in contact for a few years.

Medina: Was there a Latino Caucus meeting at that conference?

Mejía: No. If there was, I didn't know anything about it.

Medina: So, when was your first caucus meeting? Or workshop?

Mejía: I cannot remember. That wasn't my first conference though. My first conference was NCTE [National Council for Teachers of English] in, I want to say, 1986. Could've been '85 in San Antonio, Texas at the Henry V. Gonzalez Convention Center. And that's where I first met Victor [Villanueva]. I think I not only met Victor at a bar, but I might have gone to his session. And I remember very distinctly his method of presenting—he stood up and ad-libbed. And he ad-libbed for many years before he actually started to write and read-present papers.

Medina: Did he show you that there was some potential for Latinos interacting in the field and really being involved in the field in a central way because Victor already seemed to be involved?

Mejía: No. I don't want to say that Victor was inspirational [*laughs*]. By no means was he inspirational. No, we got to know each other. There were so few of us back then. You know, I'd have to look at the paperwork to see where the conferences were at, maybe that would ring some memories. But as Victor has repeated on many occasions—I interviewed him [Victor Villanueva] on video that's on YouTube—and he will tell you that for many years, when there were caucus meetings whether NCTE or 4Cs, it would be me and him, and maybe one other person. And that went on for over ten years. This is my twenty-fifth year at Texas State [University-San Marcos], which means a year or two before '91 I was already starting [to attend] 4Cs.

Medina: Can you tell in those twenty-five at which point there was a sea change in terms of going from three people to significantly more? You were saying it was about year ten [of attending 4Cs] that you finally had a few more people who you didn't know attending those meetings?

Mejía: We had a meeting in 1993 in San Diego, and there weren't many people there either, but it was an important year for me because it was the year that I would graduate and finish my PhD, after having gone to Texas State as an ABD [All But Dissertation]. And I went to San Diego with the intention of talking with Andrea Lunsford about my predicament with my dissertation director basically going-AWOL. At that 4Cs in San Diego, Lunsford decided to take over my dissertation and six weeks later I defended. A week later I graduated.

But I remember in San Diego that was the year that Renee [Moreno] had a session where her mother was there and there was some mix-up—I don't think I was there—the story goes that somebody said the wrong thing to Renee and then her mother stood up and started yelling at this person, and it was a real carnival apparently. There was some mention of it at the caucus meeting.

Medina: Would you say that it's the relationships that you've built just having gone to the meetings, having been able to meet people there, and then those times going out to dinner?

Mejía: Well, it was always certainly like, *'who's going to come back the next year?'* And who actually came back the next year. After a while, after every year passed, there would be more people, one or two more people that were coming back. So now we have maybe a contingent of fifteen people that have been coming back.

Medina: It seems like with Andrea Lunsford, you point to her as a really strong influence on you, and a really strong mentorship role—and even the people you met at the first conference who took you out to lunch in Seattle—would you say that these experiences made an impact on your role in wanting to be a mentor? I say this because I recognize you as one of my mentors, so is that something that you recognized early on? To be a mentor to those people you saw coming back again and again?

Mejía: Do I see myself as a mentor? Is that the question?

Medina: Recognizing the importance of being a mentor when you could be one.

Mejía: Let me tell you that my mentoring is a recent thing in some respects. Because I want to say first that there is no doubt that over the years that Victor was always the most knowledgeable person in our field. And I'm not talking about just content, I'm talking about logistics of working the system, of getting tenure, of getting publications, of becoming active in the 4Cs, of knowing the politics of the elections, and the politics of the policies that were being created in the 4Cs. Victor had the inside track on a lot of things. There was a period of time before and after he became Program Chair—you know he followed Keith Gilyard or preceded Keith Gilyard and Wendy Bishop—and there were people in key positions of authority in 4Cs, and I was encouraged to run and I was elected into the Executive Committee. And it was being in the Executive Committee that helped a lot, but it was always Victor who was helpful in many ways, different from Lunsford, but I've been very fortunate to have them both.

Medina: Do you have any advice for the next generation of scholars? Would you say that sticking-it-out seems like a bit part? It's like the old Alcoholics Anonymous saying, 'just keep coming?' But then you need to start recognizing your role as leadership or mentoring role and start to help the other people as well who are coming in new for the first time?

Mejía: I've told you [in earlier communication] that I'm staying with a very important mentor of mine here in Tampa, and he's been in academia longer than I have, and he got a PhD in education at the University of Wisconsin, and he was a Fulbright Scholar. This week I'm visiting here with him. He's a former dean of a college of education at a state university in Ohio, and he's a Mexican American—one of the first Mexican American PhDs in the United States. In fact, he was mentioned in a book about the first fifteen PhDs who were Mexican Americans in the United States. What he says is that it's very important no matter who you are to become professionally active and to become actively involved.

Medina: So 'actively involved' is not just teaching?

Mejía: It's not just teaching.

Medina: It's not just publishing.

Mejía: It's not just publishing. Certainly, service is big, and the way you get to publishing, service, and teaching is by becoming active professionally in organizations like this [4Cs]. For many years, I've told people that 4Cs is my home. I still maintain that, but I don't think it's my only home, although over the years it's become a significant one. I mean I've been really lucky to serve in a lot of capacities in the 4Cs: Executive Committee, NCTE editorial board, *CCC* journal editorial board, task forces (more than one), committees for best book of the year (more than once), committee member who interviewed for the college section at NCTE (flown to D.C. as a part of the interview committee).

Medina: In the same way, you would recommend any opportunities to serve NCTE or the caucus for younger people?

Mejía: I think what I would suggest, you know like you, you get the kids and you got to get them to come back every year. And then you got to get them involved. You got to get them in the Executive Committee; when you get them into the Executive Committee, that's where a lot of networking will begin. I made a lot of friends and I connected with a lot of significant people as part of the Executive Committee. Steve North, who quit 4Cs, was a friend of mine when we were on the Executive Committee. People like Keith Gilyard I met on the Executive Committee. Wendy Bishop, who died several years ago, was very significant as former Chair and certainly as officer of the 4Cs, and overseeing the Executive Committee. You know I served four years on the Executive Committee, longer than anybody else in history because someone stepped down, and they needed someone to step up for a fourth year. And I think it was Wendy Bishop who asked me to serve a fourth year and I said, "Sure."

Medina: Do you feel like—because I'm curious too—you're talking about significant people like Wendy Bishop, like Keith Gilyard—did they see you as a primary person in the Latino Caucus? Was that one of those things that they recognized you for because you were a participant in it? It helped create your credibility as someone that they would want to come to talk to because you had that community here who they could consult with you about?

Mejía: I don't think they saw me as a representative of the Latino caucus. I don't think that I necessarily represented the Latino caucus. I certainly represented Mexican American ethnicity or Latino ethnicity, and was recognized and consulted on that basis alone. When I was on the Executive Committee, we voted on a future site for 4Cs and the choices were Cleveland, New Orleans and San Antonio, and there was a case made for New Orleans and even Cleveland. But when I spoke up and said, "We need to go to San Antonio because it's a Mexican American community—we don't have enough Mexican Americans in 4Cs—we need to go there and pick up more Latinos." That settled the argument and we went to San Antonio. You know that was a key move to just draw more people in that were Latinos. And if I hadn't been on the Executive Committee arguing that case, I don't think we would have gone to San Antonio.

Medina: That's a good point too because it seems like a lot of people find it easy to be critical of Cs, but it sounds like you were able to make those kinds of cases directly to receptive audiences.

Mejía: I was the only Latino on the committee and my voice rang through. I convinced them. I said, "Hey, we got to do this," and they did it. They decided to go there. I'm very proud of taking the Cs to San Antonio. I have to tell you, I don't think while Victor Villanueva and Cecilia Milanés Rodriguez were chairs of the Caucus—to the extent that people were attending the caucus meetings—we were a small amiable group. We got along. And of course, during those years, people came and never came back. It was often the case.

Medina: So, what do you think the big suggestion then is for the future in terms of like the next leaders of the Latino Caucus? It seems like social media has been playing a role—you're staying connected with other Latinos, so people are talking about Cs again; people are talking about putting together panels. It seems like those come together a lot easier because people don't have to worry about talking to each other in person. That's just a small role, I think, but what qualities do you think have an impact?

Mejía: I think as the numbers grow, our interests grow and thereby divide us as a group. And it's good to have people with wide interests. Different people are doing different things, and the more people, the more different things, and we don't have to have unity in terms of interests. It's good to have the diversity of interests within the caucus, within the people that come.

Over time, we had an interest in pedagogy—profession wide as well as caucus wide—we had an interest in pedagogy, and I don't think in terms of the issues and problems in pedagogy that we're raising for Latinos—I don't think the questions being raised twenty-five years ago have been answered today. But what's really cool though is that other people—the profession has grown, developed and deepened, so now there are people in the caucus like you and the people out of Arizona who are doing really interesting rhetorical projects and rhetorical analyses that sometimes have nothing to do with pedagogy. I think that's the best thing that's happened.

In so far as the networking that can happen in the caucus, it's just to keep in contact with people and to support people that are developing projects: rhetorical projects, pedagogical projects... I think to the extent that there's mutual contact and support among the different members of the caucus, and just knowing that somebody else out there is doing stuff, can really be very helpful to graduate students or to an assistant or associate professor, to know that there are other people out there.

Because when I was in this twenty-five years ago, *shit*, there was nobody. The people that were out there were in literature, not in Rhet/Comp. In terms of pedagogy and teaching Mexican Americans, having best practices for academic success for students, we never in my view—and speaking as someone who published in this area—I think we need to develop more pedagogical approaches to teaching Mexican American students to become more successful in academic writing or in other professional writing. I think we need to continue that road.

People like Ralph Cintron, a rhetorician, didn't have anything to say about pedagogy. He turned his back on pedagogy. He said that "everything had been done with pedagogy." And I just disagreed, but at the same time it was important for Ralph Cintron to turn his back on pedagogy because he was going after rhetoric. And to the extent that he was through ethnography, shit, the guy was doing beautiful work. He's a beautiful writer, he's a leader in our field, and so it's important to let people go their different directions. But I still think there's a lot of work to do. We've given up on pedagogy and that's really too bad. I think we need to go back.

Medina: How rewarding has it been to maintain relationships with students who started off as a Masters student and who you've grown to see become a PhD student? Would you say that has mentoring in the more recent stages of your career has been the most rewarding?

Mejía: It's been rewarding, but I don't know if it's been the *most* rewarding. You will find out when you also take on this senior moment because students...first of all, I never thought I'd continue having a relationship with students once they left my school and graduated. It's been one of the most pleasurable surprises that I've maintained contact with a few students. And I haven't maintained contact with all of them, but to the extent that there's contact, it's been really rewarding. But you know the theme for this conference [CCCC 2015] is 'Risk and Reward?' There's also the risk that the kids won't finish, that the students will go different directions. And I've lost over the years a lot of students. I can think of several students. But there's one student, Paul Velazquez, who was a [2006] Scholar for the Dream, and then went a different direction. He came back to school and finished his Masters, which I helped him with.

Medina: Didn't he go to school at UT Austin?

Mejía: He quit school. Then he got married, he's got a kid now just like you, and his life went in a different direction, but he wasn't the first. I first said this twenty years ago.

Medina: So, there can be heartbreak on the other side of it of risk and reward?

Mejía: Professionally, you know, when you see students decide not to pursue it, it's disappointing. But you learn that it's important that they follow their own path. And that whatever path they follow, you're supportive even though you want them to follow this path. You want them to go off to earn their PhD, to become a member of 4Cs, and to become professionally active in the 4Cs. Even though that's what you want, that's not where they're going and that's disappointing, but you have to be supportive and respect their decisions.

But for the grace of God, they go on. . . I'm here for the weirdest reasons, absolutely. Had certain people not done certain things on certain days, I wouldn't be here today. And you know, who's to say that something didn't happen to my former students that they didn't come this way and something happened, and they went that way—you just don't know, man.

Medina: Is there anything else you want to make sure to document?

Mejía: Life is comprised of many things, you know, cheeseburgers, football games, children—you know—rain, desert, many things. And you know that life can become—we can become professionals in academia and members of a professional organization—these are interesting career paths, certainly life paths that people never take. And it's a different form of socializing and there are rewards and great treasures to be found in this path, to the extent that it's happened in the caucus. You know I met Raúl Sánchez [current Latino Caucus co-chair], one of the best human beings I've ever met in my life, in the caucus every year. I think we're very good friends. He's Cuban, I'm not—but we've always had something in common: we had a sense of humor and appreciated each other's sense of humor. And of course, Raúl is a monster theoretician, a very smart guy. Meeting people like him, who's culturally and ethnically different, and yet, at the same time, good friends. I can't say that about everybody in the caucus, and there was a time that I did say that about just about everybody in the caucus, but certainly the pleasures of friendships that you develop in the caucus, of meeting people who aren't just Mexican American, but also meeting people who are not, that are other Latino groups, including white folks who for some reason like to attend our meeting. To the extent that the caucus is an opportunity to learn about life and gain in life's experiences, the caucus is a good thing.

BOBBIE HOUTCHENS AND MARY CARMEN CRUZ
Interview by Anita Hernández
December 13, 2016

Anita Hernández: Thank you for your time. When and why did you choose to attend C's and/or NCTE?

Mary Carmen Cruz: One of my professors, who was my mentor, pulled me in and she said you need to get involved in this. That was Roseann Dueñas González, co-founder of the Caucus. I was one of her students as an undergraduate and also one of her graduate students, when I graduated with my BA and then stayed on to work on MA degree. She said I need to start coming to the NCTE meetings and she would take me, so I became involved in the Caucus meetings. She knew her away around NCTE working with the presidents and the executive committees. She was advocating for issues and not just Latino Caucus issues, for all teachers of color, and for all students of color, issues of students who were culturally and linguistically underrepresented. I got to meet the folks she was working with. It was rewarding, eye-opening, enlightening, mind expanding, career developing. Rewarding and career developing. Then as a graduate student, I went to one or two CCCCs. The bulk of my experience was with NCTE. It was through her efforts that I became involved.

Hernández: Did she provide a scholarship for you to attend NCTE?

Cruz: She would let me sleep in her room and that was paid for. I paid for my own transportation and I paid for my own registration. There may have been a couple of times where the college may have paid for my registration. In all the years I have been involved in NCTE, I paid my own way, never reimbursed except for the time I was on the Executive Committee and that was paid for. I received per diem when I was on the secondary section.

Houtchens: My story is like Mary Carmen. I have been active in CABE [California Association for Bilingual Education) and Washington, D.C. area TESOL regional organizations and did presentations for CABE. As a graduate student again and earning my MA in bilingualism and biculturalism degree with Dr. Barbara Flores, she encouraged me to present at the NCTE. She introduced me to Latino Caucus leaders and members, which is where I felt at home. NCTE was overwhelming. People were not community-oriented as I was used to finding at CABE and at TESOL. I felt very isolated from everyone and without Barbara Flores I probably would not have gone back. She introduced me to the Caucus and to some outstanding leaders in education for Latino Students. Meeting Sandra Gibbs, who was the liaison for the Latino Caucus and to the Black Caucus, I was connected to amazing brilliant activist black women and men in the Black Caucus. That is where I found my home, it expanded my network. When I was weary to fight those battles in our own communities, I could always find renewal at the Latino Caucus and how Latino Caucus was involved in NCTE. I was not the only warrior. There were many people in front of me and behind me . . . The caucus made me a lot smarter, being with NCTE helped me understand . . . how different states had beliefs about kids, especially Latino kids and English learners. This gave me entry to NCTE that I would not have received by myself. It changed my life. The things I have done nationally, would not have been for the Latino Caucus.

Cruz: Thank you for summarizing, it's absolutely true. We gained an awareness of activism and advocacy at the national level. The entry way and finding our home in that large organization was through the Latino Caucus. It inspired us and spread our wings to work with other leaders.

Houtchens: I think the Latino Caucus gave me voice, more than just credibility, more than just strength and power. I don't know how to frame it. Once our names were connected to the Latino Caucus, people listened to us. It was like this is the fuse you are talking to, whether it is Mary Carmen or Bobbi, we got this explosive device behind us if you don't listen to us. Especially, in the positions we had chairs of the caucus that also put us in positions to be invited where our voices would be heard. For example, at every national convention, in the past, what would happen at the convention is that we leaders of the Latino Caucus and Black Caucus, we were asked to meet with certain members of the Executive Committee, president, outgoing president, and convention chair to talk about what was working at that particular convention. what we thought necessary changes for the next convention, how NCTE was coming up with initiative with language policy or had to do with recruitment of teachers, or with how the program looked. We were always invited to come and talk. Sometimes we were the ones that prompted the invitation. We were always there and we were listened to by them. It was a debriefing. We would meet with the caucus members in order to get a debriefing before we went to the meeting, to get a feeling about the convention. Members would tell us experiences they had had, other things they had noticed, which publishers were invited, about areas of instruction might not have been addressed, or if they had been addressed, they were not very sensitively addressed, like working with Latino urban kids. . .

Cruz: I was remembering when we went to the table, we were not just talking about issues that were affecting Latino youth, but we were talking about all students of color. One session where Native American literature and stereotypes within certain curriculum were discussed, but some of the examples to resolve this were stereotypes themselves. There were authors who never lived on a reservation, were not Indian themselves, who also were being promoted. We were bringing issues to the forefront to help make the other decision makers aware of what was going on. We were the voices. It was no longer Mary Carmen. It was no longer Bobbi. It went beyond us by working with our colleagues across the nation. The struggles and the challenges, as well as the resources and successes of our students and colleagues, that was what we could bring together and that was what the other NCTE leadership were hearing. We were bringing all of those powerful experiences collectively together. It was a unified voice. There she goes, go ask her what she thinks about this. What do think about this? How about joining us?

Hernández: Was that about a twenty-year period? Was that in the 1990s to about 2014?

Cruz: Yes, about twenty years. I started going in the 80s and then I moved away to go to a small private college on an Indian Reservation in the state of Washington. I lost connection. I laugh because my mentor did not forget us. So, I lost connection with NCTE and I lost connection with my mentor because I was busy doing other things. Then when

I came back to Tucson, the year that I started working in the school districts, I got an invitation to do a presentation at NCTE. It came out of the blue. I knew who was inviting me. It was Roseann Gonzalez and Sandra Gibbs. I knew it was them because no one at NCTE knew me. I wasn't that involved at the time. Previous to that, I was a protégé following my mentors around and learning from them as much as I could. They had not given up. So, I went to give the presentation. Then I came back again and not sure how I found my way to the Caucus. Then a couple years later, I received a phone call from Sandra Gibbs. That phone call said "Mary Carmen, this is Sandra Gibbs." I was so delighted. You will hear about how instrumental Sandra was in our organization and in NCTE. Sandra did more a whole lot more than just the caucuses. She was in charge of writing scholarships for students, she was in charge of NCATE, and a lot of other initiatives. She was especially our godmother, our *nina*, she made sure that our voices were not just heard but that were paid attention to and she made sure there was communication with each other across the caucuses. We were united in our vision. She knew the history of the involvement of people of color and she knew the history of NCTE. She was a very powerful promoter of the Caucus. She invited me to become a member of the Rainbow Strand organizers. So, I became more involved in the organization.

Houtchens: Because she was on the committee on Writing, people of color were involved in the many committees she was involved with. It was a way that she spread the wealth and not to be segregated in the caucus work, but actually be involved in the main work of NCTE.

Hernández: When you were chairs, what kinds of issues did the members want to take up?

Cruz: What are the issues being taken up now.

Hernández: One issue was that Adam Banks the CCCCs chair, resigned because NCTE was acting very exclusive. The Executive Committee averted this by asking what were our demands and saying we will meet the demands. They had to acknowledge Latino and Black Caucus were not being served well in the organization. It's on video by the president, Kathy Short. Not sure if they replaced his position.

Houtchens: What were the Black Caucus demands beyond the photograph. What did they want?

Cruz: I think that NCTE as an organization has policies and statements that talk about the rights of students to their own language, committed to recruiting teachers of color, being against racism and bias in the teaching of English, promoting involvement of minority involvement, looking at diverse and multicultural education. So, if those are the beliefs that an organization professes, then there should be evidence in the actions of the organization. So, as members of Latino Caucus, we also are concerned about the success of all our students because the organization exists to bring teachers together to promote professional development and to look at issues that affect students as well as our teachers. As Latino Caucus members were very concerned about Latino students and Latino educators.

At the time when Bobbi and I were involved, those very issues came to be. For example, at time Bobbi and I were involved, those issues in terms recruiting people by headquarters, you could count the number of people of color in leadership positions at headquarters. It went back to the stock room. In terms of NCTE elections, again, it got to where we were making recommendations, that for example only persons of color are nominated on a regular basis for vice president. People of color were not being elected into the executive committee. I am talking about the presidency. Continually having regular meetings for people of color to be involved because as Bobbi said, that is a big convention. The smallest convention was 5,000 and the largest was 9,000. If you are a teacher of color, if you are a brand-new teacher, It is daunting. It can be confusing, especially if you are teacher of color who is trying to see where are others who have like interest.

It was one of the issues we wanted promoted in the organization. There was a program for Teachers for the Dream we wanted promoted for the organization. Looking at the program, how the program was not doing what it was supposed to be doing for professional development and help to enlighten our colleagues. I think those are four little issues. To make our we sessions stronger. We didn't see concerted efforts to make changes. NCTE making the same promises over and over no real change. Even in 2014, NCTE making the same promises but there was no real change.

Hernández: How have you observed CCCCs or NCTE be responsive to Latino/a scholars and educators and what actions has that organization taken that you have seen that you agree or disagree with?

Houtchens: Teachers for the Dream. The program still exists now, but it has changed from when it started. It must have been 1995 or 1996. I am trying to remember the name of Black Caucus leader. He was a short black man, older man. Teachers for the Dream was his baby. He started Teachers for the Dream. It was started to promote initiatives that would encourage students of color to join the teaching profession. That was its mission. I had a feeling that It was the Black Caucus that got it started. There were private donations in the initial year and they gave out two 10,000 grants that were available to those who had a program for people of color to join the teaching profession. A lot of those who put in proposals were from universities. Sara was her first name and I think she taught at a college and she worked with 10 students. She was from the Carolinas. She was from the Black Caucus.

In 2000, we opened a new school. I was given a grant to start a program at my school. My idea was to start this tutoring club. I taught at an urban high school in San Bernardino. Most of my kids were Latinos and most of those were English learners and long-term English learners or newcomers. My idea was to start an after school tutoring group where I would teach kids to read a book aloud to elementary school children. They could choose to work at an elementary school near their homes in case they were bused. The elementary schools let out one hour after we let out so they could tutor the last hour of school. They went and made their own contacts, but had a letter of introduction from me. They had training on child development and had to anticipate development mental needs of the kids at the grade they were tutoring. Most went five days and read stories to little kids at the elementary schools by their house. Because it was by their house, many were tutoring their nieces and nephews and making their community a better place. It became a family thing.

Their job beyond reading to the kids and making their community in a better place, contributing to their community because there was not a lot of outlets. They had to carry the message to the little kids. The more time they spent they started to believe in the motto. it was like positive affirmation. I pulled in the students from the School of Education from CSSB and they worked as mentors and supervisors. I ended up with 200 students. It was so powerful. The principals thought it was wonderful to have these kids independently going. GS would pop in and out and monitor and collect data who was reading and what books they were reading and bring back info to our club meetings to further develop their skills. The superintendent was so impressed that he said we need to connect this club to Future Teachers of Am, which was a dead club into our group. The next year, he made an announcement every high school had to have a similar program to serve their community. Everyone high school had to have a similar program.

My school would start a teaching academy to take over what Teachers for the Dreams were doing. What I was able to do with the money I got from the money was to buy materials for the kids - books, T-shirts for PR, and publicize what they were doing. If they worked 100 hours tutoring, they earned a letter which was more beautiful than the athletic letter. They got recognition from the mayor. We went on two field trips that year. Most had not been 10 miles from where they were living. We left at 7:30am and visited University La Sierra, University of Redlands, Cal State SB and these kids were promised assistance in their applications. Came to LA to a museum, we go out to a real Chinese restaurant. Many had never gone to a restaurant with table cloths and did not know how to function. It was part of what we had students experience, Russian food, including borscht. We'd go see a play where bilingual foundations for the arts had the actors come into the audience to talk with the kids. We went to see *Phantom of the Opera* We went to see a symphony. The kids arrived to the school at midnight. I wanted them to come back to school the next day because I wanted them to talk about their whole experience.

The teaching academies are still going. The teaching academy has become a mentor for other academies in California. I received Edison funding, another one from the Gas Company and another three million from federal money. They used that money to start the teaching academies, that little initiative. This blossomed into something incredible. They took over my position when I retired. San Bernardino is putting out teachers of color, most of them bilingual. It is the gift that is still giving.

Cruz: That fund has evolved differently and you don't hear too much about it. When you go to the NCTE website, you can see that. It has changed quite a bit. Grants up to $750 and it goes to an affiliate. What they do is they submit a proposal that implements recruitment initiatives during the school year through the affiliate. A teacher cannot apply for it. The money is to recruit a teacher of color into your affiliates. This is for one teacher into the affiliate. The power has been reduced. It has been reduced.

Another thing that happened during our time was with the rainbow strand. NCTE used to bring to Urbana in February the Executive Committee and all members of the different steering committees, the elementary, the middle, the secondary, the college, as well as members of the research group. Then it would bring in members of Rainbow Strand planning committee, who were members of each of the different section levels, to assist in reading proposals. We would read the proposals, two to three thousand proposals that were submitted in a given year. They were divided into the different section levels. The committees would read the proposals which would go into the program as Rainbow Strands planners. We kept an eye for those proposals, whether they were marked Rainbow or not if they met the criteria for Rainbow strand. When we saw the proposals being accepted to be on the program, we would get together and discuss what else needed to be on the program to provide greater diversity. That was valuable. What was happening at the same time was those of us on the Rainbow strands were being mentored on issues of leadership, not just for the convention, so as we went back to our own schools and our own areas with leadership skills within the organization. We grew as professionals and we grew as leaders. We were invited to different meetings with other committees and commissions. This did not happen overnight. We requested that continued. . . .

Meeting at the Rainbow stand planning was powerful. When we went the to the leadership, the secondary sections, we would go into their planning sessions as working consultants and bring expertise of working with students of color. Traditionally those groups were white. Initially people were intimidated that we were in the room, but we had been mentored where there were ways to point that was not confrontational. Being in the room, we were able to read body language. We were skilled at reading the tone of the conversation that can't get in the digital. They didn't realize we were on the same team. It was okay. That face to face meeting in February was powerful to raising the level of sensitivity of NCTE and raised the sensitivity for NCTE staff. We interfaced with the staff, made friendships and relationships to move the organization along. . . .

Cruz: When we were face to face from 7am to 8pm. We were there with everyone. Living and breathing for three days and you build those relationships that was critical when the convention happens. Something happens when the caucuses that have room apart from each other. Placement was not most effective. We went right away. Here is what our needs. How can you help us before the event happened and for next time it would be the way. Relationships with students. Relationships is at the heart of working with colleagues. The two caucuses have rooms that are apart from each other. That has happened in the past and was not most effective. We went to staff and they were happy to help us rectify before the event. We create the relationships. Relationships are at the heart. of NCTE. . . .

It took years before they became more responsive. We build It took years to become more responsive. Changed three times were there. Kent Williamson worked for the publication division and he ran the bookstore at the convention. I built the relationship with him and we already had a relationship. He became much more sensitive over the years. We talked to him along. When we started, they presented an outsider point of view of our kids and our literature. He became more open to doing that of bringing Latino and Black voices.

At the convention planning, keynote speakers are also decided. When we were first involved, the main keynote speakers are determined by chair who is the incoming president, that person will ask others, people you are interested in, depending on your concern for many years influence who you bring, Sections invited to suggest names, speakers of color who could help advance understanding to promote effective practices for all students. Often times they were. In more recent years and more brainstorming of speakers of Color to the consideration list and making it to speakers. Couple of years ago, Sonia Nazario, former LA times writer was the keynote speaker. Kathy Short brought her. I am seeing those change.

I was proud of the leadership of the Latino Caucus in using the avenues to reach out to each other and support each other, to promote each other, and help each other to grow. I am hoping that the Caucus will continue to be united again at not just at CCCCs but also at NCTE, what happens in one, will be integrated, and not separated. I want to encourage the Latino Caucus to keep doing what it is doing and finding those avenues. To continue knowing our history. When we don't know our history, then we are limited in how we go forward. Knowing the history of CCCC can give more power to what you are say, what the issues are that need to be addressed, and how we go about that change. . .

CRISTINA KIRKLIGHTER
Interview by Romeo García
October 3, 2017

Romeo García: As Co-Chair of the Latino/a Caucus as it was known back then (2009-2014), you had a fascination with the history of the caucus and reached out to a number of early caucus leaders at the beginning of your position as co-chair, such as Roseann Dueñas Gonzales, Felipe de Ortego y Gasca, and Carlota Cardenas Dwyer. You later presented papers at 4Cs and were inspired to work on the *Writing and Working for Change* Projects with Steve Parks and Samantha Blackmon. How did such interactions with these early caucus leaders shape your role in the coming years as co-chair of the caucus?

Cristina Kirklighter: I confess I've always had a fascination with history, especially autobiographical histories. I keep all these storytelling, personal essay, and autobiographical books near my bed, so my last thoughts before dozing off are usually with what someone has shared years ago. I imagine some of my elder caucus mentors liked me and took me under their wing because I never grew tired of listening to their stories of the caucuses or their experiences with NCTE and CCCCs. Both sides of my family come from the rich storytelling cultures of Honduras and Tennessee. And, it was natural to sit and listen to the stories of our elders. What they told us were life lessons intermixed with histories and sometimes tall tale histories.

The beginnings of the NCTE Writing and Working for Change projects were fueled by likeminded angry caucus folks. Samantha Blackmon and I just finished presenting on a 2009 cross caucus panel focusing on our respective histories. Steve Parks was a responder, I believe. So, after the panel, Steve, Samantha, and I started talking, and we were all fired up about how the NCTE 2011 Centennial was two years away, and we hadn't heard anything about what NCTE was doing to celebrate our histories. As usual, we said, they were going to ignore us and those who came before us. So, the like-minded angry folks said we were going to contact NCTE. Geneva Smitherman and Victor Villanueva helped us prepare and, fortunately, Keith Gilyard was going to chair this Centennial. So, after, a few rounds with NCTE leadership and executive committee, they funded us for a trip to the NCTE archives to discover our histories. It was Samantha Blackmon, Jennifer Sano-Francini, and I who flew up there for a few days. As I flew up to Urbana, my plane made an emergency landing in another city with no lights and the smell of smoke. When that plane was making an emergency landing, I started questioning my love of history, but this quickly dissipated when I arrived at NCTE. We could have spent weeks there, and the historical discoveries we found were amazing and were digitalized by Samantha Blackmon. Later, Jennifer was instrumental in publishing the Asian/Asian American Caucus book, and it started in these archives.

Steve Parks and I were the organizers of the 2011 NCTE Centennial Celebration of the Caucuses, and it was an experience I will never forget as founders and elders of the caucuses came back after many years and presented in some sessions while our emerging leaders of the caucuses presented in other sessions. Our own Tracey Flores was one of these emerging leaders, and this experience listening to these elders has shaped who she is as the current NCTE Latinx Caucus co-chair. Jennifer Sano-Francini is now the co-chair of the Asian/Asian American caucus. I'd like to believe their experiences on the *Writing and Working for Change* project had some bearing on their decisions to take leading roles in their respective caucuses.

Alexander Hildalgo who was then a graduate student at Purdue and worked under Samantha Blackmon interviewing caucus members from various caucuses. NCTE/CCCC members can watch these videos on the NCTE *Writing and Working for Change* website. As a member of both the Latinx and Queer Caucus, I know how important this project was for her and thank her for preserving these histories in visual form.

Iris Ruiz, our current CCCCs co-chair, also understands the importance of these early histories and maintains regular correspondences with Felipe Ortego de Gasca, the founding member of our caucus, as well as more current past leaders. Many Latinxs respect their elders and know what value they bring to our ability to lead. I am proud to say all the co-chairs I've known have worked with their elders in some capacity or another to help them lead and make historical and knowledgeable decisions.

Romeo García, who I mentored when he was at Texas A&M Corpus Christi, and who was mentored by Steve Parks in Syracuse, also knows the importance of these histories as he co-edits this book. If you don't know your histories as caucus leaders, it makes it almost impossible to lead, and we know how important it is for emerging leaders to have these histories as well. You are your histories.

García: During your time as the Co-Chair of the caucus, you took on a number of cross-caucus initiatives with co-chairs of the other caucuses? Would you describe a few of these initiatives and how it shaped your leadership and relationships with other caucuses? Why is it so important to work with other caucuses?

Kirklighter: In the early years when I joined the caucus and when it was a lot smaller (maybe 5-15 at most in our meetings), we seemed to have less of a voice in cross-caucus concerns. In contrast, the Black Caucus would fill up their rooms, and they had some powerful clout in caucus decisions, especially when Sandra Gibbs was at NCTE Headquarters. Sandra Gibbs though worked with all of us and would visit our meetings. It was good to have her at NCTE, but when she left, we all felt we had less of a voice at headquarters.

Gradually, the caucus started to grow as more Latinx graduate students entered Rhetoric and Composition. I became co-chair with Renee Moreno when Sandra Gibbs had already left. I believe this was the moment where caucus co-chairs realized our cross-caucus relationships needed to strengthen to send our collective voices to NCTE and CCCCs. The approaching NCTE 2011 Centennial Celebration also brought us together as we worked to document our collective histories.

We learned through these early histories how a small group of people of color, many as founders of our respective caucuses, worked together to make a difference not only at NCTE, but throughout our nation and world in literature, linguistics, creative writing, and community outreach. The NCTE *Searching for America* document where Asian American, African American, Chicano and Chicana, and Native American literature and creative writing leaders sent a strong message to this nation on how the literature our students read needed to include these group's writers. Later Geneva Smitherman and Roseann Dueñas Gonzalez and still later Victor Villanueva became the linguistic leaders. Reading these early histories and what our elders had done together I know had an impact on me and others.

So, we began coming together in force as co-caucus leaders, and it became much more difficult for others who ignored or downplayed our concerns to not hear us. Mila Fuller who worked with the caucuses at NCTE Headquarters for a few years did help as she could, but her role was not as clearly defined as Sandra Gibbs. Co-chairs at that time knew we had to create a strong voice together and work on many cross-caucus initiatives to fight the injustices of academia, NCTE, and beyond. *Writing and Working for Change* cross-caucus initiatives was what I focused on the most and encouraging our cross-caucus members to present on the same panels and workshops. Even if our attendance is still small at these panels or roundtables, we're dialoguing with each other and learning more about how our scholarship, teaching, and community outreach intertwine. For the growing number of caucus members who have multiple identities and thus affiliations with more than one caucus, going to cross-caucus sessions, workshops, working on articles, books, multimedia, digital, and films together, convening together in casual settings, speak to these collective identities and make them feel at home with who they are.

García: You were on several committees within NCTE/CCCC (Resolutions Committee, Executive Committee, Nominating Committee, Diversity Committee, NCTE/CCC Rainbow Committee as some examples) prior to taking on the role as co-chair of the Latino/a Caucus. How did serving on these committees help you when you became co-chair of the Latino/a Caucus? What would you tell other caucus members about the importance of joining NCTE/CCCC Committees?

Kirklighter: I first served on a 4Cs committee while I was a doctoral student. Victor Villanueva was Chair then in 1998 and decided I should serve on the Ad Hoc Use of Student Writing in Composition Research Committee. I was the student representative on this committee, and the rest of the committee were made up of well-established scholars in this area. Victor knew I had just finished co-editing *Voices and Visions: Refiguring*

Ethnography in Composition (Heinemann Boynton Cook 1997), and he thought I was a good choice. At that time, I was sure this committee would find out I was an imposter and didn't belong in academia. Back then, we were writing on a listserv (no Skype available then), so all they saw were my words until we eventually met up at 4Cs much later. Reflecting on this experience years later, I will say how these insecurities and imposter syndrome helped me. Before I pressed the send button on my e-mails, I spent hours researching the topic they were discussing and reading all their comments carefully. It was the best self-training I could have put myself through. I was determined to show them this Latinx could enter their conversations and had something valuable to say. I was determined not to be an imposter. As the only student on this committee, I also believed I was the spokesperson for students. Years later this spokesperson role prepared me to serve on other committees and leadership positions for my gente and others. At the end of serving on this committee, Paul Anderson as chair, told me how appreciative he was of my work on this committee and advocacy for students. I had joined the conversation as a valuable 4Cs committee member, and this was the foundation I needed for my future work at NCTE and CCCC.

I successfully entered committee conversations, and my next step with committee work was to learn the rules of NCTE/CCCC when I began serving on the Resolutions Committee. But, as I later discovered, it is not enough to learn the rules, but how others use these rules or bend these rules or do whatever else with these rules. The more committees you serve on, the better you become at gauging these rules and applying them for advocacy purposes and/or preventative measures. We've had leaders at NCTE/CCCC who have supported us, and we've had leaders who sought to derail and/or silence us. Knowing who does what and how they operate within these systems of rules is important. When you serve on a number of committees with them, you eventually can see what's coming around the corner and take appropriate measures. Both Renee and I had served on a number of committees, so we would confer together and confer with previous co-chairs and other caucus co-chairs to gauge certain situations that could hurt or help the caucuses. We seldom made decisions without conferring with others. I would say it is part of Latinx collective leadership for we are anything but silos. Also, you eventually figure out who are your allies and who are not after serving on a number of committees with them. With each committee I served on, I grew more confident and more outspoken. I figured out who to bring into certain conversations for collective purposes and who was out for their own self-interests or interests of their circle of friends.

Serving on a number of committees also demonstrates to the NCTE/CCCC leadership that you care for the organization. They may disagree with you, but they know you care, and this can gain you respect as a leader. They might say under their breath, "Oh no, what is she going to demand now" and, as Latinxs, we're used making demands for justice over again and again until someone hears us, but that's okay. We persist because of all the injustices we've faced in our lives. We have no choice but to persist, and it is a quality that can serve us well.

My last piece of advice on this matter is to serve on committees, not to alleviate insecurities or call attention to yourself. Proving yourself to others time and time again is way too exhausting. Validation comes within as I eventually learned. Serve because you want to make a difference and improve the lives of others. Others will see this in your leadership style and respect you for it.

García: In the last ten years, the membership of the Latinx Caucus has increased dramatically as more and more Latinxs pursue graduate work in Rhetoric and Composition. What advice would you have for these up and coming leaders of the caucus?

Kirklighter: First, I want to say how pleased to see so many caucus members at the last few caucus meetings. I want to thank many of caucus members who have continually encouraged and brought their graduate students to these meetings. This is how we grow through our mentoring efforts and networking. My first advice is to become engaged with this caucus and its members. As a graduate student, I had a few good mentors at my university, such as Joe Moxley and Elizabeth Metzger, but I also had mentors within the caucus, such as Victor Villanueva, Gail Okawa, Cecilia Rodríguez Milanés, Mary Carmen Cruz, Bobbi Houtchens and, later, when I discovered them in my archival research of the Latinx Caucus, Felipe Ortega de Gasca, Carlota Cárdenas de Dwyer, and Roseann Dueñe Gonzalez. I also shortly later found mentors in the Black Caucus, such as Geneva Smitherman and James Hill. And, a little later found mentors in the Asian/Asian American Caucus and American Indian Caucus, such as Lu Ming Mao, Morris Young, Malea Powell, and Joyce Rain Anderson. When I was a junior faculty member, I found Steve Parks who later mentored me when I became editor of the journal, *Reflections*.

So, the number one piece of advice is to always search for mentors no matter what stage you're at in your academic career and beyond. And, most importantly, remember all the mentors that came before you entered academia. They'll keep you grounded and remind you who you are when you start thinking you're all that and more. Whatever you do, don't fall into the "I'm too big for my britches" syndrome, an old Southern saying my grandmother taught me. Academia can lure you into this syndrome with its almost Hollywood star worship of academic stars. If you feel you might be slipping into this syndrome, pay a visit to your *familia* and let them tell you who you really are. It works every time for me.

Mentors also come in the form of those you teach. I've learned more from my students than they have from me given my Freirean approach to teaching. Remember, their combined total of years out number yours, and they are a valuable source of your learning. When you become a senior leader in the caucus, remember how much undergraduate and graduate caucus leaders can teach you.

García: When you were co-chair, you worked on several publication initiatives to promote Latinx scholarship with the caucus. Would you describe some of these publication projects and the importance of promoting our members as editors, reviewers, and co-authors?

Kirklighter: Promoting our gente's scholarship is very important to help them with getting jobs, promotion, awards, and building a community of scholarship affiliated with our scholars' work. It also helps scholars outside the caucus to understand what we value in scholarship and how it defines us. Years ago, we only had a few Rhetoric and Composition Latinx scholars and allies contributing to this body of scholarship.

Then, as we grew, we had to push publishers to go beyond just publishing these few and encourage them to discover our increasing number of emerging scholars. This didn't work out too well and publishers kept asking the same gente to be authors, reviewers, awardee nominees, etc. While the junior gente and graduate students kept encountering publishing roadblocks, some of the established gente scholars had enough of this and took matters into their own hands by becoming editors/co-editors of special issues, books, journals, videos, films, etc. They also encouraged our gente to become reviewers and review the books of our gente. We must look out for each other if we want Latinxs in R&C to thrive in academia.

Although our number of publishing allies outside the caucus are increasing, we still have a ways to go. Before I became co-caucus chair, I co-edited the book collection, *Teaching Writing with Latino/as Students: Lessons Learned at Hispanic-Serving Institutions*. A few caucus members were in the book: Isabel Baca, Dora Ramírez-Dhoore, and Beatrice Méndez Newman. I knew that this book would resonate with our caucus members, especially Latinx students, because it was about their experiences even if they were not at an HSI at the time of the book's publication. It countered many of the deficit-driven perceptions aimed at them by faculty, administrators, students, and the deficit scholarship on Latinx students. It's important for Latinx students, many of whom began at community colleges, to see authors capturing their challenges and breakthroughs as writing students. Once when I was teaching a graduate class at Texas A&M Corpus-Christi, I asked students how many of them began in "developmental" or "basic" writing classes. All of the Latinxs in the class raised their hands, and there were many great Latinx writers in my classroom many of whom went on to get their PhDs and are now professors. So, editing these types of book, is more than just helping Latinx Caucus members get published. It's also about telling their stories for other students to read and educating professors on how to work with Latinx students.

Listening to Our Elders, co-edited with Samantha Blackmon and Steve Parks, was another book, but this one was for the caucuses and Disabilities Committee. Just as I have multiple identities that speak to caucuses and/or committees, so do other caucus members. Some members must sometimes choose which caucus and/or committee they will attend given we all meet at the same time at 4Cs. They especially needed to read a book with many of their historical caucus identities in it. I am especially happy to see the after the caucus program after the caucus meetings at 4Cs, and I believe it's driven by the newer generation of scholars, teachers, and activists. I'm pleased to have mentored through this book initiative and *Writing and Working for Change* this newer generation and so pleased how they work together now in panels, books, and other initiatives. This is our future, and we are anything but silo caucuses.

The third and final major project was when I took on the editorship of *Reflections: A Journal of Public Rhetoric, Civic Writing, and Service Learning*. I edited the journal for five years ending in the summer of 2017 after my retirement from academia. I was co-chair of the caucus for two and a half of those years. *Reflections* is a small independent journal in Rhetoric and Composition, but this suited me fine. There was less politics, and I enjoyed working with our small staff, Wilma Harvey, Jess Pauszek, and Tobi Jacobi. Steve Parks did a good job of mentoring me as the previous editor, and I thank him for that. My list of reviewers became populated with cross-caucus and committee members, and I made sure at least some of the special issues focused on a diversity of issues (Latino/a, African American (reprint), Disabilities, and Veterans). Caucuses found our journal to be friendly to book reviews from their authors, so this was another opportunity. The Fall 2013 special issue co-edited with Isabel Baca focused on Latinos/as in Public Rhetoric, Civic Writing, and Service Learning. This special issue had many submissions and acceptances from our caucus members, some of whom published for the first time. It's what many of us do in the caucus, so the high submission rate from the caucus wasn't surprising. For the last seven years, the 4Cs Latinx Caucus has been one of the few caucuses and committees to reach out to the conference's local communities and ask them to present at our workshops. I enjoyed working with Steve Alvarez, Damian Baca, and Kendall Leon organizing these outreaches while I was co-chair, and I love to see how it continued with Iris Ruiz and Raúl Sánchez. If we're committed to community outreach as many caucus members are, we have to walk the walk.

The most rewarding part of promoting scholarship in the caucus was to watch as these scholars grew in confidence and began mentoring others. The cycle of giving is what's so important, not your legacy.

García: On several occasions, you've talked about your different backgrounds (Honduran, Mayan, Southern white, middle class, disabled), and you've been open with who you are. Why is it important to you to be open as a caucus leader and member? How do these backgrounds shape your leadership style?

Kirklighter: My mother taught me early on in life to take pride in who I am. She would often tell me "You are no better than anyone else and no one is better than you." I believe this was passed on to her as well. Later, as a graduate student, I had a fascination with autobiographical writings and the personal essay. What courage it took for some of these writers to be candid with who they were or are. They were my mentors too. As I was growing up with biracial parents, they never encouraged me to select one identity even though society at that time and still to this day pressures biracial children to be one or the other. They made me feel I had a strong foundation in the cultures they came from. Victor Villanueva, whose children come from similar cultural backgrounds as me, once told me he could see how open I was about my identities, and I took that as a compliment. But not all are so lucky as I later discovered, especially when I became a teacher. I did notice as I candidly talked about my identities, students and eventually caucus members would confide in me about certain identity challenges they faced. I was happy to listen and some chose to be more open and others did not. It's everyone's choice to what level they wish to open up, but those who are open know they have particular roles to play as teachers, mentors, mothers, etc. I came from a middle-class background with a father who was a successful engineer, and I know what privileges I had growing up. Later in life when I discovered I had a disability (ADHD), I decided to be open and tell my university, my students, and wrote about it in the journal I edited, *Reflections: A Journal of Public Rhetoric, Civic Writing, and Service Learning*. I was then able to mentor more students who had disabilities and wished to confide in me. More recently, I've become much more aware of my Mayan ancestors and their ways that I now know I've always strongly identified with. As I grow older, I've come to celebrate and welcome all these identities and the opportunities it affords me to connect and possibly mentor others. Each has an impact on my leadership style, and I appreciate what these identities have done for me and others. Sometimes, it's challenging living with all of these identities, but it has opened up so many cross-identifications with others. I would have it no other way.

DAMIAN BACA
Interview by Romeo García
October 1, 2016

Romeo García: When and why did you choose to attend C's or the NCTE?

Damian Baca: I joined the Latino Caucus and the C's in 2000. It was the C's Minneapolis Convention in the year 2000. I was a graduate student in the Master's program at Northern Arizona University. I am aware I am not first-generation that there are several who have come before me in the organization. But as a graduate student getting a Master's degree at Northern Arizona University in Flagstaff, I was feeling very much like first generation in that I was the first Latino to attend the Rhetoric for Master's programs which was new, with the intent of eventually earning the Ph.D. and moving on into the office of the professoriate. I was the first Latino that the faculty that I was working with in the graduate program, I guess you can describe it as first contact. It was not their first contact with Latinos, there were a number of Latinos as custodial staff at the University, the cafeteria was well staffed with Latinos. But having a Latino show up in class interested in a Master's degree in Rhetoric and Composition for the purposes of obtaining a Ph.D. in Rhetoric and Composition, that was very new for the faculty that I was working with.

Also problematic was growing up in New Mexico having Spanglish as my first language, having acclimated to standardized American English at a fairly early age, there wasn't much for faculty to do for me regarding you know fixing me linguistically. And that was another challenge for the faculty. And then also being *güero*, being *güerito* from New Mexico, being a light skinned Mexican I did not conform to the conventional stereotypical expectations of an ethnographic encounter with Mexicans. It was very much first contact and I felt very much like first generation.

Coming to the CCCC was only further alienating and it was the Latino Caucus that I discovered fairly quickly was my institutional home, my emotional home, a place of support, and a sense of belonging. Of course, this is under Ceci Milanés (the Latino Caucus chair). I was interested in language because I know you've asked about the interest in Rhetoric and Composition, so I was interested in language and identity formation, historical memory, and also the physical corporeal act of writing. It was alarming to me that the majority of the sources that were used to inform Rhetoric and Composition came primarily from Colonial-centric, Euro-centric, North Atlantic Western civilizations that really had very little beyond a 200-year history. It was thinking of the field primarily through the Enlightenment. Yes, Rhetoric and Composition studies the Greeks, but they study them through Hegel. We are really learning very little about the Greeks of the 4th century BCE in the ancient Mediterranean. We are learning more about Hegel and Hegelian visions of the intellectual kidnapping of ancient Greece as a cradle of Western Civilization. That myth. We were being asked all of us, regardless of where we came from in the classroom in the graduate level, we were being asked to take on the skin and the mentality of Euro-Centrism. So, on one hand I was interested in Rhetoric and Composition, but on the other hand the lenses that the field continues to use I felt to be highly damaging and destructive. I think the role of the Latino Caucus in the CCCC's has been incredibly important to me and I would like to especially note the role of the Latino Caucus working with former NCTE employee Dr. Sandra Gibbs who placed diversity of the forefront of all of the work we do--teaching, research, outreach, community engagement. And, a recognition that as we pursue these goals that we are not alone, that we are working parallel to other groups, other scholars, other teachers of color, who are also asking and demanding change. And, so it was Sandra Gibbs who was a very important point person for us for the Latino caucus in our interactions and correspondence with the other Caucuses of color, the co-chairs and the chair of the other caucuses of color.

It is interesting about the vision of the Latino caucus under the time of Ceci Milanés because her work comes to the world of language and text through the lens of creative writing and poetry. Her work has been a huge inspiration to me. I have always read it and engaged it as clearly as rhetoric. This can tell us much about rhetorical theory and reveals much about composition and composing strategies and the craft of writing. Ceci's work has always been stretching beyond disciplinary borders, but I was aware at the same time that the field of Rhetoric and Composition did not take her work into account and so it was very clear to me that the policed borders of what counts as rhetoric and composition and what does not. Those borders are still heavily policed even as the field claims itself as a transdisciplinary field. I do not think we have really reached that and I am not sure this intellectual work has earned that designation.

Ceci's work has broadened my horizon and I think it was very important to me. When we think about her vision of coming, again crossing borders and conventional borders, we can ask the question of who is Latino, what counts as Latino and Latina, who is in and who is out. The Latino Caucus under Ceci, and I know this even before her, had a fluidity, and I believe it still does, of accommodating, of welcoming, of including people of who actually may not be Latino and Latina. I am thinking Gail Okawa would have been one figure that comes to mind. Other members of the Latino Caucus who have been part of our community who may or may not identified with this subjectivity of the marker of Latino and Latina, so Ceci's vision was very important. I hope that the Latino Caucus will continue to be embracing those fluid categories and thinking across conventional barriers for solidarity.

García: What were your goals?

Baca: One goal was to get myself into a Ph.D. program that would allow me for options after. As a first-generation college student and as first-generation graduate student, first in my family to earn a college degree, first in my family to go on to graduate school, I had quite a bit of catch up to do in learning from a few faculty in my undergraduate degree in Texas about peer institutions, about feeder schools, about national rankings. Learning about those institutional hierarchies was very informative. And, also looking at the labor practices, the hiring practices, and particular in English departments, which is not all that encouraging. I did recognize early on that as a young punk kid from New Mexico that if I had any intentions of returning to New Mexico and returning to this part of the world that actually heading outward and getting a Ph.D. far beyond my own regional sense of place, that that may enable a possibility of returning somewhere close--close to home. I ended up finding myself at Syracuse where again though I am not a first generation that is in the Caucus, I am first generation in that I was the first student of color that was in the Syracuse CCR Program--Composition and Cultural Rhetoric program. Again, at that moment of first contact, I was a great ethnographic disappointment.

García: When you joined the Caucus, how many people were involved in that time, and what do you think was the sentiment of being involved with the Caucus at the C's when you were there?

Baca: Under Ceci, we continued to grow, our numbers continued to grow. They are not the numbers we see now. I am thinking of the numbers at the Latino Caucus at the CCCC in Houston in 2016, this past April. That would have to be the largest Caucus meeting I have seen and that is in a ten-year period of time. At least twelve or more years. There is significant growth beyond what we have seen. There have been years at NCTE, ten years ago, I went to one Latino Caucus meeting in Minneapolis at NCTE and there was only four of us in the room. There was more Latinos at the convention that year, but they were also spread in multiple directions. Not everyone can get to those meeting. It is a challenge. Sometimes, some years our numbers would be very small. I think we are moving beyond that. The days of the Latino Caucus coming and being able to count those in attendance on one or two hands, I think we have exhausted that era and we've moved on, we've moved beyond on. There are many of us, it is in every state and in every region of the country.

García: When you joined at the time what were some of the issues that you witnessed or observed at the C's in the Caucasus and how do you remember the Caucus responding to some of those issues?

Baca: One of the first things that I noticed that was a great disappointment to me at CCCC are panels that would presumably be celebrating diversity. You would see one scholar would be a prominent, one of the few prominent voices of African American rhetorical traditions, she would be there. Next to her you would have a scholar that would do Asian American rhetoric and Asian American rhetorical traditions, again one of a very small number of people, she would be there. The next presenter she would be presenting on disability, still a small circulation of scholars which is growing. And then the fourth member would be someone who is taken from literature and someone taken from another field and speak for and represent Latina and Latino rhetorical traditions. On the one hand that could be seen as a strength, but if we look at hiring practices and if we look carefully at the pipeline that actually speaks to a significant systemic problem and that is that the under-representations of Latinos and under-representations of Latina scholars in particular, women of Mexican American descent, women of Puerto Rican descent, there are very few women even today, right now in 2016. If we were to count the number of scholars in Rhetoric and Composition who are Latina, who have tenure, we are talking about people, I would probably count them on one hand right now, we are talking about a very few. I observed this at the very beginning, that if you are looking for a Latino or Latina that does scholarship in rhetoric and composition who is publishing for other scholars in Rhetoric and Composition on Latina and Latino Rhetoric and Latina and Latino Composition Practices then the CCCC is not the place to go. It is not the place for you. What I noticed I could only describe as absence, erasure, and no significant or sustained attempt to fix that situation, to tend to that, and to promote change.

The Caucus has been well aware of that sense of dread, those moments of hopelessness. I think it was important for us to be able to go even when we were in smaller number, to attend the Latino Caucus and to be able to share those moments with each other. As well as planning ahead, planning for the future, and thinking not simply what is the next step, but thinking two to three steps out how do we want to see ourselves begin making change and affecting everlasting change in the field, in the discipline.

It is very interesting about my own relationship with the C's, because some of my work as you know does touch on questions of Rhetorical history and historiography, although I really would not describe my work as necessarily rhetorical historiography, although it certainly touches on that and certainly speak into the Euro-Centric limit of what passes itself off as history of rhetoric in our field. I do not see that the field has been all that responsive. For example, in *Mestizo Scripts Digital Migrations in the Territories of Writing*, I am attempting to retell the story of Rhetoric and Writing as technologies that emerge not in Athens, because archeologists and historians will confirm that is not where writing begins. I was telling the story of Rhetoric and Writing as they emerged in the Valley of Mexico, which is not something you can do really in the expansiveness of a single book, but there was an ambitious attempt to engage in this sort of hermeneutic reconstruction with direct implications for the studying and teaching and the practicing of writing today. The reception at the CCCC was actually fairly cold, oddly enough. I have been embraced by NCTE. I will be the first to acknowledge I don't have training in English education, I don't try to pass myself off as something I am not, but, they have been overwhelmingly supportive and in the Latino Caucus, of course, through NCTE has been a huge resource of support. Also NCTE's Cultivating New Voices (CNV) for scholars of color mentorship program has been incredibly helpful to me. I was part of the cohort of 2004 to 2006. being able to work with other scholars in the field, I was the only one of my cohort, this would be significant to this conversation, that was a graduate student at the time. I was the only graduate student in Rhetoric and Composition. All of my colleagues in my cohort were coming from the school of education or were focusing on English education and that is important I think to note. Being involved in NCTE CNV scholars of color has been helpful.

García: What were some of the earliest memories that you have of the Caucus interacting with other folks outside of the Caucus and what kind of discussions on issues or matters do you remember happening and what kind of resolutions or projects were undertaken to address those issues?

Baca: I think one of the most significant developments that comes to mind would have been under Cristina Kirklighter and this was when NCTE lost Dr. Sandra Gibbs. This could have been 2006 or 2007 or right around that period of time. There was no transparency. We did not know what was happening nor were we able to really get much information, but we wanted to make sure that we communicated to the Executive Committee that we were concerned. Cristina Kirklighter and I drafted a letter to the Executive Committee encouraging them, strongly encouraging them, to reconsider their decision to release, to let her go, after around 20 years of service to the organization. I don't know the name of the letter I will have to check with Cristina Kirklighter, but we should be able to track that down.

Sandra Gibbs had worked with NCTE, I believe, for about 20 years. She was, in network theory, what we would describe as a hub. She was the connector between the Latino Caucus, the Black Caucus, and the Asian American Caucus. She was the connector across caucuses of color and caucuses of difference. She was someone that we relied on heavily. She would come and we would see her doing caucus meetings at CCCC. She'd share with us very brief necessary information about proposals that the Black Caucus was considering, for example, and which we could consider supporting. This was prior to Executive meetings. It was good for us to know ahead of time what our fellow peers and colleagues and good friends in our other Caucuses are interested in supporting so we would have the opportunity to lend our support, to explore possibilities of displaying solidarity. It was a very important position. When she was let go, I believe she was up for retirement in a couple of years, a year or two, and, so, she was let go prior to retirement. We do not have the whole story, but we were concerned and we wanted to make sure that the Executive Committee understood our concerns. There was no attempt to replace Sandra Gibbs. There was no replacement. We were at a great loss.

I drafted the letter with Cristina Kirklighter and we mobilized the Latino community and many letters were sent. We wrote one and co-wrote one of them. I know the Black Caucus also was sending letters to the Executive Committee at that time. We wanted to communicate to the Executive Committee the importance of Sandra Gibbs. We wanted to make sure this was made visible to them, that they understood the key role Sandra Gibbs played in bringing in issues of diversity to the table to be taken very seriously. Other caucuses likewise were interested in questions of race, writing, rhetoric, diversity, multilingualism and questions of representations on Executive Committees, questions of representations on editorial boards. The conversations we are still having today. Sandra Gibbs was the connector. We were able to communicate through her between caucuses. We wanted to make sure that the Executive Committee knew the value and the importance of her work. We felt the way in which she was fired from her job was a problem.

Again, we do not know why, but this was someone who was incredibly important to us and we were not hearing from NCTE and the CCCC that they were aware, that was not clear. There were other caucuses in participation, so we could describe it as a cross-caucus initiative. I do not have the hard numbers. But, it was a moment that stands out in my mind that was a cross-caucus initiative.

One of the things I will add is this past April 2016 in Houston at the CCCC, there was the after-Caucus mixer. This is something I do not know who is responsible for making that happen, but I do know there has been a push to make this happen for several years. I have been calling for it for almost a decade. It started with a question, Sandra Gibbs was still with us at the time, it started with a question, couldn't the meeting rooms be next to each other, be adjacent to each other, place them nearby. Don't segregate and put us into silo spaces far from each other at 6 pm and 7pm at night. The halls are empty and you are looking for some room several floors up. That is isolation. Do not do that. Instead take all the Caucuses, especially the Caucuses of Color, organize meeting rooms next to each other with the possibility of making some sort of connection after those meetings. In my mind that was actually a very minimal request. We weren't asking for something else other than the reservation of room assignments. It was actually a fairly modest request, but it took years of asking.

I remember several years ago there was a proposal that went up, I am not going to remember the name, offering financial assistance to teachers and professors and instructors who were employed at tribal colleges providing financial travel support to the C's for tribal college employees. That initiative came up, it was proposed by Scott Lyons, one of the few indigenous scholars of Rhetoric and Composition and that went through, I believe it was unanimous. There was cross-caucus support to ensure we are supporting those teachers and instructors who are dedicated at teaching tribal colleges. There are virtually no representations in our academic journals or conferences that would account for the pedagogies, the research, the life experiences of educators at our tribal colleges. Scott Lyons is the one who spearheaded that and there was a pronounced support from members of the Latino Caucus for that.

I think there is an understandable situation where the Caucuses can become siloed and segregated and there is some space where we need to meet in our own groups to discuss the immediate pressing of needs of our own communities. We need to have that space. At the same time, there are shared concerns, they might not be identical, so I am not interested in flattening difference, but I think there are connections across differences and there are shared concerns that we can collaborate on, that we can work together on. My perception that there has been a bit of siloing and unfortunate segregation between the Caucuses of Color. I'd like to see that changed. I do think that the Latino Caucus is in a great position. There is an advantage we have, precisely because we have a very fluid identity, a fluid Caucus identity, and even the mission statement that we have had throughout the years, going back to Ceci Milanés, the mission statement was actually never really targeting Latino and Latina scholars. The mission statement, the original mission statement under Ceci, targeted scholars who were committed to matters of Latina and Latino composition and committed to Latina and Latino contributions to rhetoric and rhetorical theory regardless of one background. It has always been rather inclusive and I'd like to see it continue to move forward in working with other caucuses in that inclusive spirit.

I think there is a great deal of ambiguity when I think about how the CCCC or NCTE has been responsive to Latino and Latina scholars and educators. I see that it has largely not been. I think that one year that stands out that we can find a clear exception to that is the year of the CCCC under Adam Banks. We can flip through the program schedule and there is a very clear effort to make sure that some of the most prominent voices in the Latino Caucus are featured not just in the program in concurrent sessions, but they are speaking as featured speakers. Featured speakers and in keynote events, that is incredibly important. We actually did see a kind of diversity at that point that had been unprecedented. It is not unprecedented outside. There is an incredible amount of diversity in our schools, in our neighborhoods, but stepping into the CCCC that is where you see an erasure. Under Adam Banks we do see a significant shift. Whether or not we have been able to mirror that in the two years past of the CCCC, I am uncertain. I think we still have a ways to go. I'd like to make sure that the C's is moving in that direction.

When we talk about what the organization has done or has not done, keep in mind that we are talking about an organization that has had only one Latino male as program chair, Victor Villanueva, and that was before my time, it might have been as early as 1999, when Victor Villanueva was serving as program chair. There has been no Latina ever in the entire history of the organization and no Latina or Latino before or since Victor. It is very easy to point to a kind of tokenizing that we see in the field. It is time for the field to shed that tokenism and begin to move forward.

The Caucus has a great history of inclusivity and alliance building and solidarity. I'd like to make sure that it continues to do that, alliance building across Latina and Latino subjectivities and experiences. For me, writing *Mestizo Scripts* was coming from a very specific Northern New Mexico perspectives and that one book simply could not account for all of the subjectivities and the histories and memories and rhetorical practices of Latina and Latino populations. No single book can do that. That is beyond the bounds of possibilities. But, it is one contribution to the question of if there is such a thing as Latina and Latino rhetoric that could not be fully articulated and accounted for and explained by Greco-Roman concepts, re-imagined through the lens of Enlightenment thinkers such as Hegel. If there is such a thing, which of course we know to be true, but if academics were to recognize that, as such, that argument would not be made in a single book. It would be made in a multitude of dissertations and books across generations and across time. So, one book is not enough. The very few other book-length works that have contributed to our understanding of Latino and Indigenous rhetorical traditions, I could probably count all of the books on one hand coming from Rhetoric and Composition. It is important for us to be thinking of alliance building across subjectivities. Even the idea of Mexican subjectivity. We are talking about a wide canvas of life experiences. I think there is a way of continuing to foster alliance building across our cultural differences, across our experiences, and then moving that and continue to move beyond to look at Afro Latino and looking at African American Black solidarity movements. I think the time is ripe for this kind of crosstalk that we need to continue moving forward.

Mestizo Scripts is a highly controversial book and people hate it. That is simply where we are at. Maybe there are other ways I could have written it to make it more accessible. I could have asked, please accommodate our difference. There could have been many more gentle and diluted calls for change that could have made it accessible, made it less demanding on the reader, I guess. But, there are so few books one could turn to if they wanted to know the story of writing as it emerges in Egypt, well there are books that you need to turn to like archaeology. Or, what about the great painted book traditions of the Valley of Mexico, well you are not going to turn to Rhetoric and Composition for that. You would turn to art history, that will give you that. What if you wanted to know the development of Sanskrit coming out of the Indus Valley several generations ago in what is now the border of Pakistan and India. You are not going to find that in Rhetoric and Composition. They are not interested in that. But at the same time, they are claiming to be interested in that, because the field wants to say that Rhetoric and Composition, and the future of writing, must be multi-modal and must be multilingual, but it is precisely multi-modal and multilingual contributions to the field of writing that the field has systematically erased out of our histories, which is why we go to Greece. I would characterize both NCTE and CCCC as primarily unresponsive.

I do not know about the vision of what the field thinks of when they think of Mexican American. They certainly do not think of me. I am aware that I am not going to be a stereotypical representation while simultaneously understanding that it is precisely the light skinned, those of us in the Mexican American community and in the Latino community that are light skinned, that will have it better off in higher education and easier than our dark-skinned brothers and sisters. But the vision of Mexican American in both the C's and NCTE seems to be someone who has arrived recently, who is in desperately need of linguistic salvation that can only come from the National Council of Teachers of English. The literacy salvation narrative, the linguistic salvation narrative, it is still that progress narrative, which is very much still part of the humanities and social sciences, it is embedded there. And, Ralph Cintron in the last *Octalog*, in the *III Octalog*, addressed this barely and he is absolutely right. We need to continue to rethink this progress narrative. They are positioning Mexican Americans as someone who has arrived recently and Mexican American also seems to be associated with manual labor not with the flowery arts of written communication. It is associated with manual labor, with custodians, food services, and being caught in cycles of low literacy. That model is still the dominant one in the field. I think the salvation and progress narrative has to do with attainment of standardized American English, that is part of it. We could go beyond it. We have those who have followed in the tradition of Freire and there is a liberatory pedagogy that goes only so far. It is liberatory pedagogy as being able to mirror the political sentiments of one's professor - and others have made that argument far better than I am right now - I think there is a fairly reductive and damaging view of the progress narrative. It is literacy as the cure all. Literacy is standardized American English, alphabetic literacy, literacy will lead the people into civilization. That was the earlier argument. It will lead people into salvation, also an earlier argument. That the rhetoric of modernity is still very much caught in that, the vocabulary words can shift, your diction can shift, you can change it at the sentence level, but the theoretical grounding is still there and still present.

I think we are better as a Caucus, we are in a better position now to respond to the narrative of salvation. I am thinking about Iris Ruiz and some of her work, *Reclaiming Composition for Chicanos/as and other Ethnic Minorities* and the co-edited collection she did with Raúl Sánchez, *Decolonizing Rhetoric and Composition Studies: New Latinx Keywords for Theory and Pedagogy*, published with Palgrave MacMillan. I think when we take that scholarship into account, we are actually in a far better place to offer a counter strike in response, a much healthier response to those very easy and, you know, paternalizing salvation narratives. I do not see us as being doomed to necessarily complicit in that language. I suspect that the scholars who have come before us had fewer options available to them than we do now.

I would say the story of the Latino Caucus is one of inclusivity and solidarity building. That is its strength. That we are inclusive of a wide range of differences within the Latino and Latino canvas. That we are not threatened by the differences. That we actually see that as a strength and that even the marker, this identity marker of Latina and Latino and Latinx, that multiplicity and the difference is not something to be erased under those mantels. Instead those markers can be used as connectors across great difference.

Doesn't publication itself suggest sort of an editing out of difference? I am thinking about just very very simple things working with my own publications with *Mestizo Scripts* and following that up with *Rhetoric of the Americas*, it is a fairly conventional practice that any word or phrase or expression that is not in English will appear in your book italicized. We can go back. Ghere has been a debate about Gloria Anzaldua's *Borderlands/La Frontera* because, of course, as she engaged in her multilingual-codeswitching and code entanglements and those linguistic innovations blurring those borders, that if you are taking something that is not English and italicizing it you are actually emphasizing difference. You are not bridging across difference. You are making the difference more evident and apparent to the reader. This is standard publication strategy. I faced it with my own two books and it was not a battle I was willing to fight. I fought other battles. There is some degree of complicity in some of our publications and maybe in the future we might be able to collectively work toward changing and making significant changes.

I think the most important thing for us to be thinking about now is how we can continue the fight for inclusivity and solidarity building. There is too much at stake for us to squabble or to fight unnecessary fights with each other. There is a time to engage in horizontal critique I guess you could say. But, we are also thinking collectively about the vertical, we are critiquing up and not across. We are at a point where I think we can continue our focus on critiquing up while working together in inclusivity and solidarity-building and that can look like different things. Sometimes, I think, I might be thinking of something very simple like how we engage each other on the Latino Caucus listserv, how we are communicating with each other on the listserv. Email, I think, is not actually a great tool for solidarity building. That is a terribly unpopular thing to say because we want to think about the creation of community in digital environments. But, I am arguing, that if we are looking at email that is actually not that helpful. I am thinking specifically about academics and how they use email. It has not been that healthy. I think maybe we need to pause when we are thinking about how we are using it as a tool. Which is more important to be right all the time and argumentative or to exist in coalition with others?

STEVEN ALVAREZ
Interview by Romeo García
August 15, 2016

Romeo García: I want you to take some time to introduce who you are, where you work, and what kind of research do you do?

Steven Alvarez: Sure, well my name is Steven Alvarez Assistant Professor in Writing and Rhetoric Digital Studies University of Kentucky. However, beginning Spring 2017. I will be assistant professor of English at St. John's university. I've been with the caucus, I guess, since about 2012 when I began my position at Kentucky. So for a few years, I guess, from both the side of C's and inside NCTE.

García: What kind of research do you do?

Alvarez: My research focuses mostly on language and literacy practices of Mexican immigrants, more specifically branching into homework practices, bilingual practices, and, now, starting to go into more food and tacos

García: Where are you originally from

Alvarez: I am originally from Safford, Arizona, a small-town Southeast Arizona

García: When did you first attend C's or NCTE and why that decision?

Alvarez: It is kind of an interesting case. When I attended my first attended C's, I had this job already accepted at Kentucky in the same year I was *Scholar for the Dream*, presenting for the first time at C's. It is little of a weird situation. As soon as I went to my first C's, however, this was in St. Louis 2012, it was there where I found the Caucus. I found people who were supportive and were really just able to give me some guidance I really did not have in graduate school. That was the first one for C's, but ever since C's I've been involved in different capacities. With NCTE beginning I believe in 2014.

García: So, when you arrived at C's, what did you see, what did you see that you liked, what did you see maybe that you did not like?

Alvarez: I guess because it was new to me, I couldn't even articulate what it was, what the structure of the organization was, what this meant for my career, and how important both the publications are and building a network. It was new to me. I guess what I noticed was that I was coming in as an outsider and also that being Latino may or may not have contributed to that. I did notice it was pretty white organization. That goes without saying. That was something I was already use to coming out of an English program.

García: The feeling as an outsider stem from that presence of whiteness or was there other elements involved in that?

Alvarez: I don't know. In the beginning, I could not really say it was even, if anything, about whiteness, but more about just learning how the organization was functioning really, just as I was going through it pretty suddenly. What I was looking for was people who, more or less, had maybe gone through some of these hoops before. That is when I started to speaking to older people in the organization, but specifically to older folks in the Caucus that had reached out to me.

García: So, you arrive in St. Louis for the C's, how did you hear about the Caucus?

Alvarez: I think it was on the program. You get the book and I was going through the book and it was some of the pre-conference. I think it was a pre-conference in the afternoon. I saw a Latino workshop and I just signed up for it. That is where I met folks such as Aja Martinez for the very first time. Cristina Kirklighter was running it at that time.

García: Do you remember why you made the decision to sign up?

Alvarez: It is funny because I guess I saw Latino and I was like, "Alright let's check it out." I was like, "I didn't see too many others, so this must be where they hang out."

García: Is it anyway connected to you maybe feeling as an outsider when you arrived at C's?

Alvarez: Typically, this was something I would have ordinarily done anyway. Seek out groups for Latinos. I think maybe it was something I didn't think about exploring as a professional or even what it meant to be or have a community. But I did see there was an identity that intersects with some of my own interests and also even my research, so I thought, let's go, maybe trying to work with people. It turned out to be that it was really a lot more mixture of junior faculty and other students, plenty cool. But I think probably not knowing anybody and seeing that I saw "Latino" in the workshop title, I thought this could be a welcoming space.

García: Do you remember at all what the sense of importance was when you arrived and joined and participated in that Caucus workshop?

Alvarez: Well, for me, I had never experienced it before. It was all very new. Come to find out through people who were on it, it was basically the same routine that was happening over and over every year. That it was sort of just a small informal roundtable, sort of informally people making complaints about the job market, maybe about different encounters of racism, on the programs, and different things like that. Stuff that was just new to me. For me, it was interesting because I had never really been around Latinos and Latinas in graduate school, at least not in English studies, so that was cool. People who were also serious about teaching. That was pretty fun. I think as I learn more about the program and the Caucus, I could see with different eyes, but the first time it was pretty cool to see so many people.

García: Do you remember some of the goals that were discussed at that workshop or some the vision? You mentioned people talking about racism a little bit, about teaching, and I remember, Isabel Baca came in, and she was talking about the community outreach programs she works with. So, what were some of the goals that you took up on your own and in your own research and that really informs what you do?

Alvarez: I did notice Isabel Baca was presenting on community service learning kind of research, bilingual communities, working where she was located. Then also Octavio was pretty cool. I remember Cristina Kirklighter was showing a book she was editing and spoke about how the Caucus came together for the project. And, then we went over the history, I did not know a lot, so it was all very new. Then meeting people who just got jobs and we were talking about the market. I gave my experience with that. I remember at the same time, Aja had just got a job, so she was able to talk about her going on the market and I had very similar experiences. It was pretty cool, because it was informal, but also it was giving us a professionalization. It gave me some sense that this was an important space. People who know each other. How that worked in my research I think I was already coming in doing stuff with community, so I saw that this was building community in a different kind of way. I could see that my research could be valued. I saw that, I think, probably more in relation to NCTE which at that time I didn't even know the difference between the two groups. I figured out K-12 was more NCTE, but that is stuff I learned later on.

García: Would you say when you participating in your first workshop that you gained maybe a sense that the Caucus was about a community, about a collective voice, or was it individual voices?

Alvarez: I think, as far as I can tell, it was always about community. I remember Kirklighter talking about buena gente, it was always about people, good people. I think for me it was always a sense that it was up to the collective to make it what it was or what it is. I didn't know a lot about the history, but, of course, at different times, there have been different leaders that have come and gone. The organization changes with leadership as well. As far as I know it has always been about a group of people who are basically are all volunteers.

García: Octavio takes up that idea of buena gente. What does that mean to you in relation to scholarship, to the caucus?

Alvarez: I guess in some ways it got me to think about who is reading my scholarship, especially, I think as we are collecting our own citations of each other. It got me think about we are not being heard even in terms of conference proposals. A lot of the sort of checks in play. To really keep the organization on its toes, to really have an organized voice of dissent, along with the Black Caucus, it kind of puts our issues that affect us into context and to have our voices be represented in the leadership capacities. On the one hand, I think that is more about the administration of organization and how that ties our scholarship is really the channels. Once you get inside the organization, it does not even matter if you are not a great scholar, being part of the organization opens up channels to be heard more and to have an active voice in the ways things are run. I think somebody I admire that has come through the Caucus is Juan Guerra and what he has done, giving back to some of the younger scholars especially through NCTE. His research has dealt with teaching and giving back to younger members as a mentor. I think if anything, it is looking at some of those folks who have been able to bridge those research interests and some of their activism has been pretty inspiring.

García: Did you gain a sense of that activism in the first workshop?

Alvarez: Not really. I think I heard more of getting to know people. I think I remember they had mentioned about NCTE previously, that they had done some kind of event where they have students do some kind of activism. I guess what I found out late is the cultural event. So that sounded really cool and I was wondering why we don't do that at our Caucus meetings. It basically was just scholars. I had heard about thinking about stuff like that with NCTE, but then, later on, I found out because they are slightly different. There is also different funding. As far as I saw for the first one for C's, I was thinking we say a lot of stuff about community, but for this one I really did not see a lot of community voices.

García: In the conversation going on in the Caucus, how do you think they translate over to the action in national organization, such as CCCCs and the NCTE, and these organizations way of being responsive to Latino and Latina scholars and other educators of color?

Alvarez: I would like to think that with the Caucus, we push back on what could easily be conversations that get pushed off as being overly politically correct or being too touchy about certain things. But I would say, for example, like at the last NCTE when the Black Caucus and the Latino Caucus teamed up to speak out about a few issues that were related, to see that kind of stuff happen is interesting, because it actually pushes back on the organization. I think there is a long way to go and I think, probably, if anything, we are seeing more people get elected to positions which is pretty cool. The fact is the organization is changing, but, if anything, it gives us a space to strategize as community and to support each other. I think, if anything, we are getting better at playing the game, especially as more members become part of the institution and learn how the game functions, how it has been excluding us for many years.

García: In many ways, you could say that NCTE and CCCCs has a way of pushing back, but that the collective voice represented by the Latino Caucus or Black Caucus is pushing back at the same time as well. Would you say then that the Caucuses are a necessary aspect of the actual NCTE and CCCCs?

Alvarez: I think so. I mean it has to be. There are some issues where I get a sense of further intersections involving different caucuses, even to the point of meeting times and meeting times that conflict. And maybe some people have made the argument about the silos that don't communicate. We have to see really the caucuses having at least one collective that is part of a larger network. We have interests we share. There is also the shared interest of social justice across Caucuses regardless. If anything, it is important only because the issues that affect Latinos and Latinas are unique. Not only for our research, but also for who we are as members of the organization and the future of the organization. Coming back to students of the classrooms and the change of demographics of students in the country. Our voices and our research matter.

García: Would you not say that the Latino voice, the student need and demands, have been marginalized, if not excluded as a whole from the actual conversations going on?

Alvarez: There is no doubt about that, especially during times, such as the political situation we are in now, the dehumanizing rhetoric of immigrants, the connection with charter schools. You get this flipped individual sense that failure is your own fault and success is your own fault as well. Looking away from some of the social contextual issues that affect students and create inequality, I think this happens at all levels, especially for many of us who are Ph.D. students who become professors. The odds have been highly stacked. It is not that any of us are supremely special, we just have different opportunities. But, also remember, we need to give back and be aware of the communities around us. We make an impact both as teachers but also as just voices to speak about some of these inequalities which other people do not always experience.

García: In regard to giving back, can you talk about the relationship between publications, mentorship, and the role of the Caucus?

Alvarez: I have grown to see a lot more that this has been a publication network and also publication assistance from older folks who have gone through some of these hoops with newer folks coming at grad school, graduate students. It has always been there. Somebody, for example, like Jaime Mejia has given me a lot of help and a lot of feedback and a lot of introductions to publishers. It has been very helpful to have colleagues who are not obliged to share the information, but who really want to share the information to help us to succeed. That also happens, I think, with even graduate students who are further along the line with graduate students. It seems very helpful in the sense that people are willing to share some of that knowledge. Unfortunately, I really never had this in my program. I wish I would have been part of the Caucus earlier because it would have helped me a lot going into being a professor, but as a young professor it was definitely very helpful. That is where I got to meet a lot of colleagues across the country who were also able to speak about similar things that they experience as junior faculty.

García: You mentioned Juan Guerra and Jaime Mejia, are these some of the leaders you see of the Caucus that help propel the Caucus as it moves forward?

Alvarez: I can give the example of Jaime Mejia and even Cristina Kirklighter. Cristina especially, because she was chair of the Caucus when I first started. Her and Renee Moreno. But someone I got to know better was Juan Guerra, partly because of CNV, Cultivating New Voices, which several other members of our Caucus have gone through the pairing up an advanced graduate student or junior faculty with a seasoned mentor. Juan was in charge of this and many of the people who have passed through this program have gone into administrative positions in the organization. It really has been an important program, huge, in terms of diversifying the organization. I saw that happening in NCTE. For CCCCs, I started seeing more a turn towards community when we started doing our workshops. What I really started to see was people coming together and accessing and researching the history who were just incredible about doing things like newsletters. Just doing a lot of work to keep people connected. So, it was really cool especially when I started doing a little bit of the history. The different people who really stepped up. When I first came into it, the people who reached out to me were Jaime, Cristina, and Juan. But it could have been a different time or any number of people who would have been there.

García: For a moment, you took on the role as co-chair?

Alvarez: Basically, my understanding was that Cristina was going to step away and there was not time for an election. I was provided the opportunity to be the interim co-chair. I said okay. We want to make sure, I said, we have an election in terms of an organization choosing who would do this. At the same time, I think Renee passed leadership on as well. I am not sure at that time who it was. I am not sure if it was Tracey or Sandra or together. I think it might have been Tracey first, then Sandra, and then they became co-chair. For a little while, I hung around Sandra and Tracey and we would have these conversations on the vision of the organization. But I stepped aside because the bad spirit of tenure and writing a book. And Raul was interested, so actually at that time I was just putting it up in the air for anyone who wanted to take on the position. Since it was already a co-chair on one side, we did co-chair on the other. So, we did a general election. I guess I did my job as an interim. I do regret that as Cristina was moving on, there were no folks who were senior scholars who wanted to step up and take the position. There were several of us as junior scholars who were a few years in. Aja specifically said we can do it together. I said, I could learn, but really no one decided to step up and take the leadership, someone with tenure basically. I said I would take it on, but it was more like until someone who knows what is going on will take it on. At that time, I think Tracey and Sandra had interesting things going on with re-writing some of the guidelines.

García: What is the story you would like to tell about the Caucus?

Alvarez: The story would have, like any other story, its ups and downs. I do not want to say the hero is a villain. Everyone's a hero. It has different personalities. And like any organization, there have been clashes and outlooks or ideologies, especially from people who study argumentation, lots of debates. But, I think it's all for the best. It keeps the organization going forward. We are starting to see more collaboration between NCTE and CCCCs, which is important because, I think, we will be only one of the caucuses, beside the Black Caucus, that has that kind of collaboration. This is important because that will connect us further with K to 12. It is a cool moment especially with so many people who are coming up as Ph.D. students that are finding jobs and becoming part of the organization. It seems really exciting. For a long time, it was always Victor Villanueva, now there are more voices and people being recognized. Not even Latino and Latina scholars, major voices in the field.

García: How would you like others to remember the caucus?

Alvarez: It is important for others to know who we are. If they remember us at all, that is perfect. If anything, they can remember that this was a group of scholars who organized themselves who had a vision, a shared vision, to give back to each other. So much of this work can be isolated and there can be a lot of back fighting and competition even amongst really good friends. The Caucus has been cool because it breaks down those smoke screens. We do not always see that competition, but more importantly, it helps us see opportunities to help each other. People publishing together, doing books, collaborations, research, writing. I mean, we are seeing more of that happen. I think the way we are using social media is a lot more savvy than other caucus groups. It is cool to see where we are going.

García: Why do you think the history of the Caucus is important?

Alvarez: I really didn't know a lot of the history until the interim position where I worked with Tracey and Sandra, when we were trying to find the newsletters. So, we found all the letters from the 60s and it was "wow." There were like recipes, poems, various accomplishments, people's birthdays. It was pretty cool. She had done this basically once a month or every couple of months. It was mass mail, folded. But just the amount of time, she took to do this, it was important to keep people together. Tracey and Sandra archived a lot of them and saved them as PDF's. Seeing them was cool because it showed me from the very beginning, it was a smaller group of people with the same interest. For me, especially, we have our different get-togethers and we see how the rooms are getting bigger and bigger. It is cool to see the community grow. It is even more important to start thinking of the kind of diversity of Latino and Latinx we need to learn amongst ourselves. A lot of more cool debates about what the identity means and, especially moving into the future, the direction we want to see the organization move.

CRISTINA RAMÍREZ
Interview by Anita Hernández
August 3, 2016
http://youtu.be/FuXszgSaZcU

Cristina Ramírez: This turns out to be my 22nd year teaching. I started teaching in the middle schools and high schools in El Paso. Twelve years into my career, I went into the Rhetoric and Composition at UTEP. Then I moved to Tucson and I just going up for tenure. I started in August 2011. I just authored, *Occupying Our Space: The Meztiza Rhetoric of Mexican Women Journalists and Activist*s published by the University of Arizona Press.

Anita Hernández: When and why did you choose to attend the CCCCs and/or NCTE?

Ramírez: I didn't get involved with the C's and NCTE until I started with my graduate work. As a public-school teacher, I did not know that much about the C's or NCTE, but as a graduate student I was introduced to this conference. As a doctoral student, the first time I attended the C's conference was in San Francisco. Attending the CCCCs and being welcomed in the Latino Caucus was formidable me as a scholar knowing that my research and my voice had a place. I became interested as a graduate student. It was not required but they told us how important to become professionals in the field.

Hernández: What was your research interest at that time?

Ramírez: My research interest as a graduate student had been into the feminist historical recovery of Mexican women journalist and activists. In recovery work, feminist historiography.

Hernández: Why did you decide to join the Caucus, who was involved and what did you sense was the importance of the caucus for others, what were your goals, what has been the role of the caucus in your career?

Ramírez: I am thinking back, if they told us about the Latino Caucus. As I looked through the conference program as a newcomer, you go through every single page. I saw that there was a Latino Caucus. I missed dinner with my friends that got upset with me. I don't know what it is about, but I am going to find out. Ever since then, I have been a member because I knew it was home for me.

Hernández: Who was involved when you went to your first Latino Caucus?

Ramírez: Victor, Cristina Kirklighter, Octavio. Those were the main people I remember. Cecilia and Alejandra Hidalgo were there. Those were the main people I remember attending the first caucus. This goes back to 2007 or 2008, almost 9 years now.

Hernández: At that time, what were some of the issues they talked about?

Ramírez: I remember representation at the conference, having our place at the conference, and also publications.

Hernández: What was it about publications? Were they encouraging everyone to publish?

Ramírez: Exactly! They were encouraging us to find our voices as Latinos and Latinas; these research projects focused on the pedagogy of Latinos and Latinas, and the recovery of these voices. We need to get our voices up there. I remember Victor told us to publish, and, since then, there has been a proliferation of publications from the Latino (a) community in the C's and NCTE.

Hernández: With that emphasis, what did you think about that?

Ramírez: I knew that my project will take off and I had a support base for my project. I knew it was important and necessary.

Hernández: Did you feel support at the University Texas in El Paso?

Ramírez: Yes. They did not in the least question my project in recovering the voices of "mujeres Mejicanas." They saw the gap between the historically Anglo voice and the emerging African-American discipline. They felt that my research was going to feel that gap.

Hernández: What were some of the issues that you witnessed/observed (such as marginalization of other Latino/as, research, publishing) at CCCCs or NCTE? How do you remember the caucus responding? Who were some the leaders that took such an initiative?

Ramírez: Raúl Sánchez, Octavio Pimentel, Victor Villanueva, Cristina Kirklighter, and Iris Ruiz. (Ruiz is now one of the co-directors). They responded by taking these concerns to the board meetings the next day. Issues with representation within the caucus have remained. One of the ways they have shifted dealing with these issues is by getting people on ballot and review boards for the conference. Jaime Mejia and Octavio Pimentel have been long-time reviewers. But we have been getting more people on the ballot. Also, in the conference at San Antonio, people commented (disparaging comments) about what they heard. They were being reported at the Latino Caucus meeting. It was taken up by the leaders, like Victor and Cristina. I have not been involved personally, but I know these issues have been always taken up at the board meetings. A combination of those complaints came at the conference in Tampa, where Adam Banks was the organizer; in that conference we felt we were seen. It was the tweeting, the positioning of our presentations at certain times. We felt we were heard. For the first time he had ribbons made for the Latino caucus.

Hernández: Did you have more people attending your session because of the tweeting and the presence of Latino and Black caucus?

Ramírez: I think so. That is still difficult because that is such a big conference and it is difficult to get people to go, be seen, and support the Latino Causes. You tried to go and see students who you represent in the university but sometimes they overlap. We need to support and represent each other.

Hernández: What are some of your earliest memories of the caucus interacting with others and what kind of discussions, resolutions, and/or projects transpired?

Ramírez: I remember having a phone conversation with Victor. He had suggested that he be on my dissertation committee. He ended up not being in my dissertation committee because it was overwhelming to have 4 people on my committee as a graduate student, but I felt his support from afar. A dissertation chair told me that if Victor was in my committee, later in my career, he could not serve as a letter writer for promotion in tenure. I was getting good counseling at UTEP. I felt "muy ansiosa" to have 4 people in my committee.

Hernández: What positive and/or negative actions have you seen between the CCCC and/or NCTE in being inclusive of Latino scholars and educators?

Ramírez: Recognition of scholarship this past year. Octavio co-edited a book that received an outstanding award as well as my book, *Occupying Our Space: The Meztiza Rhetoric of Mexican Women Journalists and Activists*, that won the Feminist Coalition Outstanding Book Award. We are starting to see our work being recognized. Victor won a prize many years ago, but we are starting to see our work being recognized.

Hernández: How helpful has CCCCs or NCTE or colleagues in the Latino Caucus been in your publishing (articles, book chapters, or books) and what kind of mentoring has there been (or not been)?

Ramírez: For the publishing, I ask for names for reviewers. I used three names from the Caucus and my final review was with Cristina.

Hernández: I noticed that Andrea Lunsford gave you a review.

Ramírez: Jacqueline John Royster wrote my forward. I was very deliberate about choosing these women because it showed a coalition, a representation from an African-American, and Andrea Lunsford, who represents the roots of feminist recovery work, and Cristina Kirklighter, a major player, advocate, and leader in the Latino Caucus for a long time. It was book- ended very nicely. I was very strategic because I wanted a coalition coalescing with the scholarship. I did not want this to be only for Latino (a) voices. I could have asked Victor Villanueva to write my forward, but I wanted an African-American scholar to do that. Jacqueline and Andrea are in the coalition of Feminist Scholars. I am active in the coalition and in the Latino caucus.

Hernández: What roles have you undertaken within the CCCCs or NCTE and what kind of benefits have you witnessed from such experiences?

Ramírez: Coalition and Latino causes. I can be a member of both, but taking a leadership in both would be very difficult. I have taken on a bigger role in the coalition. First, I was elected and voted in as a board member and then I was nominated for Secretary. I am serving a two or three year-term as a Coalition Secretary. I have seen benefits, such as reviewing scholarly work for PATHOS, and being reviewed through Alejandra's journal *Present Tense*. Working in the coalition has brought benefits, professional as well at personal, because it is gratifying. I feel I belong and that I am making a difference, which is rewarding.

Hernández: What is a story you would like to tell about the caucus and how would you like others to remember the caucus?

Ramírez: The story I want to tell about the caucus is that of an emerging voice of traditionally marginalized voices within a very traditional Anglo organization. The voices have been heard and their histories count by persistent activism, research, and outreach. The way I want them to remember is that the Latino Caucus is a "familia" and you can call on them for help. They have been advocates. When something cool happens, they blast something on the Latino Caucus page. It is nice!

Hernández: Was there a question, I did not ask, that I should have? If so, what question should I have asked?

Ramírez: How has the Latino Caucus worked with other caucuses or organizations? For example, Alejandra Hidalgo did a video for the coalition. Doing work with cross-organizational work shows that we value each other's views and talents. That took place last year 2015 or 2014. If you go to the coalition webpage and click on the archives www.cwshrc.org you can view the video.

AJA MARTINEZ
Interview by Anita Hernández
July 2016
https://www.youtube.com/watch?v=c3DtTvkPgnU

Aja Martinez: I am originally from Arizona. I went to the University of Arizona where I got my degree in Rhetoric and Composition. I had my first job after the Ph.D. at Binghamton University. It is one of the SUNY universities in upstate New York. I have just recently been hired by Syracuse University's newly titled Department of Writing Studies, Rhetoric, and Composition. We have a graduate program in Composition and Cultural Rhetoric. I am excited to get started.

Anita Hernández: When and why did you choose to attend C's and/or NCTE?

Martinez: I have gone to both, primarily CCCC because of my teaching and research in college spaces. My first time at NCTE was to promote an edited collection I did with Vershawn Young. The second time I went, I was elected to the Nominating Committee, so I went to complete my service and also to participate in the Cultural Celebration that the Latino Caucus and Black Caucus put on. I remember my first year in graduate school, my first year in Rhetoric and Composition, I was coming out of with an undergraduate degree in Anthropology and I was accepted into the Ph.D. at Arizona, into a new program at Arizona called Rhetoric and the Teaching of English. I remember during the spring semester, it was like a ghost town, everyone disappeared for a weekend in March or April. Classes were cancelled. I didn't know what happened. No one had clued me on the fact that CCCC was that weekend and everyone left. I didn't know what CCCCs was. That was the year it was in New York City. When everyone came back that was part of my miseducation, part of my lack of knowing how to navigate professional conferences that I was supposed to be participating in. The following Fall, I was encouraged to submit to CCCC because it was made clear to me that is what we do. We are participants in this conference. Everyone should be submitting and attending. I did get accepted. I was also encouraged to apply to the *Scholars for the Dream*. I did that as well. I was awarded the *Scholars for the Dream*, which made it a big possibility for me to attend that following spring in New Orleans. That was in 2008. That was the year that I met some prominent elders in the Latino Caucus, like Jaime Mejia, in particular, and everyone who was associated with him at Texas State, San Marcos. Because of the *Scholars for the Dream*, I was there at the reception. I was able to meet other people from the other caucuses and that became my home and community in the overall organization.

Hernández: Why did you decide to join the Caucus? Who was involved and what did you sense was the importance of the caucus for others? What were your goals? What has been the role of the caucus in your career?

Martinez: That year was my second year in grad school. I was already feeling a bit of displacement in my own program at Arizona. When I got to CCCCs that year, in panels but also in the Caucus meeting I attended, I started hearing people voicing similar issues at the graduate and professional level. So, I realized "I am not alone." People who have been through various stages. Some people were beginning in their graduate programs, other were early career or later career, like Dr. Villanueva. That was comforting. The other thing I thought that was strange was what with my home faculty community. Something that happened in all the *Scholars for the Dream*, fanfare happening, the opening session, and having special designated session that the *Scholars for the Dream* present at and having the reception, none of the faculty from Arizona attended any of it. They ignored the whole thing. I remember feeling very hurt, personally hurt - whether it was personal on their part or not. It was Jaime Mejia and Octavio Pimentel who attended my panel, that then took me into their arms. They said "We are excited for you. Congratulations! Come be with us." They noticed I was at this reception and I was by myself. I didn't know anyone. I didn't have faculty attending to be excited for me. They noticed I was there by myself at the reception. They were that for me. They were the ones that, after the reception, said our meetings happen on Friday, come do this thing. I would have not known otherwise. That was a big part of how I became involved, I was getting drawn in by people who were already members.

Hernández: What has been the role of the Caucus in your career?

Martinez: I think access to the organization has always been a big concern because our leadership was transitioning, at that time, from Ceci Milanés to Cristina Kirklighter and Renee Moreno. In that transfer, just from my outsider observation as a new member, and has continued to be a point of conversation, is the representation on the program and in the awards, in the many different avenues at that happen both through conference recognition to access to elected roles and leadership positions. Our leadership has continued to work on that issue. What I taken in my own work, now as a more advanced person in the Caucus because I was a participant for a few years, is to tap the social media angle of representation, making sure that the media programs are announcing not just who are members are, what we are doing, our accomplishments, our publications, but things that may be small passing exams, small things like that. What we are doing? I have tried to be the person who continues the representation. Something that is important to me, because of the way I joined the Caucus, is to make our CCCC Chairs aware of who are the new Latinos attending CCCC. Making sure that there is an email that says we exist, "Come be with us on Friday and the other events we are having." There have been more Latinos, like me, who are coming up that is creating a critical mass, so the recruitment has been a major concern for the Caucus.

Hernández: Have you seen a growth?

Martinez: A lot. All you have to look at is the group picture every year it is taken. The first year I attended it was in a pretty big ballroom, but a small circle of gente. In the past few years, we had slightly smaller rooms, but less space because the large number of people. We can't do a circle because there are too many people. It is a great story about a testament to that growth. But two years ago, in Indianapolis, I went to request the Latinx ribbon tags. It was the first year we had the tags for Latino Caucus badges. Adams Banks was in charge and he was thinking about these things. He thinks about things like that. Once again, representation. We like to show that we exist. We are walking around and for other Latinos who would see the blue badge, see we exist. I went to request a stack of them, so I could go to the next meeting and distribute them to anyone who didn't have one. The woman at the registration counter for CCCC, when I asked her 40 of that year, which was an underestimate at that, said "Oh are there that many of you?" It was rude and it was racist. "Yes, there are and there are more. We didn't have enough ribbons."

Hernández: What were some of the issues that you witnessed/observed (such as marginalization of other Latino/as, research, publishing) at CCCC or NCTE? How do you remember the caucus responding and who were some the leaders that took such an initiative?

Martinez: One that is closest to my heart that happened right in the middle of my graduate education was the ban on ethnic schools in Arizona. Mostly it was close to my heart because it was one of the schools banned, that was teaching it, the teachers were in the high school I attended. I noticed that it was one of the issues that was paid attention to in Atlanta. It was a national issue that there was space made for one of the educators, Carlos Acosta, to come and relate the issues legislatively to the entire Caucus. Our leadership at the time, Cristina and Renee, took that to the CCCCs board and up to the NCTE level. Since then, that started the ball rolling for part of what happened this past year, our resolution and our statement on Ethnic Studies that we did in cooperation with other caucuses. I feel like that is something I have seen the Caucus take serious leadership on and talk to the upper levels, that our organization as a whole is speaking on a national level about something like Ethnic Studies resolution of 2015 (NCTE, 2015c, http://www.ncte.org/positions/statements/ethnic-studies-k12-curr).

Hernández: I want to follow up on go back to something you said about the badges. What year did that happen?

Martinez: Like you said, it seems small. It is in terms of representation. "We exist." "We are part of this in an important way." The first year was the year Adam Banks was involved in the leadership of running CCCC. That was Indianapolis in 2013. That was the first moment that I saw that it was available to us. The year after that it, this year in Houston, they ran out of the Latinx Caucus ribbons that are taped to our badges by 8am Thursday morning. It was really bad. The conference had just started. People brought the issue up. I brought up the issue with senior members, like Keith Gilyard, and that this was important to us. I did not know what to say to the Chair. The entire conference. What the difference has been between Adam Banks and other chairs is that he thinks about representation. He honors that he thinks about it before we have to complain. We didn't know we could have something like that. Now that we expect it, it has to be something that we insist on. Adam set a precedent. He did that. It is something that seems small, but it is big at the end of the day. To run out on the first day made me think that none had been ordered. We were using the ones from the past conference.

Hernández: What are some of your earliest memories of the caucus interacting with others? What kind of discussions, resolutions, and/or projects transpired?

Martinez: My earliest memories are the transfer of leadership from Ceci to Renee and Cristina. That was cool to me to see women being the leaders of the Caucus. That made me feel like that this is a good organization I am joining. I remember just hearing about <u>Rainbow Strand</u>. To know what that means, how that has developed has been an interesting story to me. I remember also meeting some of the people who became my mentors to me, like Jaime Mejia and Victor Villanueva, in particular, who have both been instrumental in my publishing career, applying for jobs, and the giving advice. Those are my earliest memories of having a space that has now become for me, especially for the year which I'm less enthusiastic about participating for different political reasons that have come up. That gives me something to come back to. It is like family reunion, an academic family reunion, and coming to see everyone and catch up. There are probably new members who are feeling the way that I got to CCCC for the first time and can really use someone like myself to bring them into the fold and be there for them.

Hernández: What positive and/or negative actions have you seen between the 4Cs and/or NCTE in being inclusive of Latino scholars and educators?

Martinez: There are several things. I think what at root it is how inclusive are our publications beyond the special issues, which comes up every year. The representation of our work in the publications is what I think drives the stage 1 reviewers, in particular, and what they are thinking is important in the field at that moment. If they are not seeing our work published by the organization, they may be putting our scholarship on the backburner that may germinate at the conference. This is what happens. It sparks at the conference and then it turns into publication of scholarship. So that is one thing. As a chair, Adam Banks brought that up in his chair's address and that makes people uncomfortable, by saying that it is true that beyond special editions or special issues that our work is too sparsely featured. Representation there, then, influences the reviewers to accept work.

The other thing, when the work is there, when it is accepted, I notice our works seem to be slotted at the same time. So if people are interested in the work that is concerned with Latino issues, they have to choose and pick between two panels that are competing for audiences. Take some of the work that two of our members Sara and Steven Alvarez, a married couple, their panels are pretty consistently put in the same time slot. These are people who are related, they have to pick and choose. They can't go to each other's sessions. Their times slots have been unfortunate. That has been unfortunate. I know Joyce Carter in her chair in Houston mentioned if you can think of an app I want to hear about it. Wouldn't it be cool if there was some sort of matrix or a technology or an app, that could space things out that is more conscious of the fact that there are few of us and we shouldn't be at the same time slot. There has to be some sort of mathematical way to do this. We have a chair calling for this kind of thing. Let's call back to her and say what can we do? Is there an app that can help us do something about this? I have been hearing about it since my first year at CCCCs and up to this year. This is something that hasn't improved. Those are some of the things.

Hernández: Did you notice that in CCCC?

Martinez: Absolutely, in fact. There were cross caucus panels. There were two panels on whiteness. Guess what? These two panels were on at the same time slot. People who were interested in whiteness had to choose. It is a pretty consistent thing.

Hernández: How helpful has the Cs or NCTE or colleagues in the Latino Caucus been in your publishing (articles, book chapters, or books) and what kind of mentoring has there been (or not been)?

Martinez: The first home for my publishing was *College English* and it was special issue in College English that was edited by Damian Baca on Latino issues. Helpful. Because Victor became interested in my work early on, he took it upon himself to mentor me through a lot of the publications. I rarely submit anything without passing it by him first. My second major publication was through NCTE as a press with Vershawn Young. It was called *Code Meshing as World English,* our edited collection, an NCTE book. I think what I liked about publishing with NCTE, a book in this case, was I got to know the process early on. I was still a graduate student when I did this project with Vershawn. He as a mentor, part of the Black Caucus, at that moment, said to me, "Do you want to do this. Not knowing what I was getting into it. "Alright, Let's do it." It was at Louisville. He had me approach Kurt Austin of NCTE. Propose the book to him and to see what happens. The rest is history. We have a book. I got to know the stages of being a co-editor of an edited collection. I learned that with NCTE as a press. Helpful. The mentorship has been helpful, particularly a project through the Black Caucus and the Latino Caucus. It was important. It was imperative because I wasn't getting that mentorship necessarily from my faculty at Arizona. To have people from these other Caucuses that I would not have met, had I not been involved in CCCC, that was something that made my career what it is, at this point.

Hernández: Very pivotal. That means that is what we need to do with the new members coming through.

Martinez: Yes. There have been different conversations and efforts toward to strengthen the mentorship role. There has been a thread in the most recent listserv conversation about what our mentorship should look like, especially since our membership because we have grown so much. Some of it has been organic, people getting to know each other and who get along fine. Something more structured could definitely be needed at this time because of the sheer number of people who aren't going to pick up someone and put them under their wing. Especially when it comes to publishing because the other side of journals and the presses being more inclusive our work is that our work needs to be proposed. Walking through and teaching our members what those steps are, the navigation strategies, to put a proposal together, to get the work out there in good shape, that is the other side of the mentorship. Jaime Mejia has been instrumental to those of us he mentors to make sure it is in tip top shape. He tells us the truth about our work. It hurts. It is an important type of mentorship because he is going to tell us the things when ignorant or arrogant reviewers will tell us the same thing. Best if it comes from him to get those things in order then send it out. To have something structured in place would be great.

Hernández: What roles have you undertaken within the C's or NCTE and what kind of benefits have you witnessed from such experiences?

Aja Martinez: This is related to one of the other questions about who I have interacted with from the other caucuses. I have mentioned Adam Banks a few times because he is one of my mentors. Through having his mentorship, my name has become part of the names of people passing on when he was in leadership chair position. There are a few of us who he mentored in a writing group. I think getting the recognition of somebody who is going to pass your name along is where it starts. The networking is tantamount because then you participate in something and your name is out there. You are on a committee like deciding on the best dissertation, the other committee was the best article, the kind of things that are not elected positions, then you start working with people who you may not have interacted yet. They get to know your name and they put your name forward. I was on the ballot for the nominating committee. Now I am on the ballot for the Executive Committee. Which is great. What is not so great is that I am in direct competition with another good friend, Cruz Medina, and the way they put it to us is if we weren't in direct competition, there would be no Latinos. That needs to be fixed. I don't have the answer. But also, the word is out that I like mentoring. I am interested in mentoring others, so now I am part of the Welcoming Committee and that is a new position and that is a two-year commitment. It boiled down to they became aware of me and passed my name along and through participating in other things. It is who you know.

Hernández: What is a story you would like to tell about the caucus and how would you like others to remember the caucus?

Martinez: It dials back to what I started with say, it's about giving; the aspect of giving *un abrazo* that you need when you are new and don't know anybody. You don't even know if it is even a field or if it is a good fit. You might be getting the message from your home organization, which I was getting, that you don't fit and you are someone that doesn't belong. So, to get to a conference and to see people who somewhat look like you and some that do not. It is about Latinidad and learning about the different directions people are coming from, whether it is culturally or the heritage or the type of work that you do. Feeling that there is a place for you especially in this huge conference of both NCTE and CCCC. There are going to be people there that will be supportive and look out for you, especially now with social media. You can keep in touch with them through the whole year. Let them know what you are up to. People can keep tabs on you. What I started to do was checking in on people. "Hey, how are you doing? Did you get a job this year? If not, I heard of this." Sending those sorts of messages. Keeping track of each other. That is the story to me about the Caucus - that there is a place, there is a home for people who feel displacement in so many aspects, in their career, and in this crazy country. There is a place for us in our work and people interested in our work. That is the other aspect of the Caucus, that we have not been exclusive to people who just identify as Latinos, but are inclusive of those who are doing work that benefit our youth and our students and us as professionals. There are people who have heart and work out there. People are not turned away becoming part of who we are from our group, who we are, just because they are not the right heritage or ethnic makeup.

Hernández: Was there a question, I did not ask, that I should have? If so, what question should I have asked?

Martinez: No, I . I am looking forward. I am all in. In these crazy political times. it is hopeful that younger people are joining.

TRACEY FLORES
Interview by Anita Hernández
October 15, 2016

Hernández: When and why did you choose to attend CCCC and/or NCTE or both? What role did the Caucus play in your career?

Flores: I only attend NCTE. My first NCTE convention was in 2010 in Orlando, that is when I met you for the very first time. I was in Orlando and I attended the convention at the same time as the National Writing Project. I was invited by the National Writing Project to share work that I was doing with my second-grade students and their families in my school and in a bilingual writing workshop. That was the day before and NCTE was later. I was in Orlando for the very first time for the same convention. I was excited to be there. I remember as an undergraduate our professors did a lot with NCTE and I always said one day I would like to present my work and meet people. I never thought that I could be sharing on the national level in that space. When I was there, I did not know anyone from my university. I saw Mary Carmen Cruz, earlier that year like in September and she was the Arizona English Teachers Associate. It was the local affiliate of NCTE. She was presenting with a teacher. I had seen her at the conference. She invited me to the Caucus meeting. I wasn't sure about attending the Caucus meeting. I had not planned on going to the Caucus meeting. The more I thought I about, I thought it would be good for me to attend the Caucus meeting. When I went there Mary Carmen Cruz was there. You were there. José Montelongo was there. Bobbi Houtchens was there. At the same time, they were doing the interviews of elders of the caucuses. I remember that Dr. Hill was there. Sandra from the Black Caucus was interviewing him. At that moment, I felt it was special space. The intergenerational project. It felt really good. I remember meeting Dr. Hill and him being around at the Caucus. It felt very special and very important. I was happy I had attended.

Hernández: That is where we met Cecilia. We had met at a boat restaurant. The Black Caucus leadership came looking for us as we usually met in adjacent rooms.

Flores: Cecilia was there because it was in Florida and she is based out of Florida. It is interesting because I just got an email saying that we need to reorganize our meeting time because there is not space during our normal meeting time. I feel that was full circle and we were pushed off into that restaurant. We need to pick a new meeting time.

Hernández: We could meet at the same time and find a new meeting space?

Flores: They gave us different times to meet. We historically have met at that time. We need to figure out a new meeting time. I don't know how that works, if we say where. The reason was availability of space and they gave us different times to choose from. Historically we have met at that time that the Black Caucus also meets. I need to contact Sandra, my co-chair.

Hernández: How did you stay over one more day?

Flores: The National Writing Project paid for me to fly out early, but I had some funding from our local central Arizona Council that paid for me to stay overnight. Then I shared a room with two doctoral students from ASU. We have become lifelong friends. At the time, I was a classroom teacher. I was going through some transition. I had moved from a school site where we were undergoing reorganization. We had two organizations working with us - West Ed and Ellis Foundation. It was a complete restructuring of our school and our practices. Then at that time, I moved schools and I was in the writing project. It all came together at the right moment.

Hernández: What were some of the issues between 2010 and last year 2015?

Flores: My earlier memories was always we talked a lot about representation, historically the underrepresentation in the convention and the leadership roles and also at the national office level. As I continue to stay active and as one of the co-chairs, I continue to see those trends manifest as we have new leadership at the national office. For instances, we no longer have Dr. Mila Fuller, who we used to work with. As I stayed active, I interacted more with the Black Caucus and had conversations with the leadership. I am noticing the same trends. That is part of why Adam Banks resigned from his post and the protest of these types of occurrences. I remember hearing a lot about of the fact that the program with *Rainbow Strand* needed to be continued looked at and revitalized, that making sure we were staying true to the *Rainbow Strand* goals which was supposed to be not replicating deficit views of people of color from different backgrounds.. This was an issue among us (the Caucuses). We need to think about how we can make people aware of what *Rainbow Strand* is supposed to be. Sometimes I think that people think that it is just LGBTQ issues, but that is not true. We have to make sure we have certain topics covered, for instances there are rarely any presentations on Native American education issues, on language, on how can we get these important issues of teacher education on panels.

Hernández: How do you remember the caucus responding, and who were some the leaders that took such an initiative?

Flores: From my earliest memories, it was a lot of the leadership Bobbi Houtchens, Cristina Kirklighter, and Renee Moreno. Cristina was the more vocal voice of the Caucus. Also Mary Carmen Cruz, even though she was not one of the co-chairs, but she had that historic memory. Her work throughout was important and as we move forward we need to call on this memory. Because when I came in 2010, there were conversations about concerns and there are still concerns.

Hernández: Do you remember any Resolutions? or Projects?

Flores: What I remember, if it was a resolution or if it was something else, Iris and Raul helped and this happened more in the CCCCs side, like the resolution for ethnic studies. Lots of folks at CCCCs helped draft resolutions. Iris and Raul drafted a document that is now a resolution on the importance of ethnic studies and there was even a couple of blogs. We met with Dale, talked with him about the different sections. We drafted an important document, especially important in Arizona and all that is happening here. It was a complete process - we got signatures and then it was voted. (NCTE's position statement in support of ethnic studies initiatives in K-12 curricula can be found at: http://www2.ncte.org/statement/ethnic-studies-k12-curr/)

Hernández: What positive and/or negative actions have you seen between the CCCCs and/or NCTE in being inclusive of Latino scholars and educators?

Flores: I would say there is a lack of transparency and there are communication failures at times. I know that everyone is very busy, but I feel those things are important, especially when we voice our concerns. It is important that we are communicated with as well as how things are being communicated and how things are being handled. Yes, that directly impacts our Caucuses and our memberships and our concerns.

Hernández: Specifically, this year there is no meeting space at our regularly scheduled time.

Flores: Exactly. I just got that email [from headquarters NCTE 2015 Minnesota], here we go again.

Hernández: How have you observed the CCCCs or NCTE be responsive to Latino/a scholars and educators and what actions has that organization taken that you have seen that you agree or disagree with?

Flores: One thing that I have seen just happened last year. We had a meeting with the Black Caucus leadership and our leadership, very late night, about our letter of our demands. I thought that it was a positive direction. However, I also thought it was more or less damage control so there was not a big spectacle, that we did not interrupt the conference in ways that people would start to ask questions. They caught wind of a possible die in or protest and I think from there that is when the damage control started. They met with us and we gave them a list of demands, then agreed to apologize for moving Adam Bank's photo. There was one thing we wanted them to do the next morning and I believe it had to do with Adam Banks. So, in the presidential address, she did mention about people's feelings being hurt and since they mentioned some of those things, we did not have the protest. Then afterwards, there was a timeline and following through. There has been a breakdown. I will send you the letter. It's in our file.

Hernández: Seems like it should be discussed at the Caucus. They should be taken up. This is a good opportunity.

Flores: That is really interesting because I was thinking about the others, like the CEE. They have their business meeting and their dinner. Like, do they send them an email saying we know this is your meeting time but we have to move you? I wonder about those things. We have always had our meetings at this time in conjunction with the Black Caucus. Saturdays at noon. Friday is the executive.

Hernández: I know the past few years, we have not been able to attend because we are presenting at that time. It has been a conflict. How helpful has the Cs or NCTE or colleagues in the Latino Caucus been in your publishing (articles, book chapters, or books) and what kind of mentoring has there been (or not been)?

Flores: I have not really published, per say, with anyone. However, when I need support with my writing, I know there are people who I can call on who will look at my work or send me examples. When I applied for the *Scholars for the Dream* program, I have a friend who sent me some of her stuff and she read over mine. She is very collaborative. We are making sure we are writing every day. We met strictly through the Caucus work, it is nice to have those relationships. I presented at the Kidd Conference in New Mexico, it is meaningful because I am able to find people who are who understand me and don't judge me. I am so excited about LRA.

Hernández: What roles have you undertaken with NCTE.

Flores: When I joined the Caucus, I ran and I won and then served two times on the Nominating Committee for the elementary section. I also served as Rainbow Co-Chair with Renee. This year with Sandra, I have moved on to being a co-chair. It has been great for me because I have gotten to meet a lot of leadership across caucuses and also the Executive Committee as well as people from headquarters. I have some of the conversations I have wanted to have with people and to connect people at different levels with scholars and educators. I have read proposals and I learn a lot about, what the issues are, and what people are concerned about.

Hernández: What is a story you would like to tell about the caucus and how would you like others to remember the caucus?

Flores: I want people to know that the Caucus has come a long way from its origins. Even though there are things we are working on to get our business side going, we want to have more organization. The main objective is to come together to advocate for issues of concerns for all of us. This is a space that is inclusive of everyone, their concerns, and their needs. We are working really hard to continue to open up space for the next generation of scholars and educators and teachers. I am still very privileged to be in this space as a leader. As I look behind me, I see all the of the people who have paved the way before me. I don't take it lightly because I know that without them, I would not be here. While I honor their legacy and while I pave the way for the next group of scholars, I hope to leave the organization better than when it was handed over to us.

Hernández: When did you become a co-chair? Is that a 2-year role?

Flores: Last year, in 2015, I was the co-chair. That is why we are trying to get the bylaws passed. We need an executive board with time limits.

Hernández: You brought up a good point to have similar business meetings to CCCC.

Flores: We had the voting online, but we had to open it up again because we did not get enough people voting. We are trying to figure out the dues and how to pay the dues and what the money will be spent for. These are the questions the membership is asking. Some people have concerns, "I'm paying but what am I getting out of it?" That is what we are trying to organize within ourselves.

Hernández: Was there a question I did not ask that I should have? If so, what question should I have asked?

Flores: From my memory, I had been hearing about the Adam Banks resigning and everything and there was a plan for a protest. We had talked to David Kirkland and emails were being sent. When I got there. I guess people were talking too much. Kathy Short got wind of this. She pulled David aside and she said don't do this, let's talk. We set up the meeting that Saturday night after the presidential party. We met there to go to the meeting at 11:30pm. We were not satisfied until Sunday morning, until they met one of the demands. From there, we were alright. That is where it has been. There were emails sent even on the national email on what they were working on. Doug Hesse sent the letter in January right after the conference.

www.ingramcontent.com/pod-product-compliance
Lightning Source LLC
Chambersburg PA
CBHW021336300426
44114CB00012B/971